Monographs on
communication planning   3

In this series:

Methods
of communication
planning

Edited by John Middleton
and Dan J. Wedemeyer

Unesco

Published in 1985 by the United Nations
Educational, Scientific and Cultural Organization
7 Place de Fontenoy, 75700 Paris
Typeset by Asco Trade Typesetting Ltd, Hong Kong
Printed by Imprimerie Floch, Mayenne

ISBN 92-3-102112-5

Preface

This book is for communication planners: men and women who are engaged in the process of creating, allocating and using communication resources to achieve social and economic goals. Its focus is on communication planning as an integral part of national, social, cultural and economic development, particularly in the Third World, although many of the concepts and methods discussed have broad relevance to communication planning in a variety of settings.

The kind of communication planning considered here encompasses planning for telecommunications services, for educational uses of mass media, for non-formal education, for campaigns in support of development projects, for the development of national consciousness and identity, for the provision of news and other useful information, and for planning that seeks an integrated use of communication systems for all these purposes.

The book has two aims. The first is to define 'communication planning', both from current real-world experience and from a conceptual point of view. These pragmatic and conceptual definitions are considered fundamental to the achievement of the second aim, which is to specify and describe a range of planning methods that are useful to communication planners working with various types of communication systems for a variety of purposes. It is hoped that the concepts and methods presented will be useful to communication planners in different cultures and societies, concerned with different kinds of development problems, and operating at different levels—from projects to national planning commissions.

The idea for the book arose out of discussions in 1978 between the Division of Development of Communication Systems in Unesco, and the East–West Communication Institute (E W C I), Honolulu. The two agencies had been collaborating since 1976 in research and development activities on ways in which planned communication could be better used for development purposes. This collaboration had already led to a series of joint projects and publications which were helping to define and deepen the field of communication planning. These included the first two volumes in Unesco's 'Monographs on Communication Planning' series, *Approaches to Communication Planning* (ed. John

Middleton, 1980) and *Communication Planning for Development: An Operational Framework* (Alan Hancock, 1980), *The Development Communication Planning Simulation Game* (John Middleton *et al.*, Honolulu, East–West Communication Institute, 1979), and *Planning Methods, Models, and Organizations: A Review Study for Communication Policy Making and Planning* (S. A. Rahim *et al.*, Honolulu, East–West Communication Institute, 1978). These and a small number of other publications had set general parameters for the developing field of communication planning, established a base of professional training materials, and synthesized concepts and approaches from other areas of social planning.

What was needed was a conceptual and technical publication that would provide practising planners with a set of methods relevant to the challenges of communication planning. Such a book would be based on the needs of practising planners, would reflect the perspectives and skills of planners in both developed and developing countries, and strike a balance between relatively complex, sophisticated methods on the one hand, and simpler, more easily used methods on the other. In keeping with the spirit and philosophy of work at both Unesco and E W C I, the development of the book was to be an interdisciplinary and intercultural effort.

Work began with a survey of practising communication planners in developed and developing countries in late 1978. Through this survey a list of planning methods and planning method needs was identified which were felt by those surveyed to merit attention in the eventual book. This list was reviewed by the authors and their colleagues and a final list of methods was drawn up. Practising planners from eleven countries collaborated in the preparation of the twenty-one method chapters following a standard outline.

The intent of these chapters is to introduce the method in sufficient detail for planners to be able to appreciate the output of the method and its use in planning, as well as the strengths, weaknesses and costs that each method entails. Planners are not expected to be able to use most of the methods presented without further review of more detailed methodological presentations (though this may be possible for some of the methods presented). Thus the presentation of each method specifies its assumptions, procedures and output; provides a case example illustrating the use of the method in communication planning; and gives annotated references for more thorough treatments.

The work of defining the field and creating a conceptual framework for communication planning was carried out over a period of more than a year at the East–West Communication Institute. The institute was fortunate to have the advice and criticism of a large number of scholars and practitioners active in its Communication Policy and Planning Project during this period. The results of this effort are intended to (a) help readers locate themselves in the rather broad field of communication planning, and so to orientate themselves to the book; and (b) provide a general conceptual overview of planning to help readers see how planning methods fit with other fundamental dimensions of the planning process.

The book is organized in six parts. The two chapters of Part I provide the definition of the field and a conceptual framework for communication planning. A central element of this framework is the identification of five fundamental elements of planning: analysis, strategy, decision, action, and learning. A separate part with from three to five method chapters is devoted to each of these elements. Methods are thus clustered around the elements of the planning process where they are considered to be *primarily* useful, even though it is recognized that most methods can be used for several.

Apologies are offered in advance to readers who fail to find their favourite method included, or who would quarrel with the inclusion of others. The potential number of planning methods is indeed large, and selection was one of the most difficult tasks.

Authors have been asked, in all cases, to write in their individual capacity, and any conclusions offered are their own. The same is true of editorial contributions and choice; the opinions expressed in the book are personal and do not necessarily reflect the views of Unesco.

Contents

Acknowledgements

We are indebted to a great many people for their help in developing this book. Alan Hancock saw the need, helped in planning and provided a significant chapter. His contributions have been of fundamental importance. Our colleagues at the East–West Communication Institute (EWCI) during the period in which the book was written were unstinting in their criticism and advice. We mention especially Bruce McKenzie, Gus Root, Gerry Moriarty, Meow-Khim Lim, Melina Pugne, Mark Rasmusson and Syed Rahim. The participants in the EWCI Faculty Seminars in 1980 and 1981 gave valuable feedback. George Beal and Meheroo Jussawalla were indispensable in the conceptualization of the book and in early research, and contributed significant chapters as well. Jack Lyle, Director of the Communication Institute, provided continuous support for our work. As leader of the institute's Communication Policy and Planning Project, Syed Rahim provided our activity with an institutional base and gave us the benefit of his extensive experience as a development planner. Terry Schulze and her staff provided outstanding editorial and production support, usually under the pressure of tight deadlines.

All of these individuals contributed in significant ways. Final responsibility, of course, rests with the senior authors. Although the development of the book has been supported by Unesco and the East–West Communication Institute, the views and opinions expressed are those of the individual authors, and do not necessarily reflect the views of either of these fine organizations.

I

Conceptual bases for communication planning

Introduction

Planning is much more than the routine application of methods. It is a complex process, deeply influenced by the values and ideologies of the society in which it takes place, and by the nature of the purposes and resources to which it is applied. Planning can be greatly improved to the extent that planners are explicitly aware of the wide variation possible in the kind of planning in which they are engaged, and in the ways in which planning can be conducted. Planners need a conceptual framework which enables them consciously to create a planning approach and to select appropriate planning methods.

The two chapters in this section seek to address these needs. Chapter 1 defines communication planning, and provides a brief overview of the various types of communication planning that are practised today. Chapter 2 offers a conceptual framework which distinguishes three levels of planning: planning to plan; planning to act; and planning to learn. Five essential elements of planning are identified as fundamental to all planning processes. These are analysis, strategy development, decision, action and learning. Different planning approaches—ways of conceptualizing and organizing the planning process—are reviewed. These sets of concepts are integrated into an overall systems model of the place of planning within society.

These two chapters are intended to provide a foundation and framework for the review of planning methods that follows.

Chapter 1
Communication planning defined

John Middleton

Communication systems of many kinds have been created and used for a variety of purposes throughout history. This has always involved the application of knowledge to problems and the explicit or implicit use of theories of cause and effect as a guide to action. In short, it has involved planning.

As with many aspects of human society, planning for communication systems has become increasingly sophisticated and complex. The range of purposes for which planned communication is used has increased; we have progressed from the sending of simple messages of warning to the interactive exchange of highly complex information. We seek to use planned communication to change the nature of society itself. The technology through which information is exchanged has expanded at an exponential rate, increasing both the power of planned communication systems and uncertainty about their effects—and hence their design. The school-book remains, but it holds its place in the modern classroom amidst a welter of advanced technologies: computers, radio and television, programmed learning, simulations and audio-visual media. Scientists have advanced our knowledge not only of technology, but also of the human and social processes through which communication works and has effect. Of notable impact has been the use of theories of learning and persuasion in the design of communication messages. Political and commercial systems (governments and corporations) are more pervasive, assuming larger roles in the conduct of daily life and looking to increasingly long-range futures as they seek to control the ways in which society develops. At the same time, the increased power of large systems threatens the domination of the individual, calling forth counter-movements in the political arena and alternative models for smaller-scale participatory planning and control.

These trends in society have all contributed to the increasing formalization of a process generally known as 'communication planning'. A decade ago communication planning was primarily seen as a set of planning activities within specific sectors of society. Thus we had agricultural extension planning, community development, telecommunications planning, educational planning and so on. Increasingly, however, both practitioners and scholars have come to see a fundamental unity of purpose and process across these disparate activities, and communication planning has emerged as a field of endeavour and research, though not yet as a coherent profession.

Among the many forces noted above, two developments seem to have been especially significant in the emergence of the field. One is the increasingly widespread use of systems theory and analysis in problem-solving throughout society. A systems view of communication in society leads directly to a more fundamental conception of the ways in which communication systems inter-relate, both in form and function. The second has been steadily accumulating experience with the use of communication as part of planned social and economic development, particularly in less-developed countries. If nothing else, the relatively extensive use of centralized planning models in this arena has tended to highlight the role of communication systems as scarce resources to be allocated in the development planning process. This book rests firmly on both of these developments. Its focus is on planning of communication systems for social and economic development, with a focus on less-developed countries. Its fundamental perspective is derived from systems theory and planning.

In this chapter we shall seek to outline the broad shape of communication planning for development. The picture that emerges is far from definitive. The field is relatively new, emerging from a variety of experiences and traditions regarding the role of communication in development. It rests on widely differing and often conflicting images of the way in which societies should be developed. These social images are composite statements of the social, cultural, political and economic characteristics of current and future society, and shape in fundamental ways the goals and processes of communication planning. For example, social image determines the roles that government and private sector organizations, or systems, play in creating and using communication systems—and indeed, the role that organized planning itself should play in society. Finally, communication planning draws on many scientific disciplines, and its current diversity and lack of coherence reflect the widely varying approaches brought to the field by technologists, social scientists, economists and planners (Middleton, 1980).

Yet no matter how imprecise, such a picture is needed, if only to enable readers to identify the kinds of communication planning (for there are many) in which they are interested. In turn, this should enable them to orientate themselves in this book, particularly with respect to the planning methods which it presents. We shall begin by defining communication planning, and then turn to a review of the various types of communication planning that are currently practised.

Communication planning defined

What makes communication planning different from other kinds of planning? Simply put, the answer is that the planning is for communication goals and resources instead of something else. Communication planners seek to create communication systems, as when a telecommunications organization launches a satellite and builds ground systems necessary to use it. They allocate communication resources, as when an international commission assigns a broadcast spectrum, or a radio station decides how to fill its schedule. And they use communication resources, as when agricultural-extension campaign planners call on the services of rural radio stations and field-workers. It is through this process of creating, allocating and using communication resources that planners seek to achieve the goals of their system, and thus to maintain or expand the role that their system plays in the present and future social environment. Thus we can define communication planning as follows: 'Communication planning is the creation, allocation and/or use of communication resources to achieve socially valued communication goals, in the context of a particular social image or images.'

The processes through which communication planning is carried out are shaped by the planning approach that a particular planning group follows. There are several such approaches (to be discussed in more detail in the following chapter). These approaches are shaped in powerful and fundamental ways by the social environment and by the place of the planning system in the complex hierarchy of systems that make up society. Of particular importance in determining both the shape and content of planning is the prevailing social image in a given society.

Like all planning, communication planning is fundamentally orientated towards the future. While planning takes place in the current environment, that environment is changing even as planning goes forward. Moreover, the broad purpose of planning is to predict the direction of change, both to enable the planning organization to adapt to these changes and to try to influence the direction of change and the ways in which change takes place. This definition of communication planning fits in with two well-known, and fundamental, earlier definitions. The first is on communication policy and was developed at Unesco meetings of experts in 1972 (Unesco, 1972):

Communication policies are sets of principles and norms established to guide the behaviour of communication systems. Their orientation is fundamental and long-range, although they have implications of short-range significance. They are shaped in the context of society's general approach to communication. Emanating from political ideologies, the economic and social conditions of the country and the values on which they are based, they strive to relate these to the real needs and prospective opportunities of 'communication'.

This policy definition is balanced by Alan Hancock's widely known definition of communication planning (Hancock, 1981, p. 12):

By communication planning . . . we mean the preparation of both long-range and short-range plans (i.e. strategic and operational) for the efficient and equitable use of communication resources, and for the realization of communication policies, in the context of a particular society's goals, means and priorities, and subject to its prevailing forms of social and political organization.

These definitions emphasize the importance of 'political ideologies', 'economic and social conditions', 'values', 'means and priorities', and 'prevailing forms of social and political organization'. All of these elements go into the formation of a social image, as do other elements, such as national culture. Thus we would expect to find many different kinds of communication planning. Different societies have different social images. Moreover, each society is made up of many interrelated systems, each planned from a different perspective. Some are large and complex, such as a national telecommunication system, or a national education system. Others are smaller and less complex, such as a community health campaign or a single school. Larger and smaller systems are interrelated, but the degree to which planning for different related systems is integrated, and the way in which integration is achieved, vary as social images and planning approaches differ. Hence communication planning will differ along at least two significant dimensions: social image and the system perspective of a particular planning process. In addition, we would expect types of communication planning to vary according to the kinds of communication goals planned for, and the kind of communication resources created, allocated or used.

Types of communication planning

The four factors identified above can help us distinguish among different kinds of communication planning. These factors are: (a) the nature of the prevailing social image or images; (b) the system perspective of planners; (c) the nature of communication goals for a given system; and (d) the kinds of communication resources created, allocated or used. These four factors are shown in a simple way in Figure 1. The arrows between the ovals indicate the dominant position of social image, which determines what kinds of communication goals are considered valuable in the system environment. A free and critical press may be a broad social goal under one kind of social image, and not a goal at all in another society with a different social image. The persuasive processes of mass media may be used in support of individual competition under one social image; or to help achieve social co-operation and solidarity in another.

The way in which planners determine their system perspective flows at least in part from the prevailing social image. On the one hand, control-orientated societies tend to build large centralized systems, such as ministries, to achieve social goals. Planners in these systems tend to have large system perspectives. On the other hand, planners in a consensus-oriented society, with smaller, decentralized systems, will have a smaller system perspective. Social image also determines, in very fundamental ways, what kinds of communication resources are created, and how they may be allocated or used. Sometimes this influence comes through goals, as our example with the free press illustrates. At other times it comes more directly, as when a nation decides to establish a television system, in part, at least, to build the nation's image in the international arena.

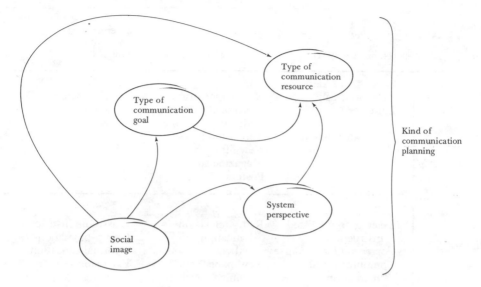

FIG. I. Factors determining a particular type of communication planning.

Finally, the system perspective of planners also affects the kind of communication resources utilized. Planners at higher levels in society, with larger perspective on more complex systems, tend to have more control over or access to communication resources than those at lower levels with smaller perspectives on less complex systems. The national-health-campaign planners are likely to have better access to mass media than the village health worker, and each will plan differently because of the different access they have to communication resources of that type.

Taken together, these factors can be used to define different kinds of communication planning. In theory, we could carry out a very complex review of existing planning efforts, using all of the four criteria. This would be a difficult task indeed, one beyond the scope of this chapter. Instead, we will focus on the two most concrete and practical factors—the nature of communication goals and the kind of communication resources created, allocated or used. These two factors will be the primary means through which we will distinguish among different planning types. In our discussion of these types, however, we will comment on the impact of social images and of system perspective. Examples of planning of each type will be given to make the discussion concrete.

Table I is a simple matrix which shows the interrelationships between six categories of communication goals and three general categories of communication resources. The matrix cells contain examples of the application of a category of resources for a particular category of goals. These applications are examples of the kinds of communication resources that planners create, allocate or use to achieve important communication goals.

TABLE I. Communication-system resources and goals

| Goals | Categories of communication-system resources | | |
	Point-to-point (telecommunications, postal communications, computer network)	Mass media press, radio, television, film, magazines, print)	Interpersonal one-to-one groups
Inform	1 Telephone call Letter Telegram Data transmission	7 Newspaper story, classified advertising Radio announcement Television news New film Magazine story Posters	13 Simple spoken statement
Educate	2 Telephone-mediated instruction Correspondence course Computer-aided instruction	8 Radio/television education Textbooks Newspaper courses Technical journals	14 Classroom instruction Group-based non-formal education Extension services Training
Persuade	3 Telephone advertising	9 Newspaper editorials and feature stories Radio/television speeches, dramas Advertising (all media) Political speeches, printed or broadcast	15 Political discussion groups Extension services Public speeches
Co-ordinate	4 Orders and directives through all media Intra-organization communication	10 Emergency announcements Announcement of deadlines (i.e. payments of tax)	16 Staff meetings Supervisory relationships
Dialogue	5 Telephone conversation on an issue or problem Exchange of telegrams Exchange of data via computer networks	11 Interactive television Radio teaching with organized feedback Letters to editor	17 Meetings Animation groups
Entertain	6 Telephone chat with a friend Exchange of letters with a friend	12 Broadcast drama Newspaper comics Cinema Various print with entertainment purposes	18 Live entertainment

Some comments on the matrix are in order. First, the two dimensions differ greatly in the degree to which their components are differentiated. The three types of communication systems are relatively easily distinguished from one another. They correspond roughly to the way these resources are organized in real world systems. Point-to-point communication systems comprise what we commonly call post and telecommunications. These communication resources are most typically used to facilitate two-way communication between two points in the system, e.g. the participants in a telephone conversation, the sender and receiver of a letter, a data base and the user of a computer terminal. Mass-media systems share messages from a single source with many receivers. With a few exceptions, these systems are one-way, with little potential for interaction. Interpersonal systems, as the label implies, comprise those organized communication acts that take place directly between and among individuals. There are, of course, examples of overlap between the systems, such as mass mailings. Another example is the radio/telephone talk show, which combines mass, interpersonal and telecommunications systems.

The goals of communication, moreover, overlap to a considerable degree. Informing is part of the process of educating, and both are components of persuasion. Co-ordination, the process through which the actions of people inside and outside organizations are directed, involves elements of informing, educating and persuading. Dialogue is the process through which interactive communication leads toward mutual understanding (though not necessarily agreement) between the participants in a communication act (Kincaid, 1979). Dialogue can, and often does, encompass all of the communication functions listed above it in the matrix. The sixth function, entertainment, is the broadest of all, potentially incorporating all of the other five functions. For this reason we have separated goal categories with dotted lines Despite this high degree of overlap, most planned communication has one or other of these functions as a primary goal. There are, of course, many instances when planners will allocate the resources of a communication system to several functions; sometimes these are integrated, as when a magazine seeks to inform, educate and entertain.

It is essential to note, also, that the same system resources are allocated in different ways to different functions. The essence of radio as a system resource, for example, is a broadcast spectrum with the technology needed to transmit and receive messages. This resource is used differently, through different programme designs and structures, in achieving different functions. A ten-second announcement of the weather (information) is a different pattern of resource utilization from a twenty-five-minute instructional programme for schoolchildren.

The categories of communication goals have been chosen in part from communication theory, and in part from review of the purposes to which planned communication seems to be put in a number of countries. The theoretical basis comes from early work by Harold Lasswell, and later Wilbur Schramm, on the broad functions of communication in human society. Lasswell identified three primary functions (Schramm, 1973, p. 28–35). The first he called *surveillance*. This is the use of communication to understand and share information about the environment. In our matrix, we have used a more common term, *inform*. The second he called *transmission*, which refers to the broad function of transmission of culture and knowledge from generation to generation, and from place to place. We have used the more common term, *educate*. The third function is that of *co-ordination*. This refers to the use of communication to manage society. We have distinguished two components of this function in our set of goal categories. One is *persuasion*, the use of communication to bring about desired change in people, groups and institutions. The other is *co-ordination*, which is the purposive use of communication resources to organize, stimulate or control the performance of individuals, groups or organizations. Charles Wright added the important category of *entertainment*. And we have added the category of *dialogue* as well.

The more pragmatic basis comes from a review of the current state of the art in communication planning as reflected in two recent bibliographies (Adhikarya *et al.*, 1979; Rahim, 1976). Most, if not all, current communication-planning efforts can be categorized as involving one or more of the goal categories in the matrix, and one or more of the three broad types of communication resources.

Any system of categories is open to question. No special claims are made for this one, other than for its pragmatic use in describing the wide range of current communication-planning efforts. The types of communication planning identified and discussed below differ from each other principally in the nature of the goals which are addressed and the types of communication resources involved. A second criterion of difference is the degree to which planners of a given type are engaged in creating, allocating or using communication resources—or in some combination of the three. The discussion of each type of planning will also cover the impact of social image on planning as well as the effect of different system perspectives. Examples of current planning efforts will serve, we hope, to make the discussions concrete.

Telecommunication planning

Telecommunication planners deal almost exclusively with point-to-point communication resources, including those systems that are used by the mass media, such as satellite and microwave transmission systems. Their orientation is primarily towards the creation (and maintenance) of communication resources for others to use. They build the systems that make possible the kinds of action shown in cells 1–6 in Table 1. When successful, planners provide resources to satisfy the needs of an important segment of society, ranging from individual telephone users to other large systems which rely on telecommunication resources to achieve their goals. Planners of postal systems are in much the same situation, although the nature of the communication resources they plan for differs from those of telecommunication planners in obvious ways, being comprised primarily of organized human effort and transportation systems. Increasingly, however, telecommunications, by such methods as electronic mail, are providing an attractive alternative to traditional postal technologies. This is leading, in cases where the two systems are quite separately controlled and planned, to inter-system conflict over goals and resources.

The impact of social image on telecommunication planning can be quite direct. As telecommunication resources are central to the flow of information in society, they are objects of great interest to governments. In some societies, telecommunication industries are closely regulated. In others, they are government-owned or controlled. Moreover, in capitalist societies, telecommunication planning is done primarily in response to projected demand for services. In centrally planned (control image) societies, planning tends to respond to needs, as articulated by social goals. Because of the size and technological complexity of telecommunication systems, planning tends to be done from a relatively high-level perspective, regardless of social image. Planning tends to be relatively long-range, too. A good example of telecommunication planning is Australia's Telecom 2000 Report (Australian Telecommunications Commission, 1973). This twenty-five-year plan for the development of telecommunication services in Australia was initiated in 1973 in response to the challenge posed by rapid technological change in telecommunication resources. This planning effort is notable for several elements. First, it was a centralized activity with a broad national system perspective in a democratic society. Perhaps in consequence, there was great emphasis on 'open' planning and the participation of a wide range of users, interest groups and so on. The strengthening of open planning, along with a call for continued assessment of the changing social and economic environment, were major recommendations of the plan.

Second, the impact of social image is seen in explicit attention to the development of a planning approach for Telecom 2000. Two contrasting approaches to futures planning were noted. The first is deterministic, holding that the future is determined by the past. Hence projections would be a primary planning method. The second is the view that future cannot be predicted, but rather created. This normative view would require building alternative images of desired futures as goals against which projections can be measured, and actions to create the desired future planned. A planning method fitting well with this approach is scenario development. In fact, the planners of Telecom 2000 felt that the truth lies somewhere between these two approaches. Their planning approach blended deterministic and normative models, and projections and scenarios.

Another interesting example may be found in telecommunications planning in Mexico (Valerae, 1977). Mexico has a strongly centralized federal system of government. Telecommunication planning and regulation are centralized, with corporations being granted concessions for the creation or use of communication resources under direct government control. The first national planning effort in telecommunications came in response to the 1968 Olympic

Games in Mexico City. A telecommunication system typical of most developing countries was replaced by a modern system using the advanced technology then available. Now, more than ten years later, technological changes in telecommunication systems pose a new challenge and are establishing goals for yet another planning and development effort. Both in 1968 and now, the system must adapt to a changing environment through the creation of new telecommunication resources.

Telecommunication planners tend to have engineering and other technical backgrounds and skills. Some are economists, and there seems to be increasing participation of other social scientists in planning telecommunication systems. The criteria that guide telecommunication planners are complex. There is an overriding concern for cost and efficiency, particularly in commercial telecommunication systems, where profit is the goal. Further, as the examples cited show, service criteria are also important and telecommunication planners are increasingly concerned with the social impact of their systems.

Mass-media planning

The orientation of mass-media planners is primarily towards the allocation and utilization of communication-systems resources. There is a secondary orientation towards the creation of systems resources, but this is done in the context of expanded or improved resources which these planners utilize. By and large, their work involves the kinds of activities shown in matrix cells 7–12 in Table 1.

Depending on the nature of the social image, planning of mass media ranges from highly centralized to highly decentralized. In some societies, the major mass media—the press, radio, television, film—are government-controlled and planned in a relatively centralized way from a broad, often national, perspective. In other societies, the media are privately held and planning proceeds in relative independence, guided by broad policies, regulations and, in capitalist economies, the nature of the market for services. The perspective of planning can be towards comparatively small systems, such as a small-town newspaper or a community radio station, privately owned and operated for profit.

The mass media have the potential to achieve all types of communication goals. One result of this wide functional capability is a great deal of interest on the part of other kinds of communication planners in using mass media, as well as in government intervention in mass-media policy and planning. This overlap of interest is most strong in control-image societies, but is manifest in various ways everywhere. Governments utilize the mass media as information channels, through direct ownership and control, or through regulation and purchase of media resources. Planners in education and development agencies seek to use the mass media for their own purposes. Thus mass-media planning seeks to allocate and use mass media resources to achieve a range of communication goals. Mass-media planners work with communication planners from other systems to achieve this variety of goals, representing and allocating mass-media resources in the context of bargaining and negotiation. Tele-communication planners create resources for others to use, but do not use them themselves for the various communication goals. Mass-media planners utilize resources themselves, primarily in achieving information goals (as in news programming and writing), but also share these resources with other systems.

The scope of mass media planning is broad indeed. In different societies, social image and different system perspectives (or 'levels of planning') combine in different ways, leading to different kinds of planning. This, of course, is complicated further by the fact that there are numerous mass-media organiz-ations (or systems). And, as we have said, the mass media have the potential to accomplish all communication goals, if wisely and imaginatively used—especially in combination with other communication-system resources, such as interpersonal communication. Thus the examples given here are illust-rations only of this broad scope.

High-level—or national-system—perspective on mass-media planning is found in both developed and developing countries. In Finland, broadcasting and press policies are set and administered by legislative committees (Sisatto, 1978). In many developing countries, a government press and broadcasting system coexists with regulated private systems. In the United States, broad-casting is regulated by policy, and both broadcasting and the press are in a sense 'planned' through the nation's legal system, through such instruments as libel laws. Below this level, mass-media organizations plan their strategies within whatever set of policies, regulations and constraints may be operating in the society. Of considerable interest are the differing ways in which mass-media-system planners work with planners in other communication systems to make mass-media resources available to achieve a variety of goals, such as education and persuasion. In many developing countries, government agen-cies in education or in one of the many development programmes either purchase radio air time from commercial stations, or compete with each other for scarce air time on the national radio network. In many countries, com-munication planners in development agencies provide to the press and to magazines news releases and feature articles designed to support the achieve-ment of their system goals. In some cases, development agencies create their own mass media—newspapers, magazines or radio broadcasting stations—to carry out their work.

Mass-media planning also takes place at the local level in systems which provide sufficient independence of action to permit this. Local newspapers and broadcasting stations (both radio and television) respond to community needs with planned communication resources. Examples can be found in many countries. In the Philippines, provincial radio stations work with family-planning communication planners to develop programmes (Domingo, forth-coming). In the United States, community radio and television stations, and newspapers as well, work closely with agricultural extension services to provide a broad range of farm and community development information resources.

Mass-media planners tend to have backgrounds in journalism or broadcasting, and occasionally (principally in broadcasting organizations) in engineering. They tend to evaluate the success of their planning by such criteria as the size of the audience they reach. Commercial mass-media organizations rely heavily, of course, on sales figures and the margin of profit in assessing the value of their output to the environment.

Educational media planning

Telecommunication and mass-media planners are defined primarily by the nature of the communication resources they create, allocate or utilize. Educational-media planners, on the other hand, are defined by their emphasis on a particular communication goal—that of education. They plan for the creation and utilization of communication resources of all kinds. They create communication resources in the form of software for media, textbooks and teaching aids, and—in a sense—when they train teachers. They utilize the resources of both telecommunication and mass-media systems. They even create mass-media resources, as when an educational-broadcasting system is developed and managed by an educational agency, or when an educational-software development centre is built. Educational-media planners are generally employed in education ministries or educational development agencies. Thus their planning perspective tends to be on large, complex systems. There are many non-formal educational efforts which utilize media, and planners for this type of project may be found in almost any type of ministry, often with more restricted system perspectives.

Social images affect educational-media planning in interesting ways. In many countries with consensus social images, education is decentralized (for example, in the United States and Canada). Educational-media planners there work with subnational perspectives. In other, more centralized societies, they tend to operate within a national perspective. Even there, however, the desire to create materials that are effective in local areas often leads to attempts to plan from more local perspectives.

There is a heavy emphasis in educational-media planning on integrated use of two principal communication systems: the mass media and interpersonal communication. The integration of these two systems comes principally through the underlying theories of learning and instruction which guide educational-media planners in creating patterns for system utilization. The same theories are applied in the design of an instructional radio programme and in the design of a training course. Thus educational-media planners are primarily involved with activities typical of matrix cells 2, 8, and 14 in Table 1. Educational-media planners have backgrounds primarily in education; some began their careers in broadcasting. Increasingly, they have training in educational communication, the hybrid field which focuses on educational media.

The work of educational-media planners is guided by communication effects. Educators are interested in helping people learn, and are accustomed to measuring this particular kind of media effect. A second criterion is cost. Much recent effort to develop educational-media systems has grown out of belief that they expand the reach of education while lowering cost per person reached. A third criterion is audience size, usually measured by enrolment figures.

There are many well-documented examples of educational-media planning (see, for example: Mayo *et al.*, 1976; Spain *et al.*, 1977). Radio has been used on a large scale in education in such countries as El Salvador, Kenya, Malaysia, Nicaragua, Philippines and Thailand. Radio is used for teacher-training, for direct classroom instruction, for support of conventional teaching and for a variety of non-formal educational efforts. Television has also been extensively used, for example in El Salvador, the Ivory Coast and Singapore. These projects have met wih varying degrees of success, but on the whole have shown the potential educational media have to bring good teaching to learners. The use of mass media for education is expanding, creating an increasingly important area for communication planning.

Development-communication planning

Development communication though varied basically comprises a wide range of planned communication activities which have as their purpose the creation of social and individual change within the development process. It encompasses campaigns in support of development programmes in health, agriculture and rural development. Governments use development communication to build a sense of national identity, and to inform people of development goals and programmes. Development-communication planning is orientated primarily towards the utilization of communication resources and, like other forms of planning discussed above, involves all three communication systems. There is a great deal of emphasis on combined uses of systems. All communication goals are at least potentially dealt with as well, although there has often been an emphasis on persuasion goals, especially in such areas as family planning. As the development theories and ideologies that are part of social image change, the dialogue function is becoming more important. In fact, the impact of different social images is especially significant in development communication. What is considered development communication in one society may very likely be considered propaganda in another.

Planners of this type of activity are found in almost any agency and sector which has development programmes. They work in information ministries; they may be found in other government ministries and in private agencies. They are deeply involved in negotiation for resources with telecommunication and mass-media planners. They tend to plan at project levels, seeking ways to use communication to support or lead development of all kinds, although national plans within a sector (i.e. family planning) can be found. Thus development-communication planners work within a range of perspectives.

31

Planning is usually quite short-term, with emphasis on evaluation and learning from experience. Planners' backgrounds are varied: many come to communication from subject- or problem-orientated backgrounds—in agriculture, in health, in community and rural development. Many have extension-education backgrounds. An increasing number have been trained in communication. Their guiding criteria relate to change: individual change, group change, and occasionally structural change. There is a central emphasis on change in information and knowledge levels of audiences and efforts are often made to measure changes in behaviour as well.

National-level integrated communication planning

The first four types of communication planning are real activities: they can be found in most societies, developing and developed. The fifth type of planning, integrated planning across systems and functions for a single society, is an idealized kind of planning, increasingly recommended and considered, but rarely done. One example of a national communication plan integrating the categories of planning noted above exists, but it has not been implemented, owing to a change in government (Unesco, 1978). Planning of this type would be done from a broad national perspective for a complex system of many elements and many goals. The idea is receiving considerable attention in developing societies. Communication resources, like other resources, are scarce in the face of increasing demand. The planned creation, allocation and use of these resources holds promise for increased cost-effectiveness. At the same time, it raises the issue of the control of a nation's communication resources in a particularly direct and tangible way. How can resources be allocated and controlled at this level while freedom and diversity remain protected? The answer, according to our framework, will flow from the dominant social image in a given society.

Planning of this type would be orientated towards the creation, allocation and use of communication resources to achieve a wide range of goals. This integration of orientation is, indeed, one of the principal benefits cited by advocates of national planning. As this kind of planning would incorporate the first four, the planners would come from the full range of backgrounds and disciplines. The co-ordination of such a planning team in itself would pose serious problems.

The guiding criteria would, like the planning team, be an amalgamation: of the criteria of the other forms of planning. National-level integrated communication planning is likely to begin with the development of coherent national policies to guide the currently fragmented efforts of the different types of planners. Councils and co-ordinating bodies may follow. While it is difficult to predict the shape that such planning will take, there is likely to be some balance between centralized resource creation, allocation decisions and priorities on the one hand, and a continuation of decentralized planning on the other. Clearly, co-ordination of organizations poses a central problem.

Communication and national development

This chapter will end with the topic which, perhaps, it might have begun. The complex questions surrounding the role of communication and development have been left last for several reasons. First, this book is primarily about planning, not about communication in development. This latter topic needs its own book—or more precisely, several books. By putting planning first we emphasize what the book is about. Second, although the chapters in this book are written from the authors' own point of view, there has been a conscious effort to be objective, analytical and descriptive. The question of communication in development cannot be dealt with in quite the same way. While there are important analytical and objective aspects of this question, there are equally important value and ideological components.

In a very wise and useful essay, Luis Ramiro Beltrán S. has analysed the cultural origins of North American communication research, shown clearly how its models, theories and methods are culturally determined, and shown further how different approaches are needed for the social and cultural context of Latin America. His analysis rests fundamentally on differences between social image held by North American researchers and the social images of Latin America. (Beltrán, 1976) The same analysis and conclusions, we believe, apply to the active role of communication in development. It has been argued that the prevailing social image is central in determining the goals of planned communication, the kinds of communication resources that are used, and the ways in which communication planning is done—and by whom. Thus the roles that planned communication can and does play in development will differ as social images differ. There is no 'role' for communication in development, but rather many roles.

Given this reasoning, planners seeking to create, allocate or use communication resources to achieve development goals will need to fashion roles for communication not only from 'objective' models, theories and information, but also from the values and ideologies which surround them. This is not an easy task. There are important questions about the roles that communication might play in development which planners might find useful. It should be clear that we believe that the answers in different societies at different times are likely not to be the same. The answers to the questions below represent the views of the author, and are offered primarily as a point of discussion and departure for others. The questions, though, may be more generally useful.

1. WHAT CAN COMMUNICATION DO IN DEVELOPMENT?

Communication has its effects through the actions of people. So whatever communication can do for development comes through what people do—or don't do—because they participate in a communication process. This is not to say that communication determines what people do or don't do, only that when communication has effects it has them through people. Human behaviour is extremely complex, determined by many factors. Some of the most important are internal to the person. We call such factors values, attitudes, beliefs, dreams, hopes and so on. Some are outside the person in the social environment. These include other people, things, organizations, expectations of others—and information and knowledge. Planned communication affects directly only knowledge and information in the person's environment. What the individual does depends more on all the other factors than on the changes in knowledge and information.

At the same time, we know that people do use information and knowledge to act. Thus we can be reasonably certain that useful information and knowledge are important to help people act. Planned communication can increase the probability that people will act, but it cannot guarantee it. If you want to provide clean water to your family, there is a better chance you will be able to act successfully if you know some basic things about sanitation; and more successfully yet if you have learned some skills in well-digging.

Information and knowledge are centrally important to the processes of thinking and reflection. The life of the mind is as important as the life of action—and to many people perhaps more important. What people are—how they see themselves and the world—is important in itself, not only because it determines much of what they do. Planned communication can have a powerful impact on these processes. It is no accident that planned communication has been a central element of all great religious and ideological movements. The creation and use of the Koran, the Bible and the *Sayings of Chairman Mao* are significant examples of planned communication. We also know that planned communication can persuade people to change both what they believe and what they do. The ethical and moral issues that surround this role of communication in development raise the question of what roles communication should play in development.

2. WHAT ROLES SHOULD COMMUNICATION PLAY IN DEVELOPMENT?

This is a central question that must be answered clearly by planners. Their answers will flow from their social image, and where images are in conflict the answers will conflict also.

Planned communication should liberate and strengthen the individual, in both the world of action and the world of the mind. We recognize that this goal can conflict with such goals as national integration, mass mobilization and social conformity. These goals are important and often valid in a given social environment. In an imperfect world, compromises between these two types of goals are perhaps inevitable. But the choice should be made explicitly and carefully.

3. WHO SHOULD CONTROL COMMUNICATION RESOURCES?

Yet another moral question, one probably not asked often enough by planners, is who should control communication resources. But the question of the role that communication should play is answered by those who control and plan for communication resources. Thus the control of communication resources leads to a significant amount of control over the nature and direction of development. Again, the answers must flow from the dominant social image. That is why communication planning is such an essentially political process. The question is a difficult one to answer. In the Third World, the absolute need for efficient use of resources seems to point towards centralization of planning and control. Yet, as we have seen all over the world, this can lead to unequal access to communication resources in society, and the use of communication for domination and exploitation.

Control must be shared if development goals such as equity are to be met. All sectors of society should have access to communication resources and to the planning and decision-making processes. There are many ways in which this might be done. Some involve radical decentralization of planning and control. Others involve the development of effective means of participation in centralized planning processes. Still others blend a degree of decentralization with participation.

4. HOW CAN WE IMPROVE OUR THEORIES?

The use of theory to guide strategy development is a crucial element of planning. Theories lie behind the 'if ... then' statements on which planned action rests. Yet most communication theory has been developed in western culture. Much of this theory base has been shown to be faulty when applied across cultures.

Communication planners in the Third World face the almost overwhelming task of developing theories and models within their own social image and culture. If the traditional western model of university-based research is followed exclusively, the task will take a long time. While universities are an increasingly important source of new knowledge, planners themselves must seize the opportunities created with planned action to learn on their own and to share this knowledge with others.

5. HOW CAN WE PLAN BETTER?

Regardless of the role that is chosen for communication, planners face the need to deal with larger and more complex systems while at the same time generating the knowledge base they need. Rapid technological changes create both opportunities and obstacles. Resources, except in a few wealthy countries, will be increasingly difficult to get, raising the importance of efficiency even higher. In this context, communication planners must look constantly at their planning approaches and methods. The challenge is to create and refine intellectual tools useful for planning. This book represents one step in that direction.

Bibliography

ADHIKARYA, R., *et al.* 1979. *Communication Planning at the Institutional Level: A Selected Annotated Bibliography*. Honolulu, Hawaii, East–West Communication Institute.

AUSTRALIAN TELECOMMUNICATIONS COMMISSION. 1973. *Telecom 2000: An Exploration of the Long-Term Development of Telecommunication in Australia*. Melbourne, ATC.

BELTRAN S., L.R. 1976. Alien Premises, Objects and Methods in Latin American Communication Research. In: Everett M. Rogers (ed.), *Communication and Development: Critical Perspectives*. Beverly Hills, Calif., Sage Publications.

DOMINGO, Z. Forthcoming. *The Community Advisory Board as the Grassroots Planning Arm of the Broadcast Media Council (Philippines)*. Honolulu, Hawaii, East–West Communication Institute. (Case Study series.)

HANCOCK, A. 1981. *Communication Planning for Development: An Operational Framework*. Paris, Unesco. (Monographs on Communication Planning No. 2.)

KINCAID, D.L. 1979. *The Convergence Model of Communication*. Honolulu, East–West Communication Institute. (Paper No. 18.)

MAYO, J.R.; HORNIK, R.; MCANANY, E. 1976. *Educational Reform with Television: The El Salvador Experience*. Stanford, Calif., Stanford University Press.

MIDDLETON, J. (ed.). 1980. *Approaches to Communication Planning*. Paris, Unesco.

RAHIM, S.A. (ed.). 1976. *Communication Planning for Development: A Selected Annotated Bibliography*. Honolulu, Hawaii, East–West Communication Institute.

SCHRAMM, W. 1973. *Men, Massages and Media*. New York, Harper & Row.

SISATTO, S. 1978. Finland's Other Broadcasting Organization. *Intermedia*, Vol. 6, No. 1, February.

SPAIN, P.L., *et al.* (eds.). 1977. *Radio for Education and Development: Case Studies*. Washington, D.C., World Bank. 2 vols.

UNESCO. 1972. *Reports of the Meetings of Experts on Communication Policies and Planning*. Paris, Unesco.

——. 1978. *Communication Planning for Afghanistan: An Eight-Year Projection of Communication Development*. Paris, Unesco. 3 vols.

VALERAE, J. 1977. A Communications Plan for Mexico (Opportunity for Discovery). *Telecommunications Policy*, September.

Chapter 2

A conceptual framework
for communication planning

John Middleton

Consider the family vacation. Planning one seems like a relatively straightforward business. One simply decides where to go, when, and how. Yet on closer examination, it is not quite such a simple thing to do. In fact, planning a vacation for your family can involve the same complex issues that are associated with planning for a national communication system. The issues appear in a simplified form, but they are there none the less.

Let us begin with your goal: to have a vacation. Actually, that is probably not your goal at all. It is a strategy you have chosen as a way to achieve your goal, which may be to relax from the pressures of work, or to see some new sights, or to spend more time with your children, or to visit your relatives—or perhaps some combination of all three. The choice of vacation as strategy means you have decided that it is the best way to achieve the goal—better than some of the alternatives you had, such as staying home to sleep and tend the garden. You made this decision using some kind of theory or cause–effect model: *if* I take a vacation, *then* I will achieve my goal. This theory can come from experience, or from information you have received (a book, a travel brochure). In choosing that strategy, you had to take into account key aspects of the system you are planning for (your family) and the environment in which it exists. You took a look at the elements of your system: the family members, your resources, and your capabilities. Who wants to go where? What can we afford this year? How much time do we have? You may have had to draw some initial boundaries around your system, deciding perhaps not to take mother along this year. Depending on the kind of society you live in, and the cultural views there about how decisions are made, you might have announced your decision and expected everyone to agree. Or you may have discussed it with the family at some length—whether to go, where to go, when to go—and worked out a compromise solution. You may have even had to struggle and fight a bit to reach the eventual strategy choice.

This 'social image' dimension of your planning was probably also reflected in the way in which it was determined, where you work, that you could have a vacation at all. It may be that your organization is very orderly, with well-established procedures and customs for such things: everyone leaves Paris in

July, and that is that. Or the situation might be more fluid, with employees negotiating the timing and duration of leave. You might even have had to argue strongly that you should go rather than someone else. Your position in the hierarchy of power probably had something to do with your ability and freedom to take a holiday. Your family's position in a similar hierarchy—of parents and grandparents, of clan allegiances—also had an effect on your freedom to choose to take a vacation. Your religion, its values and its rules, may also have had an effect in determining what your goals and strategies are— perhaps a pilgrimage to a holy place leading to spiritual renewal is more important than relaxation at the sea-shore.

So you have worked your way through all of this and have settled firmly on a vacation away from home. You now have to decide where to go. The mountains? The sea-shore? The old home town? First, though, you will probably decide how to go ahead with your planning and decisions. You recognize that there are several possible approaches to your planning. So far, you have been making your decisions in sequence: the broad general decision on a vacation away from home, first; the more detailed decision (which involves more careful analysis of alternatives), second. This is typical of one of several planning approaches, called mixed scanning—a form of rational planning. Often these approaches are quite different. As an alternative, for example, you could simply have boarded the first bus out of the city to see what would happen (a more incremental form of planning).

Let us assume you have chosen a form of the mixed-scanning planning approach. The decision on where to go then requires that you obtain information about the alternatives. What are the prices at the various places? What can one do there to relax, visit relatives, see new sights? Pick one according to your goal. You use information from the past: the Smith family went to the mountains last year, let us ask them. And you use information about the future: what will the weather be like at the sea-shore in July? Will the prices change? Sometimes the information is pretty certain. Other times, the situation is very uncertain, particularly if you are planning far in advance. Then you must rely on predictions about the future—the weather, the prices—and your uncertainty increases, particularly as the number of things that you are uncertain about increases, making the situation more and more complex. As you review the information and options about where to go, you keep your goal in the back of your mind. Which destination seems to offer the maximum chance that you will realize your goal? Will I relax more in the mountains or at the old home town? If you have several goals, which place seems to give the optimum or best balance of achievements? You may not be able to work it all out exactly because there are too many combinations of things, and may be satisfied with a good-enough choice—one that seems the best to you and your family, even though you know you have not fully considered each possibility. You are maximizing, optimizing or 'satisficing'.

Having decided where to go, you now begin planning on how to get there and what to take. In planning to implement your vacation you consider resources, alternative technologies (the bus or the plane?), time schedules and equipment (will it be swimming or tennis?). The cultural and religious values that helped you choose your goal also affect the choices you make about implementation. The timing of your trip, for example, may have to be adjusted to the schedule of religious holidays and celebrations. Finally, as you leave the house, you probably make some remark like this: 'This planning has sure been a lot of work; I am going to watch carefully to see what happens, so that planning next year's vacation will be easier. I also want to find out if, indeed, I can really relax at the sea-shore!' You are, of course, getting ready to evaluate your vacation in terms of your goal, as well as the adequacy of your own planning.

Along the way, you have probably used some methods in your planning. You made lists of alternatives with information about each. Sometimes you used these to test out your 'theory' about vacations leading to goals. You made some budgets. You and your family talked at some length about what it would be like and what might happen at each location (you evaluated alternative scenarios). You made some projections and some schedules. You probably even worked out assignments for different family members, both for planning and for implementation. The planning approach you used probably had something to do with the methods that you chose and the way you used them. If you were extremely well organized and rational in your analysis, you probably used more methods and used them more formally (I even know people who type out their lists!). The people that you worked with in your small system also had something to do with the methods you chose. Perhaps your daughter is a management student, and made a PERT chart for the whole process. And, of course, it all depended on how much time you had to plan, how much and what kind of information you could get, and on whether or not you find the planning process itself interesting and rewarding.

That was a long story about a familiar process. Let us step back from the details of planning now to look at what you were doing, overall. You were responsible for planning for a small system—your family. You probably thought about how to plan, as well as about the vacation you were planning for. So you did some planning to plan as well as some planning. And you did some planning to learn from the experience. Throughout you analysed your system and its circumstances (or environment). You created and considered alternative strategies, and made a decision for one. Then you acted. Let's hope you learned from your mistakes!

Much of what you did was aimed at preparing your family for the eventual vacation. In a general sense, you were planning to help your family adapt itself to the chosen vacation environment so that your goal would be accomplished. In essence you asked yourself what it would be like there (in the future) when you got there: what you needed to do now, and in the future, to enable you to best accomplish by our goal in that vacation environment. In planning for the adaptation of your system to its future environment, you had to take into account many other systems. You may have consulted a travel agency, or gone to a library to get a book about the area. You probably wrote or telephoned ahead to get hotel and transportation reservations. All family members had to make adjustments in their day-to-day living to go away. Depending on your culture, music lessons might have been delayed, someone may have been asked to watch the house, or perhaps a soccer game was missed. In short, you had to co-ordinate your plans with the plans and resources of other systems.

When you did this, in effect you brought those other systems into your own system, even if only briefly. The reservation clerk did things for your system; the music teacher changed her schedule; the soccer team had to start another player. Perhaps your boss had to be persuaded to let you go and your banker or a moneylender to give you a loan. Without these changes in individual and other systems, your own 'temporary' vacation system could not function. In short, you planned for them and, in doing so, made them part of your system. In a sense, you changed them—at least what they do. Of course, these others may not think of themselves as part of your system. They see themselves in a different perspective from your own, and think of themselves as parts of other systems—the bank, the soccer team, the hotel, the bus line, the music school. In fact, when they make their plans for their systems, they reverse the process you have used: they include you in *their* system. This is one of the main causes of interdependency, an important aspect of social systems. In short, who and what is considered to be within any one system is largely a matter of perspective.[1]

If you had very ambitious goals, and many resources, you may even have considered directly changing the future vacation environment itself in order to achieve these goals. For example, if you are very rich you might build your own private resort at the seaside, with a swimming pool and tennis courts, and live there half of the year. The existence of your resort would change the other elements of the vacation community. It would, perhaps, create jobs for serv- ants, take some of the beach away from the public or serve as an example to other rich people to do the same thing. This latter, of course, would greatly change the vacation community. It would change the environment to which your system would adapt in the future. If many others moved in, you might have to leave to find the solitude you were looking for originally. This simple example further illustrates the complex interdependencies of systems adapting to each other and to the environment. In building your vacation home you would have tried to change only those aspects of the vacation environment which would enable you to achieve your goal. What is important is that those elements which you chose to change would be ones which you thought you *could* change in order to achieve your goals. You could buy land for the house, but you probably could not change the shape of the sea-shore, for a number of reasons. First, it might be too expensive. Second, the local community (other elements in the vacation environment) might strongly oppose you. And if you could overcome this opposition, and did change the shape of the sea-shore by

1. For a full discussion of this idea, see Simon (1969).

blasting out your own boat harbour, there would be significant effects on other elements of the environment: the path of ocean currents would change, leading to erosion of someone else's land; there might be effects on ocean life, reducing (or increasing) the income of local fishermen; and the next large storm might wash your house away.

Thus in planning to adapt your vacation system to its future environment, you faced a range of choices about the way in which you could or would plan your system to adapt to the environment. You also faced a range of choices about the kinds of changes in the environment that might be necessary—and possible—in achieving your goal. And you may even have considered the interdependency of your vacation system with the environment and other systems in making these choices. You planned your system to adapt to the environment as it is, or as you think you can make it become. In both cases, you pay close attention to changes that are occurring in the environment—and which might be expected to occur in the future—whether you have tried to cause these changes or not. These changes are the evidence which lead you to change your plans, and even your goals, in order to maintain the successful adaptation of your system.

In the pages that follow we shall lay out a conceptual framework of planning for your inspection. The ideas in the framework will be the ideas touched on in our story of vacation planning, but expressed in a somewhat more abstract form. Why is such a framework necessary? Communication planning, like all planning, can be a very complex process. We believe, in fact, that there is no single best process. Each planner or group of planners must work out a way to plan which fits their planning environment, their system and their goals. Only then can planning be most effective. To do this, planners need a framework within which to consider the large numbers of choices they have about *how* to plan. These choices include the choice of methods to use in various elements of planning. And methods are what this book is all about. Thus the purpose of our framework is to provide you with a way of looking at planning which should help you evaluate and choose among the methods presented in this book. It may also help you look at your planning within a new perspective, seeing new or different ways to approach this complex, challenging and critically important part of human endeavour.

Planning defined

We begin our framework with some basic definitions, not because our definitions are necessarily the best ones, but because it is important that we establish a common set of these terms at an early point.

Planning is the conscious effort to adapt a system to its environment in order to achieve system goals. This is a general abstract definition that applies to all planning. We discussed this idea of planning in simple terms in our Introduction, but let us look at yet another example.

A bridge is planned to enable certain kinds of traffic (say motor vehicles) to cross a river. The bridge is part of a larger transportation system, which includes the highway, feeder roads and so on. This system links cities to farms and factories to sources of raw materials. The goal of the system is to facilitate the flow of people and goods between the places it connects, and it has been designed with this goal in mind. This system must be adapted to the environment (the river) by crossing it. Hence a bridge is planned. The bridge must be adapted to the width, depth and shape of the river, as well as to the anticipated volume of automobile traffic. It is planned for the future, for the anticipated use over a twenty- or fifty-year time span. The bridge is also planned with the existing state of technology—in construction, in materials and in design.

A communication system is, in the same way, planned to achieve a set of goals within a given social environment. These goals may include the changing of certain elements of the environment and other systems by including them in the system to be planned. For example, take development-communication planners designing instructional messages to help rural people learn new health practices. These planners study their audience carefully, finding out what the people now know and do about health practices, and the changes that these people would like to see in their lives. They identify any barriers to new health practices, such as lack of necessary materials or equipment as well as cultural values and beliefs. The capability of various media to reach these audiences is examined. Finally, a system of messages and media is designed which will get effective information to the people, and enable the people to get information back to the planners. The planners will have adapted their system—or that part of it which deals with rural health campaigns—to the village environment.

We can take even a broader view of the 'system' that the health-communication planners are dealing with. In the example above, the system included the planners, the messages and the media. By taking a different perspective, we can enlarge the view of the system to incorporate the audiences, their health problems, their needs and goals, the village physical and social environment and the mechanisms that will be used to evaluate the system in action. In this perspective, the planners are seeking to adapt this larger system to its environment. They seek to change ways in which components of the original system perform, including in this instance the rural people who want improved health. Thus, from another point of view, they are seeking to modify the environment by including those elements of the environment which they wish to change—and think they can change—within their system. This larger perspective on what a communication system is may appear somewhat unusual. However, it is generally accepted that a communication system must include both senders and receivers, and a feedback loop as well. This system, when functioning, helps people *converge* towards common understanding (see Kincaid, 1979). Thus this larger perspective on the systems which communication planners seek to adapt to an environment fits well with communication theory. It is this perspective on the boundaries of communication systems that is the foundation for the conceptual framework presented here.

National health system

Health-campaign system

Worker/villager
discussion
system

FIG. I. Hierarchy of systems

Let us take a closer look at some of the elements of our definition of planning.

SYSTEM

A system is a set of interdependent parts that work together, as a whole, towards a goal or goals, in which the performance of the whole is greater than the simple sum of the performance of its parts.[1]

In our health-campaign example, we see a number of system components: the audiences, the messages, the media, the planners, the feedback mechanism. Each component by itself will not accomplish the goal of changed health practices, yet working together, the components as a system may have this effect. Systems vary from the simple to the extremely complex. Our health-communication system is relatively complex. A component of this system might be a discussion between a health worker and a villager about boiling water. This component itself is a system, and a relatively simple one. There are fewer components, a relatively simple (and single) goal, the evaluation or feedback component is quite simple and provides almost immediate feedback, and the boundaries around the system are quite clear. This small system is part of the more complex health-campaign system, which includes many more elements,

1. This is a common definition, found in many places, including Churchman (1968).

has many more components and less clear boundaries and which has feedback loops that take a relatively long time to provide information. The health campaign itself is part of an even larger system, the national health programme. And the national health programme is part of an even more complex system, the national development programme. And so on.

It is useful to think about this interrelationship of systems at different levels as a hierarchy, from simple systems to complex systems. Alternatively, we can think of it as Chinese boxes—boxes within boxes within boxes. Depending on where they are in the hierarchy (or which box they are in), planners are responsible for some part of a larger system, and this part is itself a system (Grobstein, 1973; Simon, 1973).

In discussing the different levels of complexity of systems, we have used some key terms to distinguish among the levels. One is the *boundaries* of the system. These are the imaginary lines we draw around a set of interrelated elements for the purpose of calling it a system. We tend to define our boundaries with the system goal in mind. The worker/villager discussion has a single clear goal; the campaign is organized for a set of goals; the national health programme has an even larger set of goals. Boundaries for any one of these systems are determined by including those elements that work together for the goal or goals specified, including those elements which planners hope to change in order to achieve their goals. Establishing boundaries, of course, is a primary way in which planners choose their *system perspective*.

As we noted, more complex systems have more goals than do simpler systems. In addition, the feedback loops and processes in complex systems take longer to function and provide less reliable information than those in simpler systems. The time lag in information flow is greater; moreover, the content of the information changes significantly as systems grow more complex. The worker talking with the villager knows almost immediately what the villager knows, does and believes. At the level of the health campaign, planners may find out (roughly) how many such conversations have been held, perhaps every six months. At the level of the national health programme, planners will find out something about how the health campaign is working once a year. This is an essential feature of hierarchical systems, of course, because at each successively higher level planners have more components to deal with and less need for detailed information from the simpler systems. In fact, too much detailed information gets in their way as they plan.

Finally, the more complex a system is, the greater uncertainty associated with it and with its effects. There are several reasons for this. One is the way in which feedback works, as discussed above: in complex systems it tends to be slower and less detailed. Another is the increasing number of system components. A third is the tendency to create more complex systems to deal with more complex goals. The strategies or theories that guide the system's efforts to achieve complex goals are less clear and certain. A trained village worker knows more about how to conduct an effective discussion than does a national health planner about how to achieve a better standard of health for a nation. Finally, more complex goals take longer to achieve. Thus planners in complex systems tend to plan further and further into the future. The more we reach into the future, the less certain we can be.

Think back to our example of vacation planning. What would be the effect on your planning if you were responsible for all the vacations of the people in your organization? If, in addition, you had to plan them for three years? Or if you had to plan *all* their recreation, including weekends and evenings? Or if you were planning to develop a community of new vacation homes?

ENVIRONMENT

The environment consists of those factors outside a given system to which the system seeks to adapt in order to achieve its goals and to survive.

There are a great many such factors, far too many to list completely—even if they were all known. Some key categories of factors can be identified, however. An obvious category is resources. The type, quantity and quality of resources that a system can draw on have a great deal to do with its goals, with how it plans and with what it plans. Resources include not only money, but human resources and, what is important, information. Human resources include the planning skills available to the system; information includes knowledge of the system, of the environment, of system effects and of the theories that guide the creation of strategies. We can also think of needs as resources. Needs are reflections of problems to be solved or opportunities to be seized. To the extent that a system's goals correspond to significant needs, there is a greater likelihood of getting resources. Like most things in the environment, needs change constantly, posing a continuing challenge to planners.

Other organizations (or systems) form an important part of the environment. As we noted earlier, parts of other systems may be included in the system of the planners, depending on their system perspective. Our health-campaign planners, for example, may get the co-operation of the ministry of agriculture and find themselves planning special training for agricultural extension workers. When they are in training, and when they are giving health information to villagers, agricultural workers are included in the health-campaign system.

Of great importance is the view that planners and (and others) hold of what society should be and how it should operate, now and in the future. We call this the *social image* held, and it encompasses values, ideology and hopes for the future. The prevailing social image (or images) greatly affects both the goals that planners work towards and the way in which they plan. We will return to this idea in more detail later on, but for the moment, simply contrast the capitalist and communist views of society. Clearly, planning is done differently and for different reasons in each type of society. Values are closely related to social image, and form yet another extremely important aspect of the environment. Clearly they affect the goals of the system, as well as judgements about whether the system is successful. Individual values are important when plan-

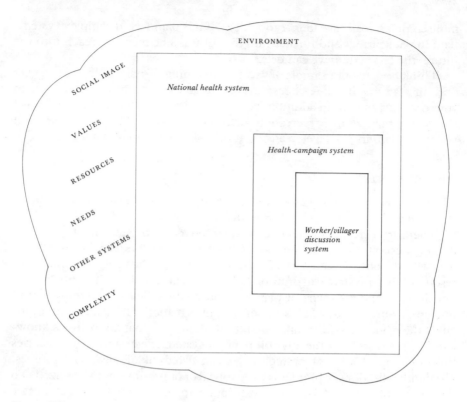

FIG. 2. Hierarchy of systems in the environment

ners deal with people, and the values of planners themselves have impact on how they plan as well as what they plan. Values that help define social image are often expressed as national goals and political ideology, and these too have a significant impact on planning.

Each of these factors can be more or less complex. Complexity leads to uncertainty, and the degree of uncertainty in resources, needs, other systems, social images and values determines much of what planners do and how they do it. Figure 2 adds these key factors in the environment to the hierarchy of systems.

What is system and what is environment? The boundaries of a system, and the importance of system perspective in establishing these, were discussed earlier. The environment for a given system may be another system or, as is often the case, parts of many systems. Given his perspective, the environment of the village health worker includes the health campaign. It also includes other systems, for example, agricultural extension. The larger national health programme is part of the environment of the campaign, and so on.

ADAPTATION

Adaptation is the process of adjusting the characteristics of a system to reach a satisfactory level of goal achievement (benefits to the environment) and resources received from the environment which depend on goal achievement (benefits to the system).

As the definition indicates, the relationship between goal achievement and getting resources is central to successful adaptation. The kinds of systems that planners deal with are open systems. Open systems take resources from the environment and return something of value. To the extent that the output of the system is valued or effective, the system will continue to get resources and will survive and achieve goals. It will have adapted successfully. We can see how this operates most clearly in a commercial firm, which makes and sells a product. If the product is needed or wanted, sales are high and the income needed to continue purchasing raw materials to make into products continues. In public agencies of the type where most communication planners work, there is no profit or loss, but the system works the same way. Agencies which produce 'good work' continue to get budgets. The process of giving value to the output of the agency is much more complicated, however. In an idealized world, this would be done with cost–benefit analysis, and evaluation does play a part in determining the resources that agencies get. However, as is well known, many other factors—often called political—enter into the process of deciding what is 'good work' and therefore what resources go to a public agency.

In planning your vacation, you adjusted several characteristics of your vacation system to maximize your goal and hence the benefits to your system. In order to get the most relaxation, you went to the sea-shore, adjusting the 'location characteristic' of your system. Our health-campaign planners adjusted the combination of messages and media they used to achieve maximum benefit in terms of health practice for villagers. They did this adjusting to key factors in the environment. These included the availability of information about the audience (including very important information about what the villagers want), the resources (such as communication channels) that were available to them, and the planners' views on whether changed health behaviours should be voluntary or required by law—views which come from their social image.

We know, of course, that the environment changes, often quite rapidly. Sometimes this is the result of the efforts of our planned system. If goals are being achieved, elements of the planned system will change (such as village health practices). These changes will in turn lead to other changes in the environment because of the interdependency of systems. Improved health, for example, may lead to increased rates of population growth and more pressure on food supply. Other changes occur independently of the efforts of the planned system. Sometimes these are the results of planned effort on the part of other systems. Sometimes they cannot be anticipated (this in fact seems to be most usual). Thus the relationship through which a system adapts to its environment must constantly be evaluated and often changed. As the environment and the system both change, the existing adaptation relationship must change as well. In fact, an important aspect of effective planning is anticipation of changes and the establishment of goals which will have value in a future changed environment. It is in this way that planning is fundamentally orientated to the future.

This is a bit abstract, but an example should help. In choosing a goal of improved health practices for villagers, our campaign planners have already rejected past goals related to curing diseases. They believe (for any number of reasons) that preventive health care is and will be more important and valuable. They project this goal in an environment where better preventive health practice is needed, and which will make a difference in terms of the higher goals of the larger system environment in which they operate, the national health programme. Thus they have adjusted their goal to important values or goals in the environment of their system. If they are successful in establishing new health practices, they will have changed part of the environment to which they must adapt in the future: village conditions. This will require them to establish new goals, thus adjusting a key characteristic of their system once again. The classic example of this was in the United States, when a large and extremely successful national volunteer agency had to change its goals from eliminating polio to working against cancer. The invention of the Salk vaccine, which the agency helped support, led to success against polio. The original system goal was no longer viable. To survive, the system had to adapt to a new goal.

Conscious effort

Conscious effort (to adapt the system) is what planners do. We commonly think of this as the planning process. Planners are those persons within a system charged with adapting the system to its environment. Very often they are called planners and think of themselves that way, particularly in more complex systems. At other times, planning is one of several activities of people in systems, as with our vacation planner or the village health worker. The planning process involves the use of rational thought and the application of knowledge to achieving system creation and/or adaptation in the future. This is what distinguishes planning from other forms of human action, such as intuitive reaction to immediate problems.

There are many ways in which to define rational thought: the five elements listed here are common, but they also appear in slightly different forms in other writings about planning. The five elements are analysis, strategy, decision, action and learning (for convenience let us call these A S D A L). Each of these elements represents a phase or stage in the process of rational thought, and hence appears in one form or another in all approaches to planning. Listing these five elements one after the another does not mean that the overall planning process is necessarily a step-by-step, linear process. Except at basic levels for simple systems, the process is almost always circular and iterative (and sometimes simultaneous), occurring over and over again. In the real world, planning begins at different points in the rational process, goes forward, goes back and skips steps. Often planners work on different elements simultaneously, such as when they plan goals and evaluation together. Nevertheless, these elements are present, in one form or another, in all planning processes.[1] Depending on the systems, the environment and other factors, planners will be planning in different ways, and the emphasis on the various elements of the ASDAL process will differ as well. We will discuss this in somewhat more detail in the next section of the chapter.

ANALYSIS

This is the element of planning devoted to learning about systems, environments and goals. It is the stage at which planners seek to investigate and to understand what must be accomplished if successful adaptation is to take place. A typical product of the analysis stage in planning is a statement of problems and causes, together with related goals.

STRATEGY

In this element of planning, planners develop alternative ways to achieve goals. They create statements of cause and effect: 'If this is done, that will occur.' In developing strategy, planners apply knowledge of theories and cause–effect models as guides to action. These theories (often called theories in planning) may come from research or from experience and common sense. Sometimes the theories are clearly and explicitly used; at other times they are hidden as assumptions underlying the actions that planners propose. Communication planners are quite familiar with this aspect of planning, especially those planners who deal with the design of messages to inform, instruct or persuade. Telecommunications planners have theories about networks, information exchange and so on.

As systems grow in complexity, and as their goals become more complex, the ability of theories to explain and predict tends to weaken. The development of alternative strategies thus becomes important at early stages of strategy-making. For example, communication theory once told us that if we had the attention of a group of listeners, and we gave them information in words that they could understand about a problem they were interested in, they would be likely to understand the meaning of our message. This is a relatively simple situation and a simple strategy. If, however, we are seeking to broadcast information to many different kinds of people with the goal of enabling them to

---

1. As we have defined them—that is, as the use of rational thought and application of knowledge to achieve system adaptations.

change complex behaviours, which themselves are only partly understood, the situation becomes more complex, theories and models offer less clear guidance and alternative strategies become more useful.

In the second level of strategy-making, planners organize actions using these theories as a guide. They arrange means (people, resources, time) in combinations which seem likely, according to their theory or cause–effect model, to lead towards goal accomplishment. And they plan the mechanisms needed to make things happen. This is often called implementation planning.

DECISION

Even with simple goals and systems, a decision is required to accept and carry out a strategy. In more complex systems with more complex goals, there are usually a number of alternatives to choose from. This choice may be made implicitly or informally, or it may be made explicitly and formally. Those making the decisions in a planning process apply a range of concepts and criteria. They think about the relationships between costs and effectiveness, sometimes formally, and almost always informally (Middleton, Bealand Pugne, 1982). They usually seek to find the 'best' or most 'cost-effective' strategy. They consider the probabilities of certain things happening. If they can truly consider all possible alternatives, they may be able to choose the single best one and optimize. Usually, this is not possible: the alternatives are too many to be identified. In this situation decision-makers satisfice: that is, they seek an alternative which is satisfactory at the time, even though other better, if unknown, alternatives may exist.

Values play an important role in decision-making. They act as guides and limits to the range of choices possible (in other words, they serve as parameters). Often the most effective strategy goes against widely held values, and is therefore rejected. The way in which things get done can be as important, from the point of view of values, as the goal. For example, the most effective way to prevent people from having unrealistic expectations about consumer products and to prevent expenditure on 'unnecessary' items may be to strictly regulate mass media advertising and content. But this may run counter to strongly held values about the freedom of the press and of commercial enterprise. If so, some other strategy to reach the goal (which itself may be questioned from a values perspective) will have to be developed.

ACTION

The true test of quality of a plan comes through action in the real world. A key aspect of action is careful attention to monitoring of what happens. Not only do strategies receive a test through action, but new theories and strategies can emerge as things get done. It is this kind of reasoning, plus a desire to avoid waste of resources, coupled with healthy scepticism about strategies, that leads to pilot projects.

LEARNING

Planners need to learn about two basic aspects of their work. First, how well did planned action work? In answering this question, planners seek to assess the effects of planned action and relate these to the strategy. In the best of all worlds, this assessment will deal not only with what happened and what did not happen, but also with reasons why and why not.

Second, in assessing the effects of planned action, the planners will reach some judgements about the planning process itself. The basic question is: how can our planning be improved?

Learning of both types is essential if planning, and planned action, are to improve over time.

SUMMARY

We have defined planning as the conscious effort to adapt a system to its environment in order to achieve system goals. Systems, as sets of interrelated components working together to achieve goals, are arranged in hierarchies or Chinese boxes. Systems are defined by their purposes. Consequently, what is included within the boundaries of any given system is a function of the goals for which it is created, and thus of the system perspective of planners.

Systems exist in and must adapt to environments. The characteristics of systems must be adjusted so that the system provides benefits of value to the environment in return for resources. Successful adaptation requires planners to develop system goals for future environments. Accomplishment of these goals contributes to the constant change that characterizes environments and the ways in which systems adapt. Key factors in the environment are resource needs, other systems, values and social image. The conscious effort to achieve successful system adaptation is the core of the planning process. The planning process rests on the use of rational thought and the application of knowledge to system adaptation. Five elements of the planning process were identified: analysis, strategy, decision, action and learning (ASDAL). These elements are thought to be found in planning of all kinds, though not necessarily with the same degree of emphasis, and certainly not always in a linear, step-by-step way.

Three levels of planning

The discussion so far has remained at a relatively simple level, treating planning as if it were a single process. We are now going to inquire more deeply into the different kinds of planning to be done in order to achieve effective system adaptation.

Planners face three related but separable tasks. They must organize themselves to plan; they must plan for action; and they must learn more about how they plan and what they plan so that they can improve. Each of these challenges requires the application of rational thought and knowledge (hence the elements of ASDAL), and is thus a form of planning within the overall planning process. For convenience's sake, we will call these component planning processes *levels* and give them names: planning to plan, planning to act and planning to learn.

PLANNING TO PLAN

Most practising planners recognize immediately that they are part of an identifiable subsystem within their organization. In larger, more complex organizations this subsystem may even be formally recognized as the planning branch, division or office. In smaller or less complex organizations, without formally designated planning subsystems, individuals will often create a temporary planning subsystem at certain intervals, often for specific duration, during which time they plan more and carry out other kinds of duties less. In yet a third general type of situation, planning is a fully ongoing process completely integrated with the other actions of people in a system. This too tends to be found in smaller, less complex organizations. Even in this third type of situation, people will be able to distinguish their planning tasks from other kinds of work.

The relationships of the planning subsystem to its larger system and to the system task environment are shown in Figure 3. The systems in Figure 3 are greatly simplified. However, they show the planning subsystem as a component of the larger system. The planning enclosure has been placed close to the boundaries of the larger system to emphasize its critical role in adaptation of the larger system to the environment.

As we discussed earlier, the larger system puts something of value into the environment in return for resources. This input–output relationship is the system's adaptation strategy. The planning subsystem draws resources both from the task environment and from the larger system itself. Money and people are important resources to the planning subsystem. Information and knowledge are also important, because they make it possible for the subsystem to plan successfully at all three levels—to plan, to act and to learn. The planning subsystem produces outputs for the larger system. We can conveniently think of these outputs as 'plans', as long as we recognize that the term includes all forms of information useful in the adaptation of the larger system. Figure 4 translates Figure 3 into a more common example, that of our health campaign.

Planning to plan is the conscious effort to adapt the planning subsystem to the larger system and to the task environment.

There are many different approaches to planning. To achieve successful adaptation to the system in which they work, and to be most effective in planning for the adaptation of the larger system to its environment, planners must develop an approach to planning which fits their system and their environment. Because systems and environments are different, and change

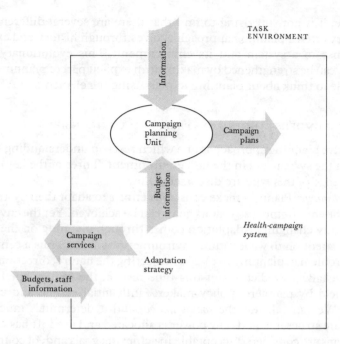

FIG. 3. Planning subsystem in its environment

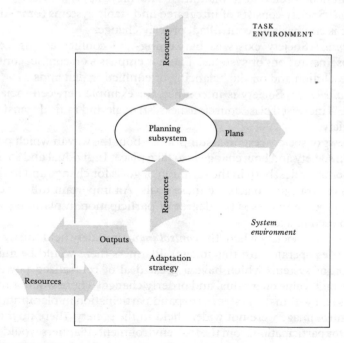

FIG. 4. Planning subsystem in its environment: example

over time, it is not surprising to find that there are several different ways to plan. Very often a planning approach evolves through history and experience in response to a system and its environment. This evolutionary process, however, can be strengthened by making it an explicit part of planning. Thus it is possible to think about planning to plan using the elements of ASDAL.

ANALYSIS: UNDERSTANDING SYSTEMS AND ENVIRONMENTS

An effective planning approach is one which rests on understanding of the key factors in the system and in the task environment. Three of the key categories of knowledge of this type are discussed below.

Social image. Planners make conscious efforts to adapt their system effectively to the environment so that its goals can be achieved. Yet the environment is constantly changing. Adaptation comes through planning on the run with constant attention to what future environments will be. Thus a central intellectual problem in planning to plan is projecting the nature, direction and pace of social change. Predictions of this type rest on the fundamental image of society held by planners, policy-makers, influential people and citizens in general. We can call this the *social image,* and it determines much of how systems are structured and how power is allocated and used. It has bearing on what means are considered acceptable in achieving goals and, of course, on the selection of goals themselves. Three contrasting types of social image have been identified as relevant to planning (Thornley, 1977):

1. *Control:* Society consists of integrated and stable systems (or institutions). There is emphasis on controlled, orderly change.
2. *Consensus:* Society exists as bargaining and conflict among competing groups, institutions or systems. There is emphasis on conflict containment and resolution and on the balancing of conflicting demands.
3. *Radical change:* Society is in conflict, for example between social classes. There is increased class consciousness, struggle and radical transformation of society.

These views of society rest on assumptions about the way in which power is to be used in society and how change is to take place. Individual and social values play important roles, both in the selection of goals for change and in the choice of means or strategies to achieve these goals. An important difference among the three types of images is the degree of participation in planning which fits well with each image.

Let us take a society where the *control image* is widely held (many developing countries operate with this image). Planners there would be guiding the adaptation of systems which have a great deal of centralized power. There would be high value on gradual and orderly change. There would probably be little pressure within the system to expand participation in planning, although if the control image were not widely held in the society, there might be some demand for participation from the task environment. Planners would probably see participation, for example of key officials and village leaders, primarily as a way to get information and to get people to agree with plans in order to strengthen implementation.

In a society with a *consensus image*, things might be quite different. Power would be shared by a number of competing groups and agencies. A key problem in planning would be that of establishing a power base through bargaining and negotiation with other agencies. Change goals would also be worked out through bargaining and competition. The participation of various groups and individuals in planning might be essential to achieving power and support. In a consensus society, there is likely to be considerable ideological support for participation as a good thing in itself, and planners are likely to share these values.

When the social image is of *radical change*, participation in political action to restructure society might be a central means of acting and, in effect, be required of citizens.

Systems complexity. Complex systems have several characteristics. The number of interacting components is relatively high; there are often long delays in the feedback systems, making it difficult for the system to know how well it is adapting. The goals of the the system tend to be long-term and deal with several interrelated problems in the environment. A health ministry is a relatively complex system compared to a discussion between a field-worker and a villager. Complex environments have similar characteristics. There are many interrelated systems. Social images may be changing or confused, and it may be difficult to identify future goals which will enable the system to adapt successfully.

The principal implication of the level of complexity in planning is the degree of uncertainty that planners face. As the complexity of the system increases, planners can be less certain about what the system can do. The information they get from and through the system comes slowly and is often distorted. As the environment grows more complex, planners are less sure of their information about the environment, especially about the causes of the problems which they seek to solve. At the same time, they are more and more uncertain about the theories and models they use as the basis for their strategy. And as they plan further and further into the future, these uncertainties increase. The levels of complexity and uncertainty which planners face have a great deal to do with the planning approach that they choose. Planning approaches which emphasize control and accountability are more possible where there is a relatively high level of certainty and relatively less complexity. Where uncertainty is high, planning approaches which emphasize continual learning from experience and constant adjustment of goals and strategies are often more appropriate.

Uncertainty is present at some level in all planning. We are talking about a matter of degree. It is possible to plan health-worker visits to villages in a controlled way, emphasizing schedules of accomplishment and accountability, even though there are many uncertainties associated with carrying out that plan: the weather, finding people at home, reliability of transportation etc.

However, when planning a national telecommunication system to help create a national consciousness and social integration in a multi-ethnic society, uncertainty increases considerably. A planning approach that emphasizes learning and constant readjustment is likely to be more effective.

Resources. The third major variable in planning to plan is resources. Clearly, different levels of resources have direct impact on what planners can do. Two categories of resources have been distinguished: physical and knowledge resources. Physical resources include such obvious elements as money and people. We can also include here technology as a resource and in communication planning; technological changes are a major factor to be dealt with. Knowledge resources are extremely important. These include not only data about systems and environments, but also the theories and cause–effect models available to planners as the basis for developing strategies.

Given few physical resources, limited data and few strong theories for strategy-making, planners will tend towards planning approaches that emphasize learning, even though they may use more comprehensive, accountability-orientated approaches on the surface. Where resources of both kinds are in good supply, rational comprehensive planning would seem to be more effective. There are, of course, other factors in the system and task environment which affect the way in which planners plan. The three categories discussed above are among the most important and serve here principally as examples of the kind of analytical information which is useful in evaluating alternative strategies in the second stage of planning to plan.

STRATEGY: ALTERNATIVE WAYS TO PLAN

In general, a strategy is a way of achieving a goal. When planning to plan, the goal is to develop a planning subsystem which can guide the system successfully in achieving goals and adapting to the environment. The strategy is a planning approach—or a way in which planners organize themselves and their resources.

We are also accustomed to thinking of alternative strategies, especially for more complex planning assignments. Alternative strategies give decision-makers a range of choices, each with strengths, weaknesses and costs. In planning to plan, there are several alternative strategies available as initial paradigms or guides to practising planners. These strategies are known as planning procedure theories or theories of planning. Developed largely in western industrialized countries as part of urban planning and development, these theories provide several contrasting ways to go about the planning process. They serve not as ideal models to be carefully followed, but rather as reasonably coherent descriptions of alternative processes from which practising planners can draw and adapt ideas.

Think back again to your vacation planning. While you probably made your plans in an organized and rational way, thinking ahead about different ways to accomplish your various relaxation goals, you could have just taken the first bus to see what happened. These two alternative planning approaches, in fact, correspond in a simple way to two of these theories of planning. To further illustrate the range of strategy options available to planners, a number of these theories are briefly reviewed below.[1] In these reviews the ideal form of the planning approach under each theory is emphasized. In the real world, of course, the ideal form invariably changes to meet reality. By stressing the ideal form of each theory, however, we can see the alternatives that they represent more clearly.

Rational/comprehensive planning. As Barclay Hudson (1979) has noted, rational/comprehensive planning is 'the dominant tradition and the point of departure for most other planning approaches, which represent either modifications ... or reactions against it'. This is the planning approach with which most planners are familiar. It is a linear and logical process, which begins with needs assessment and goal setting and proceeds through the development and evaluation of alternative strategies, implementation planning and evaluation. Though the process is linear in form, it is often implemented in an iterative way, with planners moving back and forth among the stages as the plan is developed. In the ideal form of this planning there is a great deal of emphasis on analysis as the basis for planning. All possible strategy alternatives are developed and evaluated, with the optimal alternative being selected, usually on the basis of some form of cost–benefit analysis. In practice, it is usually impossible to develop all alternatives, especially for complex planning environments and systems, and planners satisfice by choosing the best of several alternatives even while recognizing that other alternatives are possible.

This planning approach emphasizes the rather formal use of information, theories and cause–effect models in planning. Consequently, there is also a tendency towards the formal use of relatively complex methods. Very often goals and policies are developed outside the planning unit, and planners see themselves primarily in a technical role. Planning is also separated from implementation, and there is considerable emphasis on the plan itself as a basis for decisions and implementation.

There are several assumptions underlying rational/comprehensive planning. Because of the formal and generally linear nature of the approach, there is great emphasis on the use of processed information about the system and the environment as the basis for developing and evaluating alternatives. This is also true for the use of theories and models for developing strategies. Thus, the approach assumes a relatively stable environment and system, both of which can be understood in the present and projected into the future. There is the assumption that good data are or can be made available. Environments and systems like this are likely not to be too complex, or, if they are complex, to be changing relatively slowly. The theories and models that planners use are

1. For a more complete review, see Middleton (1980).

assumed to be strong and tested, shown to be capable of predicting the effects of planned action. There is also an assumption that the power necessary to implement a plan is available: the linear and rational process does not, in its pure form, give much emphasis to bargaining and compromise. In short, this form of planning tends to be associated with a social image of control.

The heart of rational/comprehensive planning is to bring a great deal of information to bear in decision-making. Because of the large volume of information needed to operate an effective rational/comprehensive planning approach, a number of procedures have been developed to organize both information and decisions (Faludi, 1973). One is called *routinization*, in which a number of rules or procedures are developed in advance to apply to certain kinds of information and activities. Some of these are familiar planning methods, such as programme budgeting or decision trees. A second procedure is *sequential decision-making*. Problems are broken into small pieces and put in a certain order. Rules are set for decision-making. Each small problem is then solved in turn. Planning methods used here include decision tables. In yet a third procedure, called mixed scanning, fundamental decisions are made based on the information that is available, and these basic decisions are used in turn as rules for making later, smaller decisions. These later decisions are made with more detailed information, and can cause planners to return to original fundamental decisions and revise them. Mixed scanning is the broadest and most flexible of the three procedures, and leads to the most learning. For example, a fundamental communication-planning decision, based on available information, might be to expand access to educational opportunities by extensive use of educational broadcasting. In working out details for this, planners might find that this fundamental decision was not feasible—perhaps because costs were underestimated, or because the amount of effective learning of the type desired from broadcast lessons was overestimated. The fundamental decision might then be revised (Etzioni, 1973).

Thus it can be seen, even from this brief description of decision-making strategy, that there can be considerable variation within the rational/comprehensive approach, even though the basic elements and assumptions remain. Most people planning their vacation would use some form of the rational/comprehensive approach, as was done in the example earlier in the chapter. The system and environment are relatively simple and stable. Information is available. 'Theories' about cause and effect for various alternatives are available from past experience, friends and travel agents. The chief planner in the family has the power to implement the plan. The separation between the policy decision on vacations (in the employing organization) and planning (in the family) is quite clear, although planning and action are the responsibilities of the same people.

Incremental planning. This planning approach grows directly out of criticisms of the rational/comprehensive approach, most notably of its assumptions. A central premise of incremental planning is that systems and environments are too complex to be understood at the level of certainty that rational planning assumes. Information about the environment and systems is not reliable, and most theories and models which are available to planners to guide strategy development are relatively weak in explaining complex environments and problems (Lindblom, 1959). Incremental planners also question the separation of goals, planning and implementation that characterizes rational/comprehensive planning. This is seen as artificial and weakening implementation. They also question the assumption of centralized power that seems to go along with rational/comprehensive approaches: in other words, they question the social image of control.

Incrementalism (sometimes called disjointed incrementalism) proceeds from opposite assumptions. The system and the environment are seen as complex and uncertain; consequently, there is much emphasis on short-range planning. Planners propose short-term actions with heavy emphasis on learning from experience. Problems are analysed 'on the margin', that is, in terms of the next best step given limited information. There is much less attention to the evaluation of alternatives.

The social image of incremental planners is one of consensus. Power is achieved through bargaining and compromise. Planning is decentralized, and planning, decision-making and action are rather completely integrated. This facilitates learning. Planners working this way tend less to use formal and complex methods, partly because the short-range nature of their plans requires less projection into the future, and partly because there is more reliance on informal and intuitive knowledge than on formal processed 'data'.

Critics of incremental planning often call it 'non-planning'. In fact, the approach describes much of the planning that goes on in the world. Incremental-planning theorists, however, have provided a rationale for planning of this type, helping us see the conditions under which it may be an appropriate approach. Incremental vacation planners may just get on the bus and go exploring. Perhaps they have little information about alternatives and little theory or experience to draw on. They say to themselves, 'I will plan today now; tomorrow I will see what is happening and plan again.' They are willing to let their strategies evolve from experience and intuition.

Innovative planning.[1] Thus far in our review of planning theories we have contrasted two approaches which differ primarily in social images held, the ways in which planners go about developing strategies, the way power is used and the roles that planners play. There are other planning approaches which are similar in whole or part to rational/comprehensive planning or incremental planning but which are different in different ways. One of these is innovative planning. Planners taking this approach step back somewhat from the planning process to look directly at how society is structured. Innovative planning emphasizes action through institutional change. Planners set up new systems to carry out programmes in response to problems. In short, they create new systems and turn them loose to adapt to the environment. These systems tend

---

1. This summary, and that of allocative planning which follows, is based on Friedman (1973).

towards incrementalism in planning because planning and action tend to merge in response to the problems the system has been set up to address. The emphasis is on the mobilization of resources through the creation of the new system.

The establishment of new systems can lead to a competitive, relatively uncoordinated environment. Thus innovative planning can be seen as an overall strategy to fit with or introduce a consensus form of social image. Over time, however, these new systems may stabilize and become part of relatively co-ordinated networks of institutions. Planning may then turn to yet another approach, allocative planning.

Under innovative planning you might question a vacation as the system to meet your relaxation goal. Instead, you might try to restructure your work and life to get more relaxation all the time.

Allocative planning. This planning approach is concerned essentially with the distribution of limited resources among competing users. It is the kind of planning which often goes on in bureaucracies competing for budgets. It appears with both control and consensus social images. Power and planning may be relatively decentralized, but there are rules and formally established procedures for planning and decision-making.

Planners in allocative systems tend towards rational/comprehensive planning, even if only on the surface. This planning approach is often laid out in formally established rules and procedures. However, as many practising planners will recognize, planning processes—especially in smaller system components—are often quite incremental. In an allocative family, the head of household would announce that certain resources were available for vacations. Family members would then prepare plans in competition with each other for these resources.

Transactive planning. This is yet another approach to planning, one which differs sharply from the others discussed so far in the purpose of planning. Rational/comprehensive, incremental, innovative and allocative planning approaches all see the primary value of planning in producing effective action— in adapting the system to the environment. Transactive planning sees another equally if not more important purpose. Participation in planning is seen as central to human growth and learning, both of which are seen as the highest goals in society. Thus a purpose of planning is to involve as many people as possible in planning for action which affects their lives. Transactive planning changes knowledge into action '... through an unbroken sequence of inter-personal relations (Friedman, 1973, p. 171). These interpersonal relations are between planners, who rely on processed and abstract knowledge, and clients of planning, who rely on personal knowledge.

Planning is radically decentralized to permit this kind of close inter-personal contact between planners and clients. Planning can be either rational or incremental, although extreme decentralization probably pushes it towards incrementalism. The social image underlying this form of planning is one of consensus; the approach itself is a structure for consensus generation. Here the important part of vacation planning would be what family members learn from planning together and with a consultant from the travel agency. If they felt better able to plan for themselves afterwards, more confident and capable, planning would be successful.

Radical planning. The social images underlying the planning approaches discussed so far have been either control or consensus. Radical planning comes in two forms (Hudson, 1979). Each reflects a social image of radical change.

One form emphasizes collective action at the 'grass roots' to solve problems and foster self-reliance. The role of large systems, especially government systems, is minimal. The 'people' are seen as struggling against the oppression of large systems to establish their own forms of planning and action. This approach to planning differs from transactive planning in the absence of technical or professional planners: instead of an unbroken interpersonal dialogue between planners and clients, the clients are the planners. The writings of Paulo Freire and Ivan Illich reflect this approach. Father would find his relaxation goal attacked or ignored. Different family members would advance their own goals and plan for themselves in their own way.

The second form of this approach is most closely aligned with radical change. Because society is seen as oppressive and structurally wrong, large-scale restructuring is required. The conflict may be between social or economic classes or among rival ideological groups. Planning as we customarily know it is not done; the emphasis is on radical restructuring, often through violent methods. The theories that guide radical action are political and ideological.

While our vacation-planning analogy is stretching a bit thin, we might say that under this form of radical planning the family itself might be called into question as the ideologically correct social structure, and vacations as a wrong social goal. A revolt from the younger members would lead to new social structures with new goals. Vacations might be replaced by collective action to combat oppression.

Participatory planning. This is sometimes thought of as a distinct planning approach. However, as we have seen, there are different purposes of participation in planning, depending on the dominant social image. These different purposes lead to different forms of participation by different groups of people in society. Some form of 'participation', in fact, can be built into any planning approach, depending, of course, in part on available resources.

Rational/comprehensive planning can and often does include participation of key interest groups and influential individuals, often in the analysis phase of planning as well as in the review of draft plans. The purpose is to get important information from the environment, and to improve the probability of successful adaptation by identifying key obstacles in advance and by winning the support of those who participate. Incremental planning tends to be associated with a consensus image in which participation of influential people and systems is required as a part of bargaining and negotiation. Participation may also be seen as a good thing in itself. Transactive planning, of course, sees participation as the central element in planning. Thus the question is not so much whether to have your family participate in vacation planning, but rather how they should participate and why.

DECISION: CHOOSING A PLANNING APPROACH

Even the brief review of planning approaches above indicates the wide range of alternative ways to plan available to planners planning to plan. In many if not most planning situations the approach that planners follow emerges over time from experience. In many cases, this is satisfactory. Yet as planners become increasingly aware of alternatives, more formalized decisions among alternatives may emerge. Certainly in newly created planning subsystems conscious choice of a planning approach would seem not only possible but desirable.

The task in the decision stage is to use knowledge of the system and its environment as a guide in searching through alternative planning approaches for an approach, or combination of approaches. Planners will seek to choose an approach which fits with key elements of the environment and the system, now or in the future. This choice is central in effectively adapting the planning subsystem to the larger system and to the task environment. Like all planning choices, it requires that planners work not only with a current image of the environment, but also with their predictions about the way the environment will or should change. It is a complex choice, one about which little is known from experience or research. A full theoretical discussion, moreover, is beyond the scope of this chapter. However, we can look at some of the kinds of decisions that planners face in matching planning approaches with the environment in which they plan.

The fit between planning approach and social image is clearly important. Rational/comprehensive planning is not likely to work when the social image is that of radical change. Incremental planning fits well with a consensus social image, and may also fit in societies with control images. In this later case, however, there will be pressure on incremental planners for increased accountability, stronger promises and longer time frames than this approach assumes. In a control-orientated society, the decentralization of power and planning that incrementalism requires if problems are to be attacked in smaller steps is likely to be hard to get. Transactive planning likewise does not fit with control-orientated societies, though it would fit well with a consensus social image and might be combined with grass-roots radical planning in a society undergoing radical change. Few task environments, of course, hold strictly to only one of the three social images discussed in this chapter. Various mixtures of the different images are more often found, even though one image may be dominant. In these circumstances, planners may be faced with a choice among images as a first step in selecting a planning approach. This puts planners face to face with a gamble on the future. If they select well among these images, they will be more successful in helping their system adapt to the future environment. If they select poorly, their system will not adapt well, and may not survive.

The values that planners themselves hold play an important part in such choices. Authoritarian planners are likely to be biased towards more stable social images, such as control; democratic planners towards consensus images; and revolutionary planners towards radical images. The social image itself is created out of sets of dominant values. These values, and therefore the images, can change and be changed. Thus planning is intimately linked with political action, and indeed all action designed to change systems and environments. Remember, the planners' task is to adapt their system to the environment. If their values and analysis combine to predict a future environment with a different social image, or a different combination of social images, they will choose a planning approach now which will enable their system to adapt to that future.

The degree of complexity in the task environment makes a significant difference in choice of planning approach. We have noted the different assumptions about complexity and uncertainty that distinguish between rational/comprehensive and incremental approaches. The former is associated with relatively high levels of certainty, and consequently with relatively less complex environments. The later approach explicitly recognizes complexity and uncertainty, and indeed is built around this recognition. In emphasizing extreme decentralization of planning, the transactive approach implicitly recognizes the difficulty of dealing with large and therefore complex task environments. Again, the correspondence between real world environments and systems is not simple, nor are the features of these approaches. For most systems and task environments, some things will be complex and uncertain, other things less complex and more certain. Planners will thus find themselves combining approaches to meet this reality, planning rationally for some aspects of adaptation, incrementally for others. Other systems in the environment are part of the issue of complexity. If there are many systems to be adapted to, planners may have to adjust their planning approach to fit with the ways these systems plan, particularly if other systems have control over the resources that planners need. We see this quite clearly when planners prepare a proposal for funding from another agency. Very often the proposal must meet planning requirements of the agency supplying resources. This in turn affects how planners plan. Thus we often see planners using different processes for different plans. One might be for a regular government budget—a form of allocative planning done incrementally. Another might be for a large grant or loan and be done with a form of rational/comprehensive planning. These requirements for different kinds of plans, and thus for different planning approaches, underscore the value to planners of knowing several alternative approaches.

Finally, the quantity, quality and type of available resources make a difference in the choice of planning approach. Rational/comprehensive planning relies on heavy use of processed data and theories, on long-term projections and on more complex planning methods. This kind of planning requires more time, more money and more skills if it is to be done well. Incremental planning requires less time and money (for example, for the collection of extensive data in the analysis stage), but requires skills in bargaining. Transactive planning places a premium on the interpersonal skills necessary if planners are to interact continuously and well with clients. In short, while analysis may call for a particular planning approach, the decision to adapt that approach depends in large part on the resources available.

ACTION: USING A PLANNING APPROACH

Choice of a planning approach among the alternatives available—or the creation of a unique approach drawing on various alternatives—is the first step in evolving a vital and successful planning process. The second step comes as planners seek to plan following their approach. Like most planning decisions, the choice of a planning approach is likely to be only partially correct. As experience accumulates, planners will find themselves continually adjusting the way they plan.

Beginning with a well-defined planning process helps a great deal in making these adjustments. Planners who know why they are planning in a particular way are better able to identify aspects of their planning process which need to be changed. They know what kinds of information to get as they monitor their planning process. For example, planners following a rational/comprehensive approach will give special attention to their ability to collect and use processed information in the analysis stage. They will search for new and stronger methodologies for using this information for decisions. When planning incrementally, planners will be concerned with the mechanisms they have developed for bargaining with other systems and for learning from experience. Radical planners will seek to strengthen and inculcate the ideology which justifies action.

LEARNING: IMPROVING THE PLANNING APPROACH

The purpose of the kind of monitoring suggested above is learning. Planners need to be open, experimental and critical with regard to their approach to planning. It is not only that the initial choice or creation of a planning approach or set of approaches is imprecise and subject to error, but also that—as we have emphasized—systems and environments change. This year's planning approaches may not be effective in helping the system adapt to the environment tomorrow. This sounds easier than it is. Change in a complex system like a planning process is difficult. Explicit recognition of the value of clearly defined planning approaches and of the importance of learning and change helps. It also helps to remember that a planning approach that does not fit well with the system and the environment has less of a chance of leading to effective planning—and successful adaptation of the system to the environment. A system that is not adapting well will have to make significant adjustments. One of the first places to look is the planning subsystem itself, and the people who operate within it. If that subsystem is not well adapted itself, to the larger system and the environment, it will have to be changed—or even replaced. Perhaps this is why planning subsystems, whether permanent or temporary, are always subject to the authority of others in the system—those directly charged with system management and sensitive to factors in the environment. A family surviving two terrible vacations in a row will have to get a new vacation planner if they want to achieve their goals.

PLANNING TO ACT

The first level is planning to plan, in which planners choose or create a planning approach based on an analysis of key factors in their system and its environment. They then test this approach—and learn how to improve it—in the second level of planning: planning to act. Planning to act is the conscious effort to adapt the system to the environment in order to achieve system goals, given a particular planning approach. This definition, of course, is much the same as our general definition of planning. The difference is that the outcomes of the first level of planning—whether conscious or unconscious—shape the way in which effort is made.

In our discussion of planning to plan we noted several ways in which the structures and assumptions of different planning approaches affect the planning process. Put more simply, the elements of ASDAL are given different emphases and combined in different ways under different approaches. The elements of rational thought—ASDAL—and planning approaches function somewhat like foods and menus. The same foods can go into several different kinds of meals, depending on the menu. The meals that result can be quite different, depending on what the menu says about the quantity and quality of each: rice, meat, vegetables and tea can be combined to produce one meal fit for a growing child, another for a malnourished adult, or a third for an overweight executive with heart disease. The relationships between the elements of planning, planning approaches and planning to act are shown in Figure 5. This diagram merely puts in graphic form the relationships that we have been discussing. The important thing to note, perhaps, is that there are many different possible processes for planning to act. They will all contain the elements of ASDAL in some way; the differences among these real-world planning processes will be explained at least in part by differences in the underlying planning approach. That planning approach, of course, has resulted explicitly or implicitly from analysis of key factors in the system and in the environment. Let us look at two selected examples of the ways in which different planning approaches lead to different emphasis on the elements of planning: analysis, strategy, decision, action and learning.

In a relatively pure rational/comprehensive approach, considerable emphasis will be given to the analysis element. Planners will seek to create a large body of information about the environment and their system as the basis for strategy development. They will make projections from this information about the future, seeking at all times to achieve a high level of precision in their

65

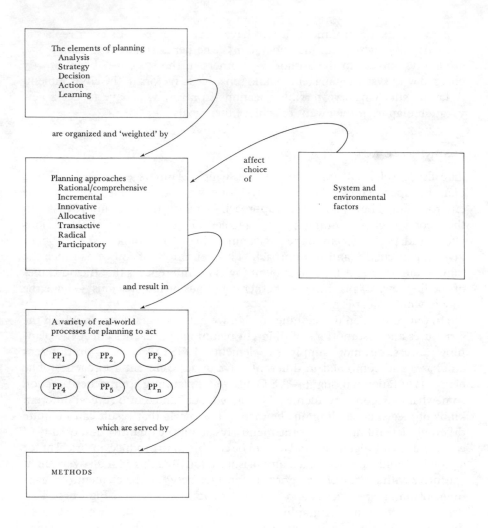

Fig. 5. Logical relationships between elements of planning, planning approaches and real-world planning processes

analysis (and a correspondingly low level of uncertainty). Alternative strategies will be formally developed and evaluated. Because planning of this type is a staff function, there will be an emphasis on formal plans for decision-making by others. Action will be the responsibility of various implementing units. The planners may plan for evaluation and learning or this may be done independently by implementing units or independent research/evaluation systems. Evaluations are likely to be rather formal, and consequently take a rather long time to do and to use for decision-making (reflecting a long time-lag in feedback on system adaptation). There are likely to be formally established time frames for planning and replanning.

There will be analysis in incremental planning but it will be much less comprehensive and formal. There will be more reliance on intuition and judgement. Strategies are likely to be incremental as well, representing changes in current strategies without much formal consideration of alternatives. Strategy decisions will also be relatively informal and closely linked with action. Planners and implementors are likely to be the same people. Learning receives the greatest emphasis in this approach, and there will be much evaluation, although, again, it may be relatively informal. Planning is a more constant process, with strategy changes being made whenever learning indicates that change is needed. Much planning effort goes into bargaining and co-ordination with competing systems.

These differences in emphasis would clearly lead planners to organize their resources in different ways. To take one example alone, the amount of time and resources devoted to analysis would be quite different. Moreover, the use of planning methods would be quite different. In a rational/comprehensive approach, the need for extensive analysis, alternative strategies, formal decisions based on plans and formal evaluation will call for formal application of relatively complex methods. Incremental planning, on the other hand, would be less likely to involve complex methods in analysis and strategy-making, although there might be more use of formal methods of evaluation in the learning element. Methods for co-ordination and bargaining would be quite important.

It seems important here to recall one of the central assumptions underlying this planning framework. The choice or evolution of a planning approach depends on the system and the environment. There is no single best way to plan. Instead, the planning approach should be consciously devised to fit with a particular situation at a particular time. For some systems in some environments, rational/comprehensive planning would be most effective. In other situations, incremental, transactive or radical planning would be more appropriate.

PLANNING TO LEARN

Planning to learn is the conscious effort to get and use information about the effectiveness of the adaptation of the planning system to the system and about the adaptation of the system to the environment in order to improve both planning and system adaptation. This is the third level of planning. Here planners apply the elements of ASDAL to create effective evaluation strategies. There are two essential aspects. One is a set of values or attitudes within the system and planning subsystem. The other is more technical. This is the use of a variety of methods and subsystems to gather information and to process it for use in decision-making.

The value aspect. The value aspect is critically important. The most sophisticated and effective evaluation methods and systems possible will have little impact if planners and decision-makers are not willing to learn and change.

67

One of the unfortunate values which seems to be associated with planning is a certain level of arrogance linked with defensiveness. It is not the plan that is wrong in some respects, but the planners themselves. When this attitude prevails, planners are understandably reluctant to learn openly. While recognizing the limits of planners, we must also recognize the complexity of systems and environments and the weakness of many of the theories on which our plans rest. Having made this recognition, the importance of learning from experience becomes obvious. Planners (and decision-makers as well) need to be encouraged to learn, even if this means admitting mistakes. Only when this attitude prevails will learning be maximized and improvement in plans and planning take place.

The technical aspect. The technical aspect is important as well. There are two elements to be considered here. One is the structure that planners develop to guide their efforts to learn; the other consists in evaluation methods.

   Structure. Planners often speak of *summative* and *formative* evaluation. These terms distinguish between two purposes of evaluation and learning. The first, summative evaluation, is intended to aid decisions on the overall effectiveness of a particular planned action (or in our terms, a particular adaptation strategy). Is it good or bad? The second, formative evaluation, is concerned with more or less continuous learning for the purpose of improving a strategy (or a planning process) as it is being developed and carried out.

   Some of the types of evaluation are shown in Figure 6 (Gallagher, Lim and Middleton, 1979). As shown here, there are five important kinds of evaluation comparisons that can be made at various points in the planning and implementation of an action programme. Each involves a judgement, usually based on data, about the fit between key stages in planning and acting. The evaluations that come earlier in the process tend to have formative purposes. *Need* evaluation compares a need in the environment with the goals that are established to reflect that need. This assessment is made early in planning and is, in effect, an initial judgement of the potential for a particular kind of adaptation of the system. Is the need sufficiently important so that, if we achieve the goal, our output into the environment will be judged important enough to get resources for our system?

   Design evaluation compares the goal with the way resources are allocated to meet the goal. In effect, this is evaluation of the fit between the goal and the plan. In addition, it includes evaluation of the planning process, leading to the kind of learning about the planning approach which helps planners modify the way they plan. *Management* evaluation compares plan and implementation. This is the monitoring of action that is an essential part of the action element of planning. The comparison is between the plan and immediate outputs. In a communication plan, outputs might include such things as the number of radio programmes, the number of telephones installed or the number of farmers enrolled in discussion classes.

   Outputs are related to effects in *performance* evaluation. With this kind of

68

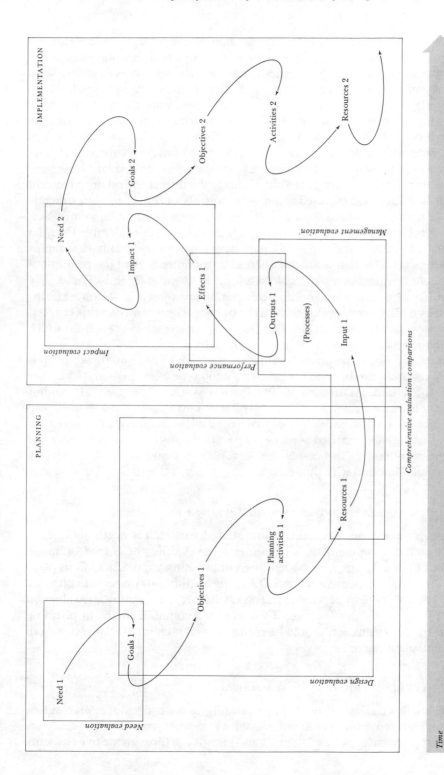

FIG. 6. Impact evaluation

evaluation, we begin to ask questions about changes that the outputs are making. Are people learning from radio programmes or discussion classes? Are they using telelphones? These kinds of changes are often called effects. With this type of evaluation, summative kinds of judgements begin to made.

The final type of evaluation is *impact* evaluation. With this mechanism, we seek to find out what differences effects are making in comparison with the original need. Is learning leading to more effective participation in development programmes and to higher productivity on farms? Is the use of telephones improving health-care delivery, or the sense of solidarity between people in the country and in the city? This is the ultimate kind of judgement about the value of the planned action—in sum, about the adaptation strategy. This is where evaluation with summative purposes most often takes place. Note that by the time impact evaluation is carried out, considerable time has passed. The need at the beginning may have changed, especially in complex environments. Hence it is shown as Need 2 in Figure 6. And the continuous nature of planning is shown, as Need 2 leads to a new goal, and so on.

In Figure 6, planning and implementation are shown as separate efforts, linked by management evaluation. In the framework presented in this chapter, these two activities are considered to be part of an overall process from which and about which planners constantly seek to learn.

Methods. There are many evaluation methods. Some of these, such as survey research, can be used for practically any type of evaluation. Others are more specialized. Management information systems are used to monitor action. Field experiments are used to pilot test strategies. Cost–benefit and cost-effectiveness methods are used in design evaluation to evaluate alternative strategies; they are also used as part of impact evaluation. Case studies generate insight into complex processes, helping planners and decision-makers to understand how and why things happen.

PLANNING TO LEARN AND PLANNING APPROACHES

Although we have discussed this at some length earlier, it is worth noting here that learning as an element of planning receives different emphases and is carried out in different ways under different planning approaches. Thus planners applying the elements of ASDAL, in planning to plan, can apply the same rational thought process to the task, whether of designing an evaluation structure or a plan for learning. In fact, it is a common theme in planning literature that evaluation should be planned as an integral part of planning to plan and planning to act.

THREE LEVELS OF PLANNING: SUMMARY

We began this framework by defining planning as the conscious effort to adapt a system to its environment in order to achieve system goals. This process rests on the application of rational thought and knowledge through the five elements of analysis, strategy, decision, action and learning. This basic planning process can be applied to three levels of planning. One is planning to plan, through which planners choose or create a planning approach which enables the planning subsystem to adapt to the larger system and to the environment. This planning approach (or set of approaches) is developed from analysis of the system and of key factors in the environment on the one hand, including the prevailing social image or images, complexity and resources; and of characteristics of different planning approaches on the other.

The second level is planning to act, in which the elements of ASDAL, organized by a particular planning approach, are applied to develop strategies to adapt the system to the environment in order to achieve system goals. The output of this level of planning is something we call 'plans', recognizing that the exact nature of these plans differs under differing planning approaches. Sometimes these are formal documents with much analysis. At other times they may be memos, reports or even verbal recommendations.

The third level is planning to learn. The goal of planning to learn is to get and use information about the effectiveness of planning and of planned action in order to improve both. The elements of ASDAL can be used in planning for learning as well, making planning to learn an integral part of both planning to plan and planning to act. In planning to learn, planners consider two purposes for evaluation: formative and summative. They deal with technical aspects of learning by creating a structure of types of evaluation and fitting appropriate methods of evaluation to this structure. The results are evaluation strategies. Of special importance to planning to learn is the attitudinal aspect. If learning and improvement are to occur, planners and decision makers need to recognize the complexity of most planning efforts and be willing to learn openly by accepting and learning from imperfect planning, plans and action.

A systems framework for planning:
summary

A summary diagram of the planning framework developed in this chapter is given in Figure 7. There is always danger, of course, in presenting a complex set of ideas in a simple diagram. However, the diagram does enable us to see the various parts of the framework in relation to one another. First, the planning subsystem is shown within the larger system, which itself exists in a task environment where such factors as social image, complexity and resources are important. The system establishes an adaptation strategy through which resources are acquired in return for achieving goals. The planning subsystem and the larger system both draw two kinds of resources from the environment: physical resources and information. The planning subsystem also draws information and physical resources from the system itself. The three levels of planning are shown within the planning subsystem. Planning to plan leads to planning approaches, which in turn organize the process of planning to act.

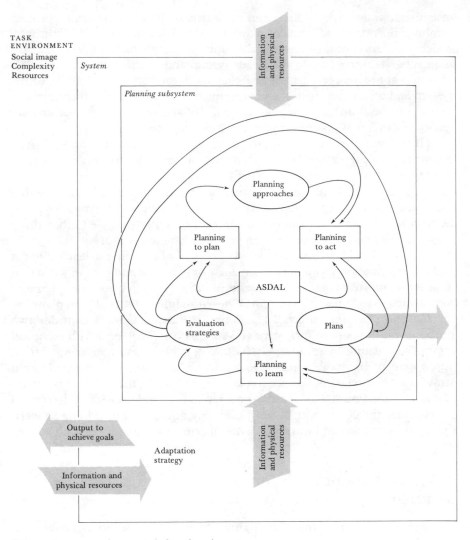

FIG. 7. A systems framework for planning

Planning to act results in plans for the system itself. Planning to learn leads to evaluation strategies. The learning that results from these affects all three levels of planning.

The elements of rational thought and application of knowledge are shown as central to the planning subsystem. Analysis, strategy, decision, action and learning (ASDAL) can serve as a guide to planning at all levels.

Planning methods

Throughout the development of the conceptual framework for planning we have emphasized the role that information plays at all levels of planning—information about the environment and about the system, past, present and future. We have also, from time to time, mentioned planning methods. Planning methods are clusters of techniques used to create and organize information for specific planning purposes. Notice that in this definition we distinguish between methods and techniques. The line between the two concepts is not precise. In fact, some of the things called methods in this book are called techniques elsewhere. However, a method may be distinguished from a technique in that it creates or organizes information for a particular purpose. Techniques, on the other hand, may be used for a variety of purposes. Let us look at some examples. Survey research is considered a method for gathering information from large numbers of people. It includes a number of techniques: sample design; questionnaire construction; and various techniques of statistical analysis. Programme planning and budgeting as a method encompasses the technique of establishing logically related goals and objectives, as well as the technique of using matrices to interrelate different kinds of information. The techniques mentioned can be used in a variety of combinations within other methods. Sample design can be important in developing and administering tests as measures of learning; questionnaire construction is useful in the Delphi method; statistical tests are used in trend projection; matrices are used in cross-impact analysis and in simulations.

There is yet a third term which is often used by planners. This is *methodologies*. Like method and technique, this term is often used in different ways. Here, we will define methodologies as clusters of methods used to carry out a particular planning approach. For example, planners following a rational/comprehensive approach may combine the methods of trend projection and scenarios into an integrated set of actions taken in several of the elements of planning. This combination would be a particular planning methodology. Alternatively, they might add Delphi analysis (with or without cross-impact matrices), creating yet another methodology. Sometimes planners consider these methodologies to be their planning approach. However, as discussed earlier in the chapter, a planning approach is a more general and fundamental aspect of planning, one which is capable of utilizing more than one methodology—and an even greater variety of methods.

We have chosen to focus on methods in this book because they are the basic building blocks out of which planning methodologies of various kinds can be fashioned. Methods, moreover, can be categorized by the planning elements they serve. Techniques, on the other hand, are generally too small in themselves to be clearly useful alone to a planning element. We have identified five elements in planning: analysis, strategy, decision, action and learning. Each of these elements requires planners to create different kinds of information, and to organize it for different uses. Thus most planning methods can be catego-

TABLE 1. Planning elements and planning methods

Planning elements	Planning methods	
Analysis. Methods which create and organize information about the system and environment past, present and future	Systems analysis Resource assessment Trend extrapolation Delphi Brainstorming	Surveys Case study Cost–benefit Goal-achievement matrix
Strategy. Methods which create and organize information and means–ends, cause-and-effect relationships	Scenarios Simulation/gaming Cross-impact Input–output Compact policy assessment	Systems analysis Delphi Flow charting Brainstorming Research/evaluation methods*
Decision. Methods which create and organize information about choices	Decision analysis Cost–benefit Zero-based budgeting Goal-achievement matrix	Programme planning/ budgeting* Scenarios Simulation/gaming Cross-impact
Action. Methods which create and organize information for co-ordination, control and modification	Inter-organizational co-ordination Work planning PERT Flow charting	Management information systems* Routine reporting* Conferencing*
Learning. Methods which create and organize information for change and improvement	Communication indicators Surveys Case study	Cost–benefit Research/evaluation methods*

rized as most useful for one or more of these elements, given the information-processing requirements of each element and the unique characteristic of each method in terms of the kind of information created and organized.

Table 1 is a matrix in which different planning methods are categorized by the five elements of ASDAL.[1] You will note that several methods, such as systems analysis, cost–benefit analysis, surveys, scenarios and brainstorming, are seen as useful for more than one element of planning. Each of these methods has characteristics which enable it to create or organize information for different purposes, depending on the kind of information to which the method is applied. Surveys as part of analysis can tell us what people want; as part of learning they can tell us what they say they have. Systems analysis helps us understand a system and its environment, and it also helps us build causal

1. Most of these methods are dealt with in this book. Those which are not are indicated by an asterisk (*) in Table 1. These either are too complex to be dealt with here and well covered in widely available publications, or are already part of the tool kit of most practising communication-planning teams.

relationships. Brainstorming and Delphi are methods for applying the judgement of groups and individuals to problems in analysis or in strategy. Scenarios are pictures of the future environment, and they can include expected results from planned actions: cause-and-effect relationships.

Cost–benefit analysis can be used to evaluate alternatives for decisions, or as part of summative evaluation to aid learning. Other methods are less widely useful. PERT is primarily a way of organizing information about action in order to monitor progress and the effects of changes. Simulation is primarily useful for testing cause-and-effect relationships. Zero-based budgeting is clearly a decision method. Each method has its own set of costs and benefits. Some require considerable resources—in skill, in information and in time. Others require much less to operate. Some yield relatively precise information, depending on the quality of information that they operate from. Others lead to more general information based on judgement. Each method also rests on certain assumptions. Trend projection, for example, is based on the idea that past trends can be projected into the future; in short, that the environment is unlikely to change in any significant way during the projection period. Delphi assumes that collective judgement of experts provides reliable information about the future. Zero-based budgeting assumes that decision-makers will make choices based on comparison of costs and objectives for different activities. The costs, benefits and assumptions of the methods in this book have been explicitly laid out to aid planners in choosing among them.

As discussed earlier, different planning approaches tend to lead to different methods. A primary reason for this is that planning approaches themselves rest on different assumptions about the system and the environment. Under a rational/comprehensive approach, planners assume a relatively stable environment for the period of the plan. Trend projection, discounting and zero-based budgeting share this assumption, as well as the assumption that a relatively extensive data base is available or can be assembled. This planning approach, and its associated methods, also assumes a relatively high level of resources for planning, particularly in terms of planning skill and time to use methods. By way of contrast, incremental planning assumes that the environment is too complex to be known well, that reliable information is hard to get, and that relatively fewer resources are available to planners. Judgemental techniques—such as brainstorming and scenarios—fit better with this approach.

Under some planning approaches, including incremental planning, planners may tend to use methods informally. That is, they may use the ideas behind methods without the collection of extensive data and the formal application of techniques. Cost–benefit and cost-effectiveness analysis often seem to be used this way in certain kinds of communication planning. In other planning approaches, notably radical planning, central assumptions clash sharply with the assumptions of most methods—and few methods are used. Most methods help planners impose order of one kind or another on an essentially chaotic environment. Radical planning may find this need to impose order contrary to the high value it puts on radical change.

In sum, the choice of a set of planning methods is complex. In fact, many communication planners seem to work primarily from the methods that they know, regardless of the fit between those methods and a planning approach, the availability of resources or the value of the method in creating or organizing information of the right kind for a particular planning programme. There have been good reasons for this approach to the choice and use of methods. A conceptual framework for communication planning has not been widely available, nor have communication planners had access to a range of planning methods. This book is an attempt to provide planners with both.

Bibliography

CHURCHMAN, C.W. 1968. *The Systems Approach*. New York, N.Y., Delacorte Press.
ETZIONI, A. 1973. Mixed Scanning. In: Andrew Faludi (ed.), *A Reader in Planning Theory*. Oxford, Pergamon Press.
FALUDI, A. 1973. *Planning Theory*. Oxford, Pergamon Press.
FRIEDMAN, J. 1973. *Retracking America: A Theory of Transactive Planning*. Garden City, N.Y., Doubleday/Anchor.
GALLAGHER, M.; LIM, M.K.; MIDDLETON, J. 1979. Evaluation. In: John Middleton *et al.*, The Development Communication Planning Simulation Game. Honolulu, Hawaii, East–West Communication Institute.
GROBSTEIN, C. 1973. Hierarchical Orders and Neogenesis. In: Howard H. Pattee (ed.), *Hierarchy Theory: The Challenge of Complex Systems*. New York, George Braziller.
HUDSON, B. 1979. *Comparison of Current Planning Theories: Counterparts and Contradictions*. Los Angeles, Calif., B. Hudson Associates. (Mimeo.)
KINCAID, D.L. 1979. *The Convergence Model of Communication*. Honolulu, Hawaii, East–West Communication Institute, September. (Paper No. 18.)
LINDBLOM, C.E. 1959. The Science of Muddling Through. *Public Administration Review*, No. 19, Spring.
MIDDLETON, J. 1980. Images and Action: Theories in and of Communication Planning. In: John Middleton (ed.), *Approaches to Communication Planning*. Paris, Unesco.
MIDDLETON, J.; BEAL, G.: PUGNE, M. 1982. The Use of Economic Concepts in Communication Planning Practice. In: M. Jussawalla and D. McL. Lamberton (eds.), *The Economics of Communication*. Oxford, Pergamon Press.
SIMON, H.A. 1969. *The Science of the Artificial*. Cambridge, Mass., MIT Press.
—— 1973. The Organization of Complex Systems. In: Howard H. Pattee (ed.), *Hierarchy Theory: The Challenge of Complex Systems*. New York, N.Y., George Braziller.
THORNLEY, A. 1977. Theoretical Perspectives on Planning Participation. *Progress in Planning*, Vol. 7, Pt 1, pp. 1–57.

II

Methods
for analysis

Introduction

Planning rests on the understanding of systems and environments. In this section we present five methods for creating and organizing information about systems and the environment—past, present and future. These methods enable planners to identify the problems and needs which in turn become the basis for setting goals for adaptation strategies. Planners employ these methods for a variety of specific analysis tasks. In a general sense, each of these tasks entails increasing understanding about one or more elements of the system and the environment, and about interactions and relationships among these elements. This understanding, in turn, becomes the basis for the design of strategies designed to accomplish goals.

Among the specific tasks of the analysis element of planning we find needs assessment, in which planners seek to find out what services are wanted/needed in the environment in order to establish goals and an adaptation strategy. A related task in communication planning is often called audience analysis. Here planners seek to understand as much as possible about the people who will be involved in planned action, including those who will benefit (clients) and those who will play influential roles in planning and implementation.[1] A second task is analysis of institutions and trends which shape the social environment, and which determine both the way in which planning is done (planning approach) and the nature of the adaptation strategy chosen. Of particular importance are the patterns of interaction among these elements in the environment. A related third task is analysis of the policies which guide and constrain system development, and the distribution and nature of political and economic power. This analysis includes a close examination of the values and ideology on which policies rest. Thus, in sum, it is an analysis of existing social image.

Analysis of the system which planners seek to direct requires assessment of system resources and capabilities. Also important is an understanding of current adaptation strategies. This requires planners to use evaluation information, providing a concrete illustration of how the element of learning in the planning

1. For an expanded analysis of this point, see Middleton and Root (1979).

process is closely connected with analysis. In carrying out these analysis tasks, planners use information about the past and the present to project the nature of the environment and their system into the future. As we shall see, different methods approach the projection task in different ways. These projections require differing assumptions about the degree of certainty in the environment, and about the extent and kind of data available. These assumptions thus tend to associate different methods with different planning approaches.

Methods presented

Five selected methods are presented in this section: systems analysis, resource assessment, trend extrapolation, Delphi and brainstorming. As we have noted in Chapter 2, other methods are useful in the analysis element and some of the methods presented here can be used in other elements of planning.

SYSTEMS ANALYSIS

In our view of planning, systems analysis is a fundamental method for understanding systems and environments, with emphasis on the complex patterns of interaction among system and environment elements. In the broadest sense, systems analysis serves as a guide to thinking and planning, and provides a framework for the use of other analytical methods. The method can incorporate a wide range of information of many kinds. When applied with good data and strong planning skills and resources, systems analysis can lead to complex dynamic models of systems and environments, which embody the patterns of interaction among system elements, and which enable planners to study how the system might function under different strategy assumptions.

Because of its fundamental nature, systems analysis can be applied at varying levels of detail and complexity. In the most simple applications, systems analysis is a way of thinking, requiring only an understanding of basic principles and data derived from personal knowledge of planners. In its most complex form, the method requires extensive data, mathematical formulation of patterns of interaction, advanced skills and the use of computers (Root, 1980). This flexibility makes systems analysis an appropriate method for several planning approaches. In its complex form it fits well with the assumptions of rational/comprehensive planning. Less complex forms are appropriate for incremental, allocative and transactive planning. The potential of systems analysis as a participatory method also rests on the level of complexity with which the method is used. More complex applications, requiring extensive data, skills and resources have less potential for widespread involvement of non-technical planners and clients. As a guide to thinking, however, systems analysis can be learnt and used widely.

RESOURCE ASSESSMENT

A key aspect of systems analysis is assessment of the resources available to systems planners. As the chapter on resource assessment (Chapter 4) makes clear, the method is useful at all stages of planning, and is concerned with identifying and assessing a wide range of resources. These latter include not only physical resources (such as technology, skilled persons and budget), but also information resources, which enable planners to create the base of information necessary to all elements of planning. Thus Chapter 4 provides a comprehensive listing of the kinds of data planners should have, under ideal conditions. The extensive nature of the list fits best with rational/comprehensive planning approaches. The categories of data, however, provide in themselves a general guide to resource assessment for less formal planning approaches. They would be useful to an incremental planning team, and could provide the basis for interaction between clients and professional planners in a transactive approach. Thus the method has potential for participatory planning. As the chapter makes clear, data of the kind listed would be extremely useful in allocative planning, in which the assignment of resources to different systems is a central task.

TREND EXTRAPOLATION

Trend extrapolation is a widely used method for using information about the past to project the future. Most usually the method is applied to a single variable, such as demand for telephone services. It requires quantitative data. Expanded versions of the method (described in Chapter 5) enable planners to incorporate more than one variable into their projections, and to assess the probable impact of future events on trends. Trend extrapolation requires a considerable amount of data, and assumes that past trends will continue into the future. Thus it fits best with rational/comprehensive planning approaches. Requiring a relatively advanced level of technical skill, the method is not particularly well suited to participation of non-technical planners. The results, however, can be simply and usefully displayed and explained to non-technical persons.

DELPHI

The Delphi technique is also a projection method. However, instead on relying on past data for future projections, Delphi draws on the combined judgement of 'experts' to identify future trends and events. It deals directly with a relatively large number of variables, and thus yields more complex projections than trend analysis. The relatively simple procedures of this method, plus its reliance on pooled individual judgement instead of processed data, make it useful in most planning approaches. Depending on the nature of the systems being planned, and the environmental needs to be served, Delphi can be simple or complex. Judgement may be sought from planners or technically qualified experts, or it may be sought from non-technical clients of planned action. This latter feature strengthens the participation potential of the method. Although computer analysis of large-scale, complex Delphi applications is usually necessary, simpler versions can be analysed by hand.

BRAINSTORMING

The purpose of brainstorming is the generation of creative thinking and the production of a large number of ideas related to a specific problem or task. As a method of analysis, brainstorming is useful in identifying system and environment elements of significance, and in creating insights into the nature of these elements and of their interaction patterns. The method requires the use of formalized rules with small groups. No formal data are required, nor are formal analytic techniques applied. Thus the method is useful in incremental and transactive planning, and has strong potential for participation of a wide range of persons.

Other uses of presented methods

The underlying principles of systems analysis can be used throughout the planning process. More formal application of the method is especially useful in developing strategies, particularly in the construction of models which embody expected cause-and-effect relationships among system elements. Likewise the Delphi method, as a technique for identifying future trends and events, is also useful in developing strategies. As a creativity technique, brainstorming can be used as a problem-solving method throughout the planning process. Each of these methods, by revealing the nature of problems and needs, helps planners establish goals for their strategies.

Other methods for analysis

The five methods for analysis presented here are not the only ones useful in this element of planning. Surveys,[1] for example, are widely used to generate information for various forms of analysis, including needs assessment and audience analysis. Case-study methods[1] are also used for these purposes and for policy analysis. Scenarios[1] can be constructed to organize information about future environments. Cost–benefit analysis[1] and the Goal Achievement Matrix[1] can help planners gain insight into alternative existing strategies as part of using information from the learning element of planning.

---

1. Methods presented in other sections of this book.

Bibliography

MIDDLETON, J.; ROOT, G. 1979. Human Systems in Communication Planning. In: John Middleton *et al.*, *The Development Communication Planning Simulation Game*. Honolulu, Hawaii, East–West Communication Institute.

ROOT, G. 1980. Modelling and Simulation. In: John Middleton (ed.), *Approaches to Communication Planning*. Paris, Unesco.

Chapter 3
Systems analysis

Manuel Gómez-Ortigoza

Dan J. Wedemeyer

The process of communication planning is increasingly experiencing the need to consider more and more variables. It is becoming more complex. Systems analysis is one approach that allows planners to consider these broader-based variables and the interaction among them. Systems analysis encourages a more holistic approach to the development of communication systems and services as they relate to broader development goals.

Definition

Systems analysis is a method for applying the 'systems approach' or general systems theory (GST) to problems in planning. Van Gigch (1974) has described this approach as 'a way of thinking, a practical philosophy, and a *methodology of change*' (emphasis added). In communication planning, systems analysis can be viewed as a technique that encourages those engaged in planning to view problems more broadly. Systems are composed of subsystems, all of which are interrelated. Therefore, a change in one subsystem changes the entire system. In order to understand this approach more fully, it is useful to define several concepts fundamental to systems thinking. The concepts generally associated with designing or improving a system are as follows (Van Gigch, 1974):

Elements. Elements are components of each system. In many cases, they are considered systems themselves; that is, they are subsystems of larger systems. For example, a telephone system can be viewed as system unto itself, but at another level of analysis it is only a subsystem (an element) of the larger national communication system or, larger yet, a national development plan.

Conversion process. Conversion process is that which goes on within the system. Usually this process takes 'inputs' and applies some process of change and produces 'outputs'. This is sometimes referred to as the process that operates within a 'black box'. For example, in a telecommunication/computer system the computer takes the data inputs, converts them using programming rules and produces some outputs—the internal unspecified process is referred to as the 'black box' or the conversion process. This process need not remain unknown—it can be the subject of a systems investigation.

Inputs and/or resources. Inputs can be viewed as system resources. They are in many cases that which initiates action within a system. System inputs can be in physical form such as unedited film or video stock or can be pure information or data.

Outputs. Outputs are the results of the conversion process within a given system. These can be considered by-products of the 'conversion process'. In some cases, the outputs of one system can be inputs for other systems. These terms can be understood more easily by example. A television news team is sent to shoot footage of some media event—the raw footage can be considered input to a newsroom. The 'conversion process' is the activities involved in cutting and editing the raw footage. The output is the finished (edited) version of the media event. This output becomes input into a larger system called 'the evening news'.

Environment. The environment of a system is defined by boundaries around the system under study. It is immediately outside the system under analysis. A national communication system operates within many environments at once. Some of these are cultural, social, political, economical or technical systems. The environment influences the internal workings of the system under study.

Purpose and function. The purpose of a system is determined by its relationship with other systems (both sub- and meta-). It is important here to understand the concept of hierarchy of systems (sometimes referred to as level of analysis). The function or purpose of a system can also be the focus of the

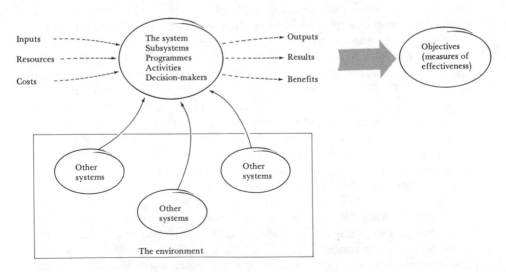

FIG. I. A system and its environment

system under study. For example, the planning of a government information office may be approached by first determining its purpose or function. The system can then be designed that best serves those purposes or functions.

Structure. The relationships that bind the subsystems together form the structure. The structure, for the most part, determines the efficiency and effectiveness of the system. It is defined by the links between (among) the elements in the system. These linking structures are often represented as organizational charts or communication networks. Communication planning sometimes deals directly with the links within a given system.

States and flows. The system 'state' is defined by the properties of the elements (which may be subsystems) at a given point in time. These change from state to state and constitute the system 'flow'. A systems 'behaviour' can be characterized by determining the system's states over time. Figure 1 is useful in understanding the definitions and functions of the above terms.

Assumptions

The key assumption of systems analysis as related to communication planning is that the system behaves as a whole and that any change in one part of the system will somehow affect the entire system. Sub-assumptions here are that 'the whole is more than the sum of its parts' (the concept of synergy) and that the 'whole determines the nature of its parts'. Finally, in systems thinking the parts cannot be understood if considered in isolation from the whole and all parts are dynamically interrelated or interdependent.

To understand the history of systems analysis one must first understand the history of general systems theory (GST). GST can be traced back to Aristotle, Descartes and Hegel. Aristotle noted that the 'whole is more than the sum of its parts'. Later, Hegel set out some of the principles mentioned in the assumptions section of this chapter. Ludwig von Bertanlanffy enlarged the idea of GST and its application to science. He is known as the 'father of general systems theory'. Bertanlanffy explained the aims of GST by defining the concept of 'wholeness'. He said the GST is an alternative to traditional scientific investigation. GST solved problems of organization and dynamic interaction that could not be solved by reducing phenomena into units independent of each other. Cybernetics (control of systems), information theory and theory of games were directly related to the development of general systems theory.

Systems analysis is a general method which can be applied to any problem. Areas of application range from microproject planning to national or regional development planning. One of the earliest examples of systems approach applied to planning was the first moon landing by the American National Aeronautics and Space Administration (NASA).Here, analysis and planning were essential in order to understand and co-ordinate the extreme complexity of the project. It was important that each subsystem was linked most efficiently

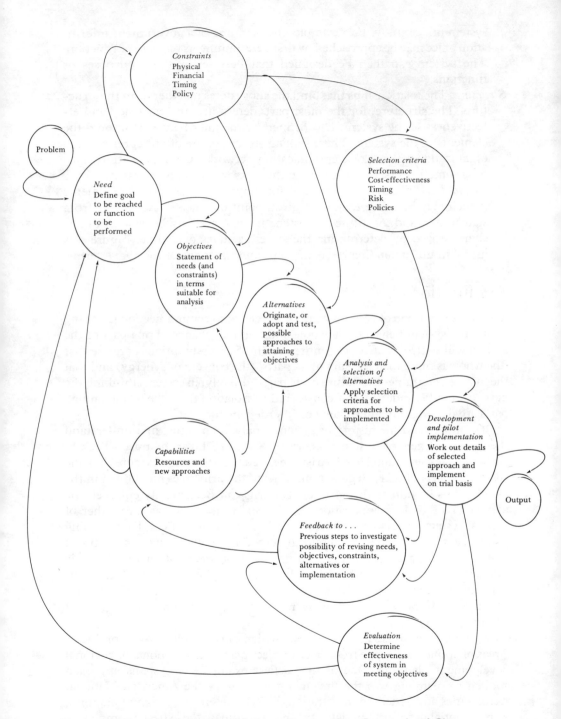

Constraints
Physical
Financial
Timing
Policy

Problem

Selection criteria
Performance
Cost-effectiveness
Timing
Risk
Policies

Need
Define goal
to be reached
or function
to be
performed

Objectives
Statement of
needs (and
constraints)
in terms
suitable for
analysis

Alternatives
Originate, or
adopt and test,
possible
approaches to
attaining
objectives

*Analysis and
selection of
alternatives*
Apply selection
criteria for
approaches to be
implemented

*Development
and pilot
implementation*
Work out details
of selected
approach and
implement
on trial basis

Output

Capabilities
Resources and
new approaches

Feedback to . . .
Previous steps to investigate
possibility of revising needs,
objectives, constraints,
alternatives or
implementation

Evaluation
Determine
effectiveness
of system in
meeting objectives

FIG. 2. Relationship of systems analysis to planning (from International City
Management Association, 1972, p.2)

and effectively in order to accomplish the very complex goal of safely landing a man on the moon by 1970. In communication planning, systems analysis is useful in developing an overall scheme of the problem and of the alternative solutions. Figure 2 depicts the relationship of systems analysis to planning.

Limitations, product and communicability of results

Systems analysis can suffer most from shortcomings of the analyst(s). That is, the person or team may incorrectly define the appropriate level of analysis; they may incorrectly identify the systems, subsystems or higher systems or essential links which bear on the problems at hand. Usually a systems analyst will have to 'push back' the boundaries of the system in order to consider the problem links which bear on the problems at hand. Usually a systems analyst will have to 'push back' the boundaries of the system in order to consider the problem from a whole-system perspective. Caution should be exercised not to approach the communication-planning problem too narrowly and to consider the relationships of the system under analysis to larger and smaller systems.

Systems analysis is unique. It was developed because other analytical mechanistic approaches had severe limitations when taken from the physical world into the sociological, political, economic or behavioural worlds. The earlier analytical methods could not explain organizational or regulatory processes. Systems analysis provides a broader, more comprehensive framework, which is meaningful across complex systems and different disciplines.

The products of systems analysis are many. Some of the more obvious include: (a) a well-defined problem(s); (b) an identification of system and subsystems; (c) a better understanding of the actual 'state' (condition of behaviour) of the system under analysis; (d) an understanding of the differences between the expected and actual state of the system; and (e) a model of the system and its processes. Finally, systems analysis can provide a comprehensive framework for planning a particular system (e.g. telecommunication) within other systems (e.g. transportation, electrification, etc.). It can provide a system design for change without adversely affecting external planning goals in other subsystems.

The level of detail of systems analysis is set by the analyst(s). These can range from broad/general or simplistic systems diagrams to specific/complex algorithms (often performed on computers) that seek optimization of the systems under analysis. One of the early tasks in systems analysis is to determine the appropriate level of investigation. After selecting a particular level, the system larger than the system under study becomes the environment, and the systems smaller than the unit of analysis are considered subsystems.

Systems analysis lends itself to ease of communication. In many cases, the process can be depicted in schematic form, which promotes understandability even in the most complex systems.

Resources needed and procedures

Systems analysis requires little more than a competent analyst(s). In some cases, it is useful to have access to computer-modelling capabilities, but again, this depends upon the level intent and extent of the analysis. Much can be accomplished by simply sketching (detailing) systems with pencil and paper. Mathematical simulation of a system would obviously require more and different resources than are required to conceptualize and detail a communication planning or development process.

The procedures vary with each application. In general, there are four important areas in any analysis. They are:

1. Specifying the boundaries of the system and its environment (setting the appropriate level of analysis).
2. Defining the key objectives (goals) of the system under study.
3. Indentifying the key subsystems and determining the structure and relationships of each to the other.

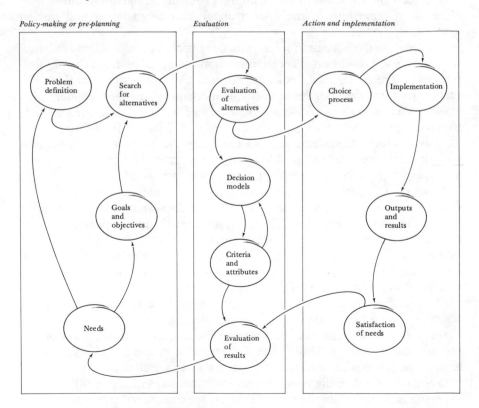

FIG. 3. Systems analysis cycle (from Van Gigch, 1974, p. 59)

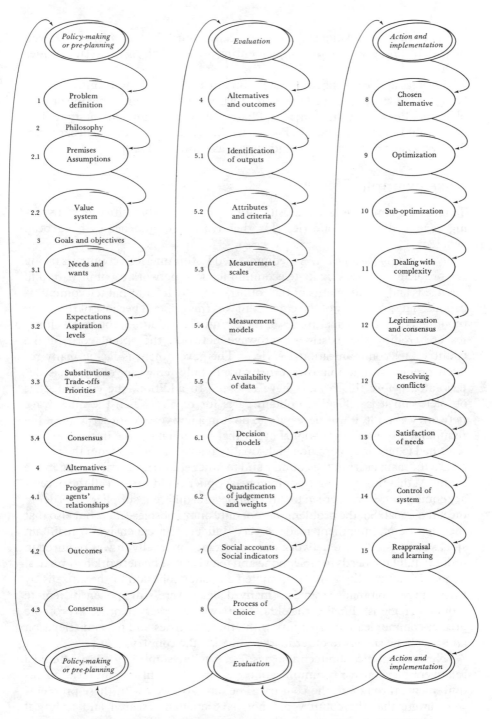

Column 1 — Policy-making or pre-planning

- Policy-making or pre-planning
- 1 — Problem definition
- 2 — Philosophy
- 2.1 — Premises Assumptions
- 2.2 — Value system
- 3 — Goals and objectives
- 3.1 — Needs and wants
- 3.2 — Expectations Aspiration levels
- 3.3 — Substitutions Trade-offs Priorities
- 3.4 — Consensus
- 4 — Alternatives
- 4.1 — Programme agents' relationships
- 4.2 — Outcomes
- 4.3 — Consensus
- Policy-making or pre-planning

Column 2 — Evaluation

- Evaluation
- 4 — Alternatives and outcomes
- 5.1 — Identification of outputs
- 5.2 — Attributes and criteria
- 5.3 — Measurement scales
- 5.4 — Measurement models
- 5.5 — Availability of data
- 6.1 — Decision models
- 6.2 — Quantification of judgements and weights
- 7 — Social accounts Social indicators
- 8 — Process of choice
- Evaluation

Column 3 — Action and implementation

- Action and implementation
- 8 — Chosen alternative
- 9 — Optimization
- 10 — Sub-optimization
- 11 — Dealing with complexity
- 12 — Legitimization and consensus
- 12 — Resolving conflicts
- 13 — Satisfaction of needs
- 14 — Control of system
- 15 — Reappraisal and learning
- Action and implementation

FIG. 4. Breakdown of steps within the general systems-analysis cycle (from Van Gigch, 1974, p. 73)

4. Specifying the relationships of the decision-makers and agents involved with planning, evaluating, implementing and controlling the system under study.

These areas are perhaps better understood in a systems design context. Here, key elements can be grouped into three phases: Phase 1, policy-making or pre-planning; Phase 2, evaluation; and, Phase 3, action and implementation. The cycle would appear as shown in Figure 3. This general cycle can be broken into detailed systematic steps. It would appear as shown in Figure 4.

Case example

This case example is a composite drawn from real-life situations involving several different countries (for that reason specific names have been avoided).

Definition of the problem. A medium-sized Latin American country is facing the problem of increasing its telecommunications network capability to fulfil the needs and requirements of the country, mainly its internal telecommunications. The geography of the country makes this difficult because of the many mountains and the high altitudes of the country. In addition, the harsh climates are eroding the existing microwave network, the spinal cord of the country's telecommunications services. The government is facing many related problems. The microwave network is only ten years old yet has deteriorated before thirty years have elapsed. In addition, the equipment is obsolete and it is difficult to obtain parts for repair. When the microwave network was built, it was necessary to do it in a few years in order to meet the requirements of an international event that was to take place in the country. This had to be done to provide high-quality television signals from the capital city to the main cities of the country and to other countries participating in the event. At that time no single equipment-supplier could furnish all the necessary equipment. It was agreed to buy from several different suppliers in order to meet their goal. So, the problem was not only one of obsolescence, but also that the mixture of equipment made it very difficult and expensive to maintain stocks of parts. The old network was important. Internally, it was required in order to fulfil the needs for telephone and television. The network had vertical and social desirability also. It promoted a greater cohesion of the citizens by furthering a dominant language (many dialects were still spoken in remote mountain regions). Finally, the old network was necessary in order to promote greater communication capability with other countries and to send television and telephone signals to other markets outside the country.

New communication technologies (e.g. satellite communication) offered a relatively inexpensive communication resource to fulfil communication requirements throughout the country. The officials faced with these problems were aware that the country did not have enough research and technical development to design or build their own satellite. There was not even a technical staff trained to handle the tracking and telemetry of a satellite. It

seemed advisable to lease transponders from a developed country, most probably the United States. Before making the final decision of leasing satellite
capability from the United States, the military was consulted in order to determine whether the decision would affect the sovereignty (defence integrity) of
the country. The decision had to be made quickly because telecommunications
demand already exceeded capability, and the building and launching of a satellite would take several years.

It was known that other Third World countries, such as Brazil, Colombia,
India and Indonesia, were experimenting with and considering satellite technology as an alternative to solve their internal communication problems.
Politically, it seemed advisable to consider satellite technology because the
country could become integrated for the first time. Today, it is easier to
communicate with New York or Tokyo than with some of the most remote
parts within the country. It was known that communication promotes urbanization. Cities with good communication facilities tend to grow faster than those
with lesser capabilities. So, if well designed, the communication system could
promote a decentralization goal of the country. Future technological alternatives like direct broadcast satellites, space stations, reflection of signals on the
moon, etc. were also considered but rejected. The officials of the country
decided to follow the satellite solution, but not before making an overall
systems analysis of the problem.

Systems-analysis application

Objective. To provide internal and external state-of-the-art communication
services (television and telephone mainly) at the earliest possible time.

Performance measure. Feasibility of the different alternatives as measured
economically, politically, socially and culturally.

Cost-effectiveness. A cost-effective analysis of microwave and satellite alternatives provided the following results:
1. Over short distances, satellites are more expensive than microwave.
2. Satellites are distance-insensitive, i.e. while inside their 'footprint' communications between two points will cost the same, no matter how far away
   they are from each other.
3. Satellites require an infrastructure for end points only, while microwave
   systems require an infrastructure of receivers, amplifiers and transmitters
   every 40 miles (60 kilometres) depending on the geography. In addition,
   each station requires electricity and maintenance.
4. Also, in a microwave system a failure at one point of the network will
   interrupt the signal, thus affecting the rest of the network. In satellite
   communication, failure in one earth station will not affect more than that
   particular point.
5. In a country of about 1,500 square miles (3,885 km^2), where many villages

93

and towns are scattered throughout, satellites would provide cheaper means of communication than microwave, in the shortest time.

6. A microwave system have to be ordered with a lead-time of one year, while satellite earth stations can be purchased with only thirty days' notice.
7. Satellite transponders, if leased, can start operating as soon as the up-link and first down-link are installed.

Resources for the system. The cost of both alternatives was considered, and whether there was enough money for either or both. In this case, the country decided on the less expensive, that is, satellite. It was important to determine the cash-flow requirement of leasing the space segment of a satellite, and if there were any financing problems at hand. In addition, the number and cost of terminal equipment, up-link earth stations (five) and down-link earth stations were calculated.

Interrelated components of the system
1. Number of up-link earth stations.
2. Number of down-link earth stations.
3. Satellite space segment.
4. Types of signals to be sent through satellites and time schedules (telephone and television signals).
5. Microwave situation, operable links.
6. Future growth and future needs.

Management of the problem
1. Determination of the number of up- and down-links depending on an optimization of the financial possibilities.
2. Reallocation of the microwave use, such as for creating certain earth stations, networks of microwave signals to complement and expand the communication capability via satellite.
3. Determination of the hierarchy of installation and of the turnover (if required) date from microwave to satellite communication.
4. Determination of the need for insurances, and the amounts and items to be covered.
5. Determination of the future expansion of the system, and potential side uses that can develop.
6. Analysis and evaluation of the expected and achieved results.
7. Preparation of the operational plans for the routines of operating the system, maintenance and keeping stocks of parts.

Results of the analysis. If it is intended to keep the microwave operating—while complementing it with satellite communication—and also for military and political reasons to update the microwave network, then the main constraint will be financial. Again, a subsystems planning model can be used to look at a cost formula. For reasons of space this is not included here, but the results might be such as to make each television and telephone outlet interested in

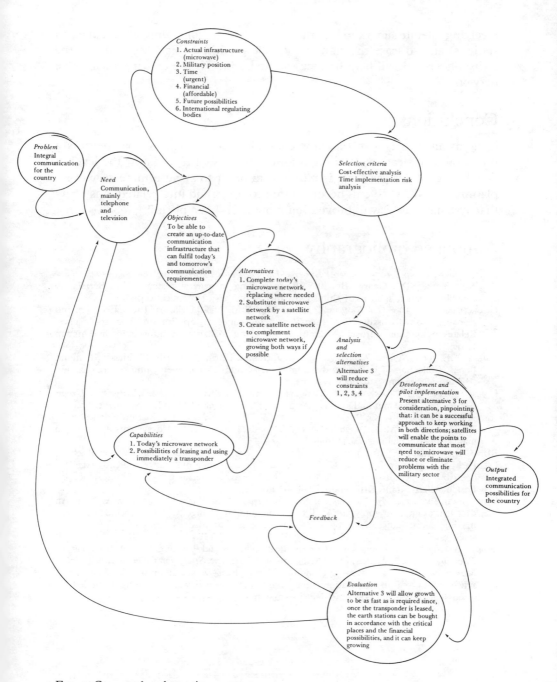

Fɪɢ. 5. Case-study schematic

receiving satellite signals to buy their own earth station (deregulation of earth stations) and to lease the signal from the satellites; this lease will pay the transponder and will help finance the upgrading of the existing microwave network.

Conclusions

Systems analysis is a method for communication planning that permits a universal investigation. It is important, when using it, to know the level of detail (level of analysis) that is required in order to avoid unnecessary over-planning. As the problems become more complex and interrelated, it is likely that systems analysis will prove even more useful as a planning tool.

Annotated bibliography

BERTALANFFY, L. VON. 1975. *General Systems Theory, Foundations, Development, Applications.* New York, N.Y., George Braziller. Basic reading in general systems. Von Bertalanffy contributes much in terms of philosophy, theory and basic system concepts.

CHURCHMAN, C.W. 1968. *The Systems Approach.* New York, N.Y., Delacorte Press. Excellent and readable book discussing fundamental systems concepts, applications and approaches. Relates the systems approach to planning, budgeting, management information and human values.

EMERY, F.E. 1969. *Systems Thinking: Selected Readings.* Harmondsworth, Middlesex, Penguin Books. Collection of background readings on systems management, human organization system environments and open systems.

INTERNATIONAL CITY MANAGEMENT ASSOCIATION. 1972. *Applying Systems Analysis in Urban Government.* Washington, D.C., Department of Housing and Urban Development.

JOHNSON, R.; FREEMONT, K.; ROSENZWEIG, E. 1976. *Theory and Management.* Providence, R.I., The Institute of Management Science. A good example of applied systems approach to management, including case studies.

RUBEN, B.D.; KIM, J.Y. (eds.). 1975. *General Systems Theory and Human Communication.* Rochelle Park, N.J., Hayden Book Co. Collection of materials from a number of sources. Excellent contributors include such notable systems thinkers as von Bertalanffy, Boulding, Rapoport, Laszlo, Alfred Kuhn, Krippendorf, Thayer and others.

VAN GIGCH, J.P. 1974. *Applied General Systems Theory.* New York, N.Y., Harper & Row. An excellent example of applying GST to the planning of change. Contents include decision-making, social indicators, programme planning and problems of measurement in social sciences.

WEDEMEYER, D.J. 1978. Long-Range Communication Policy and Planning. In: S.A. Rahim *et al.*, *Planning Methods, Models, and Organizations. A Review Study for Communication Policy Making and Planning*, p. 122–30. Honolulu, Hawaii, East–West Communication Institute. A synthesis of GST and its relationship to communication policy and planning. Included is a discussion on system design and decision-making.

Chapter 4
Resource assessment

Alan Hancock

The majority of the chapters in this book deal with the application of specific techniques to communication planning. The reader might well expect that a chapter entitled 'resource assessment' would be of the same order: setting out to provide a series of operational formulae and routines for the identification, evaluation and distribution of communication resources. In fact, the chapter adopts a different perspective. It treats resource assessment not so much as a technique but as a component process of planning which reaches into all aspects of the planning cycle and is a necessary adjunct to all planning approaches. As such, it draws upon many of the methods decribed elsewhere, but it does so in a more complex setting: while it includes the identification of resources, their evaluation and finally their distribution, these must be carried out in such a way that the needs of users are reflected throughout and the characteristics of decision-makers understood. In this composite process, questions of judgement, subjective data, conclusions based on experience and consensus-seeking approaches share an equal weighting with allocative techniques. The chapter is, therefore, contextual, and it is important to state clearly what it attempts to do, in a short compass, and what it does not attempt. It seeks to place resource assessment in a planning context, but it does not seek to evolve a planning strategy (that is the subject of many other books, including my own) (Hancock, 1980, p. 11). It seeks to identify, within this context, techniques which are useful in information acquisition and processing, as a prelude to resource distribution, but it does not attempt to amplify these techniques (many of which are considered in other chapters). It seeks to provide the elements for media inventories, and a typology for data collection and presentation, but it does not try to develop this typology in other than general terms (that exercise is problem-specific and could only be attempted, even illustratively, in a much larger compass). It is, therefore, a framework within which many of the techniques described elsewhere in the book can be located, and one which attaches itself, fairly readily, to a variety of planning approaches.

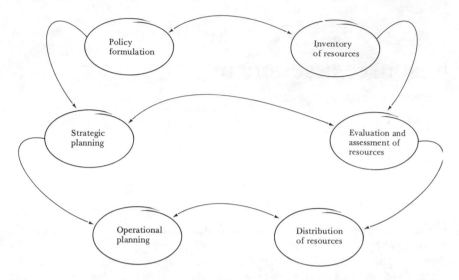

FIG. 1. Relationship of resource-allocation stages to the principal policy planning activities

Resource assessment and communication planning

Resource allocation is neither a planning theory, nor a technique. It is, rather, an indispensable component of the planning process, irrespective of the planning approach adopted. And as such it is made up, in turn, of a number of stages: these include not simply the allocation of resources but, as a prerequisite, their inventorying, assessment and evaluation. In Figure 1, these are seen in relation to the principal planning activities of policy formulation, strategic planning and operational planning, which they parallel.

RANGE OF RESOURCES

To approach the matter in this way raises a number of questions. First of all, there is the matter of defining resources, since it is apparent that these cannot be considered as purely material. As a basic categorization, I would propose their division into material, infrastructural and human. Material resources include hardware, and such discrete items as programmes, information sources etc. Infrastructural resources include the institutions and organizations involved in the production and distribution of messages, while human resources include not simply people, but also their ability to conceptualize.

WHO IS CONCERNED WITH RESOURCE ALLOCATION?

Evidently, all planners are concerned with the estimation and allocation of resources. However, in communication planning we must assume that information-handling for resource allocation is carried out by some kind of cadre or core unit, which provides technical support to other planners and decision-makers. This is important, in that the same people will probably be concerned with needs assessment as with resource assessment and allocation, and the two activities are intertwined. In reality, it is also evident that decision-makers are just as much concerned with resource allocation as are planners. Most of what has been said so far draws upon the rational-comprehensive planning mode, and the identification, evaluation and distribution of resources according to national criteria, usually following traditional lines of systems planning. In fact, however, the allocation of resources in this way is of little use if it is arbitrary; it needs the agreement of all concerned, and a broad consensus (as indeed do all stages of planning and decision-making, down to the operational level).

AN INFORMATION PROCESSING ROUTINE

In summary, we might say that resource allocation, as a component of planning and as a support to decision-making, is essentially a form of information-processing routine. My intention in this chapter, therefore, is not so much to superimpose efficiency as an overriding goal for communication planning, as to help plan for the distribution of resources in such a way that planners, managers and, above all, decision-makers are aware of what they may be giving up when their judgements are made on non-efficiency grounds. In this process, what is being sought is a routine for distinguishing between alternative propositions, according to clear criteria. For this somewhat complex process to succeed, not only is a good deal of information necessary, but the data must be carefully coded and presented in a way that allows the recipient to make clear perceptions and judgements. In other words, resource allocation is seen to have a direct connection with needs assessment, and the two are linked in an information-processing routine in which normative, political, qualitative and economic judgements are intermingled. Figure 2 illustrates such a routine (and acts as a guide to the sections which follow). In this diagram (which expands upon Figure 1), activities associated with a characteristic planning sequence in the rational-comprehensive mode are related to their main information needs at each stage.

It is evident from this figure that information is needed not only regularly, but also early and speedily. Much of the information is required at the policy-making stage, as decision-makers, when they formalize policy, often delimit, sometimes without realizing it, the nature of resources and the manner in which they can be aggregated, combined and apportioned. Early collection and coding of data should have the effect of expanding the range of alternatives upon which strategic planning is based, and of making the presentation of alternatives more rational. Similarly, at the strategic stage which follows, a quick response is needed to whatever alternatives are put forward in such a way that the implications of each alternative are clear, in concrete and, where

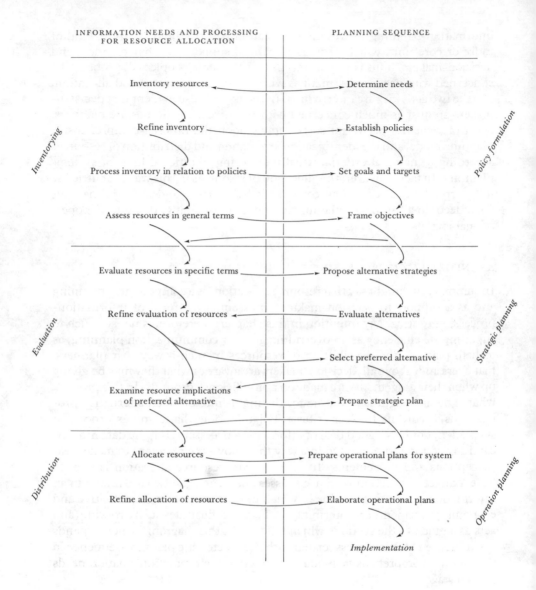

INFORMATION NEEDS AND PROCESSING
FOR RESOURCE ALLOCATION

PLANNING SEQUENCE

Inventorying

Evaluation

Distribution

Policy formulation

Strategic planning

Operation planning

Inventory resources — Determine needs

Refine inventory — Establish policies

Process inventory in relation to policies — Set goals and targets

Assess resources in general terms — Frame objectives

Evaluate resources in specific terms — Propose alternative strategies

Refine evaluation of resources — Evaluate alternatives

Select preferred alternative

Examine resource implications
of preferred alternative — Prepare strategic plan

Allocate resources — Prepare operational plans for system

Refine allocation of resources — Elaborate operational plans

Implementation

FIG. 2. Resource allocation/needs assessment linking to information-processing
routine

possible, quantified terms. For this, once again, an adequate data bank needs to
be prepared in advance, as decision-making at the strategic level will normally
reflect pressures of time, and a refined analysis of alternatives, especially
economic analysis, may well be impossible. I shall, therefore (in the next three
sections) take in turn the policy, strategic and operational stages, with a
primary emphasis on the first.

Policy formulation

A MATRIX FOR DATA ACQUISITION AND PROCESSING

Information-gathering and processing is most complex at the stage of policy formulation, because at this time the sources of information are considerable, but largely unspecified, and the uses to which the information will ultimately be put are not yet clear. With data needs of such complexity, some kind of instrument is required for their identification, collection and categorization. The matrix proposed in Figure 3 is based upon a model which I developed in an earlier book, where I tried to pinpoint the focus of communication planning (Hancock, 1980, p. 14–15). The content of communication planning is illustrated by Figure 4, where a simple Venn diagram shows the basic influences that converge in its practice. Taking as a starting-point, therefore, the three main categories of social and political development, communication infrastructure and technology, these are used to form the vertical axis of a matrix for data acquisition and presentation, proposed in Figure 3.

Subdivision of the horizontal axis is according to the kinds of data to be acquired. A basic distinction is between quantitative and qualitative data (i.e. between objective, descriptive and regulatory items on the one hand, and subjective, normative and evaluative items on the other). Both kinds are clearly necessary; while descriptive and statistical items are required for operational planning, policy-making and strategic planning depend, to a considerable extent, upon the establishment of social norms, on the articulation of need and upon an evaluation of the capability and potential of existing programmes and institutions. Consequently, the horizontal axis follows a seven-point typology, which has been evolved from an analysis of previous communication plans and from my own experience: it is an attempt to provide a set of categories which is characteristic and comprehensive, but at the same time compact, employing a minimal number of groups. As such it has no particular authority or validity; information collected and processed in this way should, however, correspond in broad terms to the preoccupations of planners.

Among the quantitative and descriptive items, a distinction is made between statistical data, descriptions of historical evolution, organizational structures and legal and regulatory aspects. In the more subjective, qualitative category, the subdivision is between stated goals and targets, social norms and values, (including information on attitudes) and future-orientated data on long-term developments and trends.

AN INFORMATION CHECK-LIST

Figure 3 is, therefore, a general matrix, which can be put to use in different ways according to planning needs and the planning environment. For a full-scale national planning exercise, for example, it is assumed that a separate version of the matrix would be used to collect information for each sector, with

Area	Data	Statistical data	Historical growth	Organizational structures	Legal and regulatory	Goals and targets	Norms and values	Future trends
Social and political development		1	2	3	4	5	6	7
Communication infrastructures		8	9	10	11	12	13	14
Technology		15	16	17	18	19	20	21

FIG. 3. Matrix for data acquisition and presentation

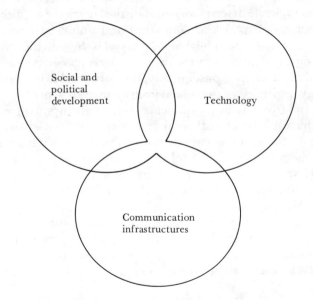

FIG. 4. Basic influences on communication planning

extensive processing and synthesis to follow. In the case of sectoral planning, the single matrix would suffice, and in the case of institutional planning, many of the categories which seek to place communication in a broad social context would be too detailed, unnecessary to complete in detail. In the check-list which is printed as an appendix to this chapter, an indication is given of the broad range of data needs that might be required for a large-scale plan, at the national level, and of information sources. The check-list is indicative rather than complete, and it would need adaptation for each sector to which it is applied (as well as considerable reduction in the case of smaller, institutional planning exercises). The numbers in the check-list correspond to those given in Figure 3.

INFORMATION PROCESSING

Policy formulation, however, needs something more in the way of processing: decision-makers and planners, if they are to formulate a coherent range of alternative proposals (which may be reviewed at the outset of strategic planning) need a comparative account of existing policy and practices. Figure 5 extends the dimensions of Figure 3 to assist with this kind of synthesis. By putting together different blocks of the matrix, it should be possible to draw out relevant information on, say, norms and values, or on organizational structures, in which not only is the overall background to the theme clear, but also particular aspects relative to communication and technology. Similarly, sectoral positions can either be presented independently, or be compared and synthesized.

Each kind of processing is carried out for different purposes. Certain kinds of information need collation for the benefit of planners, and a main purpose in doing so is to reveal duplications, redundancies or waste. Analysis of data on statistical areas, regulatory issues or organizational structures is likely to reveal such elements. On the other hand, a synthesis of sectoral perspectives on norms and values, or goals and targets, is likely to reveal anomalies of a different kind: disagreements or discrepancies on policy and philosophy, which need to be brought to the attention of decision-makers because they require discussion, and probably arbitration.

NEEDS ASSESSMENT

There is, however, another dimension of information needed for the policy-maker which will not be satisfied by an analysis of the status quo; this is the dimension of need. Here, the intention is to ascertain the basic needs of communication users, both to reveal fundamental needs and to establish what is not being met by existing provisions. In practice, needs assessments are of two kinds. In the first place, there are the needs of what we might term the 'clients' of a communication system: the sectors themselves, specific groups (professional or community), public and private agencies. Second, there are

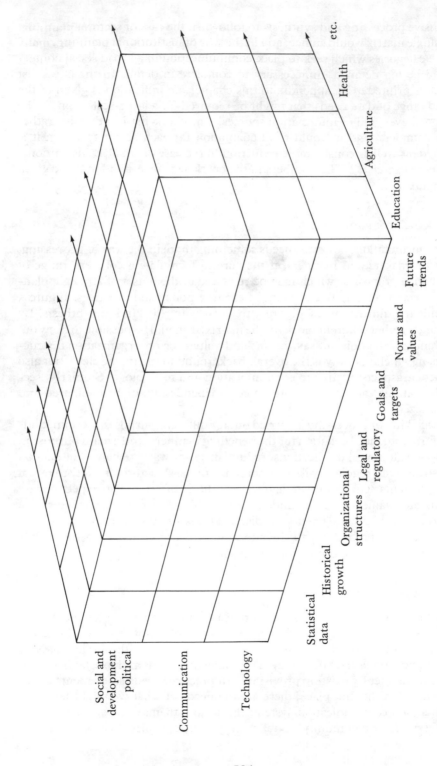

FIG. 5. Extending the matrix for data acquisition and presentation

the needs of the general public, and of the individuals who make up that public.

Below, some characteristic questions are listed which are likely to require answers in the course of policy formulation. They are listed under three headings, relating to: the adequacy of existing provision; the accessibility of users to communication infrastructures and materials; and degrees of participation by users in communication planning, management and operation.

Adequacy

Reliability and capacity of communication channels. Imbalances of communication between regions, urban and rural sectors, population groups

Domestic capacity to acquire, generate, produce, implement and maintain communication channels

Quality and quantity of information available to users (institutional and individual)

Accessibility

Accessibility of all demographic and geographic segments of the community to communication channels

Indentification of major barriers to improved access ... physical, technical, economic, cultural and institutional

Channel requirements of information providers and consumers within society

Information needs of users (institutional and individual) in terms of resources, cost, awareness, expertise

Participation

Degree of participation by users (institutional and individual) in the planning, management and operation of communication channels

Because they are projections of social needs and objectives, the data requirements here are of a rather different kind. To some extent, they may be compiled from existing sources (e.g. data on imbalances), but in the main they will have to be specially gathered, through field surveys or studies. In most cases, too, they can only be tentative answers. A statement of need, by definition, implies that the need is not being met: information acquired in this way will be intended to direct policy, not to state existing positions.

AN INFORMATION SYNTHESIS

The end result, at this stage of policy formulation, should be an information synthesis: an edited corpus of data on existing provisions and a statement of future needs. From this information base, more detailed policy formulation and strategic planning can proceed.

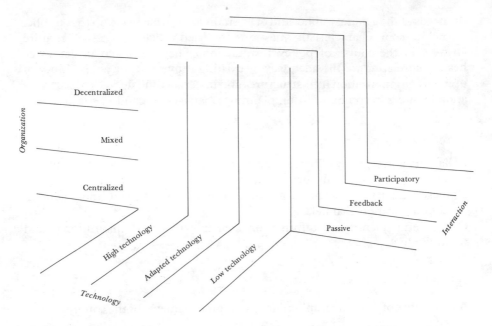

FIG. 6. Evaluation of alternatives: a matrix for choice

Strategic planning

The data base proposed in the previous section was cast deliberately wide, as it should also serve as a base for the phases of strategic and operational planning which follow.

THE EVALUATION OF ALTERNATIVES

The key to at least the rational/comprehensive mode of planning is the preparation, and relative assessment, of alternative proposals to meet stated objectives; as such, this is a critical stage in the information-processing routine shown in Figure 2. There are two particular needs. The first is for a clear framework within which alternative propositions can be devised and compared, so that the parameters of choice are clear to decision-makers. The second is a precise and, where possible, quantified assessment of the resources attached to or required by each alternative, and an evaluation of their quality and viability.

A matrix for choice is given in Figure 6 which helps define parameters for the selection and development of alternatives. Here, three critical characteristics of a communication system are presented in a three-dimensional grid: the level of technology sought (i.e. high or low technology, or an adapted form which attempts to relate technology quite specifically to local goals, irrespect-

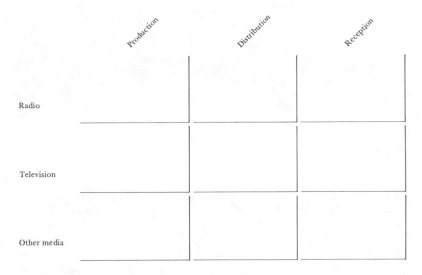

FIG. 7. Matrix for costing alternatives

ive of whether it is 'high' or 'low'); the kind of organization proposed (centralized, decentralized or a mix of the two); and the degree of interaction assumed between planners and decision-makers and publics (e.g. a passive system, a system which seeks to create feedback or a genuinely participatory system of decision-making). This kind of matrix can be helpful in delimiting the range of choice, provided that a realistic assessment of priorities and intentions is sought (i.e. a participatory system must imply a genuine desire to involve the public in decision-making, with all its attendant complexities, compromises and tensions, rather than a rhetorically stated intention to increase social participation which is not backed up by suitable infrastructures. This matrix can obviously be modified to suit individual circumstances (it might, for example, include axes of public–private ownership and management of media institutions).

Matrices can also be developed to assist with the evaluation and comparison of alternative systems. Figure 7 shows a simple matrix for the costing of alternatives which was developed some years ago during a pre-investment survey of educational mass media in Thailand. The following is an account of its use (Hancock, 1980, p. 41–2):

The team also developed a costing matrix, covering a variety of system possibilities, which became the basis of a good deal of scenario construction and decision-making. In outline, this matrix is produced in Figure 7, relating various combinations of basic mass media (radio, television and support media), ranging from centralized to local forms, to the key processes of production, distribution/transmission and reception/utilization, across a variety of potential audiences. The matrix itself was primarily a costing tool, but the accompanying commentary considered the educational and social impact of different permutations; taken together, therefore, these gave a guide to alternative

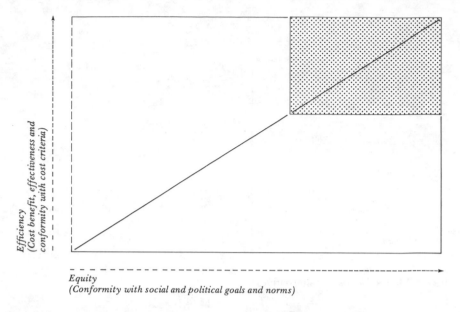

FIG. 8. Locating alternatives between efficiency and equity

systems. Various media strategies could be produced by tracing maths through the matrix, each fixed according to different system objectives, to logistical demands and to cost.

This matrix, admittedly crude, is limited to the costing of alternatives, and deals purely with electronic media. But it does provide a framework within which alternatives can be viewed as a whole; greater detail is provided by the accompanying prose commentary and cost estimates and analyses. In reviewing alternatives, however, a major difficulty is to find a balance between cost factors and issues of social equity. This is illustrated in Figure 8, which seeks to locate each alternative proposal along a grid of efficiency (i.e. conformity with stated cost criteria) and equity (i.e. conformity with social and political goals and norms). A simple presentation of alternative proposals, for overall comparison, can be made in this way.

In this figure, the vertical axis (efficiency) moves along a path of cost-effectiveness from least to maximum; similarly, in the horizontal axis (equity), the path is from least to maximum equity. Thus, alternative proposals and solutions which are to be seriously considered or recommended should fall within the shaded section of the diagram (which surrounds the upper portion of the vector bisecting the efficiency/equity grid).

While the diagram is simple, the problem of establishing criteria for mapping efficiency and equity is clearly less so. The criterion of efficiency, if seen in costing terms, is the less problematic. Here, techniques of cost–benefit analysis, described elsewhere in this book, can be used to isolate solutions which provide least-cost alternatives (in relation to unit costs of the alternative systems proposed, in which both development and recurrent costs are considered). The question of equity is more difficult, as its parameters will be different for each context in which it is to be plotted. Factors to be taken into consideration will include:

Relevance to developmental goals and objectives

Degree of centralization and decentralization of system planning and management

Degree of public participation

Relevance and benefit to the rural sector

Relevance and benefit to other marginal sectors, e.g. the poor, disadvantaged and minority communities

To establish such criteria it may also be useful to employ models similar to that illustrated in Figure 7.

The function of such tools is deliberately restricted: they are not sophisticated models for decision-making, nor are they instruments for the analysis of resources. They exist to help delimit the range of alternatives chosen, on the one hand, and to place the results of comparative analysis in a holistic perspective, for decision-making, on the other. In this way, they provide a framework for the application of specific techniques described elsewhere in this book.

Operational planning

DISTRIBUTION

The final task of resource distribution, once the preferred system has been identified and agreed upon by planners and decision-makers, is a more mechanistic process, but again, it comprises several stages. There is an element of needs assessment even at this allocative stage; the existence of a coherent strategy does not mean that all the information required for operational planning is available, and more specific inquiries and data analyses will be needed. The plan as a whole has to be broken down to allow for the identification and distribution of resources shared among various agencies involved in the overall communication programme. This implies not simply the consideration of resources *per se*, but also of the means required to generate such resources for the programme's sustenance (i.e. manpower needs imply the creation or strengthening of training institutions etc.). Consequently, in designing programmes for communications development, the following types of assessments should be made:

Need and benefits of intended beneficiaries and users

Needs of programme and project managers and implementers

General performance needs of communication distribution channels and networks

General performance needs for the production and consumption of information

Technology implementation support and requirements
Short-term and long-term budgetary needs
Project priorities
Extent to which intended services are self-sustaining or require continued
    support
While operational plans vary considerably in format and content from case to
case, a good plan should always contain a clear and detailed statement of
resources available, their quality and the grounds upon which resource allocation has been based. It can then be used by implementers as a main reference
document in which the programme's information base has been consolidated.

Conclusion

Information needs do not, evidently, end at this point; they recur throughout
the period of monitoring and evaluation, as a prelude to the reallocation and
adjustment of resources. Throughout all these processes, however, there is the
same need for an adequate and detailed information base to improve the
quality of decision-making. The allocation of resources is finally a political act,
but its efficiency and equity will be much affected by the character of the
information base provided, before a decision is formulated and entrenched.

Bibliography

CLIPPINGER, J. H. 1980. A Framework for Needs Assessment in Communication Development.
    In: *Telecommunications Policy*. Guildford, Surrey, IPC Science and Technology Press.
EICHER, J. C. 1977. *The Economics of New Educational Media*. Paris, Unesco.
ETZIONI, A. 1969. *The Active Society: A Theory of Social and Political Processes*. London, Collier-
    Macmillan; New York, N.Y., Free Press.
HANCOCK, A. 1980. *Communication Planning for Development: An Operational Framework*. Paris,
    Unesco.

Appendix   Check-list

A. SOCIAL AND POLITICAL DEVELOPMENT

[1] Statistical data
Basic data on:

Geography:
Area; topographical distribution; distribution of main cities and business centres and their
    hinterland; climate and weather conditions
Administrative, political and social units; transportation network (railways, waterways, airways);
    volume of traffic and pattern of mobility reflected in physical transportation; isolated areas
    and reasons for isolation; areas vulnerable to natural disasters; incidence of natural calamities
    and disasters

Population:
Size of population, rate of population increase
Sex and age composition
Density, distribution of population in urban and rural areas

Religion and ethnic groups: composition and distribution
Internal and external migration and movement of population
Number of housing units and housing density

Economy:
Gross domestic product and gross national product and their distribution by economic sectors
Income per capita and income distribution
Government income and expenditure
Income and expenditure in private sector
Capital formation and investment, balance of payment
Principal financial sources of national budget; amount of foreign aid, by source
Imports and exports by countries
Major trade and commercial activities within the country
Market structure in urban and rural areas; type and number of urban and rural market-places
Cost of living indices; family expenditure on different categories of items

Political institutions:
Election and voting rates; expenditure on election campaigns
Political parties, composition and number of members
Local-government organizations and co-operative societies: number, functions, sources of finance
Private voluntary agencies: number, functions, sources of finance

Diplomatic and external agencies:
Overseas missions, trade missions, membership of regional and institutional organizations

Employment:
Human resources by sector and type of employment: approximate number of employees, distri-
    bution and professional background or training
Current unemployment rates and trends; distribution by various occupational categories, age and
    sex
Training institutions: type, number, enrolment
Overseas training and use of foreign experts: type and number

Languages:
Number of languages and proportion and distribution of speakers

Education:
Structure of education: levels and stages, forms and types
Illiteracy rate: by age, sex, region
Educational levels: primary, secondary and higher education; enrolment by age and sex; drop-out,
    wastage and repeat rates; academic performance and success rate
Number and type of educational and cultural institutions and enrolment or membership figures

[2] Historical growth
Historical development of areas listed under 1

[3] Organizational structures

(*a*) *Institutional forms and organizational procedures of areas listed under 1*

(*b*) *Structures of planning:*
Constitutional, legal and organizational status of planning in the country
Responsible central entity (ministry) or authority; planning councils or boards; departments of
    planning in other ministries, institutes etc.; mechanisms of co-ordination, subordination etc.
Ideological and political elements of planning (planning and private activities; compulsory and
    indicative aspects)
Organization and administration of planning activities by sector
Planning procedures: diagnosis, formulation, targeting, format, evaluation, mechanisms of
    control

Project identification (government and administrative levels at which it takes place); decision-making processes for project selection and financing; control mechanisms of execution; application of evaluation techniques; planning and financing strategies (subsidies, loans, inflationary budgets, special taxes, national and international loans, bonds etc.)

[4] Legal and regulatory

Legal framework and infrastructure
National constitution
Pattern of formulation and adoption of legal instruments
Principal international (bilateral, regional and multilateral) agreements covering political organization and affiliation, trade, transportation, cultural exchange, security etc.

[5] Goals and targets

Goals and targets articulated by development plan and by sectoral plans
Goals and targets as evidenced by politicians and political parties, researchers and investigators, reports of task forces and study groups

[6] Norms and values

Attitudes to family unit, community and state; economic organization and industrial practice; political organization; religion and morality; language, artistic and cultural development; racial and minority groups
Basic constitutional or habitual rights: assembly, organization, special protest etc.

[7] Future trends

Views of medium- and long-term social, political and economic development, as held by experts, specialist groups and general public
Manpower projections by sector, for skilled and specialist services
Aspirations for long-term regional and international affiliation, as evidenced by reports, studies and research
Future-orientated reports and plans on specific aspects of development

B. COMMUNICATION

[8] Statistical data

Postal services:
Number of post offices by region and urban/rural location
Postal staff by categories: salary structure; professional qualifications and experience
Income and expenditure, budget and financing
Volume and flow of mails: national and international
Charges and tariffs; use of postal services by region, class and per capita

Telecommunications:
Telephone network: number of telegraph offices, telephone exchanges and telephone receivers in urban and rural areas
Microwave network: area covered and type of services
International telephone, telex and other telecommunication services
Satellite transmitting and receiving stations
Production of telecommunication equipment
Telecommunication staff by categories; salary structure; professional qualifications and experience
Type and volume of message flow
Extent and nature of breakdowns
Income, expenditure, budget and financing
Costs and tariffs of various services and rate structures: use of telecommunications per capita

Radio:
Number of stations and coverage
Breakdown of stations by public or private ownership
Transmission capacity and types of equipment
Transmission time by programme categories
Transmission time by network, regional, local output
Transmission time by public/private ownership
Number of radio receivers and their distribution (e.g. by region, class per 1,000)
Community or group listening services, if any
Radio staff by categories: salary structure; professional qualifications and experience
Radio programme production facilities: number and distribution
Programme production by network, regional, local output
Programme production by public, private ownership
Import and export of programming
Performing staff: full-time, part-time and contract
Income, expenditure, budget and financing
Production of radio transmission and receiving equipment
Import and export of equipment
Cost and availability of receivers: details of licensing system, if any
Total licences and licences per 1,000
Advertising rates, if any
Audience research figures, broken down by channel, programme, type, region, class
Audience-reaction surveys

Television:
Number of stations and coverage: broadcast and cable systems
Breakdown of stations by public or private ownership
Transmission capacity, quality and type of equipment
Hours of transmission and distribution of time by programme categories
Transmission time by network, regional, local output
Transmission time by public/private ownership
Number of television receivers and their distribution (e.g. by region, per class, per 1,000)
Community and group listening facilities, if any
Television staff by categories: salary structure; professional qualifications and experience
Television-programme production facilities and actual volume of production by type
Programme production by network, regional, local output
Programme production by public/private ownership
Imported and exported programmes by type and sources
Performing staff: full-time, part-time hire and commissioned
Income, expenditure, budget and financing
Television-receiver production and imports; cost and availability of receivers
Licensing system, pay system etc., if any
Total licences and licences per 1,000
Advertising rates, if any
Audience-research figures, by channel, programme type, region, class
Audience-reaction surveys

Cinema:
Number of cinemas and other outlets (including mobile units): volume of business, ownership
Number of distributors: volume of business, ownership
Number of producers and production organizations: volume of business, ownership
Staff employed in cinema industry; by number, categories, salary structure, professional qualifi-
    cations and experience
Number and type of films produced
Number and type of films distributed
Income, expenditure, budget and financing of cinema industry (production and distribution)
Import and export of production and distribution equipment: volume and cost
Import and export of films
Total seating capacity and number of seats per 1,000
Total annual attendance and annual cinema visits per capita

Newspapers and periodicals:
Number of newspapers: type, frequency, format, language
Newspaper and periodical circulation: by region, social class, age and sex structure
Total circulation and circulation per 1,000
Newspaper ownership: production and distribution
Staff employed in newspaper and periodical industry: by number, categories, salary structure, professional qualifications and experience
Distribution outlets: number and location
Income, expenditure, budget and financing of industry (production and distribution)
Advertising rates
Sources and breakdown of news and information
Readership surveys
Importation of production equipment, local production and export
Import and export of newspapers by region, language, audience

Printing (excluding newspapers and periodicals):
Number of printing firms by category
Number of printing presses by type and capacity
Volume of business and capacity of printing houses by type of printing, ownership, clientele
Staff employed in printing industry by number, categories, salary structure, professional qualifications and experience
Income, expenditure, budget and financing of printing industry
Importation, production and exportation of equipment
Paper consumption: total and per capita
Paper production, import and export

News agencies:
Number of news agencies, volume of business, ownership, clientele
Staff employed by number, categories, salary structure, professional qualifications and experience
Subscription to foreign news agencies: number and usage
Words produced daily by domestic news agencies (by agency)
Words consumed daily from external news agencies (by agency)
Language and time breakdown of production and consumption of materials
Subscription rates, charges and tariffs
Membership of regional news agencies and pools

Publishing, libraries, documentation centres:
Number and type of publishing sources
Number of books published, by type and year, language, average price of different type of book
Volume of publishing business
Number of booksellers
Number of libraries and book holdings
Volume of borrowing and attendance of readers
Number of documentation centres
Staff employed in each sector by number, categories, salary structure, professional qualifications and experience
Income and expenditure, budget and financing of publishing industry
Investment and cost of library services
Import and export of books

Advertising:
Number of advertising firms: origin, functions and activities
Staff employed: number, categories, salary structure, professional qualifications and experience
Volume of advertising business by media: newspaper, radio, television etc.
Income and expenditure, budget, financing
Advertising rates, by media
Government advertising: cost and distribution over various media

Popular culture:
Number and type of popular culture groups and organizations

Performance and attendance records
Production and sale of records, cassettes, tapes (audio and video)
Import and export figures for recording industry
Staff employed by number, categories, professional qualifications and experience
Income, expenditure, budget, financing of industry (production and distribution)
Rates for performing rights, reproduction, copyright

Sectoral communication agencies and services
(e.g. education, health, agriculture, rural development, public information, law and security services, weather information, religious and private groups):
Types of communication media and channels employed: number of functions
Production data: number of production agencies and units, volume and nature of production, ownership and management
Transmission data: number of transmitting sources (if separate from main transmission sources); volume, nature and timing of transmissions; ownership and management
Transmission/distribution coverage (in relation to overall potential target audience)
Volume and sources of imported programming/materials
Staffing by categories, salary structure, professional qualifications and experience
Income, expenditure, budget and financing by sector or organization
Audience data: numbers, breakdown by educational level, function, social status, urban/rural composition, age and sex
Production seen as a proportion of overall sectoral activity
Manpower seen as a proportion of overall sectoral manpower
Expenditure seen as a proportion of overall sectoral expenditure
Evaluation data on use and acceptability/quality/utility of output
Content analysis of programming/materials
Sources (local and external) of programming and programme inserts
Unit costs of output by various categories
Types and region of equipment employed: numbers, origin, maintenance conditions
Utilization services: number, function and distribution of utilization and extension staff

External services:
External broadcasting, press and public relations: number, type, objectives, outputs
Production data: materials produced, type, objectives
Transmission data: intended audience, audience coverage
Sources of income, expenditure, budget and financing
Utilization data: audience surveys and reactions

[9] Historical growth

Historical development of all communication sectors and agencies listed under 8 above

[10] Organizational structures

Degree of organization of communication as a coherent sector: division of communication responsibilities
Organizational structures, planning and operational procedures for all communication sectors and agencies listed in 8 above
Professional and industrial structures and groups for all communication sectors listed in 8 above
Type, number and function of research and training institutions, for communication sectors and agencies listed under 8 above

[11] Legal and regulatory

Development and present structure of communication law, rules and regulations by sector (see 8 above), procedures and methods of enforcement
Communication law *vis-à-vis* the individual (e.g. Citizen Band access)
International (bilateral and multilateral) agreements and pacts on communication, covering all sectors listed in 8 above, in respect of external activities, or participation in bilateral, regional

and multilateral activities (e.g. space, news distribution, marine and air traffic, meteorology)
Copyright law
Agreements for the exchange of persons and materials
Regulations on censorship

[12] Goals and targets

Specific goals and targets for communication development, as expressed by: development plan, sectoral plans; media organizations; professional groups; academic and reseach institutions; community and public groups

[13] Norms and values

Codes of ethics of professional groups and media organizations (see list of sectors and agencies in 8 above)
Attitudes to freedom of expression, information flow, censorship; access to media by individuals and community groups; participation in media planning, management and operation by community and individuals; attitude to importation and exportation of information and programmes
Patterns and norms of social and interpersonal communication
Attitudes towards multinational communication organizations and agencies
Existence of and attitude on folk and traditional media
Attitudes towards international communication agencies and programmes
Perception of communication rights and responsibilities by leaders and by political groups

[14] Future trends

Trends in mass communication; regional and international communication; information and data exchange; alternative and community media
Projection of volume and flow, supply and demand of communication sectors and agencies listed under 8
Manpower projections for communication sectors and agencies listed under 8

C. TECHNOLOGY

[15] Statistical data
Basic data on the following:

Imports and exports of technology hardware and software (including spares and maintenance)
Industrial organization and growth
Production and consumption of technology
Trends of mechanization and automation by sector
Production and distribution of electric power: extent of electrification in rural areas

[16] Historical growth

Historical dvelopment of science and technology; industrial development; science policy
History of dependency (sources of technology and technological expertise)

[17] Organizational structures

Organizational structures of science and technology sector; industrial sector (public and private); research and development agencies
Structures and procedures for technology importation, adaptation, exportation

[18] Legal and regulatory

Regulations covering technology sector: import/export arrangements; agreements and tariffs; patents; controls
Industrial law and its provisions

[19] Goals and targets

Goals and targets of public and private sectors for science and technology as expressed by: development plan; sectoral plans; research and development organizations; science and technology organizations; industry, professional and unionized groups

[20] Norms and values

Attitudes towards technology and modernization; automation; appropriate, alternative and intermediate technologies
Attitudes towards scientists and technologists; relative views of white-collar and blue-collar workers, science education and research
Science policy and technology policy, as perceived by specialized groups, research institutions, public and private sectors, general public

[21] Future trends

Views of research and development institutes, academic institutions, professional groups, individual experts on future technological trends
Studies and reports on future technological needs, capacity, orientation, functions
Specific forecasts of needs in field of technology: power, industry, information services, computerization, transportation
Manpower projections for science, technology and industry sectors
Forecasts of contribution of technology to role and function of the society *vis-à-vis* other societies; future bilateral, regional and international groupings

Chapter 5

Trend extrapolation

Benjamin E. Suta

Trend extrapolation is the general name for a variety of mathematical forecasting methods, all of which determine future values for a single variable through
some process of identifying a relationship valid for the past values of the
variables and a solution for future values. Although the technique is generally
useful for only a single variable, this variable may be highly complex in that it
may reflect numerous trends. The technique is only useful on quantifiable
variables; however, ingenuity can frequently be used to express qualitative
trends in quantitative forms. A major limitation of extrapolatory methods is
that they have not been able to deal with unanticipated patterns in the historical data. Recognizing this limitation, the Futures Group Inc., of
Glastonbury, Connecticut, United States, developed a technique called Trend
Impact Analysis (T I A). T I A allows an extrapolated trend to be impacted by a
set of specified unprecedented future events. Trend extrapolation includes
such methods as 'eyeballing', moving averages, exponential smoothing and
linear and non-linear regression. In this paper we describe trend extrapolation
through the use of linear regression techniques and then discuss modification
of the extrapolated trends in consideration of potential unanticipated future
events.

Definition

Trend extrapolation is a family of quantitative forecasting techniques, all of
which depend on extending, or extrapolating, time-series data in accordance
with specified, usually mathematical, rules. The extrapolations constitute the
forecast. The specific method of extrapolation involves developing a 'best-fit'
curve to represent the historical pattern in the data. Statistical regression-
analysis techniques may be used for this purpose where a number of different
types of curves may be tried. The data used are usually actual counts of the
phenomenon under investigation, such as population, number of units sold,
events per units of time, or dollars earned. The methods also can be used with
proxy data or other kinds of indicators, provided they are available for a long

enough period to reveal a pattern of development that can be used as a basis for extrapolation.

Trend extrapolation depends on the hypothesis that past and present trends will, in the future, develop in the same direction and at the same rate as in the past, unless there is a clear indication of a shift in trends. Such shifts—not always foreseen—account for some recent spectacular errors in extrapolatory forecasts. Population, inflation and oil prices are recent examples, along with that perennial American favourite, the Dow-Jones average.

History

The instinctive use of trend extrapolation goes back to the dawn of man. Surely, even the most primitive man was confident that day would follow night simply because 'time-series analysis' showed no exception. In a more sophisticated fashion, many ancient civilizations developed theories of cosmology by noting changes in positions of stars over many years.

Trend analysis and projection has in recent decades enjoyed an expansion that amounts to a boom. Among the causal factors explaining this rising interest are:

The growing complexity and interdependence of civilization. Trends in one sector are apt to cause important effects immediately or in the future in many other sectors. The human environment is increasingly human-made, abstract and subject to rapid shifts resulting from human decisions and actions. Trend analysis and forecasting has become an indispensable tool for understanding what is happening to us.

As society grows more complex, more and more transactions are formalized and recorded. One result of this is more and more —and in some cases more and more accurate—time-series data. Thus, opportunities for trend projections based on existing data are more and more widely and readily available.

The 'computer revolution' has encouraged the development and use of diverse, sophisticated and often powerful methods that enable us to analyse and project trends rapidly and at relatively low costs.

For such fundamental reasons as these, much—perhaps even most—contemporary research in economics, political science and the other behavioural and social sciences is centrally dependent upon or makes heavy use of trend analysis and projection methods.

Procedures

GENERAL

In general, trend extrapolation is easy to do, requiring a relatively small expenditure of time and money. Once the appropriate time-series data are available, they are plotted as value versus time. The rhythm of the trend is often self-evident from the plot. In some cases, all that is required to extrapolate is use of a ruler or a french curve. Regression-curve fitting is preferred because it gives a mathematical expression that can be used for extrapolation and it gives an indication as to how well the curve fits the historical data. The regression curves can be calculated with a hand calculator or with the use of a computer. Standard software packages for regression analysis are available for most computers.

UNIMPACTED TREND EXTRAPOLATION

The unimpacted (or surprise-free) trend extrapolation involves the fitting of one or more curves to the historical data and the subsequent selection of one of the curves that appears to represent the trend better. The mathematical assumption underlying trend extrapolation is that a relatively orderly progression of historical data will continue into the future. Examples of the types of curves that have been found useful for trend extrapolation are as follows:

$$V = a + bT \qquad \text{linear curve} \tag{1}$$

$$V = a + b/T \qquad \text{inverse curve} \tag{2}$$

$$V = a\,e^{bT} \qquad \text{exponential curve} \tag{3}$$

$$V = aT^b \qquad \text{power curve} \tag{4}$$

$$V = a + b\,ln(T) \qquad \text{logarithmic curve} \tag{5}$$

$$V = L/(1 + ae^{-bT}) \qquad \text{pearl curve} \tag{6}$$

$$V = L\,e^{-ae^{-bT}} \qquad \text{gompertz curve} \tag{7}$$

where: V is the value of the trend; T is time, L is some limiting value, and a and b are constants.

The general shapes of these curves are shown in Figures 1 to 7. The pearl and gompertz curves are useful when it is known that a trend cannot exceed some predetermined value. In Table 1, we give the regression equations that are used to determine the values of the constants (a and b) for the linear curve. The linear regression can be used with a suitable transformation of the dependent or independent variables to determine the values of the constants for equations (2) to (7). For example, the constants for equation (2) would be determined by letting $X = 1/T$ and $Y = V$. Similarly, the constants for equation (3) would be determined by letting $X = T$ and $Y = ln(V)$.

The coefficient of regression (r^2), shown in Table 1, gives an indication of how well the curve fits the historical data. The coefficient of regression ranges in value from 0 to 1, with 0 indicating a complete lack of fit and 1 indicating a perfect fit. A procedure that is sometimes used is to fit several different types of curves to the data and to select the curve with the largest coefficient of regression. This procedure may, however, be overridden by other factors. Another useful feature of the coefficient of regression is that it can be used to

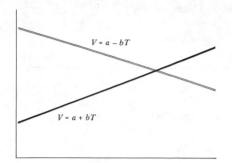

FIG. 1. Linear curve

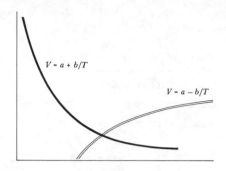

FIG. 2. Inverse curve

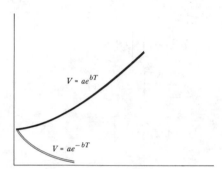

FIG. 3. Exponential curve

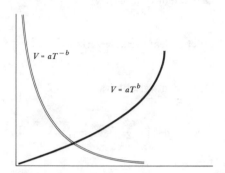

FIG. 4. Power curve

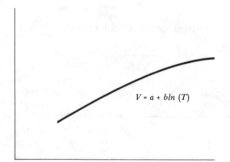

FIG. 5. Logarithmic curve

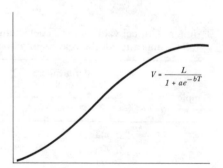

FIG. 6. Pearl curve

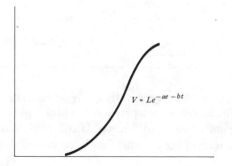

FIG. 7. Gompertz curve

TABLE 1. Equations for simple linear regression ($Y = a + bX$)

Independent variable $= X$

Dependent variable $= Y$

Sample size $= n$

Independent variable average $= \bar{X} = \sum\limits_{i=1}^{n} X_i$

Dependent variable average $= \bar{Y} = \sum\limits_{i=1}^{n} Y_i$

Independent variable variance $= S_x^2 = \left[n \sum\limits_{i=1}^{n} X_i^2 - \left(\sum\limits_{i=1}^{n} X_i \right)^2 \right] \Big/ n(n-1)$

Dependent variable variance $= S_y^2 = \left[n \sum\limits_{i=1}^{n} Y_i^2 - \left(\sum\limits_{i=1}^{n} Y_i \right)^2 \right] \Big/ n(n-1)$

Slope $= b = \left(n \sum\limits_{i=1}^{n} X_i Y_i - \sum\limits_{i=1}^{n} X_i \sum\limits_{i=1}^{n} Y_i \right) \Big/ \left[n \sum\limits_{i=1}^{n} X_i^2 - \left(\sum\limits_{i=1}^{n} X_i \right)^2 \right]$

Intercept $= a = \bar{Y} - b\bar{X}$

Coefficient of regression $= r^2 = b_x^2 S_x^2 / S_y^2$

TABLE 2. Critical values of the coefficient of regression (r^2) used for testing the significance of the regression equation[1]

Sample size (n)	Significance level		Sample size (n)	Significance level	
	5%	1%		5%	1%
3	0.994	1.000	20	0.197	0.315
4	0.903	0.980	30	0.130	0.214
5	0.771	0.919	40	0.092	0.154
6	0.658	0.841	60	0.063	0.105
7	0.569	0.765	100	0.038	0.065
8	0.499	0.696	200	0.019	0.033
9	0.444	0.636	500	0.008	0.013
10	0.399	0.585			

1. Used to test if the regression equation $Y = a + bX$ is significantly better than $Y = \bar{Y}$. Critical values are based on the student's t-test of significance.

---

determine if the regression curve is statistically significantly better than simply using the average of the values as a predictor. Table 2 gives critical values to be used to determine statistical significance. If the computed value exceeds the tabulated value, statistical significance has been attained.

TABLE 3. Gross product expenditures for communications in the United States

Year	Gross product (thousand million 1972 U.S. dollars)	Year	Gross product (thousand million 1972 U.S. dollars)
1950	6.3	1972	29.4
1955	9.1	1973	32.0
1960	12.1	1974	33.6
1965	16.9	1975	36.5
1970	25.6	1976	39.1

Sources: Bureau of the Census (1978).

TABLE 4. Example of various equation forms fitted to gross-product expenditures data for communications in the United States

Equation type	Equation form	Coefficient of regression (r^2)
Linear	$Y = 1.044 + 1.279(T - 1949)$	0.946
Logarithmic	$Y = -0.963 + 9.594\,ln(T - 1949)$	0.681
Exponential	$Y = 5.790\,exp[0.070(T - 1949)]$	0.998
Power	$Y = 4.644\,(T - 1949)^{0.507}$	0.855
Pearl	$Y = 100/\{1 + 17.441[exp\,-0.087(T - 1949)]\}$	0.994

There are a number of statistical books that describe regression analysis in more detail. As examples, the reader is referred to Draper and Smith (1966) or Daniel and Wood (1971).

Unimpacted trend case example

For a case example, we have taken the annual gross product expenditures for American communications. The data for 1950 to 1976 are shown in Table 3. These data are plotted on Figure 8. We have fitted five of the different type curves to the data (Table 4). The pearl curve was fitted assuming an arbitrary limit of $100,000 million/year. We have transformed the time variable by subtracting 1949 from the year. This is rather arbitrary and transforms 1950 (the first year of data) to a value of 1.

The exponential curve was found to have the largest coefficient of regression (0.998), providing an almost perfect fit to the historical data. The pearl curve provides almost as good a fit (coefficient of regression of 0.994). Both of these curves are plotted along with the data on Figure 8. Thus, either curve might be used to extrapolate gross product expenditures for U.S. communications. However, as is illustrated on Figure 8, the two curves provide quite

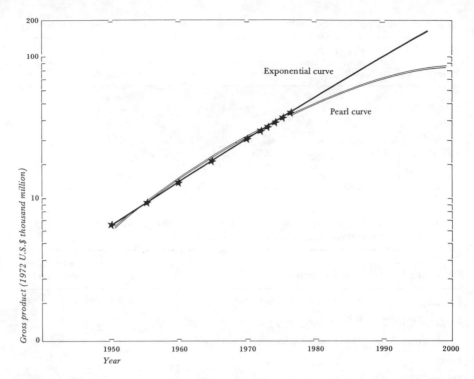

FIG. 8. Gross product expenditures as a function of time for American communications

different extrapolations at the year 2000. This illustrates the fundamental difference between the two curves: one is unconstrained while the other is constrained at $100,000 million/year. One, therefore, should not myopically select the best-fit curve but should combine the selection with whatever additional knowledge is available regarding the trend being extrapolated.

Impacted trend analysis

Extrapolation of a historical trend into the future using the curve-fitting procedure described above assumes that no unusual or extraordinary events will occur that might have a significant effect on the trend. A review of history shows that such events occur rather frequently. Examples of these events might be a war, global inflation, introduction of a new product, restriction of the supply of a crucial resource, change in government or widespread adoption of a new or different life-style. It is, of course, not possible to predict accurately when such events might take place, if at all. However, it is possible to estimate subjectively the probability of their occurrence over time. It is also possible to predict the effect that such events might have on the extrapolated trend, should they occur. These two factors (probability of occurrence and expected effect on

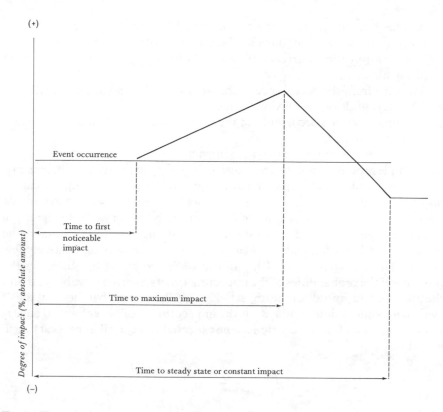

FIG. 9. Event-impact assessments

the trend, should the event occur) can be used to estimate statistically the expected future trend values when impacted by these events.

The trend-impact analysis procedure was developed by the Futures Group as a useful forecasting technique. It permits extrapolation of a historical trend to be statistically modified in view of expert opinion about the future events or trends that could affect the basic trend in question. (See Gordon and Stover, 1976, for a discussion of T I A.) The procedure starts with the unimpacted trend curve, as previously described. Expert judgement is then sought regarding potential unprecedented future events that might occur during the forecasting time period and that might have a significant affect on trend. The source of the information regarding the trends might come from a review of the literature or from assembled or unassembled groups of experts. Several subjective judgements are required for each event regarding (a) its probability of occurrence over time and (b) its potential impact on the trend over time after its occurrence. The probability of occurrence can be expressed in tabular or graphic form, and contains the subjectively determined probability of the event occurring in each of the forecasting time periods (monthly, annually etc.). The potential impacts are characterized by the stylized procedure illustrated in Figure 9. It requires the following subjective judgements:

1. The time from the occurrence of the trend until it begins to impact the trend (delay time).
2. The time from the occurrence of the trend until its maximum impact.
3. The magnitude of the maximum impact.
4. The time from the occurrence of the event until a steady state or constant impact is attained.
5. The magnitude of the steady-state impact.

This simple procedure gives a great deal of flexibility in the type of impacts that can be described. For example, the maximum and steady-state impacts can be positive, negative or zero in value. The impacts can also be specified in terms of the trend value or as a percentage of the unimpacted trend value. Generally, a computer program is used to assess the expected impacts of the events on the trend, although hand calculations can be used for cases having relatively few events. The expected value of the impacts are computed by summing the products of the probabilities of the impacting events for each possible year and the predicted magnitude of the impact. Thus, if P_{ti} is the probability that the ith event will occur at time t and $I_{t'-t,i}$ is the impact that the ith event would have $t' - t$ time periods after its occurrence, the expected value of all impacts at time t' would be

$$E_{t'} = \sum_{i=1}^{n} \sum_{i=t_0}^{t'} P_{ti} \cdot I_{t'-t,i} \qquad (8)$$

where: $E_{t'}$ = the expected value of all impacts at time period t'; P_{ti} = probability of ith event occurring at time t; $I_{t' \times t,i}$ = impact of ith event $t' - t$ years after its occurrence; n = number of events; and t_0 = first year of extrapolation. The probabilistic nature of the specified events can also be used to develop statistical confidence limits about the extrapolations.

Impacted trend case example

We will illustrate the T I A procedure by a continuation of the unimpacted case example of gross product expenditures for American communications. Three sample events were selected from those determined by Wedemeyer (1978) for communications in Hawaii. These are a recession, the advent of electronic shopping and petrol rationing.

Table 5 provides estimates regarding the possible impacts of the events and Table 6 provides estimates of the probability of event occurrence. The values given in Tables 5 and 6 are purely hypothetical and are given here only for illustration of the TIA procedure. Equation (8) was used to estimate the expected impacts of the events. An example of the estimated expected impacts of a recession is shown in Table 7. The total expected impacts of each event along with the estimated impacted and unimpacted trends are given in Table 8.

TABLE 5. Estimated event impacts

	Recession	Electronic shopping	Petrol rationing
Years to first impact	0	0	0
Years to maximum impact	−3	3	5
Years to steady state	−5	4	6
Maximum impact	−10	9	10
Steady-state impact	0	6	10

TABLE 6. Estimated probability of event occurrence

	Event				Event		
Year	Recession	Electronic shopping	Petrol rationing	Year	Recession	Electronic shopping	Petrol rationing
1981	0.10	0.05	0.25	1986	0.10	0.05	0.00
1982	0.10	0.05	0.25	1987	0.10	0.05	0.00
1983	0.10	0.05	0.25	1988	0.10	0.05	0.00
1984	0.10	0.05	0.25	1989	0.10	0.05	0.00
1985	0.10	0.05	0.00	1990	0.10	0.05	0.00

TABLE 7. Hypothetical expected impacts on communications expenditures from a recession

Year of event occurrence	Year of impact									
	1981	1982	1983	1984	1985	1986	1987	1988	1989	1990
1981	−0.3	−0.7	−1.0	−0.5	0.0	0.0	0.0	0.0	0.0	0.0
1982	0.0	−0.3	−0.7	−1.0	−0.5	0.0	0.0	0.0	0.0	0.0
1983	0.0	0.0	−0.3	−0.7	−1.0	−0.5	0.0	0.0	0.0	0.0
1984	0.0	0.0	0.0	−0.3	−0.7	−1.0	−0.5	0.0	0.0	0.0
1985	0.0	0.0	0.0	0.0	−0.3	−0.7	−1.0	−0.5	0.0	0.0
1986	0.0	0.0	0.0	0.0	0.0	−0.3	−0.7	−1.0	−0.5	0.0
1987	0.0	0.0	0.0	0.0	0.0	0.0	−0.3	−0.7	−1.0	−0.5
1988	0.0	0.0	0.0	0.0	0.0	0.0	0.0	−0.3	−0.7	−1.0
1989	0.0	0.0	0.0	0.0	0.0	0.0	0.0	0.0	−0.3	−0.7
1990	0.0	0.0	0.0	0.0	0.0	0.0	0.0	0.0	0.0	−0.3
TOTAL	−0.3	−1.0	−2.0	−2.5	−2.5	−2.5	−2.5	−2.5	−2.5	−2.5

TABLE 8. Impacted trend adjustments

Year	Recession	Impact source			Unimpacted trend[1]	Impacted trend
		Electronic shopping	Petrol rationing	All impacts		
1981	−0.3	0.2	0.5	0.4	55.0	55.4
1982	−1.0	0.5	1.5	1.0	60.0	61.0
1983	−2.0	0.9	3.0	1.9	64.0	65.9
1984	−2.5	1.2	5.0	3.7	69.0	72.7
1985	−2.5	1.5	7.5	6.5	74.0	80.5
1986	−2.5	1.8	8.5	7.8	80.0	87.8
1987	−2.5	2.1	9.5	9.1	85.0	94.1
1988	−2.5	2.4	10.0	9.9	90.9	99.9
1989	−2.5	2.7	10.0	10.2	99.0	109.2
1990	−2.5	3.0	10.0	10.5	105.0	115.5

1. Based on extrapolation using the exponential curve.

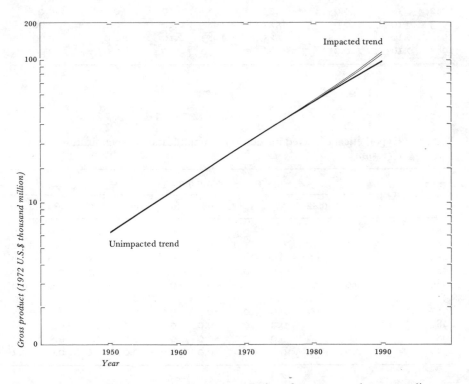

FIG. 10. Impacted and unimpacted trend predictions for gross product expenditures for American communications

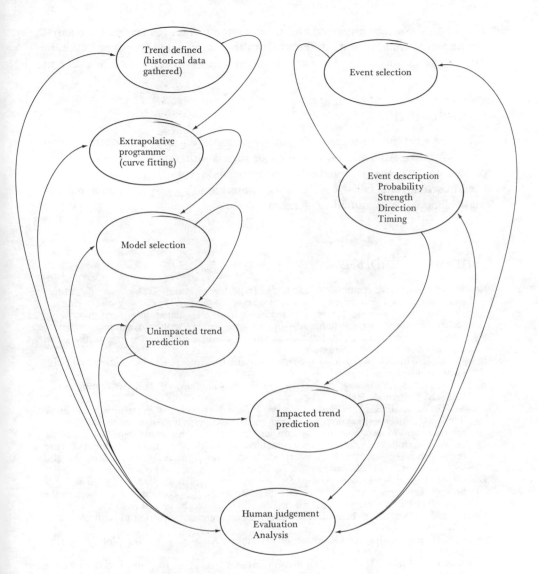

FIG. 11. Trend extrapolation procedure

Figure 10 shows the impacted and unimpacted trends. As frequency occurs, the impacted trend is quite different from the unimpacted trend; however, in our simple example, the difference between the two is about 10 per cent in 1990.

Conclusion

We have presented methods for making impacted and unimpacted trend extrapolations. An overview of the procedure is illustrated in Figure 11. The procedures, whether stopped at the unimpacted trend or continued through the impacted trend, consist of a series of steps blending historical data, mathematical models and human judgement.

Annotated bibliography

BLOOM, M. F. 1975. Deterministic Trend Cross-Impact Forecasting. *Technological Forecasting and Social Change*, Vol. 8, No. 1, p. 35–74. Presents a method of analysing past trends and projecting them into the future. The model includes a combination of three forecasting techniques: trend extrapolation; cross-impact analysis; and system dynamics simulation. These are applied in a an illustrative example to a simple five-trend system of the Israel population–economy–welfare system.

Box, G. E.; Jenkins, G. M. 1970. *Time Series Analysis: Forecasting and Control*. San Francisco, Calif., Holden-Day.

BROWN, R. G. 1963. *Smoothing, Forecasting, and Prediction of Discrete Time Series*. Englewood Cliffs, N. J., Prentice-Hall.

DANIEL, D.; WOOD, F. S. 1971. *Fitting Equations to Data*. New York, N. Y., John Wiley & Sons. This book is an exposition on the problems encountered in fitting equations to data. It helps the reader: (a) to recognize the strengths and limitations of his or her data; (b) to test the assumptions implicit in the least-squares methods used to fit the data; (c) to select appropriate forms of the variables; (d) to judge which combinations of variables are most informative; and (e) to state conditions under which the equations chosen appear to be applicable.

DRAPER, N. R.; SMITH, H. 1966. *Applied Regression Analysis*. New York, N. Y., John Wiley & Sons. This is a good reference book on regression analysis. It contains a description of the equations used in regression analysis, information that can be gained from the analysis of residuals, procedures to be used in selecting the best regression equation and a discussion of non-linear regression.

ENZER, S. 1972. Cross-Impact Techniques in Technology Assessment. *Futures*, Vol. 4, No. 1, p. 30–51.

GORDON, T. J.; STOVER, J. 1976. Using Perceptions and Data about the Future to Improve the Simulation of Complex Systems. *Technological Forecasting and Social Change*, Vol. 9, p. 197–202. Many of the techniques used to forecast the future are basically extrapolative, that is, they assume that the future will be an extension of the past. This assumption will eventually be incorrect, as new forces cause future changes. This paper describes methods for incorporating data and perceptions about unprecedented forces and events in otherwise extrapolative procedures. Two specific techniques incorporating these methods, trend-impact analysis and probabilistic-systems dynamics, are described.

JENKINS, G. M. 1979. *Practical Experiences with Modelling and Forecasting Time Series*. Jersey, Channel Is., Gwilym Jenkins & Partners.

KANE, J. 1972. A Primer for a New Cross-Impact Language—K S I M. *Technology Forecasting and Social Change*, Vol. 4, p. 129–42. This article describes the K S I M cross-impact simulation technique. K S I M is a mathematical means of articulating and visualizing what people sense to be the relationships among a number of interacting variables. As a simulation, too, it combines expert opinions with analytical computing techniques to analyse relationships among broadly defined variables in environmental and socio-economic systems. The technique enables a team of people, first, to define and structure a set of variables describing a perceived problem and then, using an interactive computer program, to calculate and display the changes in the variables over time.

LIPINSKI, H.; TYDEMAN, J. 1979. Cross-Impact Analysis: Extended K S I M. *Futures*, Vol. 11, No. 2, p. 151–4. This article presents an extension of K S I M that allows the inclusion of events and trends and describes the basic issues of forecasting and compatibility of forecasts.

MITCHELL, A., *et al.* 1975. *Handbook of Forecasting Techniques*. Menlo Park, Calif., Stanford Research Institute.

SHAW, R. 1979. Forecasting Air Traffic. *Futures*, Vol. 11, No. 3, p. 185–94. The author reviews the econometric techniques, and their attendant methodological problems, used in air-traffic forecasting. He goes on to discuss the reliability of such forecasts, particularly where they predict large increases in traffic.

UNITED STATES OF AMERICA. BUREAU OF THE CENSUS. 1978. *Statistical Abstracts of the United States: 1978*. Washington, D.C., U.S. Department of Commerce.

WAKELAND, W. 1976. O S I M 2: A Low Budget Heuristic Approach to Modeling and Forecasting. *Technological Forecasting and Social Change*, Vol. 9, p. 213–30.

WEDEMEYER, D. 1978. Forecasting for Communications Policy and Planning in Hawaii: Summary of an Application. In: S.A. Rahim *et al.*, *Planning Methods, Models, and Organizations. A Review Study for Communication Policy Making and Planning*. Honolulu, Hawaii, East–West Communication Institute.

Chapter 6
The Delphi technique

Dan J. Wedemeyer

Delphi is a technique useful in forecasting and structuring group communication. Developed in the early 1950s, it utilizes experts to collect opinion data when problems do not lend themselves to more empirical analytical techniques. Delphi involves two to three rounds of anonymous expert debate and group estimates. The results are a set of forecasts or higher understanding of the problem at hand. As a decision-making tool, Delphi is most useful during the early stages of planning (goal-setting, scenario development etc.). Its most serious limitations concern criteria for expert selection and potential for sloppy execution. Few resources are required, usually one to two monitors, a panel of experts, questionnaires and some clerical support. The procedures are simple and straightforward, yielding results that are useful in planning decisions.

Definition

Delphi is a group technique that organizes and utilizes expert opinion in order to deal with complex problems. It is a structured communication system which involves two or three rounds of experts' estimates. Anonymous feedback is provided to the participants after each round. This method enables each participating expert to make independent estimates and then revise them with supplemental information provided by the other Delphi panel members. Usually each round is administered via mailed questionnaire, but variations involving in-person interviews, computer conferencing or physically assembled groups are also common. The technique is administered by a monitor or monitors to a selected group of individuals who have notable expertise on the problem at hand. The monitor(s) develops the questionnaires, coordinates the panel members, summarizes the estimates and feeds back the information to the group. The experts then use the information from the past rounds to make subsequent round estimates. The final round produces a consensus of opinion (or lack of consensus, which can be equally valuable) on the particular topics at hand.

Assumptions, history and main uses

The primary assumption of this technique is that group estimates of complex problems are superior to individual estimates. It also assumes there is a reasonable availability of experts on any selected subject-matter. It assumes that experts can make better estimates on complex problems than the lay person. The inventors of Delphi also assumed that a central problem of using experts is the tendency for some people's opinions to be influenced by the status or personalities of other members of the group, and that group decision-making is particularly susceptible to the 'bandwagon effect' (i.e. individuals abandoning their individual position to be swept along with the group's feeling). Delphi's use of anonymous responses was designed to overcome this problem.

The Delphi technique originated at the Rand Corporation in the early 1950s. The co-inventors, Olaf Helmer and Theodore Gordon, developed the method as part of a US Air Force contract in order to forecast the details and consequences of a major nuclear attack on the United States. This problem obviously required speculation on the part of a large number of partici-pants.

Helmer and Gordon needed to develop systematic methods to deal with the problem. Delphi was born, according to Helmer, 'once that it was apparent that the only way to deal with the problem was intuitive judgements (i.e. no empirical data existed). We were faced with the problem of systemizing the process to remove as much ambiguity as possible from the deliberation' (personal communication). The first unclassified example of the Delphi techniques came out of the Rand Corporation in 1963 (Helmer and Gordon, 1963). Since that time, the Delphi method has been applied to thousands of problems in hundreds of corporations and nations around the world. Today, Delphi is viewed by many as the cornerstone of future research. It is a method that is capable of creating future-orientated information (opinion data) that is especially useful in planning situations.

The Delphi method is most useful in planning situations that do not lend themselves to precise analytical techniques. In addition, Delphi can be used when:

The individuals needed to contribute to the examination of a broad or complex problem have no history of adequate communication and may represent diverse backgrounds with respect to experience or expertise.

More individuals are needed than can effectively interact in a face-to-face exchange.

Time and cost make frequent group meetings unfeasible.

The efficiency of face-to-face meetings can be increased by a supplemental group-communication process.

Disagreements among individuals are so severe or politically unpalatable that the communication process must be referred or anonymity assured.

The heterogeneity of the participants must be preserved to assure validity of the results, i.e. avoidance of domination by quantity or by strength of personality ('bandwagon effect') (Turoff, 1975, p. 4).

The adoption of Delphi as a planning tool requires a shift towards 'adoption of some of the methods of operations research, notably the construction of simulation models and the systematic use of expert judgement' (Helmer, 1973, p. 4).

Delphi is most useful in the early designing stages when setting planning goals and requirements—the so-called creative-search aspects of normative and strategic planning. Delphi has traditionally been used in forecasting long-range developments, group decision-making and alternative explorations, as well as in a host of other applications. It is also well suited to: evaluating possible budget allocations; exploring planning options; constructing a planning model; exposing priorities of personal values and social goals; developing causal relationships in complex economic or social phenomena; and gathering data not accurately known or readily available.

Delphi can be used as a forecasting method and a system for structuring communication among planners. It is useful in promoting interaction among participants in the planning process with a minimum of cost or adverse social/psychological effects.

Limitations, product and communicability of results

Obviously no method is without its drawbacks. Delphi is no exception. The technique has been used and reviewed by many. Some general criticisms have been set out by Linstone (1975, p. 174–586). Potential problems associated with Delphi include:

Discounting the future. The occurrences of developments that appear further in the future are heavily discounted because uncertainty increases and there is always the hope that additional options or solutions will surface. Therefore, the need for a decision will ease or disappear.

The prediction urge. The human need for 'certainty' and a search for 'truth' or the single best model. This is most problematic in the interpretation phase of the Delphi inquiry.

The simplification urge. The human preference for simplicity over complexity is compounded by Delphi. There is an urge to oversimplify large, complex, multiple interactive patterns.

Illusory expertise. The problem of over-reliance on the concept of expertise and the operational definition of an expert is ever present in the technique.

Poor/sloppy execution. The Delphi monitor is sometimes guilty of selecting 'like-thinking' participants and superficial analysis of his/her responses.

Optimism–pessimism bias. This refers to short-term forecasts, which are usually biased toward over-optimism and long-term forecasts that are plagued by pessimism.

Overselling. Overenthusiasm for applying Delphi for any or all problem situation, and overstatements regarding the 'truth' of Delphi results.

Deception. Manipulation of data or interpretation of results. This is further complicated by the anonymous character of the Delphi process.

While many of these limitations can be applied to any research technique, Delphi is particularly susceptible to weaknesses involving expertise (How do you identify real experts?) and weaknesses involving consensus (How do you know whether the consensus is real and describes some underlying agreement on an issue?). Both problems are real, but they can be minimized by strict attention to expert selection, definition of panel members and the execution of the study.

Although almost every application of the Delphi technique involves some modification, no real substitutes exist. The most related methods which carry separate names yet similar processes are E T E (estimate, talk, estimate), Delbecq, the Policy Delphi and the Mini-Delphi. Each of these has some advantage over conventional Delphi. E T E and Delbecq are similar to what many refer to as the 'Mini-Delphi'. They involve less time to execute, and require that group members be physically present. The results are perhaps less reliable, but the trade-offs in time and expense are sometimes justifiable. The Policy Delphi is structurally similar to the conventional Delphi, but seeks out differences and alternatives rather than trying to obtain consensus. All of the aforementioned methods are excellent strategies for promoting communication and decision-making in groups. They are especially useful in the early stages of planning projects.

The outcome of a conventional Delphi is usually a set of forecasts and higher understanding of the planning problems, issues, values, etc. at hand. Depending upon the application, the results can be consensus (or identified non-consensus, which often indicates polarization on an issue) concerning prioritized budgets, goals, needs or values, trends, probabilities of event occurrences etc. The conventional Delphi results are usually quantitative, which are then integrated into qualitative terms (ranking, priorities, ranges etc.) useful in planning decisions.

The *level of detail* of the results depends very much upon the level of detail of the Delphi questions. For example, one could pose a scale-orientated question concerning the general need for telephone service in a particular region. Such a question would obviously result in very different information than an open-ended question asking for the best estimate of the number of telephones in the particular region by the year 2000. In other words, the level of detail is very much dependent upon specific data needs; Delphi is flexible in this regard.

The *confidence level* of Delphi depends very much on the quality and control of its execution. Many of the aforementioned limits and cautions are tied to questionnaire formulation and the actual execution of Delphi. While the level of confidence of the method results is still widely debated, reliability and accuracy tests have produced relatively high marks for the technique. As with most methods, caution should be used in over-interpreting the results or basing decisions on a single source of information. Delphi is but one method that provides information helpful in complex planning decisions.

Delphi results are easily understood by those who are not intimately involved with the process. The outputs of the exercise are usually much more understandable, and therefore communicable, than the internal workings of the exercise. And, unfortunately, communicating the Delphi results to decision-makers is much easier than getting them to act on new information at hand.

The problem of credibility has been associated with the Delphi technique since its inception. Recent studies (Jones, in Linstone, 1975; Wedemeyer, 1978*a*) have eased this concern somewhat. Sackman's (1974) assessment, which is highly critical of Delphi, has been countered by an entire issue of the *Journal of Technological Forecasting and Social Change* (1975) (see Coates, 1975). While non-credibility rightfully remains a concern of Delphi users, the observance of possible pitfalls and rigorous execution should ease even the most adamant critics.

Delphi, like all planning exercises, involves future problems and environments. Shorter-term concerns (one to five years) usually can be addressed by other methods such as trend extrapolation, regression etc. Delphi is most useful when forecasting five to thirty years hence. Anything past thirty years suffers from problems of forecasting accuracy and reliability.

Resources needed and procedures

Carrying out a Delphi survey requires little in the way of personnel or special equipment. Delphi does require time, however. Depending upon the sophistication level, experts involved and number of rounds, it can range from three to six months, with some elaborate studies requiring up to a year. In terms of resources, a typical two-round Delphi study may take six months, utilize one or two monitors, twenty to thirty selected experts, questionnaires and some clerical support. More sophisticated versions of the technique can be carried out via computer conferencing, which obviously increases the required resources while substantially decreasing the required time.

A typical Delphi procedure involves the selection of a group of experts and the preparation of a first-round questionnaire which poses precise, pre-tested questions, both quantitative and qualitative, about the specific problems to be studied. The questionnaires are either administered by personal interview or, more commonly, mailed to the individual panel members. After the experts respond to the questionnaire, the results of the round are tabulated by computing the semi-interquartile range (i.e. the middle 50 per cent of the responses) and a measure of central tendency, usually the median. The second-round questionnaire is then prepared. The questions include the first-round items as well as any new questions suggested by the panel. Summary statistical information from the first round is also included in the second round as feedback to each of the individual experts. The experts are then asked to consider carefully the feedback in responding to the second-round questionnaire. If their response on the second round is outside the interquartile range, they are asked to provide information regarding their rationale for the response. Each 'rationale statement' is summarized and fed back to the experts for the third round (if there is one).

The third (usually final)-round responses are collected and again the interquartile ranges and medians are computed. These statistics are accepted as the final group estimate of an occurrence of an event or a trend level.

Case example[1]

OVERVIEW

This example addresses long-range forecasting of communication needs, supplies and rights as inputs to the policy and planning process in the State of Hawaii. Three rounds of Delphi inquiry were conducted using sixty communication experts in the State of Hawaii. The experts were asked to estimate the levels of communication need, supply and 'right'[2] for twenty-four communication concepts for the years 1976, 1991 and 2006, and to indicate the years by which there would be a 10 per cent, 50 per cent and 90 per cent chance that each of the seventeen communication-related events will have occurred.

The study results provide specific trend-level forecasts and rankings for twenty-four communication concepts for the years 1976, 1991 and 2006. The rankings reveal the relative importance ascribed to each communication need and right, as well as the availability of particular communication supplies. Two indices, a policy urgency index (PUI) and a dynamics index (DI), were developed to indicate possible future imbalances and growth of each of the twenty-four communication needs, supplies and rights over the thirty-year period. These indices play a major 'foresight' role in revealing particular areas in which planning action should be undertaken.

SELECTING THE EXPERTS

The choice of experts is of primary importance to the outcome and utility of the forecasting effort. For the purpose of this study, the selection process was greatly simplified by the Hawaii Communication Directory Project, sponsored by the University of Hawaii Social Science Research Institute. Approximately 500 names of persons who were directly concerned with the communication sector of the state were compiled. These persons were initially identified using both Hawaii communication conference attendance lists and professional dir-

---

1. This section is a summary of Wedermeyer (1978b).
2. 'Right' refers to a 'societal obligation' to provide communication access and resources to meet communication needs. Entitlement is by just claim, legal guarantee, moral principles etc.

ectories compiled during the past three to five years. From these 500 communication specialists, seventy experts were selected and were asked to participate in the inquiry.

The expert selection was accomplished by having four professional communication specialists designate from twenty to thirty people who had distinguished themselves as being exceptional in the field of communication in the State of Hawaii. An expert was operationally defined as a person who had notable experience, knowledge or special skill acquired through professional training or practical experience in the field of communication. The four specialists making the initial participant selections represented a wide range of expertise (engineering, research, community action and futures research) in specific areas of communication in Hawaii. Each of the communication experts was selected on the basis of notable expertise balanced by such factors as island location, sex, race, technical, social and political orientation. Each expert received a personal letter requesting his or her participation in the Delphi forecasting study. Included with this initial request was a letter of endorsement from the Hawaii Research Center for Futures Study and a brief profile sheet to be completed and returned.

SELECTING THE QUESTIONS

The procedures for selecting the appropriate questions for inclusion in the Delphi inquiry were also critical to the study and subsequent use of the data. Since there is no single theoretical framework which adequately accounted for the various roles and functions communication plays in a society, another approach to question development was adopted. The first step in selecting the questions entailed the identification of a large number of potentially important long-range developments from previous communication forecasting studies and literature. This extensive list of developments was then subjected to the following criteria for inclusion in the study:

Event questions

Is the event likely to occur within the next thirty years?
Is the impact of the event significant to communication in the State of Hawaii?

Trend questions

Is there a strong likelihood that any of the levels of the needs, rights or supplies
　　will deviate from the anticipated level?
Will there be a direct or indirect impact on communication in general if the
　　deviation occurs?
These guidelines required an affirmative response for each of the events and trends included. An excessive number of items (more than 150 trends and nearly fifty events) remained. Substantial reductions were accomplished by clustering the many specific items into broader conceptual items. For example,

television, radio, newspapers etc. were grouped into 'one-way' communication, and electronic mail, electronic funds transfer and telefacsimile were grouped into 'electronic message flow'. The conceptual grouping also had the added advantage of reducing the necessity of correctly anticipating presently unknown technologies and of removing some of the media-specific biases from the forecast.

Two problems remained in the final selection of questions. First, although the number of communication concepts had been reduced to about twenty, each question had to be posed in terms of a need level, supply level and a right level. Second, each concept's need, supply and right levels had to be estimated for three time periods (1976, 1991, 2006) in order to generate trend lines. These requirements brought the total number of trend questions to 180. Still too large, the number of questions was reduced by shifting the written questions to 'graphic' questions for each of the twenty-four concepts. The list of concepts and working definitions included in the final questionnaire is as follows:

TREND QUESTIONS: COMMUNICATION CONCEPTS

Trends: *Definition*

T1   *Mobile communication*. Ability to communicate without being stationary. Examples include two-way telephones, citizen band radios, walkie-talkies, etc.
T2   *Security communication*. Ability to have life and property monitored electronically.
T3   *Openness of government*. Open, prepared and posted agendas, and provision for citizens to attend all government meetings.
T4   *Citizen information*. Consumer information, schedules for services and events, legal, medical and health information open and conveniently available to citizens.
T5   *Two-way, interactive communication*. Bi- or multi-directional communication, involving exchange of mutually developed messages (demand-pull communication).
T6   *One-way communication*. Traditional, centralized, one-directional flow. Examples include broadcast television and radio, newspapers, magazines and books.
T7   *Persuasive communication*. Messages intended to change behaviour, to persuade (for example, advertising).
T8   *Entertainment communication*. Pleasurable (i.e. enjoyable or stimulating) messages via electronic media and film—not including plays, operas etc.
T9   *Citizen involvement in political decisions*. Voting, polling, calls or letters to representatives.
T10 *Capital investment in communication infrastructures*. Availability and expenditures of money for internal communication development and maintenance.
T11 *Face-to-face communication*. Physically present communication (not electronically interposed).
T12 *Civil-defence communication*. Warning systems alerting citizens of tsunamis, fire, military attack etc.
T13 *Electronic message flows*. Electronic mail (i.e. direct digital transmission of personal and business mail to home or office).

T14   *Small-group communication.* Three to twenty persons interacting electronically (i.e. linked by computers, telephones, video conferences etc.), not physically assembled.

T15   *Citizen participation in local community.* Social and cultural interaction of people that promotes a sense of community or neighbourhood.

T16   *Self-expression.* Ability of an individual to signify or symbolize feelings in a creative and open manner (examples include plays, operas, poetry, music, public speaking etc.).

T17   *Education communication.* Formal and informal electronically interposed and/or augmented learning.

T18   *Serendipitous communication.* Communication resulting from accidental meetings or unplanned encounters.

T19   *Privacy.* The control over information about oneself.

T20   *Cross-cultural communication.* Social communication with individuals and groups external to Hawaii's culture.

T21   *Societal communication in general.* This item is an overall indicator; it includes the concepts of all previous trends.

T22   *Access to means of communication.* Individual citizens and citizen groups have equitable and practical means to develop and disseminate messages (examples include television cameras, editing equipment, appropriate airtimes, computer terminals, technical assistance etc.).

T23   *Monopolistic control of communication.* More than 60 per cent control over a specific communication system.

T24   *Anticipatory communication skills development.* Development and teaching of communication skills not presently recognized as important, but having a high probability of importance in ten years (for example, visual media literacy).

EVENT QUESTIONS

E1   The establishment of the first public video conferencing centre of the state.

E2   The utilization of optical fibres instead of traditional coaxial cables by the telephone company.

E3   An energy crisis equal to (or greater than) the crisis of 1973.

E4   Twenty-five per cent of Hawaii's homes have installed a digital storage device on the television or telephone.

E5   The establishment of a 'dial-up' (telephone or similar device to a specific programme) pay-television service to the home.

E6   The passing of legislation requiring a telephone in every island home.

E7   The passing of legislation requiring that Hawaii be included in U.S. mainland telephone averaging.

E8   The first occurrence of an electronic delivery (television-screen display) of a newspaper into an island home.

E9   The occurrence of electronic home polling (other than telephone polling) of citizen opinion by the state government.

E10   The passing of legislation which establishes a severe tax ($500 per year) on second family cars.

E11   The establishment of free mass transit on Oahu.

E12   The occurrence of state petrol rationing on a regular basis.

E13   The physical establishment of neighbourhood communication/work centres (not shopping centres) with the intent of decentralizing the work location.

E14   A statewide requirement of 'keyboard skills' (typing, ten-key calculators etc.) in public schools.

E15   The passage of a state communication 'Bill of Rights' (the right for each citizen to the communication resources required to satisfy his/her communication needs).

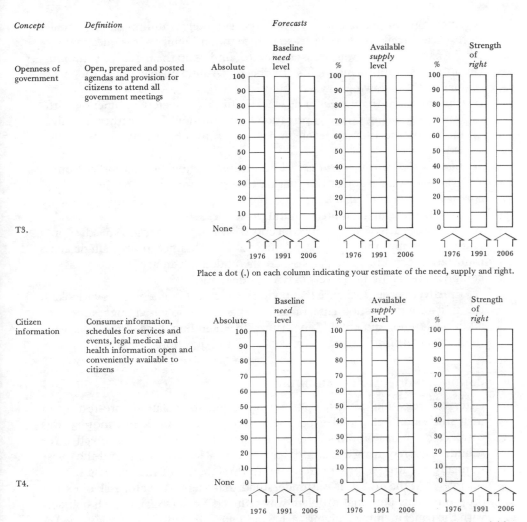

FIG. I. Page from questionnaire collecting estimates of need, supply and rights levels

EI6 Some 25 per cent of all shopping transactions are performed remotely (i.e. the buyer and seller are electronically interposed by computer, audio, video etc.).

EI7 A technical breakthrough (other than optical fibres or coaxial cables) that provides inexpensive and virtually unlimited spectrum space.

Each of the trend items was posed with nine graphic scales requiring estimates of need, supply and rights levels for 1976, 1991, and 2006. Figure 1 shows an actual page from the questionnaire. The zero-to-100 scale represents the following relationship with respect to needs and rights: zero represents 'no need' or 'no right', and 100 signifies an 'absolute' need or right. Zero supply represents no available supply, while 100 symbolizes unlimited or virtually unrestricted availability. In order to reduce the ambiguity of the questionnaire for the participants, it was necessary to expound upon the nature of communication needs, supply and rights. In the first-round instructions, they were defined in the following way:

Baseline communication needs. The level required for society to function without experiencing urgency, privation or destitution. It is neither the minimum nor the utopian level; rather it is somewhere between these two extremes.

Available communication supply. The means, technology and/or personnel available in a particular time period to serve communication needs.

Strength of communication right. The intensity of that which is due anyone by just claim, legal guarantees, moral principles, etc.

By providing each of the twenty concepts with a 1976, 1991, 2006 need, supply and rights graph, nine forecast points could be obtained from a single communication concept. The graphs had the added advantage of being easy to complete and being intuitively easy to understand.

Finally, in order to assure that no important development was overlooked, the first-round questionnaire provided space and solicited suggestions for additional trends and events. The criteria for including these suggestions were the same as the initial selection of concepts and questions.

CONDUCTING THE DELPHI INQUIRY

After the selection of developments, question formulation, pre-testing of instruments and the final expert selection, the actual Delphi inquiry was conducted. It was administered in the State of Hawaii and involved three rounds, each requiring about fifty days to complete. At each round the questionnaire required approximately one to three hours of the expert's time to complete. At the outset, it was understood that there was some risk of expert drop-out. This potential problem was reduced by personalizing all contacts with the panel members, giving each expert an airline discount card (valued at U.S.$5.00) and offering participants final results of the study. One to two weeks after each round's questionnaire was sent out, the experts were sent a personal letter and/or contacted by telephone to remind them gently to return the questionnaire. The monitor's telephone number was also included on all Delphi questionnaires, and the panel members were encouraged to call if any problems developed.

All returned questionnaires for the round were processed by the monitor, and medians and semi-interquartile ranges were computed. These statistical summaries, along with a synthesis of anonymous comments, were provided to each panel member after each round. More specifically, during the second-round questionnaire, the panel members were requested to justify any forecast which did not fall within the semi-interquartile range as reported in the feedback statistics calculated from the first round. All justification statements

TABLE I. Communication needs rankings

1975	1991	2005
75.16–T11 Face-to-face communication	80.38–T19 Privacy	85.86–T4 Citizen information
74.55–T9 Citizen involvement in political decisions	79.82–T9 Citizen involvement in political decisions	83.51–T5 Two-way communication
72.93–T19 Privacy	78.84–T3 Openness of government	83.24–T9 Citizen involvement in political decisions
69.30–T3 Openness of government	77.41–T11 Face-to-face communication	82.46–T15 Citizen participation in local community
67.82–T15 Citizen participation in local community	76.36–T12 Civil-defence communication	81.79–T20 Cross-cultural communication
67.68–T6 One-way communication	75.93–T4 Citizen information	80.48–T19 Privacy
67.52–T12 Civil-defence communication	75.73–T15 Citizen participation in local community	79.85–T12 Civil-defence communication
65.96–T5 Two-way communication	75.34–T5 Two-way communication	79.55–T21 Societal communication in general
53.57–T4 Citizen information	72.89–T6 One-way communication	79.16–T3 Openness of government
61.93–T20 Cross-cultural communication	71.53–T20 Cross-cultural communication	78.58–T11 Face-to-face communication
61.00–T21 Societal communication in general	70.74–T21 Societal communication in general	76.68–T6 One-way communication
60.83–T16 Self-expression	68.03–T16 Self-expression	75.53–T10 Capital investment in communication infrastructures
51.06–T8 Entertainment communication	64.09–T10 Capital investment in communication infrastructures	75.03–T17 Education communication
50.45–T10 Capital investment in communication infrastructures	59.23–T8 Entertainment communication	74.29–T16 Self-expression
38.81–T17 Education communication	57.68–T17 Education communication	67.93–T13 Electronic message flow
38.80–T22 Access to means of communication	52.96–T24 Anticipatory communication skills development	67.80–T24 Anticipatory communication skills development
36.19–T18 Serendipitous communication	50.93–T14 Small-group communication	65.86–T14 Small-group communication
35.87–T24 Anticipatory communication skills development	49.76–T22 Access to means of communication	64.60–T1 Mobile communication
32.70–T7 Persuasive communication	48.12–T13 Electronic message flow	63.75–T8 Entertainment communication
31.13–T2 Security communication	45.10–T2 Security communication	62.40–T22 Access to means of communication
29.96–T14 Small-group communication	43.90–T1 Mobile communication	59.26–T2 Security communication
24.60–T1 Mobile communication	39.00–T18 Serendipitous communication	41.11–T18 Serendipitous communication
24.58–T13 Electronic message flow	35.73–T7 Persuasive communication	34.80–T7 Persuasive communication
22.51–T2 Monopolistic control	24.10–T23 Monopolistic control	25.10–T2 Monopolistic control

TABLE 2. Communication supplies ranking[1]

1975	1991	2005
70.20–T7 Persuasive communication	80.27–T6 One-way communication	87.10–T6 One-way communication
70.03–T6 One-way communication	75.53–T7 Persuasive communication	79.06–T8 Entertainment communication
61.68–T11 Face-to-face communication	58.60–T8 Entertainment communication	78.10–T5 Two-way communication
57.20–T8 Entertainment communication	67.23–T12 Civil-defence communication	76.53–T7 Persuasive communication
52.92–T5 Two-way communication	85.67–T5 Two-way communication	76.20–T12 Civil-defence communication
52.20–T9 Citizen involvement in political decisions	64.57–T9 Citizen involvement in political decisions	73.42–T9 Citizen involvement in political decisions
51.06–T12 Civil-defence communication	63.10–T11 Face-to-face communication	73.00–T1 Mobile communication
44.57–T23 Monopolistic control	56.60–T4 Citizen information	72.92–T21 Societal communication in general
41.20–T19 Privacy	56.00–T20 Cross-cultural communication	72.43–T20 Cross-cultural communication
40.53–T16 Self-expression	54.16–T16 Self-expression	71.96–T4 Citizen information
40.40–T21 Societal communication in general	52.62–T1 Mobile communication	66.34–T17 Education communication
40.13–T15 Citizen participation in local community	52.06–T19 Privacy	65.96–T3 Openness of government
38.83–T20 Cross-cultural communication	51.76–T10 Capital investment in communication infrastructures	65.80–T10 Capital investment in communication infrastructures
38.22–T10 Capital investment in communication infrastructures	51.32–T21 Societal communication in general	64.58–T2 Security communication
37.73–T18 Serendipitous communication	51.20–T3 Openness of government	64.33–T11 Face-to-face communication
37.54–T3 Openness of government	51.06–T15 Citizen participation in local community	64.23–T13 Electronic message flow
36.82–T4 Citizen information	49.75–T23 Monopolistic control	61.32–T14 Small-group communication
29.76–T1 Mobile communication	45.03–T2 Security communication	59.79–T15 Citizen participation in local community
23.96–T2 Security communication	43.80–T17 Education communication	58.86–T16 Self-expression
23.30–T22 Access to means of communication	42.26–T18 Serendipitous communication	55.00–T24 Anticipatory communication skills development
22.83–T17 Education communication	40.17–T14 Small-group communication	54.85–T19 Privacy
20.45–T24 Anticipatory communication skills development	39.19–T24 Anticipatory communication skills development	54.06–T22 Access to means of communication
16.75–T14 Small-group communication	38.96–T22 Access to means of communication	53.75–T2 Monopolistic control
13.46–T13 Electronic message flow	38.65–T13 Electronic message flow	49.72–T18 Serendipitous communication

1. Ranking by means.

TABLE 3. Strength of communication right rankings[1]

1975	1991	2005
85.80–T12 Civil-defence communication	87.06–T12 Civil-defence communication	88.23–T12 Civil-defence communication
82.57–T9 Citizen involvement in political decisions	85.53–T9 Citizen involvement in political decisions	87.86–T4 Citizen information
82.03–T19 Privacy	85.31–T6 One-way communication	87.65–T6 One-way information
81.86–T3 Openness of government	84.89–T4 Citizen information	87.10–T3 Openness of government
81.24–T6 One-way communication	84.83–T3 Openness of government	87.07–T9 Citizen involvement in political decisions
80.72–T4 Citizen information	84.30–T1 Privacy	85.50–T19 Privacy
79.03–T11 Face-to-face communication	82.03–T11 Face-to-face communication	84.51–T16 Self-expression
77.93–T16 Self-expression	81.58–T16 Self-expression	83.81–T21 Societal communication in general
76.86–T15 Citizen participation in local community	81.50–T15 Citizen participation in local community	83.43–T15 Citizen participation in local community
76.06–T20 Cross-cultural communication	79.62–T21 Societal communication in general	83.32–T5 Two-way communication
74.66–T5 Two-way communication	78.64–T5 Two-way communication	82.24–T11 Face-to-face communication
73.81–T21 Societal communication in general	78.06–T20 Cross-cultural communication	80.86–T20 Cross-cultural communication
65.28–T8 Entertainment communication	67.16–T8 Entertainment communication	75.53–T17 Education communication
58.50–T10 Capital investment in communication infrastructures	66.30–T22 Access to means of communication	74.66–T22 Access to means of communication
56.03–T22 Access to means of communication	64.82–T10 Capital investment in communication infrastructures	70.74–T24 Anticipatory communication skills development
53.16–T18 Serendipitous communication	63.36–T17 Education communication	70.51–T8 Entertainment communication
51.96–T24 Anticipatory communication skills development	62.64–T24 Anticipatory communication skills development	68.78–T10 Capital investment in communication infrastructures
51.23–T17 Education communication	57.18–T14 Small-group communication	68.09–T14 Small-group communication
43.31–T14 Small-group communication	55.00–T18 Serendipitous communication	64.32–T13 Electronic message flow
42.64–T7 Persuasive communication	54.28–T13 Electronic message flow	62.65–T1 Mobile communication
41.00–T2 Security communication	51.87–T1 Mobile communication	58.63–T2 Security communication
38.75–T13 Electronic message flow	50.07–T2 Security communication	56.46–T18 Serendipitous communication
36.93–T1 Mobile communication	49.54–T7 Persuasive communication	49.24–T7 Persuasive communication
24.24–T23 Monopolistic control	25.79–T23 Monopolistic control	29.10–T23 Monopolistic control

1. Ranking by means.

TABLE 4. Urgency-index rankings

1976	1991	2006
2605.60–T3 Openness of government	2387.3–T19 Privacy	2191.3–T19 Privacy
2602.8–T19 Privacy	2344.7–T3 Openness of government	2054.7–T7 Persuasive communication
2159.2–T4 Citizen information	1985.93–T15 Citizen participation in local community	1891.35–T15 Citizen participation in local community
2128.2–T15 Citizen participation in local community	1971.69–T7 Persuasive communication	1303.9–T16 Self-expression
1845.4–T9 Citizen involvement in political decisions	1640.9–T4 Citizen information	1203.6–T4 Citizen information
1756.9–T20 Cross-cultural communication	1546.22–T21 Societal communication in general	1171.92–T11 Face-to-face communication
1599.9–T7 Persuasive communication	1304.3–T9 Citizen involvement in political decisions	1149.72–T3 Openness of government
1581.97–T16 Self-expression	1212.27–T20 Cross-cultural communication	1079.5–T8 Entertainment communication
1520.4–T21 Societal communication in general	1176.85–T11 Face-to-face communication	913.3–T6 One-way communication
1420.8–T12 Civil-defence communication	1174.4–T16 Self-expression	905.47–T24 Anticipatory communication skills development
1065.3–T11 Face-to-face communication	892.10–T17 Education communication	855.02–T9 Citizen involvement in political decisions
973.6–T5 Two-way communication	862.55–T24 Anticipatory communication skills development	833.75–T23 Monopolistic control
868.46–T22 Access to means of communication	799.23–T10 Capital investment in communication infrastructures	756.8–T20 Cross-cultural communication
818.6–T17 Education communication	794.85–T12 Civil-defence communication	669.22–T10 Capital investment in communication infrastructures
801.2–T24 Anticipatory communication skills development	760.4–T5 Two-way communication	656.3–T17 Education communication
715.4–T10 Capital investment in communication infrastructures	716.04–T22 Access to means of communication	622.66–T22 Access to means of communication
572.1–T14 Small-group communication	659.70–T23 Monopolistic control	555.6–T21 Societal communication in general
534.7–T23 Monopolistic control	647.50–T6 One-way communication	525.0–T1 Mobile communication
430.9–T13 Electronic message flow	629.28–T8 Entertainment communication	486.1–T18 Serendipitous communication
400.8–T8 Entertainment communication	615.25–T14 Small-group communication	450.76–T5 Two-way communication
293.97–T2 Security communication	514.03–T13 Electronic message flow	322.92–T12 Civil-defence communication
190.9–T6 One-way communication	452.3–T1 Mobile communication	311.91–T2 Security communication
189.45–T1 Mobile communication	179.3–T18 Serendipitous communication	309.1–T14 Small-group communication
81.86–T18 Serendipitous communication	3.5–T2 Security communication	236.6–T13 Electronic message flow

TABLE 5. Dynamics-index rankings

Needs	Supply	Right	Total (needs + supply + right)
43–T13 Electronic message flow	51–T13 Electronic message flow	26–T13 Electronic message flow	120–T13 Electronic message flow
39–T1 Mobile communication	45–T14 Small-group communication	26–T1 Mobile communication	108–T1 Mobile communication
37–T17 Education communication	44–T17 Education communication	25–T14 Small-group communication	106–T14 Small-group communication
36–T14 Small-group communication	43–T1 Mobile communication	24–T17 Education communication	105–T17 Education communication
32–T24 Anticipatory communication skills development	41–T2 Security communication	19–T24 Anticipatory communication skills development	86–T2 Security communication
28–T2 Security communication	35–T4 Citizen information	18–T22 Access to means of communication	86–T24 Anticipatory communication skills development
25–T10 Capital investment in communication infrastructures	35–T24 Anticipatory communication skills development	17–T2 Security communication	73–T22 Access to means of communication
24–T22 Access to means of communication	34–T20 Cross-cultural communication	10–T21 Societal communication in general	64–T4 Citizen information
22–T4 Citizen information	32–T21 Societal communication in general	10–T10 Capital investment in communication infrastructures	62–T10 Capital investment in communication infrastructures
20–T20 Cross-cultural communication	31–T22 Access to means of communication	9–T5 Two-way communication	60–T21 Societal communication in general
18–T21 Societal communication in general	28–T3 Openness of government	7–T4 Citizen information	58–T20 Cross-cultural communication
18–T5 Two-way communication	27–T10 Capital investment in communication infrastructures	7–T7 Persuasive communication	53–T5 Two-way communication
15–T6 One-way communication	26–T5 Two-way communication	7–T16 Self-expression	44–T3 Openness of government
15–T15 Citizen participation in local community	25–T12 Civil-defence communication	7–T15 Citizen participation in local community	41–T15 Citizen participation
14–T16 Self-expression	22–T8 Entertainment communication	6–T3 Openness of government	40–T12 Civil-defence communication
12–T8 Entertainment communication	21–T9 Citizen participation in political decisions	6–T6 One-way communication	39–T16 Self-expression
12–T12 Civil-defence communication	19–T15 Citizen participation in local community	5–T8 Entertainment communication	39–T8 Entertainment communication
10–T3 Openness of government	18–T16 Self-expression	5–T23 Monopolistic control	38–T6 One-way communication
9–T9 Citizen participation in political decisions	17–T6 One-way communication	5–T9 Citizen participation in political decisions	35–T9 Citizen participation in political decisions
8–T19 Privacy	13–T19 Privacy	4–T20 Cross-cultural communication	24–T19 Privacy
5–T18 Serendipitous communication	12–T18 Serendipitous communication	3–T18 Serendipitous communication	20–T18 Serendipitous communication
3–T11 Face-to-face communication	6–T7 Persuasive communication	3–T11 Face-to-face communication	15–T7 Persuasive communication
3–T23 Monopolistic control	5–T23 Monopolistic control	3–T19 Privacy	13–T23 Monopolistic control
2–T7 Persuasive communication	3–T11 Face-to-face communication	3–T12 Civil-defence communication	9–T11 Face-to-face communication

from round two were retyped and included with the appropriate concept in the round-three feedback. The experts were asked to utilize these statements in making their final round forecasts. The final round results were analysed and disseminated to the experts, along with an invitation to attend a conference at which a summary of the study was presented.

RESULTS OF THE DELPHI INQUIRY

The final-round means were computed for each of the twenty-four concepts. These means represented the experts' final forecasts for each trend for the years 1976, 1991 and 2006. These means were then used to rank-order in terms of importance of each need, supply and right. These rankings are shown in Tables 1 to 3.

One cannot conclude from the data that these lists are in exact order from highest to lowest need, supply or right. However, it is reasonable to conclude that the top five often are of higher magnitude (in the case of need and right) or availability (for supply) than the bottom five or ten. Given limited resources in policy and planning for communication in the state, it would be reasonable to take action on the top-ranking concepts before taking action on the bottom-ranking concepts.

PLANNING DECISIONS BASED UPON DELPHI RESULTS: THE URGENCY INDEX

As an emample of how Delphi opinion data can be used in planning communication, an urgency index (U I) was developed. The following equation was used to determine which concepts were most 'out of balance' in respect to supplies meeting needs as weighted by rights:

(NEEDS score *minus* SUPPLY score) × STRENGTH OF RIGHT score = URGENCY

Simply stated, the need level minus the supply level leaves a quantity which is an unmet communication need. This quantity multiplied by the strength of the right yields a quantity called the urgency index (U I). The rank order of each of these U I quantities provides an indication of which of the concepts are most 'out of balance' when weighted by human rights. The rankings for 1976, 1991 and 2006 are as shown in Table 4.

In summary, the U I is the mechanism that can be used to indicate priorities or data collection which, in turn, should indicate what specific policy planning actions should be taken. The U I reduces uncertainty by providing an 'early warning' of potential problems before crises occur and therefore more lead time is available to assemble information or develop adequate plans.

THE DYNAMICS INDEX

The final index developed concerned the dynamics of each concept need, supply and right over time. By subtracting the 1976 level from the projected 2006 level, a growth index can be derived. The equations are as follows:

NEEDLEVEL 1976 *minus* NEEDLEVEL 2006 = NEEDSGROWTH

SUPPLYLEVEL 1976 *minus* SUPPLYLEVEL 2006 = SUPPLYGROWTH

RIGHTSLEVEL 1976 *minus* RIGHTSLEVEL 2006 = RIGHTSGROWTH

NEEDSGROWTH + SUPPLYGROWTH + RIGHTSGROWTH = DYNAMICS INDEX (DI)

The dynamics index provides an indication of which concepts will exhibit the most growth over time and, therefore, are most likely to require policy and planning attention. The dynamics rankings are shown in Table 5.

The dynamics index is an important indicator of potential policy problems associated with rapid growth. The more dynamic and concept (for example, the higher the change per unit of time), the less lead time there is available to correct an evolving crisis situation. Therefore, those areas reflecting high overall dynamics rankings require greater monitoring. It is this alerting function, provided by the dynamics index, that reduces some of the uncertainty in the communication policy and planning process.

Annotated bibliography

CENTER FOR THE STUDY OF SOCIAL POLICY. 1975. *Handbook of Forecasting Techniques*. Menlo Park, Calif., Stanford Research Institute. Summary of Delphi and expert opinion includes uses, procedures, strengths and weaknesses of the Delphi technique.

COATES, J. 1975. In Defense of Delphi: A Review of Delphi Assessment, Expert Opinion, Forecasting and Group Process by H. Sackman. *Journal of Technological Forecasting and Social Change*, Vol. 7, p. 193–4. An entire issue of a journal devoted to assessing the Delphi methods and its critics.

FOWLES, J. (ed.). 1978. *Handbook of Futures Research*. Westport, Conn., Greenwood Press. An excellent discussion of the Delphi technique and the use of experts' opinions in forecasting and planning. Also discusses other procedures and challenges of futures research.

HELMER, O. 1973. *Accomplishments and Prospects of Futures Research*. Los Angeles, Calif., University of Southern California, Center for Future Research.

LINSTONE, H. A.; TUROFF, M. (eds.). 1975. *The Delphi Method: Techniques and Applications*. Reading, Mass., Addison-Wesley. An entire book devoted to the background, uses, strengths and weaknesses of the Delphi technique.

SAHMAN, H. 1974. *Delphi Assessments: Expert Opinion, Forecasting and Group Process*. Santa Monica, Calif., Rand Corporation.

TUROFF, M. 1975. The Policy Delphi. In: H. A. Linstone and M. Turoff (eds.), *The Delphi Method: Techniques and Applications*. Reading, Mass., Addison-Wesley.

WEDEMEYER, D. J. 1978*a*. Delphi: Long-Range Communication Policy and Planning. In: S. A. Rahim *et al.*, *Planning Methods, Models, and Organizations. A Review Study for Communication Policy Making and Planning*. Honolulu, Hawaii, East–West Communication Institute. A chapter describing Delphi as a technique in communication policy and planning. Includes philosophical foundations, problems and one variation called the Policy Delphi.

——. 1978*b*. Forecasting Communication Needs, Supplies and Rights for Policy Making and Planning in the State of Hawaii. Los Angeles, Calif., University of Southern California. (Dissertation.)

Chapter 7

Brainstorming

George M. Beal

Wimal Dissanayake

Brainstorming is designed to stimulate creative thinking and the production of a large number of ideas related to a specific problem or task. During the creative phase no criticisms, evaluations or questions of feasibility are allowed. After the brainstorming sessiion, the ideas produced are organized and processed into a form that can be integrated, along with other ideas, into group discussion and decision-making. The assumptions behind the technique, group formation and sessions procedures, cautions, the organizing of ideas produced and a case example of use are presented.

Definition

Brainstorming is a small-group technique designed to stimulate creative thinking, expression and interaction leading to the production of a large quantity of ideas related to a specific problem or creative task without imposing the limitations of feasibility and without the challenge of critical evaluation from fellow group members. Brainstorming is a relatively simple technique. A group of people are assembled and are presented with a relatively well-defined problem or creative task. The members of the group are encouraged to contribute as many ideas as possible, as rapidly as possible, in a relatively short period of time. It may be seen as the use of the brain to 'storm' (attack) a problem—brainstorm. Brainstorming does not usually result in rationalized decisions or problem solutions. What it does accomplish is the generation of a large number and a broad range of ideas which can serve as leads to problem-solving. It develops ideas which can subsequently be further processed, evaluated and, if useful, incorporated into problem solution.

Two general principles govern group interaction in brainstorming sessions. The first principle deals with the individual group member's contribution of ideas. In contributing the ideas the individual should not be concerned with the feasibility or practicability of the idea. No concern need be given to how the idea might contradict existing policies, structures, values and norms. Group members are encouraged to take advantage of the ideas and stimulation provided by other group members. Taking cues from, 'piggy-backing' or 'hitch-hiking' on the ideas of other group members is welcomed. Elaborating, combining, dividing, extending or otherwise modifying or improving (without evaluation or criticism) on the ideas of others is highly encouraged. The goal is to involve the members so that they will be 'free-wheeling' with the introduction of new ideas—the wilder the ideas the better. The unique, the daring, the dramatic, the remote, the apparently unworkable idea is desired. It is hoped the rapid interaction and stimulation will develop a contagion and set off a chain reaction involving all group members in idea generation.

The second principle dictates that no member will challenge, disagree with, evaluate, be negative towards or question (except possibly for clarification) the ideas presented by other group members. Ideas are not appraised or discussed. The objective of brainstorming is to generate as many and as broad a range of ideas as possible dealing with a problem or creative task in as short a time as possible. Quantity, not quality, is the goal—though striving for quality is acceptable. To meet the norms of quantity and speed, group members often do not even evaluate their own ideas before communicating them, hoping thus to unleash additional creativity. After the brainstorming, the ideas must be organized and processed into a form that can be used in group discussion, deliberation and decision-making. This activity will be discussed in more detail later in the presentation.

Assumptions

It is recognized that no idea is generated except in the individual human mind. However, it is observed that in many instances of problem definition, analysis, goal-setting and the choosing of means and problem solutions, we are very unimaginative. We may be unimaginative because of our background, experience, training and traditional values and approaches. If we are a part of formal bureaucratic organizations, we are aware of such things as status-prestige patterns, those in positions of authority, the importance of seniority, dominant personalities and institutionalized ways of approaching problem analysis and solution. We may see the reward patterns favouring those who perform routinely, who do not take risks on who do not seek to be creative or innovative. As individuals, we may not suggest new ways of doing things because we do not like to be involved in arguments or disagreements or be criticized—we lack self-confidence. In many cases, we are dominantly action-orientated—we do not take time to analyse, reflect and explore a wide range of possibilities, including new alternatives. Often we try to move rapidly to compromise, consensus and closure. We really have had little opportunity to pursue creative thinking.

However, it is assumed (with some evidence to back the assumption) that many people possess a high degree of creativity. The challenge is to develop the atmosphere or climate that will allow for the release and the stimulation of that creativity. Brainstorming attempts to create that atmosphere and provide the freedom and the stimulation for interaction and free-wheeling creativity. It is not seen as a substitute for individual creativity, but as a supplement to it.

History

The concept and technique of brainstorming is usually traced back to Alex F. Osborn. From our perspective, it may be of interest to note that Osborn was in the field of communication. He was a member of an advertising firm—in the business of creating advertising programmes, campaigns and 'copy'. He was searching for a way to encourage creativity; to stimulate innovative ideas. He developed the technique that creates an atmosphere in which a group of people are stimulated to interact and, with creativity and imagination, to suggest many new ideas. In 1953, Osborn published the first edition of his book *Applied Imagination*, which dealt with imagination and creativity and included a detailed discussion of the background, rationale, procedure and process of brainstorming as an aid to problem solution. Over the past twenty-five years, the technique of brainstorming has been used by hundreds of different groups, including those in business, government, religion, education, health, the military and the professions. It has been used for a wide variety of purposes, such as: new product development, improvement and adaptaion; proposing solutions to social problems; labour–management relations; managing administrative changes; the provision of improved services; communication and marketing campaigns and strategies; more effective use of communication media and messages. There are a large number of case studies and controlled experiments that support the conclusion that group brainstorming—used properly and under appropriate conditions—can create a larger number of ideas than do individuals in isolation—and that many of these ideas are useful in problem diagnosis or solution. Brainstorming also may contribute to group productivity through individual involvement and to long-run individual creativity by releasing individual creativity in brainstorming sessions.

Main uses

*Purposes.*The technique can be used for a wide range of purposes. It can be considered for use when there is need to 'break out' of usual or traditional ways of thinking about such things as: problem definition, dimensions, causes; innovative approaches to planning; programme, project and activity goals; alternative strategies, approaches or means to ameliorate or solve problems; different approaches to organizational structures, roles or personnel; developing concepts, criteria and methods for evaluation; creating new, unique products, images, materials, messages or media mixes. It can also be used for ideas about the outcomes, effects, consequences (intended and unintended) of programmes and specifying possible limitations or shortcomings of projects or programmes, including the communication components of those projects. Ideas judged as valid then could be used as a basis for working to improve the plan and strategy for implementation.

Group characteristics. The technique should be considered for use when it is judged that the group leaders and members are sufficiently mature and flexible enough to offer the potential for breaking out of traditional perspectives and behaviours and entering into a creative, interactive endeavour.

Time and stage. The technique should be considered when there is a time, or time can be allocated, for processing the ideas and discussing them in operational terms and considering them as inputs into a decision-making process.

Individual creativity. A latent purpose for using brainstorming may be the impact it has on individual group members beyond the brainstorming session(s). In many cases, involvement in brainstorming and finding one can express new ideas—finding they are considered or accepted, and are not criticized—leads to continued increased creativity on the job and in other situations.

Limits and cautions

Like any technique, brainstorming is no panacea—it has its limitations. However, in many cases, the limitations can be overcome with proper planning and discussion leadership. Probably the greatest 'limitation' on the use of the technique is unrealistic expectations. The technique is not designed to solve problems, make decisions on goals or means, design a product or campaign. Its purpose is to play an important role in those processes, namely, create a large number and wide range of ideas, dimensions, solutions, alternatives etc. for further clarification, elaboration, rationalization, consideration and decision-making. The objectives and role of brainstorming in the larger planning process should be understood by all group members and realistic expectations set.

It may be difficult to change traditional perspectives and behaviour. People may find it difficult to ignore status differentials and to express ideas without consideration of constraints, without constantly evaluating their own and other group members' ideas. Some may think the technique is 'silly', juvenile, unrealistic—a waste of time. They may find it difficult to release their creative ability. Providing a background on past successful use of the technique, specifying ground rules, developing an atmosphere of free expression and stimulating and encouraging interaction should help overcome this problem. In some cases, it may be difficult to obtain the creativity desired, especially in the first experience with the technique. Because emphasis is often given to group-member interaction and 'piggy-backing', or building on the ideas of others, discussion sometimes focuses on a limited line of discussion and creativity and becomes channelled into stimulating ideas introduced early in the discussion. Judicious suggestions for redirecting discussions or throwing out ideas on different themes can often alleviate this problem.

If successful, brainstorming results in rapid-fire contribution of ideas and the adding to, dividing or combining of many ideas. In the process the identity of those who contributed the idea or contributed to the ideas is often lost. This lack of recognition may bother some group members. If group norms can be established that reflect the importance of the number and the usefulness of ideas, rather than of those who contributed them, this problem may also be alleviated.

The spontaneous, free-wheeling, dramatic and 'way-out' suggestions often lead to a degree of humour and levity in the group. Often this relaxes and stimulates the group members. However, in some cases group members may strive to gain status through obvious attempts at humour or becoming the 'group comedian'. If this behaviour is detrimental to group productivity, it should be discouraged by the group leader and other group members.

Resources needed

The importance of considering leader and group-member maturity and flexibility, and the time and a method to process the ideas generated, have been discussed above.

GROUP COMPOSITION

There is no specific guideline on group composition. In many cases, the organizational structure, the situation (e.g. planned or spontaneous) or timing will heavily influence the composition of the group. One can conceive of groups varying in composition from those in which the brainstormers are identical with those who process and make decisions (using the ideas generated) to those in which the generators of ideas, processors and decision-makers are all different.

Though there is no conclusive research evidence, many who use this technique believe that, while there should be some degree of continuity of membership through the process of topic definition, brainstorming, processing and decision-making, the most effective procedure involves some people in the brainstorming session who do not have the continuing responsibility for processing of ideas and decision-making. Two possibly contradictory influences run through this consideration. On the one hand, if people can be involved in brainstorming who do not have to be similarly involved in processing and decision-making, the possibility is open of seeking out highly creative people in the brainstorming session. Further, if those involved in brainstorming do not have conscious (or unconscious) responsibility for processing or decision-making, greater creativity may be released—in no way do they face the consequence of their idea creation. On the other hand, if people are asked to process, use and make decisions using ideas they have had no part in creating, they may not be motivated to explore fully the potential of ideas.

An optimizing strategy may be continuity of some group members throughout the process by the addition of members at the brainstorming session and the inclusion of other members who are responsible for aiding in the processing and decision-making. Including new members or rotating members in the brainstorming sessions has been found by some to add to the creativity. The number of individuals that can effectively be involved in a brainstorming session probably varies from a minimum of five to a maximum of thirty. The optimum size is probably around twelve.[1]

TIME

The amount of time scheduled for brainstorming may vary depending on the group, group members, topic and task. In some cases people argue that, in certain situations, placing a time constraint (for example, ten minutes) on a group may stimulate a high degree of productivity. Others suggest timing be structured so that a specified time (say, three minutes) is reserved for verbal interaction, while a specified time (say, five minutes) is reserved for quiet individual contemplation, with both activities being continued in sequence. In general, the guidelines recommend the leaders not to be afraid of some silence (no discussion) for periods of several minutes, but not to try to extend discussion beyond the productive period. Enthusiasm and creativity are energy-consuming and wearing—the productive bounds should not be exceeded. Productive periods may vary from fifteen minutes to two hours. Optimum time is usually around thirty to forty-five minutes.

The seating of leaders, recorders (secretaries) and group members in a common-level circle (with the leader unidentifiable by position or equipment) in a bright, clean room of pleasant atmosphere facilitates interaction and creativity.

Procedures

While general guidelines will be presented for the procedures to use in brainstorming, it should be recognized that there are many variations in how the technique has been and can be used. For example, although brainstorming can be used as a highly rationalized, pre-planned, even regularized activity and process, it may also be used very much on the spur of the moment, spontaneously. Further, regardless of the situation or use, there is often no agreement on the 'right' or 'correct' procedure. A relatively wide range of personal and group styles seem to be effective. What is presented here are suggestions.

BEFORE THE BRAINSTORMING SESSION

When it is possible, or when the use of brainstorming is deliberately planned, a more rationalized approach to brainstorming is recommended in which there

---

1. There are group techniques designed for the involvement of participants in large groups (into hundreds) in group idea creation, and decision-making. Techniques such as 'Buzz' groups and 'Phillips 66' are designed to break large groups into small (six to eight people) groups for discussion and then through a written or verbal reporting system to enable them to communicate and consolidate their ideas for further discussion and/or consideration.

is communication with the participants, usually in writing, several days prior to the brainstorming session. The communication with the participants will usually include: a clear statement of the topic to be discussed (a simple, rather than complex topic); brief background on the topic; why it is judged important; if relevant, the present state of affairs related to the topic; and several examples of ideas that could result from the brainstorming. Often this can be communicated in a page or less. The participants are encouraged to read the communication, research the topic if needed, think creatively about the topic and jot down ideas that come to their minds and bring them to the meeting.

BRAINSTORMING SESSION

There are two structured roles needed for the brainstorming session: the leader and the recorder(s).

The discussion leader and his/her role. Flexibility in choosing the person to lead the brainstorming session will depend upon the situation and whether brainstorming is used in a pre-planned setting or spontaneously in the middle of a planning or discussion activity. However, even in the case of spontaneous brainstorming, the person taking leadership responsibility for the session does not necessarily have to be the person in a position of authority or who is leading, or in charge of the activity, just prior to the brainstorming. If possible, the leader for brainstorming sessions should be a person who is highly respected for his/her openness and fairness, skilled in group processes and involving others and skilled in playing facilitative roles. He/she should not be a dominant authority-figure, or the type of person who is heavily dependent on formalized roles and procedures for group leadership.

In pre-planned brainstorming situations, the leader is usually involved in the pre-planning and communication with group members. The leader gives considerable thought to the topic suggested and the procedures, and thinks through his/her ideas on the problem or creative activity. This may provide a first test for how well the topic was stated and how well it lends itself to brainstorming. Also, the list of ideas the leader develops may help to stimulate other group members, build on their ideas or provide a basis for introducing new ideas to give breadth to the brainstorming session.

At the session, the leader presents the topic, states the ground rules for the discussion, sets the expectations for group interaction and productivity during the session, asks for any questions of clarification as to procedures and, in some cases, may want to start the meeting by suggesting one or two ideas of his/her own. During the meeting, the leader maintains as low a profile as possible, but does facilitate contributions and interactions of group members, tries to stimulate wide participation and contribution related to the topic and enforces (or reinforces) the guidelines for the meeting, including those of no criticisms, judgements, disagreements or evaluations of ideas presented. It is the leader's responsibility (alone or in consultation with the group members) to decide when the group has reached the end of its productivity and to terminate the brainstorming session. At the end of the brainstorming session, the leader should inform the group members on how the ideas will be organized, processed and used. If brainstorming is used in a spontaneous fashion and the group must move forward to further consideration of the problem or creative activity, the group may be involved in organizing and processing the ideas, or a short break may be taken for the leader and/or small working group to carry out this task. The group then moves forward to using relevant ideas produced in their further deliberations. However, if brainstorming is used in a more deliberate, rationalized process, organizing and procession of the ideas will probably be done after the meeting (see 'Post-brainstorming session' below). In the latter case, group members should be informed as to the feedback (if any) that will be made to them regarding the use of the ideas produced.

The following more specific ideas may be of value to the group leader and members. If the group is being introduced to brainstorming for the first time, it may be well to complete a brief (say, five-minute) 'dry run' brainstorming session on a simple stimulating topic unrelated to the major topic to be discussed, so that group members can get a 'feel' for brainstorming. A brief evaluation and discussion of the 'dry run' should be made before moving on to the main topic. In the case of pre-planned brainstorming sessions, members are encouraged to do pre-session thinking and to write their ideas down. However, in the meeting session, ideas should not be read from the list—rapid verbal expression adds much more to the spontaneity of the session. Present only one idea at a time, with little detail or elaboration. Encourage adding to, modifying, building on and elaborating the ideas of others. Often, ideas may come rapidly from many members. The leader may have a difficult role of maintaining interest and motivation and still keeping some degree of organized participation. Raising a hand and being recognized (by a nod or slight gesture rather than formal recognition) may build towards an acceptable degree of organization. When most of the group wants to contribute, going round the group members in order may help facilitate wide participation and orderly contribution. Groups which work together can rapidly develop their own cues, gestures and symbols to facilitate rapid communication. For example, some groups adopt the idea of raising the hand to be recognized as one form of entering the discussion. If the hand is raised and the fingers snapped, it signifies the group members wants to add to or elaborate the idea just presented, rather than introduce a new trend of thought. To facilitate building on the ideas of others, the person who snapped his/her fingers would be recognized. Since interaction is often very rapid and it may be difficult to get into the discussion, it is recommended that group members jot down notes themselves so that they will not lose ideas in the rapid fire of others' contributions.

Rather than to present a detailed recommended plan of action and rules governing behaviour, or a long list of specific ideas, it is more important to communicate the point that getting the most out of a brainstorming session is in itself a creative task. The leader and group members working together can develop their own most productive creative process to fit their needs and preferred style of interaction.

Recorders. The ideas produced must be recorded. If interaction, stimulation and creativity are high, many ideas will be produced. Therefore, it is often advisable to have at least two recorders. Since recording will usually be a full-time job, it is usually advisable to use someone who is known by the group but from whom idea contribution is not expected—full-time recorders. Recorders may be designated members of the group, or a respected secretary or clerk who is conversant with the topic and concepts being discussed. Recording is usually done directly on notepaper, since ideas normally flow so fast it is impossible to keep pace with them on a chalkboard or easel pad. It has been found that, if an attempt is made to record the ideas on the board, participants will wait for the recorder to write down the ideas, with a loss of spontaneity and quantity. A compromise sometimes used is a chalkboard recorder (in addition to the other recorders), not located in a central or focal location, who records the ideas so that they may be returned to at designated times during the session for review, clarification or new take-off points. Group members are informed of this procedure so that they will not be waiting for the recorder or constantly referring to the visual recorder.

POST-BRAINSTORMING SESSION

The objective of brainstorming is the generation of a large number of ideas. The pay-off from the activity comes from the use of these ideas. Again, there is no single, specific agreed-upon approach to utilization. The utilization process may include the following ideas. The members of the brainstorming group may be encouraged to take the initiative to submit additional ideas that come to them during a designated period (perhaps two days) after the brainstorming session. In other cases, the group members are contacted to see if additional ideas have developed during an 'incubation' period. The leader or designated group members, working with the recorders or from recorder notes, attempt to organize the ideas produced at the brainstorming session under logical headings. However, in most cases, no attempt is made to consolidate or collapse ideas under more general headings at this time. If needed, attempts are made to clarify the ideas developed, going back to the person who contributed the idea, if necessary. Often attempts are made at this stage to elaborate and operationalize the ideas. In some cases, preliminary judgements may be made about the ideas at this time. This information is then communicated to relevant persons for their study prior to informal or formal meetings at which the information assembled is used as one of the information inputs into the discussion and decision-making process.

In those cases where the users of the ideas generated are different from those who generated them, the ultimate uses made of the ideas may be fed back to those participants who generated them in the brainstorming session.

Case example

WIMAL DISSANAYAKE

This is an example of a pre-planned brainstorming session conducted in Colombo, Sri Lanka. Its objective was to generate ideas regarding the cultural barriers to family-planning communication, and to suggest a range of means on how best to overcome them. The brainstorming session was held under the auspices of Community Development Services, a voluntary organization primarily concerned with family planning. The location was a room in the Community Development Services Building.

The group consisted of ten members: four lecturers from the University; an assistant director of the organization who had a legal background; two executive officers from the organization (one had experience of over twenty years in sales and marketing and the other experience in family health); a physician; and two students from the University. The organizer of the group and the leader at the meeting was a senior lecturer of the University. Each member of the group was contacted by the leader about four days prior to the meeting, and the topic that was to be discussed and the nature of the discussion explained. Each member was requested to think about the subject and, if necessary, to jot down ideas. However, it was categorically stated that during the session they should not read from their notes; they needed to interact spontaneously. The leader explained to all members of the team that the objective of the brainstorming session was to generate as large a body of ideas as possible without being constrained by questions of viability, practicability etc.

The group met at 10 a.m. on a Saturday. It was the most convenient day for all the members in the group. One of the younger lecturers acted as the recorder. The leader introduced the subject and briefly explained the ground rules and then sought to maintain as low a profile as possible. He envisioned his role as that of a catalyst and connector. The recorder assiduously took down all the ideas that were generated during the brainstorming session. Before the group actually got down to the business of discussing cultural barriers to family-planning communication, a 'mock session', lasting for about five minutes, was held. The theme of it was, how could one improve the bus service of Sri Lanka? It was felt that this would indeed be a useful means of 'warming up' for the main session, and also of acquainting oneself with the technique of brainstorming (all but three members had had no experience with this method of generating ideas).

The brainstorming session lasted for about one hour and generated a multitude of ideas related to barriers to family-planning communication and how best to overcome them. Religious injunctions, taboos, questions of ethnic imbalances, linguistic problems, neo-colonial machinations, issues pertaining to masculinity, negative rumours regarding pleasures of sexual intercourse and diseases, old age and security were among the barriers mentioned. Similarly, the need to make imaginative use of the services of schoolteachers, native physicians (as opposed to the western-trained doctors), youth leaders, community leaders, entertainers, folk artists etc. was suggested. All the ideas generated during the brainstorming session were meticulously noted down. A few days later, three members of the group, together with the director of the organization and one other official, discussed the ideas that were generated. As a result, it was decided that the native physicians offered great potential for overcoming cultural barriers to family-planning communication and should be made the nucleus of this educational effort. These native physicians were held in high esteem in the villages and the people often confided in them on matters of family health.

Soon a survey was conducted, with the aid of the Department of Mass Communication in the University, of the knowledge and attitudes of native physicians relating to family planning. On the basis of the data obtained, an extensive programme has been launched by Community Development Services to educate the native physicians more thoroughly in family planning, and to make use of them for the purpose of supplying the basic information and services.

Those participating in the brainstorming session and the decision-makers and planners in the Community Development Services agreed that the technique had stimulated group members to generate a large number of highly relevant ideas. The session and ideas produced led to a major decision to use the native physician and also to a clearer basis for planning strategies to overcome communication barriers.

Annotated bibliography

BEAL, G.M.; BOHLEN, J.M.; RAUDABAUGH, J.N. 1973. *Leadership and Dynamic Group Action.* 5th imp. Ames, Iowa, Iowa State University Press. A practical book dealing with medium-size (ten to forty) group productivity, group techniques and group evaluation. Brainstorming (p. 246–50) is one of seventeen group techniques presented.

BOUCHARD, T.J., Jr. 1972. Training, Motivation, and Personality as Determinants of the Effectiveness of Brainstorming Groups and Individuals. *Journal of Applied Psychology*, Vol. 56, No. 4, p. 324–31.

BOUCHARD, T.J., Jr.; DRAUDEN, G.; BARASALOUX, J. 1974. A Comparison of Individual, Subgroup, and Total Group Methods of Problem Solving. *Journal of Applied Psychology*, Vol. 59, No. 2, p. 226–7.

GRAHAM, W.K.; DILLON, P.C. 1974. Creative Supergroups: Group Performance as a Function of Individual Performance on Brainstorming Tasks. *The Journal of Social Psychology*, Vol. 93, p. 101–5.

HAETELE, J.W. 1962. *Creativity and Innovation.* New York, N.Y., Reinhold Publishing. Broad approach to creativity and innovation by a research chemist in the private sector. Many approaches to creativity discussed (brainstorming in several contexts). Eight index references to brainstorming including description (p. 142–5) and evaluation (p. 155–7).

OSBORN, A.F. 1953. *Applied Imagination: Principles and Procedures of Creative Problem-Solving.* 3rd rev. edn. New York, N.Y., Charles Scribner's Sons. A very detailed approach to imagination and creativity, with detailed discussion of the background, rationale, procedure and use of brainstorming. The early classic.

POTTER, D. ANDERSON, M.P. 1976. *Discussion in Small Groups: A Guide to Effective Practice.* Belmont, Calif., Wadsworth Publishing Company. A straightforward, understandable presentation dealing with discussion, discussion leadership, technique and evaluation. Brief, clear presentation of brainstorming (p. 54–5).

III

Methods
for strategy

Introduction

Central to planning is the application of knowledge and theories about cause and effect to problems. In this part we present five methods that planners use to create and organize information about means/end, cause-and-effect relationships. Through analysis, planners determine what has been and what is—and what might be if things continue unchanged. The very purpose of planning—to create a successful adaptation relationship for the system—requires anticipation of how things can and should change in the future. For any system, this requires planners to develop a strategy for the creation, allocation and/or use of communication resources. This strategy is a statement of how the services provided by the system to the environment will meet important needs, and thus enable the system to continue to get resources from the environment. Thus a strategy is an 'if, then' statement in which planners propose that *if* certain actions are taken in a certain sequence, *then* goals will be achieved. Statements of this kind rest on theories about the cause-and-effect relationships between proposed actions and desired changes. In communication planning, theories come from many sources: from the academic disciplines of communication, sociology, economics and psychology; from previous experience; and from the personal knowledge of planners.

Planning methods used in developing strategies enable planners to translate abstract theories into concrete actions. Thus they typically enable planners explicitly to lay out the assumptions underlying proposed actions, and to test the strength of these theoretical assumptions in predicting what will really happen once action gets under way. By employing methods of this kind, planners can expose their assumptions for criticism, not only from experts, but also from other persons participating in the planning process. These methods also help planners with the task of organizing resources into action, making implementation planning possible.

Methods presented

Five selected planning methods are presented in this section: scenarios; simulation and gaming; cross-impact analysis; input–output analysis; and compact policy assessment.

SCENARIOS

The scenario method enables planners to study the impact on the system of a wide range of possible future developments in the environment. Scenarios describe alternative futures, enabling planners to see how different future environments can call for different strategies and to test strategies against these possible futures. To develop these pictures of the future, planners draw on a wide range of information about the environment and trends of change. A number of other planning methods can be used for scenario construction, including surveys, trend extrapolation and Delphi.

The method is relatively complex, and requires a great deal of information as well as skill in application. Thus it is typically found in rational/ comprehensive planning approaches, although simplified versions could be applied in less formalized planning—as when a small group of planners or experts uses brainstorming to 'imagine' what the future might be like. Scenario development can involve a large number of experts, though participation of clients—or 'non-technical' persons—appears difficult.

SIMULATION AND GAMING

This planning method creates a simplifed but dynamic version of a future system and environment, enabling planners to participate directly in the process of trying out alternative strategies to see how they might work. Simulations and games can also be used for education training.

Simulations and games rest firmly on thorough analysis of the environment and the system. This analysis enables the planner to construct a model of the expected interaction between the system and the environment; that is, of the proposed strategy. This requires a relatively high degree of planning skill and extensive data, and simulations and games are therefore typical of rational/comprehensive planning. Once constructed, however, simulations and games can be effective tools for expanded participation in planning, enabling non-planners to obtain the same personal experience with the strategy that planners experience. Depending on the complexity of the simulations, it may be necessary to create simplified versions for non-technical participants.

CROSS-IMPACT ANALYSIS

Cross-impact analysis is a particular method for simulating the future interaction of trends and events. It is a form of dynamic modelling through which planners can analyse the mutual interaction of trends and events, thus enabling them to test elements of strategies. Like all modelling techniques, cross-impact analysis rests on the assumption that an acceptable model of the future can be developed. It therefore requires considerable data, computer analysis and a relatively high level of planning skill. It is a rational/comprehensive planning method. The technical nature of this method restricts its potential for widespread participation in planning.

INPUT–OUTPUT ANALYSIS

Input–output analysis is a method for modelling the interaction of major sectors of a national economy. It enables planners to trace out the effects of changes in one sector, such as information, on other sectors, such as agriculture. It is thus useful in helping planners assess the effects of investment strategies at a national level, and is appropriate for such communication-planning tasks as telecommunications system development.

This is a relatively complex method, requiring a great deal of information, advanced planning skills and computer analysis. It is therefore useful in rational/comprehensive approaches, and primarily for planning at a national level. It has no real potential for widespread participation in planning.

COMPACT POLICY ASSESSMENT (COMPASS)

This planning method uses group discussion and analysis to assess strategies or other components of planning, and to design policy and strategy. It provides a low-cost, relatively quick way to test strategic ideas using the combined judgement of a group of persons. Compass requires little data or resources, and a relatively low level of planning skills. It is similar to both Delphi and brainstorming in that it is essentially a set of rules to guide and structure the interaction of a group faced with a policy or strategy problem. The method is ideally suited for incremental and transactive planning approaches. Its simplicity and ease of use gives it considerable strength as a participatory planning method.

Other uses of the presented methods

Scenarios provide a useful way of organizing analytical information. Early stages of scenario construction involve a great deal of data analysis, and thus the method can also be considered useful in the analysis planning element. The same is true for simulations and games, as well as for cross-impact analysis. Each of these methods contributes to the decision element of planning by creating the rationale for alternative strategies, thus providing decision-makers with well-structured information.

Other methods for strategy

Systems analysis, of course, provides a basic framework for structuring strategy alternatives, as does the Delphi technique. Flow charts can be helpful in depicting interrelationships of strategy elements. Brainstorming is, once again, generally useful as a way to develop creative ideas and to test strategies for their probable effectiveness.[1] Various research/evaluation methods—such as message pre-testing and pilot testing of project components—are used to test the adequacy of strategy elements.

1. Methods presented in other sections of this book.

Bibliography

MIDDLETON, J. 1980 Images and Action: Theories in and of Communication Planning. In: John Middleton (ed.), *Approaches to Communication Planning*. Paris, Unesco.

Chapter 8

Scenarios

John Spence

Scenario analysis is a systematic approach to studying the impact on an organization of a wide range of possible future developments of a social, political, economic and technological nature. The objective is, through this approach, to devise a forward plan which best accommodates this range of futures together with suitable procedures to monitor events that may require adjustments to the plan over time. It may also be appropriate to develop contingency plans to facilitate quick responses if events deviate significantly from those anticipated in the preparation of the forward plan.

Definition

A scenario is a full description of the socio-economic, political and technological environment of the future relevant to the organization's activities and regions under review. A scenario relates the different future elements in an internally consistent way and describes those aspects which could significantly influence the key factors for the organization, e.g. population growth and its impact on communication demand. A range of scenarios is normally developed. These scenarios are not chosen just for their likelihood of being responsible descriptions of the future but also to expose those extreme conditions which could occur and have significant impacts on the organization's plans.

Communication scenarios are most effectively developed using a three-stage process. Figure 1 shows the conceptual outline of the methodology used to develop communication scenarios and their relationship to communication demand forecasts. These three stages involve the development of:

Scenarios for selected social, economic and political futures.

Descriptive analysis of the prospects for technological developments (technology prospects, or T Ps) identified as being in areas of importance to the communications industry.

Communication scenarios, by cross-impacting the scenarios with the T Ps to assess likely future needs for, and directions of, communications.

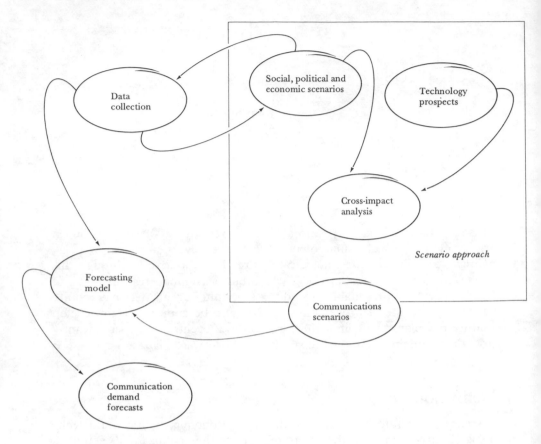

FIG. 1. Outline of communication methodology

History, advantages and main uses

The concept of scenario construction is not new. The military have used this concept in 'war games' for more than one hundred years. What is relatively new is the systematic application of scenarios to industrial and government planning to help overcome the deficiencies of 'single forecast' planning. This usage of alternative scenarios for industrial and government planning was popularized by Kahn and Weiner in their writings about 'surprise-free' futures (Kahn and Weiner, 1967). Today, it is increasingly being applied by management to plan future facilities and markets effectively even when faced with considerable uncertainty.

There are a number of advantages of the scenario approach:
It improves an organization's preparedness to handle possibly different future eventualities, because the scenario approach takes into account the impli-

cations of alternative futures and does not rely on a unique forecast of the future.

It encourages an organization to develop contingency plans in advance, to facilitate quick responses when events deviate significantly from those previously anticipated.

It leads an organization to develop a formalized procedure for monitoring important future developments. This monitoring programme concentrates management effort on those factors in the environment that could significantly influence the organization.

Overall, the scenario approach and the monitoring programme greatly reduce the uncertainty that generally surrounds environmental change.

Scenarios are used when organizations are faced with decisions affecting future investments, construction programmes, market developments and major forward planning generally. The main use of the scenario approach is to provide an effective substitute for subjective judgement and single forecasts, both of which have been recognized in recent times as being inadequate to meet the complex changes that the future increasingly seems to hold.

Limitations and form of output

In addition to using soundly based statistics, scenarios require, for their preparation and analysis, the objective inputs of qualified and experienced personnel. The reliability and/or usefulness of the scenario approach is therefore limited by the level of experience and capability drawn on for these inputs and the depth of scrutiny under which the inputs are placed to ensure reasonableness and consistency. In addition, should key factors and/or significant technological prospects not be identified, then this will limit the reliability of the scenarios developed.

Four types of output are derived from the process depicted in Figure 1:

1. A detailed statement and table of data for each selected scenario, describing the social, economic and political developments which are likely to occur under those future circumstances.

2. A research paper for each technological development of interest, outlining its future prospects and, in particular, depicting the rate, timing and impact of its acceptance. (For the communications industry these are likely to be, primarily, communications technologies, but they will also include other areas of potential influence such as transportation and technologies which could enhance or render obsolete the industries in the region and hence the region's demand for communication services.)

3. A report outlining the communication scenarios (i.e. the future development of the communication environment) resulting from the cross-impacting of the social, economic and political scenarios with the technological prospects.

4. Quantified forecasts of demand for communication services for each social, economic and political scenario under the impact of relevant technology.

Level of detail and level of confidence

The scenarios can be developed in broad outline or in great detail, depending upon the nature and significance of the decisions to be made. The scenario approach, correctly applied and drawing on experienced personnel, can greatly reduce uncertainty and increase the overall level of confidence in communications planning. It can help eliminate alternatives, clarify which decisions can safely be made and identify where additional information is needed for management action. It must be recognized however that no approach can forecast the future with certainty. With this realization, the scenario approach aims greatly to increase management's level of forecasting confidence by realistically narrowing the range of possible futures and by anticipating the 'unexpected'.

Forecasts can be made to cover any required time horizon, with the period usually chosen to reflect the life of the 'investment' to be made. However, it is normally found most appropriate to plan for a period of from seven to twenty years (with data beyond ten years usually diminishing rapidly in reliability).

Resources needed

People. Scenario development normally requires a team approach, with the team comprising several different types of people, as follows:
Those with a specialized knowledge of the communications sector (or the problems that planned communication will address) who can help identify all of the key factors and technological aspects likely to be significant.
Those with a strong analytical capability who can define the data needs related to the key factors, organize data-collection surveys, review and analyse the data and develop for review the technological prospects and the social, economic and political scenarios selected.
Those with specialized knowledge of a social, economic, political and/or technological nature who can critically review scenarios and TPs for consistency and completeness.

Time. The range in elapsed time will be from six weeks to twelve months, depending upon the complexity of the scenarios and TPs, and the size and experience of the team involved. Normally the elapsed time is around six months.

Money. This ranges from modest ($10,000) to high ($150,000), depending upon the level of detail and complexity of the scenarios and TPs, the extent to which experts are used and the appropriateness of computer facilities to handle data.

Case example

DEVELOPMENT OF COMMUNICATION SCENARIOS

The case example described below is based on an actual study carried out by a management consulting firm, W.D. Scoot & Co. Proprietary Ltd, for an Australian organization involved in the communication industry. This organization is called Communications Australia Ltd in this case. The study involved forecasting the development of communications in Australia.

OBJECTIVES OF THE STUDY

The objectives of communication scenarios in this case are to:
Provide a basis for forecasting the level of demand for communication services.
Identify those key factors and technological developments that might significantly affect communications traffic in terms of demand, type of traffic or sudden change in demand.
Expose critical thresholds and events requiring major decisions.
Identify the need for policy decisions.
Appraise the impact of possible new technologies under these various situations and the effect of various technological options.
Encourage analysis of extreme conditions that might require preparation of contingency plans and/or monitoring programmes in the near future.

SCENARIOS

The starting-point in our case was to describe the future social, political and economic conditions in Australia over approximately twenty years. As the number of possible combinations of events was very great, the first step was to decide on the number and themes of scenarios to be developed. These themes were chosen not just because of their likelihood of emergence as an accurate description of the future, but also to highlight those extreme conditions that would evoke special economic, technical and/or social demands on Communications Australia Ltd. Four themes were identified in this study:

Scenario A was designed to explore demand for communication services under conditions in which:
There is a relatively unplanned society which has gradually evolved towards a comprehensive welfare state.
Cyclical conditions characterize the economy, political attitudes and public versus private issues.
Historical trends and growth rates prevail.

Scenario B was intended to examine an environment characterized by:
Vigorous competition between the public and private sectors.

Intense competition in the communications industry.

Responsiveness in government and business as well as the community to technical threats and opportunities as distinct from social pressures.

Emphasis on economic growth rather than life-style consideration.

Scenario C was designed to examine environmental conditions involving:

Growing dependency on, and acceptance of, the government for decisions and actions for individuals' material well-being and protection against misfortunes.

Emphasis on the quality of life and self-actualization rather than material considerations.

Attitudinal restraints on growth and entrepreneurship.

High discretionary time, leading to high interest in education, hobbies, leisure time and mobility.

Rigorous ecological restraints, raising costs and causing shortages, restricting industrial activity and locations.

Scenario D described an environment characterized by:

Low demand.

Limited budget for Communications Australia Ltd.

Socially fragmented society with dissatisfied people, lack of co-operation, poor workmanship, poor maintenance etc.

Special-interest, self-appointed groups attempting to dictate policy, procedures etc.

Troubles with and between unions, environmentalists and special-interest groups as each struggles to strengthen its own position.

IDENTIFICATION OF CRITICAL FACTORS

Once the scenarios were developed to a draft outline stage in accordance with the themes selected, and had undergone initial reviews, factors important to communication planning were identified within each scenario. A composite list of these factors was then produced and where possible each was quantified. The purpose in doing this was to:

Allow the future directions of the scenarios to be related to communications.

Quantify the various sections of the scenarios to allow ready comparison of the different futures being examined, and to ensure that the scenarios were adequately testing the range of futures themes that had been agreed with the client.

Facilitate more precise internal consistency checks by the study team.

The critical factors actually used and quantified in the scenarios are listed in the scenario range table described below.

TREND ANALYSIS

Historical data were collected and analysed on each of the critical factors which had been identified and on important related data. This was done for several reasons:

To provide reference data base for the socio-economic variables.

To facilitate calculations related to the variables to be used in scenario A.

To enable the values of each factor for the year 2000 to be assessed against the historical trend, i.e. to provide a check on the validity of the ranges being considered.

To facilitate the assessment of past relationships between factors as a guide to future behaviour.

USE OF EXPERT PANELS AND FURTHER DEVELOPMENT
OF SCENARIOS

Once the scenarios were prepared they were checked for consistency, clarity, completeness and relevance. The check for internal consistency was particularly important. It was achieved initially through an internal review by the study team, and secondly by having the scenarios reviewed by experts in various socio-economic and political fields who were not involved in their preparation. The scenarios were submitted to over forty experts in small groups who were asked to consider:

In what ways was the scenario internally inconsistent?

Was the description of the Australian society and economy possible?

How far did the description depart from what the group as a whole, or individual members, felt was the most probable future situation?

In the light of the comments arising from these questions, further research was undertaken where necessary, and modifications and alterations made to the scenarios. The scenarios were resubmitted to the experts for any further comments they might have had. The final scenarios incorporated many of these comments, although inevitably they did not encompass all the diverse requirements of the various experts.

SCENARIO RANGE TABLES

Control over the choice of critical factors, the internal consistency of each scenario and the relationships between stated themes and quantitative data on the one hand, and between themes of different scenarios on the other, was maintained by a device called a 'range table'. A range table (see Table 1) endeavours to set out a complete list of critical factors used in development of the scenarios, and shows the ranges and actual values (where applicable) for each factor for each scenario. A quick glance at the table indicates the range for the value of all factors across all scenarios. Consistency of the scenarios in terms of their respective themes can be inspected easily. For example, it is

TABLE I. Example: scenario range table

| | Reference | | Scenario | | | | Measurement |
Critical factors	Data	(Year)	A	B	C	D	unit
A. Demography[1]							
1. Population size	13	(73)	18	18	16	16	Million
2. Population growth rate	2	(61–73)	1.4	1.3	0.7	0.7	Average percentage p.a.
3. Age distribution							
0–4 years	28 ⎫		24	27	23	23 ⎫	
15–64 years	63 ⎬	(73)	66	64	66	66 ⎬	Percentage
65 + years	8 ⎭		10	9	11	11 ⎭	
4. Labour-force size	5	(71)	9	8	8	9	Million
5. Labour-force growth rate	2	(61–71)	2	1	1	2	Average percentage p.a.
6. Labour-force participation rate	42	(71)	49	43	48	55	Percentage of population in labour force
7. Urbanization of population	61	(71)	67	63	60	75	Percentage of population in metropolitan areas
8. State distribution of population Victoria and New South Wales	64	(71)	62	65	61	65	Percentage of population
9. Immigration	70 000	(60–70)	70 000	50 000	0	0	Immigrants p.a.
B. Economic base							
C. Leisure							
D. Trade unions							
E. Education							
F. Mobility of population							
G. Transportation							
H. Housing							
I. Consumption							
J. Energy							
K. Natural resources							
L. Environment							
M. Government							
N. International conditions							

1. For example purposes only subfactors and numbers have been shown for the critical factor 'Demography'.

consistent for scenario B to have a higher level of GDP (gross domestic product) per capita and a lower level of unemployment than scenario D.

TECHNOLOGY PROSPECTS

In parallel with this work, action was initiated to develop statements of relevant technological prospects. A 'technology prospect' (TP) is a positive statement about the prospective performance, use and meaning of a particular technological device, system or related service over a future time period. Although emerging new technologies and changes in existing technologies can have a direct impact on the social, political and economic conditions of today and in the future, technological considerations were initially kept separate from the development of scenarios about future social, political and economic conditions. This was done because it was noted that:

The interactions of social, political, political, economic and technological forces at work in any society are very complex indeed. A great deal of time can be expended in debate about cause and effect without much real progress being made. There is need to simplify, and this approach is a logical simplification in theory and in practice.

A great deal of prospective future technology of consequence in this study will be imported to Australia. It was very unlikely for this technology to be 'home-grown'. For this reason, the approach of examining the impact of a technology on prevailing social, political and economic conditions in Australia was seen to be most appropriate.

It should be mentioned that broad technological assumptions were built into some of the scenarios. For instance, in scenario D it was postulated, without detailed consideration of the technology prospects, that communications will be poor. The effects of this broad technical condition on the social, political and economic conditions of the day were considered in the scenario as it was developed.

DEVELOPMENT OF TECHNOLOGY PROSPECTS (TPS)

The process of developing TPs relied on inputs from many sources, including experts in communication-orientated organizations, consulting organizations and universities. Initially fifteen TPs, such as electronic message systems, electronic fund transfer systems and optical fibres, were developed and examined under five broad headings: (a) likely technical form and potential application; (b) state of development; (c) potential impact on the communications organization; (d) potential impacts on the individual user and/or society as a whole; and (e) policy issues.

Then, initial TPs were reviewed by experts and led to a long list of TPs, classified into the type of impact the TP would have on the communications organization, such as technologies, linking mechanisms, services and legal and/or institutional matters. Each formal technology-prospect paper had the following sections:

1. *Proposition for the year 2000.* A short statement, identifying concepts and some of the variations that may appear during implementation of the prospects.
2. *Present state of development.* A statement and history of the present stages of development of the TP, or the elementary forms of it.
3. *Known plans (if any) for this TP.* Statements about any known plans that may exist anywhere in the world relating to the development of the T P—whether the T P is a service or a device/system.
4. *Trends.* Any attempt to look twenty years into the future must also look as far into the past as possible for trends of similar introductions or technology developments. Therefore, this section sought to establish, where possible, information about performance, substitutions of alternative services, times between stages of development in the past and identification of analogous introduction or developments of other devices/systems—particularly where direct information on the TP being examined was not yet available.
5. *Technical problems to be overcome.* This section of the TP identified particular technical problems that would need to be overcome before the TP, as a prospect (as outlined in section 1 of each paper), would be available.
6. *Likely implementation problems.* This section sought to identify the particular social, political and non-technical-type implementation problems that would need to be addressed before the stages of development for the T P could be postulated. Other matters in this section included legal questions, potential organizational constraints, regulatory problems and standardization needs.
7. *Probable costs and timing of availability.* As far as possible, costs and availability estimates were included in the TPs. Most of the base information included in the TPs related to their development without considering specific constraints that may apply in Australia.

Then T Ps were not forecasts of what will happen but rather were propositions which needed to be examined against the background of the social, political and economic scenarios, i.e. to identify the societal inhibitors or stimuli that could affect the rate of implementation of each T P.

CROSS-IMPACT ANALYSIS

Cross-impact analysis was then used to assess the likely acceptance of the relevance and technology prospects in the social, political and economic conditions defined in each of the four scenarios. The cross-impact analysis involved several key steps:

1. Analysis of the independent impact of each technology prospect on each of the four scenarios described above.
2. For those T Ps which are considered to have at least general acceptance in a given scenario, analysis of the interaction and impact of each pair of tech-

nology prospects (TPs one on the other, to identify complementarity, dependence or other forms of interaction between the TP pair in the contact of a particular scenario).

3. Analysis of the combination of all TPs considered to have at least general acceptance in a particular scenario to examine system effects, sequencing of impacts and other interactions, leading to development of a description (or scenario!) for a prospective future communications environment of relevance to Communications Australia Ltd. This led to the development of the communications scenario, commented on further below.

It is not intended to discuss cross-impact analysis in detail in the case study because the technique is the subject of another part of this book. It should be appreciated, however, that in all of this work a great deal of subjective judgement and informed opinion is used to assess and quantify the various impacts and interactions among the various technology prospects and between the TPs and the conditions previously quantified in the scenarios.

COMMUNICATION SCENARIOS

The end result of the overall process after cross-impacting was the development of a set of communication scenarios (one for each of the four social, political and economic scenarios described above). These described the level and rate of acceptance likely to be achieved by each of the technology prospects under the conditions of that particular future. In this way, it was possible to see which developments were likely to continue, even in difficult socio-economic circumstances, and which were unlikely to be successful in other than growth times. For example, of the four communication scenarios described for the technology prospect 'Electronic Fund Transfer System' three forecast high growth rates, while under scenario D it was predicted that this technology prospect would not be implemented.

Collectively, then, the scenarios were able to provide guidance as to which communications developments justified support and/or close monitoring attention, thereby assisting management with its immediate plans for action and its longer-term policy stance on a range of important issues.

MONITORING

It should be noted that this process left the organization, Communications Australia Ltd, in the position of knowing not only which developments were likely to be significant but also where changes in key factors were most likely to change the forecasts. In this way the scenario approach provided the basis for continuously monitoring those few key factors and thereby maintaining an updated set of forecasts to aid in communications planning.

Annotated bibliography

CENTER FOR THE STUDY OF SOCIAL POLICY. 1975. *Handbook of Forecasting Techniques*, p. 190–205. Menlo Park, Calif., Stanford Research Institute. An excellent discussion of scenarios and related forecasting methods. Provides definitions, backgrounds, uses, cautions and so on.

DELP, P.; THESEN, A.; *et al.* 1977. Scenarios. In: *System Tools for Project Planning*, p. 164–7. Bloomington, Ind., Indiana University, International Development Institute. Short description of scenarios, their advantages, limitations and procedures for use.

KAHN, H.; WEINER, A. 1967. *The Year 2000*. New York, N.Y., Macmillan.

LITTLE, A. D. 1976. *Telecommunication and Society, 1976–1991*. Report to the Office of Telecommunication Policy, Executive Office of the President (C79119). One of the best examples of how scenarios can be used in communication planning. Excellent format for scenario presentation and commentary.

WILSON, I.H. 1978. Scenarios. In: Jib Fowles (ed.), *Handbook of Futures Research*, p. 225–47. Westport, Conn., Greenwood Press. Covers purposes and uses of scenarios as well as scenario development. Complete with short examples of alternative scenarios.

Chapter 9
Simulation and gaming

Gus Root

Problems seldom exist in a simple cause–effect environment. Complex factors and networks can be studied to identify the most critical factors and functions, and these can be represented in manageable form in a 'simulation'. This simulation can then be played as a game, to help the participants have a first-hand experience with the dynamics of the problem situation. This experience is almost always stimulating to the participants, helps them realize the import-ance of new knowledge and skills for dealing with the problem and leads to a degree of involvement that is seldom found in conventional academic situ-ations. Another way that simulations can be used is by managers and decision-makers who wish to try out alternative policies on a simplified replica of the complex problem situation in order to observe the probable outcome of each alternative. The outcome of such an analytical use (rather than educational use, as noted earlier) of simulations can aid the decision-maker in his or her effort to initiate effective action with the fewest unexpected costs or negative side-effects. Two examples of simulations are given: one very simple and the other complex.

An introductory fable

The prime minister of Siabad[1] was worried. The Siabad ministers of health, agriculture and education all wanted new radio stations, printing facilities and computers. They were each able to present strong arguments supporting their needs for these facilities in order to meet their urgent five-year goals. But their combined budget requests amounted to three times the available resources! The prime minister and his advisers were convinced that the different minis-tries needed to plan together for the joint use of common communication systems (radio networks, printing operations, district offices) and shared cen-tral facilities (office buildings, research departments, computer services). A simulation of the national planning processes was prepared. The prime minis-

---

1. Siabad: the hypothetical Asian nation which is the focus of the 'Development Communication Planning Simulation-Game', developed by Unesco and the East–West Communication Institute.

ter watched carefully as many decision-makers went through the entire planning process in the five-week simulation. National goals were clarified.
Objectives for individual ministries were prepared. The activities and resources required were specified. Co-operation between projects and ministries
was found to be essential if national goals and separate ministerial objectives
were to be achieved within the limits of available resources.

The fifty people who worked through this simulated experience together all
gained new insight into how their individual planning efforts contributed to
the achievement of national goals.

Simulation: an informal definition

A simulation is a simplified working model of a problem situation. Small
groups of people try to understand and solve certain problems when they are
assigned roles in a simplified representation of that problem situation. The
cause–effect relationships of the 'real life' problem situation are maintained,
but the participants have to make decisions and act within relatively short
periods of time. In successive time periods, they learn from the results of their
decisions and actions, and try to improve their performance in solving problems and achieving desired results. In contrast to what occurs when information is obtained about problems from reading or lectures, the participants in a
simulation learn from their own experiences and usually become much more
emotionally involved in the problem, the factors which contribute to the
problem and their own efforts to reduce or solve the problem. Therefore, a
simulation is a working replica of a problem within its cause–effect network,
with which people can 'play' in order to have a first-hand experience with the
factors affecting the problem. A simulation imitates the essential performance
of a problem situation, but in a simplified and speeded-up manner. Examples
of simulations are:

War games, in which armies and officers act out defensive and offensive moves
   under controlled conditions.

Management training exercises, in which business leaders work in a hypothetical company and make decisions on sales, manufacturing, engineering
   and budgeting in order to achieve business objectives.

Medical diagnosis, at which doctors-in-training can ask for information on a
   simulated patient in order to make a diagnosis and prescribe correct treatment before the 'patient' dies.

The Siabad Communication Planning Simulation-Game, in which planners
   practise analysing national and local needs in order to prepare co-ordinated
   plans for meeting those needs.

Assumptions, history and main uses

When we construct a 'simulation', it is important to realize that we are making
certain assumptions, such as:

That we know the critical factors and relationships affecting the problem situation.

That our simulation expresses these factors and relationships realistically, so that the simulation acts (behaves) in ways that accurately reflect the 'real' situation.

That the results of the simulation can be meaningfully related to the outcomes of 'real world' situations.

That what we learn from using and manipulating simulations will be useful (helpful) in acting wisely in 'real world' situations.

A simulation, necessarily, is a simplification of some 'real world' problem situation. It will leave out many factors and features which we believe (assume) to be relatively unimportant or irrelevant to the problem. It will also speed up 'real world' time schedules, so that 30 minutes in the simulation may represent three months of 'real world' time—and we assume that the events in those 30 minutes are a realistic image of the important factors in the 'real world'.

Who knows when humans first began 'pretending' and acting out important events in advance of the 'real' thing, in order to become proficient before those skills were critical? Parents probably encouraged their children to 'play' at hunting, war and housekeeping even during prehistory periods. Formal education has frequently included drama, games, problems, drill exercises and stories (parables, folk tales) to provide opportunities for actual or vicarious practice of behaviours believed to be important for effective life within a particular society or culture. The formal study of simulations and the development of theories about what makes for effective simulations are quite recent, beginning just after the Second World War when military experiences were extrapolated to the preparation of 'simulation games' for elementary- and secondary-school students. When it was demonstrated that certain types of learnings were facilitated and accelerated through simulation-games, various signs of professionalism began to appear: a professional journal was started; national professional societies and meetings were organized; research was conducted to test the relative importance (effect) of variations in simulation characteristics; commercial groups were formed to produce and sell simulations which had been found to be effective in achieving prescribed objectives.

There are two major ways that simulations are used:

1. As *teaching-learning experiences*, whereby participating in a simulation-game, and then working to improve the experience for others, provide significant educational exercises. First, the participants have to learn the problem parameters and the cause–effect relationships in order to perform appropriately. Second, they can compare and contrast the simulation with their own understanding of the problem situation and other learners like themselves, and invent new ways to make the simulation more effective. Simulations can be designed gradually to add more and more complexity in successive 'rounds' or cycles of play, until something very close to the complexity of 'real life' situations emerges to challenge both the participant and the leader-instructor.

2. As *management decision aids*, whereby the building and use of a simulation can serve many possible functions, for example as:
   (a) A tool for clarifying a common perception of some problem situation on which decision-makers must act. The simulation can help expose and reconcile different perceptions among those who work in or manage the problem situation.
   (b) A tool for working out a number of alternative policies, each representing one person's or group's concept of an effective approach to the solution of the problem; the simulation helping the decision-makers to be sure that each proposed policy is comprehensive enough to include consideration of all major problem factors.
   (c) A tool for forecasting the probable outcome of alternative policies or problem-solving approaches, if the current factors and relationships were to act over an extended period of time.

Limits and cautions

The limitations of simulations are directly related to the assumptions noted above. Yet, in each case, there are actions we can take to minimize (even if we cannot eliminate) these potential shortcomings. Each potential limitation described below will be followed by suggestions on how to control for the effect of that particular difficulty. When used within appropriate safeguards, they can provide valuable experiences and tools.

A simulation is not the 'real' thing. It includes only a selected number of the factors affecting the 'real' problem situation. A simulation is a simplification of some problem situation. Learning how a simulation works may give people a false impression of how the 'real' situation actually works. They may learn to 'play the game' but not learn how to perform effectively in the more complex 'real' situation. Decision-makers may make serious mistakes if they base their decisions on the simulation, because the simulation cannot include all of the relevant factors that are present in the 'real' problem environment.

Suggestions. When preparing a simulation, ask a variety of 'experts' to help you include the most critical factors and relationships. As the number and complexity of these characteristics increases, the simulation will, of course, become more complicated. Few educators or managers take the time and spend the energy needed for this kind of problem analysis without the use of demanding tools (such as simulations, cross-impact matrices and other 'modelling' approaches). It is likely that good simulations will help educators and managers perform their most complex tasks better than could be done without such tools. But there are also steps that educators can take to make even the best simulation more effective in helping participants learn something that will be useful to them later:

Talk with participants before the simulation to set the stage for the experience and the 'reality' which is being simulated.

Provide the appearance of 'reality' with maps, photographs and charts related to the problem and its setting; hang them on the walls; give out copies.

Assign people realistic roles and positions within organizations, give them appropriate titles and job responsibilities.

Use spaces in the physical setting of the simulation to represent distances between people or groups, and schedule realistic events with normally controlled structure (such as meetings with enforced rules of order).

Talk with the participants after the experience to relate their activities and feelings back to the 'real life' situation which was the basis for the simulation.

A simulation is only someone's perceptions and beliefs about the problem, and he/she/they could be wrong. There is no way to be 100 per cent sure that the factors and relationships in a simulation represent that which really produces and affects the problem. Any simulation is someone's theory about the problem, and the theory may be wrong, misleading or inappropriate. Also, different people may have different theories about the problem, and one of those theories may be much better than the others—any attempt to get agreement among those many people on a common theory (a simulation) may leave you with just some set of inconsequential factors upon which they agree.

Suggestions. Bring together the most knowledgeable people you can find and ask them to help you make a good simulation which represents what is known about the problem and its cause–effect relationships. Work with these people to conduct and evaluate the simulation.

If there are strong differences among experts, prepare simulations of the major different points of view. Ask these experts to compare these alternative theories.

If someone loudly says that you are wrong (!), listen carefully and ask your critic to contribute to the development of an alternative model (theory, simulation).

After playing a simulation game, ask the participants to help you make it better and more realistic.

It is a lot of work to prepare and conduct simulations; it may not be worth while. It takes the time and effort of good people to develop a simulation, and that is a costly investment. What are the benefits which result from this cost? Students and employees are not always easier to work with after they have participated in a simulation. They are likely to ask more, and more difficult, questions. They will want more complicated answers. They often want to examine and explore decisions and policies in order to be personally convinced of the quality of proposed actions. All this makes it harder to work with them.

Simulations do not make decisions easier and simpler for managers. It is often harder to make decisions, as a good simulation helps to clarify the issues and relationships that affect a problem.

Suggestions. There are at least two ways to deal with this issue of increasing complexity: (a) avoid it; prepare only simple simulations, limit the information and alternatives provided to participants; or (b) embrace it; encourage participants, educators and managers to regard uncertainty as a natural and unavoidable thing which needs to be dealt with constructively. To limit the disturbing effects of complexity, include in the simulation only those factors and relations you know you have to work with. Use the simulation selection-and-design process to clarify your own thinking about the problem. Play the simulation-game to teach the problem-solving approaches you think are most appropriate, or to explore the outcomes of the approaches you think you and others should take. Use a simulation as a personal tool to demonstrate the quality of a particular approach.

To help yourself and others deal constructively with increasing complexity, you could:

Within yourself, recognize that 'reality' is both complex and uncertain, and may be filled with unexpected adversity and bad luck. Accept errors in yourself and others as natural opportunities for learning, rather than as 'sins' to be avoided. State publicly what you know and believe, also what you do not know, and the differences between experts which indicate that nobody knows 'for sure'.

In dealing with others, give full recognition to what they know and can do well, and also to their uncertainties and errors. Demonstrate publicly your knowledge and acceptance of life as complex, uncertain and turbulent.

In preparing simulations, plans and decisions, prepare for alternatives. Be ready to change (to another simulation or plan) as conditions change or as relationships become more clear. Prepare simulations and plans in order to learn from them, so that you can plan better another time.

'Real life' problems and relationships change rapidly, so that any simulation may be inappropriate for current conditions. The social factors and relationship which affect problems (causing them and contributing to their solutions) will change from time to time, and from one community to another. Educators and decision-makers need to understand and work with current problems and relationships in order to achieve desired future results. Out-of-date ideas and simulations could be misleading and costly.

Suggestions. There are several ways to deal with these issues:

Select, develop and use simulations of problems which are common to many cultures, societies and settings; e.g. simulations of agricultural development, the economics of rural development, the dynamics of health and nutrition. Certain fundamentals of these problems are shared by many cultures, so that the simulation may need to be adjusted for only the social structures of a particular group of participants.

Learn to develop and use small, quickly prepared simulations to represent an immediate problem of a group or institution. Do not take the time to prepare unique, large simulations because these are likely to be out of date by the time they are ready to use. Rather, concentrate on many small problem simulations, each of which can be designed and modified easily to keep it relevant to its participants.

At the end of any simulation, have the participants help you redesign the experience to make it more current and relevant for others like themselves. They may learn more from this redesign effort than from participation in the simulation. This is also a good way for them to learn the art of exploring any problem situation in order to discover the underlying cause–effect relationships that can be changed. This general skill may be more valuable to the participants than a knowledge of a particular set of factors affecting a particular problem.

Other related techniques

The main emphasis of this chapter is on simulation-games which are played by groups of people without major dependence upon computers. In these situations, individuals act out roles within fairly well defined organizations, and there are criteria for evaluating effective–ineffective performance. But there are many variations in the characteristics of simulations:

The role of a computer may vary from none to dominance. No computer is used in the examples at the end of this chapter. But in another situation, a business man may sit at a computer console, the computer may provide information on a simulated company and ask for a proposed yearly budget, the business man may allocate budget amounts to various activities, and the computer print-out will describe the year-end performance of the business as a result of those budget decisions.

The degree of control of participant actions may vary from allowing complete freedom to permitting only a narrow range of behaviours. In 'role playing' simulations, the participants must invent their own actions based on their personal backgrounds. At the other extreme, the simple simulation at the end of this chapter permits the participants only the choice between two very simple acts.

The existence and certainty of performance evaluation criteria may vary from none to clear and unambiguous criteria. Some simulations are only designed to provide an experience, without any indication of what is good or undesirable performance—the participants are asked to judge the strengths and limitations of their own behaviour. In other simulations, the achievement of objectives may depend upon chance factors such as the draw of a card or roll of dice. In still other cases, success or failure may be measured against tightly defined criteria.

The goals of most simulations focus on the human learning of the participants as a result of the experience. Rarely are simulations used for the benefit of an analyst or manager who wishes to observe the probable effect of variations in the simulation's roles and relationships of the overall performance of the simulated problem situation. Another type of simulation is known as a 'dynamic model' and is operated wholly within a computer without human roles or participants. Such a computer model is designed to represent the perceived relationships as expressed in mathematical form and acting in many interactive feedback loops. The effect of alternative decisions and policies on the model's performance can be observed in successive 'runs' of the model over simulated time periods. Examples of such 'simulations' are cross-impact matrices, interpretive structural modelling and system dynamics models. Of course, a non-computer simulation (a simulation-game) can be played repeatedly with variations in its roles and relationships, in order that an analyst or manager can observe the effect of alternative decisions or policies on the overall performance of the simulation.

Variations in simulations have been called role-playing, socio-drama, business games, experimental theatre, laboratories in human relations and experiential learning. Each is useful for a range of problems and desired outcomes; each has its particular demands on its developers, on those who lead the experiences and on those who participate.

Level of detail and level of confidence

Simulations vary widely in the amount of detail that is provided or needed in order to 'play the game' and learn something significant from its outcomes. When preparing a simulation, the designer must make many decisions about the number of factors to be included and the detail that is appropriate for each factor. For example:

What outcomes are desired? How much detail will be used in an evaluation of the simulation experience? If a simulation is only an 'awareness' experience for the participants, the demand for detail in the evaluation and in the simulation itself will be rather low; roles and relationships do not need to be carefully prescribed. On the other hand, if the experience is to develop very specific skills, then the roles, relations and performance criteria would need to be detailed and precise.

What is the nature of the problem underlying the simulation? How much is known about its cause–effect relationships? What level of detail is required to understand the problem and take action to solve it? Some problems can be solved only after the analysis of detailed and precise information on a small number of factors, and this will determine the level of detail included in the simulation. On the other hand, some problems require decision-makers to consider a large number of poorly defined and ambiguous factors, so that an appropriate simulation would provide a lot of information but none of it would be very precise.

How much time is available for the simulation? How much information can participants be expected to take in and manipulate in the available time? In short simulations (thirty minutes to three hours), the amount and complexity of the information provided must be severely limited. In longer simulations (two days to five weeks), participants can be expected to deal with a lot of information, complex interactions and fine detail.

Who will be the participants? How old will they be; how much ability do they have to use the language and ideas of the simulation? Greater levels of ability and experience with the problem will permit higher levels of detail in the simulation.

LEVEL OF CONFIDENCE

Can we be confident that a simulation provides a realistic picture of the problem situation which is of concern to the educator or manger?

Can we be sure that the results from using a simulation will be useful and constructive for the participants?

These are both good questions. Their answers depend upon the ways in which a particular simulation is selected, developed, used and evaluated for particular purposes. When the responsible persons carefully identify a set of goals and objectives for a specific group of participants, choose and develop a simulation that reflects the critical features of a problem that is of concern to those involved, and conduct the experience in an open and thoughtful manner, then the outcomes are likely to be meaningful and rewarding. As in most human endeavours, our confidence increases when we are working with competent people who are well intentioned, well informed and have adequate support, as they are systematic in developing, conducting and evaluating their work.

Communicability and credibility of results

A primary advantage of simulations is the personal, 'hands-on' experience with the problem elements and relationships—this does not depend upon another person's descriptions. This experiential learning is persuasive and enduring. Coleman (1973) examined seven years of research with simulations and concluded that there were two distinctly different ways in which people learned: (a) information-processing, through some symbolic media that represent principles and examples; and (b) experiential learning which is not mediated by symbols but is derived from personal action and experiencing the consequences of that action. The first of these is very rapid and efficient if those involved have high skills with the language of the symbols, but depends upon external motivation (school grades), is difficult to translate into effective action and is quickly forgotten unless used regularly. On the other hand, the kind of experiential learning that comes from simulations is intrinsically motivating (participants do become involved and excited) and easily remembered, although it is slower learning and hard to transfer learning from one simulation to another type of situation. Simulations are easily understood by those who participate, but participants often find it hard to tell others about their experiences.

Do people who use simulations tend to act upon the results of their experiences? Yes, if several things have happened:

If the simulation was designed around a problem which is pertinent and important to the participants.

If the participants were selected, prepared and orientated in ways that demonstrated why this simulation was important to them.

If the experience leads the participant to practise important behaviours and provides open, non-punitive feedback on the quality of that behaviour, with opportunities to try again.

If there is ample time after the experience to discuss the implications of the experience for future performance.

The greater the person's involvement in the experience, the greater its credibility and impact upon future performance.

Resources needed

Let us consider the resources needed to (a) design a simulation, and then (b) conduct the simulation-game experience.

Designing a simulation. Three kinds of people need to be involved in the process of designing a simulation: problem experts; simulation designers; and potential participants. People who know about, work with and have studied the problem to be simulated are essential contributors to the design process. They are the ones who must be responsible for identifying the characteristics of the problem and the cause–effect relationships which act to increase or decrease the problem. Educational and simulation-game developers have the special knowledge and skills required to bring together the materials and activities of a short time experience that will be interesting to learners and still reflect the insights of the problem experts. Potential participants are needed during the development process to 'test' early versions of the simulation, make suggestions on its improvement and be willing to be observed for the possible impact of the experience on their subsequent performance.

During this development phase, the designers will need only minimal support through secretarial assistance, spaces to hold experimental experiences and the services of an artist in making attractive visuals and displays. One resource that should *not* be liberally available during this design phase is *time*. The time allocated for this design-development should be as short as possible. Experience has suggested that busy, responsible people will not maintain high levels of interest and participation beyond a three-month period—and the simulation should be developed and conducted within that period if at all possible, before these important people move on to other concerns.

Conducting a simulation. There are three aspects to conducting a simulation: preparing the participants; leading the experience; and evaluating and reporting on the experience. Invitations to the participants should go out from the highest-level decision-maker, who should also be involved (but not make the final decision) in assigning persons to roles in the simulation. It is important that the descriptive material sent along with the invitation be well prepared, attractive, informative and call for a response to assist in planning the event. When the participants arrive on the scene, they should be greeted, given assistance with simple routines such as the location of facilities and helped to meet the others. The opening discussion of the simulation experience should be done slowly and carefully. The leader should be open about why these persons were invited and what this experience will involve for them now and in the future. Introductory materials should be provided, and the participants given adequate time to read the materials and ask questions about them as needed. Leading an effective simulation can be a demanding activity. Guiding the participants through the details of the experience demands the close attention of someone who knows the simulation intimately. Frequently a team of leaders is required, with the director circulating regularly and getting feedback through frequent meetings with the team of leaders. The post-simulation discussion should involve all of the leaders, participants and the high-level decision-makers who are concerned with the participants and their ultimate performance.

After the simulation, evaluative data should be gathered and brought together for a comprehensive review and analysis. An evaluative report should be prepared to record what happened and the outcomes of the experience, with suggestions on any further action by those who were involved.

Thus, the major resources needed for a simulation are skilled people, minimal support for these people and as little time as possible still to get the job done well. Other resources will include adequate space and privacy, paper and office supplies, and the money required to permit busy people to participate.

Procedures

As has been suggested above, there are three broad phases involved in the preparation for and conduct of a simulation: developing or selecting-modifying the simulation; conducting the experience; and evaluating and reporting on the outcomes. These three phases can be seen in both very simple and very complex situations (such as the two examples at the end of this chapter).

PHASE ONE: DESIGN OR SELECTION—MODIFICATION OF A SIMULATION

1. *Identification of a problem* that is significant to a particular group of participants or a manager who wants to analyse the probable outcome of a decision. Analysis of the problem and the cause—effect network that surrounds it.
2. *Establishing the objectives* for the proposed participants and/or institutions involved.
3. *Designing simulation materials, strategies and contingencies* to represent the most important factors and relationships within a realistic set of experiences.

4. *Preparation and validation of evaluation instruments and procedures* for use before, during and after the experience.
5. *Preliminary try-out* of the experience on persons who resemble the intended participants, and the revision of the materials and experiences until the desired results are achieved.

PHASE TWO: CONDUCTING THE SIMULATION

1. *Inviting the participants.* It is important that potential participants be identified by a responsible decision-maker, and receive an invitation along with descriptive materials indicating the experience as a chance to learn new and important skills relative to current and future responsibilities. This is important whether the simulation is being conducted for educational purposes or as an aid to a decision-maker in exploring the probable outcome of an intended decision or policy.
2. *Preparing the participants.* Do not start too quickly. Arrange for the participants to feel comfortable with each other and the setting. Be as open as you can about the experience and its history and intended outcomes (without 'giving away' the key issues that you want them to discover for themselves). Distribute material and give the participants time to become orientated and ask questions.
3. *Guide the simulation experience.* Begin! Get the participants engaged in the activities and materials. Keep time schedules. Provide many opportunities for the analysis of participant reactions; be ready to make adjustments whenever it becomes clear that some part of the experience is not quite the way you would like it (for this reason, it is wise always to have a team of leaders who can check each other and add separate insights).
4. *Conducting a 'debriefing'.* As soon after the experience as possible, lead a review and analysis of the experience to get answers to such questions as: 'What happened to you and how did you feel about that?' 'What were your goals and what seemed to help or hinder in achieving them?' 'What could have happened instead of what did, and what would have made that possible?' 'What is the relationship between this experience and the "real life" situations you know?' 'How could this experience have been made more valuable to people like yourself?'
5. *Ending the experience.* Express your appreciation and close the activities. Help people gather their things and leave. Yet, still provide time for anyone who wants to talk more deeply about some aspect of the experience. After everyone has gone and you have had time to settle down, send letters of appreciation and any follow-up material that was planned or promised.

PHASE THREE: EVALUATING AND REPORTING
ON THE EXPERIENCE

1. *Completing the evaluations.* Although most simulations are good experiences for the participants, that is generally not enough. Did it make a difference in their performances later? You will need to complete the post-simulation

190

evaluations as planned in Phase One, to make judgements about the impact of the simulation.

2. *Analysing the data.* Do statistical analyses and collect all subjective data, and make estimates of the features of the experience that contributed to successes and failures. Identify changes that would make it more effective another time.

3. *Reporting the results.* Document your findings and circulate copies of your report to appropriate persons (you may want different reports for different people). Get these reports out as soon as possible; if you planned for a six-month follow-up, do not wait at this time, but distribute another report later. The value of this report will decrease rapidly if it is delayed more than a few weeks.

In the examples that follow, you will see evidence (sometimes very little) of these three phases, but you will also see that they do not always appear in the 'neat and tidy' sequence suggested by the above description. We hope you will read and then try these simulations yourself, as they may be appropriate to your situation.

Two case examples

Simulations come in all sizes, forms and styles. They can be fun (even when they have serious intentions) and they can be hard work (even with the excitement of significant challenge). Two examples of simulations are presented to illustrate the wide range of possible simulations; the first is very short and simple yet represents a fundamental human problem, and the second is long and complex as it develops many interrelated principles.

SIMULATION-GAME I: THE 'FINGER GAME'

This simple simulation-game will contrast sharply with the second example, the Siabad simulation-game. This 'finger game' needs only about twenty to thirty minutes of time, little advance preparation, a minimum amount of structure, almost no special materials and can be done in almost any setting. It has been used with small groups of eight to ten persons as well as in large auditoriums with over 300 students. The following description is a listing of what the leader-instructor would say in introducing and directing the activity, and includes copies of the charts (matrices) the leader would display so that participants may score their own performances. The leader-instructor would study this simulation-game and make the decision that the problem underlying the experience is appropriate for a particular group, at a particular time. The group would be told that a fundamental principle of human decision-making would be presented through a small simulation-game, and that discussion of those principles would follow the game. When the 'game' is to be conducted, the leader-instructor would say something like this:

1. 'Hello. In the next few minutes, I will introduce you to a simplified

example of a situation which we all face from time to time. This "game" will simulate the experience of making a decision on the basis of choosing between the alternatives that are open to you, but having your success or failure depend upon the joint actions of yourself and the others in your environment. For most individuals, companies or nations, success or failure depends upon the combination of what they do and what others do at the same time. So, here we go!

2. 'In this game, you will have only two actions your can take. When I say, "Go", you must throw out either *one* or *two* fingers—like this: "*Ready-set-GO!*" and demonstrate by raising your arm so that, on saying the word "Go", you thrust out your hand and hold out either one or two fingers.

3. 'Try it with me now, just to be sure you have mastered this very complicated procedure.' (Openly laugh at yourself.) '"*Ready-set-GO!*" and see if you can get every person to do it. Laugh with them at this simple foolishness (but which has a serious purpose as will be shown later). Repeat only once more, until almost everyone understands the procedure. Then, move along quickly.

4. 'OK, very good. Now we will count off by twos to make pairs of players all around the room. Starting in one corner of the room, say—"You will be 'A' "', as you point to the first person. Moving to the person beside him or her, say—"You will be 'B' "'. Then, pointing to the next person, "You are 'A' and your partner is 'B' "'. And so on around the room until every person is paired with someone next to him or her, and each is identified as either "A" or "B".

5. 'Good! Now here is the way you can earn points by throwing out either one finger or two' (and again demonstrate the quick out-thrust of one or two fingers). Draw the simple 2 × 2 matrix (*without* numbers) on the blackboard or project the same matrix on an overhead transparency (Fig. 1). Explain how the combination of A's and B's actions determines the cell of the matrix in which their individual scores will be given: 'If A throws out one finger, then we look across the first *row* of the matrix. If, at the same time, B throws out one finger, then we are in the first *column* of the matrix, therefore their individual scores will be in the "1,1" cell of the matrix, right here!' Trace this example to show that this combination leads to the 1,1 cell. Most people will understand, but several will be totally confused. Give one or two other examples, as A and B throw out different combinations of fingers. As soon as at least one person in each pair seems to understand, move right along to keep a sense of fun!

6. Now add numbers to the matrix cells to show the number of points to be gained or lost in the first round of the game. Move quickly through an explanation and a practice trial where everyone throws out one or two fingers, and each pair of players calculates their individual scores.

7. Tell them, 'No talking with your partner from now to the end of the game!', and caution any pair that seem to be talking about game strategies that they should *only* talk about procedures for the play of the game. You

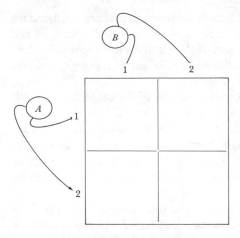

FIG. I. The 'finger-game' matrix

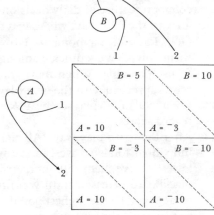

FIG. 2. 'Finger-game' matrix: first score

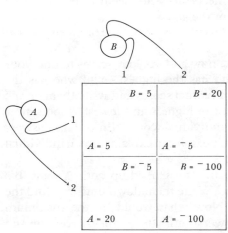

FIG. 3. 'Finger-game' matrix: second score

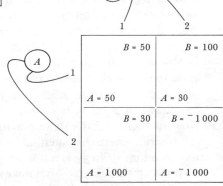

FIG. 4. 'Finger-game' matrix: third score

are sure to have some persons who do not understand and are confused by the matrix and determining their individual scores. Ask others in the group to help them just once or twice. If they still do not seem to understand, smile and say, 'Yes, it is a different way of earning points, but you will understand as we move along.' Proceed!

8. 'Now, we will play this game ten times, and you will want to record both A's and B's scores on each of those ten plays. One person in each pair should keep a record of the points each person earns on each play. Be sure you have paper and pencils for this, or borrow them from a neighbour.' As they prepare for this recording, you may want to emphasize that the whole game consists of ten plays, and that then they will see who has the highest individual and group scores.

9. Laugh with them at their uncertainty (because this uncertainty is a common feature of daily decision-making). But *begin!* 'All right, here we go with the first play, where you throw out one or two fingers. *Ready-set-GO!*' Pause just a moment. 'Now figure your individual scores and write them down.' Walk quickly among the participants, helping any that seem to have trouble. When most (not necessarily all) seem to have written scores, proceed with the next play of the game.

10. For a total of ten plays, repeat '*Ready-set-GO!*' with time between plays to record scores.

11. After the tenth play, say, 'All right, now add up your scores to find your individual totals so we can see who has the highest—and who has the lowest!' Have them call out their individual scores and write them on the blackboard or easel, until you find the highest and lowest. 'Good, now what would be the highest possible individual score?" Encourage answers until you get the correct one and that person can explain how an individual would get that score.

12. Say, 'Good, now what are your team scores? Add up both A's and B's scores and tell me your team scores.' Write them down until you find the largest and the smallest. 'Good. Now what would be the maximum possible team score?' Draw out answers until you get the correct one and an explanation of how that maximum team score would be achieved.

13. Then slow down the pace of the game and begin a discussion of the reasons why it is hard to achieve both individual and team benefits considering the factors of risk, trust and information about the other person's intentions. Have them consider what would really be the best strategy of play if each person really had the other person's welfare and probable strategies in mind, as well as his or her own.

14. Now ask them to think about playing the game again with a different 'pay-off' matrix, where the potential loss in the 2,2 cell is somewhat higher and the optimum strategy is not a simple one. (Most people will play a conservative, a 1,1 strategy—but not everyone, and that makes for an interesting discussion as to why they played a risky option.) After several plays, stop and ask them to discuss their own strategies.

15. Now ask them to relate this experience to that of nations, where the head of state (president or prime minister) must act relative to other states, with the possibility of gain or loss, with the ultimate loss being war and mutual devastation.

Although you have now completed the simulation-game, pause long enough for one or two perceptive comments (let us hope from perceptive persons) about the relationship of this game to real-life situations, and the importance of trust and open communication about intentions and actions. Some will have been confused and may protest at the use of matrices and numbers to represent important human events. It may be advisable to recognize that some people look at life that way, as you are unlikely to change anyone's mind on that issue in this situation.

SIMULATION GAME 2: THE SIABAD
COMMUNICATION PLANNING SIMULATION–GAME

This large and complex simulation-game was developed over several years with the support of Unesco, in Paris, and the East–West Communication Institute, Honolulu, Hawaii. The set of workshop materials (which includes this simulation-game as the central feature) was published in a limited edition by the East-West centre in the autumn of 1979. As the history and character-istics of this simulation are presented, you will see the general relationship between this developmental sequence and the 'idealized' structure suggested earlier in this chapter. Every simulation developer and user should expect some variations in this pattern of activity.

Phase One: Conceptualization and initial development

In the spring of 1976, Unesco invited a number of communication planners and educators to Paris to consider possible curriculums and teaching materials for the rapidly growing field of communication planning. At the end of this consultancy, the two representatives from Syracuse University (Dr Norm Balabanian and Dr Gus Root) submitted a proposal for the development of an extended simulation-game which would be the core experience in a four/five-week workshop on communication planning. The proposal incorporated the agreements reached during the consultancy—that the materials should be prepared for middle-level persons in the communication field, should show the relationships between planning at three organizational levels (the project, ministerial and national levels), should be suitable for those from South-East Asian countries, and should include at least a leader's guide, participant materials and a reference reading package. This proposal was accepted, and a South American university agree to use the materials in a trial course in order to make suggestions for revision by Syracuse University.

In the autumn of 1976, Balabanian and Root guided a group of inter-national graduate students (from Syracuse's schools of education, communication and political science) in the development of a draft version of a five-week workshop centred around the Siabad simulation-game. Copies of these initial materials were forwarded to Unesco, in Paris, and the South American university for review and comment. Unfortunately, the South American experience was not completed. Using all available suggestions, second draft materials were prepared for a major trial in Penang, Malaysia, to be held in late 1977. These materials consisted of four packages: a leader's guide for each of the five leaders; participant's materials for each of the fifty persons who would attend; a data base of information on the hypothetical country of Siabad (patterned after Thailand); and selected papers to serve as instructional and reference reading materials. Within the simulation itself, there were three stages of activity (three major 'rounds' of play, each requiring substantially different actions by the participants); the conduct of the simulation-game will be described in terms of these three 'stages'.

Phase Two: The conduct of the simulation-game

Unesco personnel arranged for the workshop to be held in Penang, Malaysia, and sent out descriptions of the experience to many persons and communication agencies throughout South-East Asia. High-level managers were invited to send in the names of possible participants, from which Unesco selected a balance group consisting of communication educators, practitioners and researchers, all of whom had competence in reading and speaking English. Letters of invitation were sent to the accepted applicants, with the request that each bring a current communication problem to which the principles of the workshop would be applied.

Stage One: Project development. The simulation began with a 'plenary session' which brough together all of those who would be working together over the following few weeks. It was a quieter and more informal atmosphere than that of the formal orientation of the day before. Each person had had time to settle into the situation and had read much of the material. After informal greetings and friendly 'small talk' the simulation began.

The participants were divided into small groups representing several of the major Siabad ministries that would be active during the entire simulation (education, health, agriculture and information). The leaders had assigned the participants in a way that balanced the number of educators, practitioners and researchers on each ministry, and brought people together with similar levels of language ability. A workshop leader was assigned to each group as an observer-facilitator (not to be a chairperson or instructor). Each simulated ministry began to identify its highest-priority problems relative to Siabad's national goals and needs as these were described in the data base of information on Siabad. As the participants struggled to establish objectives for specific projects aimed at meeting these high-priority needs, the workshop leaders organized and conducted seminars on pertinent topics such as 'problem identification' and 'project objectives'. Thus the participants were faced with realistic problem situations in the simulation which required new knowledge and skills, and then the required knowledge and skills were presented in reading materials, self-instructional modules and professional seminars and discussions.

At the end of Stage One, each ministry had identified a number of high-priority development projects, and had prepared plans for each project which included enough detail to estimate the personnel, facilities and budgets required.

Stage Two: Within-ministry co-ordination. When the reports of the separate ministries were available, the workshop leaders met and reviewed them in detail in order to provide similar feedback to all groups. It was apparent that each group had planned many separate projects without considering the needs and activities of the other projects even within the same ministry (and this is commonly seen in 'real life' situations). There was little or no evidence of concern for such things as: projects that were serving common communities and audiences; activities demanding the same scarce resources (skilled personnel, production facilities, distribution networks, liberal budgets); and evaluations that used similar approaches and research facilities.

Feedback to each ministry indicated the need for close co-ordination among the previously separate project staffs, facilities and budgets, and a revision of its budget request to a figure substantially below that submitted on the first round of the budget preparation process. At the same time that this feedback was provided, the long-range plan for the Ministry of Information (MoI) was distributed. The MoI plan introduced the possibility of several ways in which the different ministries could co-operate for both economy and increased effectiveness; there could be: (a) an expanded radio and television network serving the entire country of Siabad; (b) a selection and training centre for communication personnel; (c) a number of interrelated production centres for messages on radio, television, film, arts, pamphlets etc.; (d) a network of information centres to serve all ministries throughout the country; and (e) an expanded evaluation and research function to serve all ministries, having a distributed information and computer network.

Each ministry was asked to prepare a second draft of its plans and budgets for the next five years, and was invited to consult with representatives of the MoI. Instructions and pre-prepared forms were given to simplify this process. The submission of this Stage Two report marked the end of this part of the simulation. A long weekend with field trips and social activities provided a break for the participants. It also gave the workshop leaders time to review the submitted documents and prepare for the final stage of the Siabad experience.

Stage Three: Integration into one national plan. In this final phase of the simulation-game, each participant was asked to represent the ministry in which she/he had been working for the past weeks and meet with representatives of the other ministries on the Siabad National Communication Planning Council (NCPC). The task of this NCPC was to integrate the plans of the different ministries, develop one national five-year plan for communication to support Siabad growth and development and allocate budgets to the ministries for communication facilities and functions. Three such councils were formed so that every participant had the opportunity to speak for the projects, plans and budgets they had worked on. In each of the three councils, one of the workshop leaders performed as the Siabad prime minister, and assisted each council to analyse the strengths and weaknesses of the separate plans and decide on the most appropriate resolution of conflicts, duplications and omissions. Each council worked out its own resolution of these problems and came to a unique set of conclusions regarding the best way to organize the personnel, facilities and budgets to meet the communication needs of the country and its various ministries.

The presentation and discussion of the three different set of solutions provided the setting for a review of the principles of communication planning and the activities and ideas involved in this extensive simulation-game.

Phase Three: Evaluation, revision and publication

Based on the suggestions of the Penang participants and leaders, the workshop and simulation materials were revised and prepared for additional 'trial runs'. The workshop was then conducted two additional times: in Hawaii and in South America (in Spanish translation). When shown to be appropriate, additional revisions were made in the materials and new papers and experience added. A set of final materials was prepared for publication in late 1979. As can be seen from the extracts of the workshop materials and publicity releases printed below, the materials have retained and developed the concepts that were stated at the Unesco consultancy in 1976.

The Development Communication Planning Simulation-Game[1]

Communication planning is a newly emerging tool with important applications for national and social development. It is a field of social action requiring the application of knowledge and techniques drawn from a wide range of scientific disciplines. Few individual communication planners are likely to have all these necessary thinking tools to execute every aspect of a development communication plan.

A simulation-game workshop, originally developed for Unesco by a team at Syracuse University in 1977, tested in a Malaysian workshop later that year

---

1. A five-week packaged workshop organized by the East–West Communication Institute and Unesco.

and revised by the East–West Communication Institute, has been created to assist men and women with communication-planning responsibilities to develop and broaden their thinking skills in this vital area, and to practise communication planning in teams.

EXPECTED GOALS

After completing the workshop, participants will be able to relate ideas of development communication planning to their own situations, combining their professional experience with concepts of social and economic development, social change, communication and systems thinking. Participants will be familiar with approaches to development communication planning at project, ministry and co-ordinated, cross-ministry levels. They will also be acquainted with a range of techniques for communication planning.

THE GAMES: PLAY, ENJOY, LEARN!

Participants work in teams in which simulated problems and challenges are introduced and plans are developed. Personal ideas and experiences are applied by everyone. Ideas and data eventually grow into a series of cumulative communication plans. Review, feedback and analysis are part of the process.

THE SIMULATED NATION: SIABAD

The simulation-game workshop revolves around the Asian nation of Siabad, steeped in tradition and long-cherished values, and rich in agricultural land as well as in cultural and religious heritage. Siabad's 40 million people want an improved economy, greater social justice and reduction of urban–rural inequalities. Communication is seen as an important resource in achieving these broad social goals.

WHY THE SIMULATION–GAME APPROACH

Simulation speeds the learning process. Participants retain ideas longer because they practise actively with regular feedback. Knowledge-transfer skills are strengthened since the simulations are designed to be quite similar to situations in which new knowledge and skills will be applied.

The lecture/reading/discussion format is less effective in developing higher-level intellectual abilities of analysis, synthesis and evaluation. Simulation requires active participation in complex situations which are more likely to lead to higher-level skills.

Communication planning requires attention to emotional as well as to intellectual challenges. Simulation-games emotionally involve participants, providing them with valuable experiences to work through as they acquire additional intellectual resources.

TABLE I. Basic workshop schedule

Monday	Tuesday	Wednesday	Thursday	Friday
		Week One		
Welcome and orientation	Learning unit	Learning unit	Learning unit	Learning unit
		Week Two		
Introductory planning game	Introductory planning game	Planning game I	Planning game I	Planning game I
		Week Three		
Planning game I Presentations and review	Planning game 2	Planning game 2	Planning game 2	Planning game 2
		Week Four		
Planning game 2 Presentations and review	Planning game 3	Planning game 3	Planning game 3	Planning game 3
		Week Five		
Planning game 3 Presentations and review	Planning game 3 Presentations and review	Generalization/ projection unit	Generalization/ projection unit	Review, evaluation and wrap-up

HOW THE WORKSHOP IS STRUCTURED

The workshop comprises five components. It is designed so that planning done early on, at the project and ministry levels, builds up to provide a basis for development of national communication plans. The participants will employ the following elements;

Learning unit. Four instructional modules help participants establish at the beginning a common language for and general orientation to economic and social development, communication, communication planning and systems thinking.

Planning games. There are three planning games. The first requires development of communication projects for Siabad's ministries of health, education and agriculture. In the second, ministry teams plan co-ordinated projects within budget constraints. The third game brings ministry teams together to negotiate towards an integrated 'national' communication plan. Moderators with certain rules guide the games through their roles as chairman of the national economic planning board and as minister of information.

Data base. Siabad's socio-economic structure is reflected in a data base covering key aspects of the nation; agriculture, education, government, health, family planning, transportation, economy, co-operatives, communication, culture.

Tool box. Planners draw on various planning techniques. Technical papers are provided on goal-setting, human systems, evaluation techniques, economic indicators, cost–benefit analysis, management objectives, scheduling and budgeting, management information, an organization in its task environment, inter-organizational co-ordination and media utilization.

Generalization and projection unit. Activities are provided to enable the participants to relate workshop ideas and experiences to their own home setting.

WORKSHOP CONTENTS

Learning unit. Four instructional modules on: economic and social development; communication; introduction to communication planning; systems thinking.

Workshop leader's guide. Full instructions for managing the workshop, including prototype audio-visual aids.

Participant instructions. A complete guide to the three simulation games, including planning worksheets and planning problems.

Data base. Qualitative and statistical data on various aspects of Siabad.

Bibliography

ACADEMY FOR EDUCATIONAL DEVELOPMENT. 1973. *Let's End the Confusion about Simulation Models: A Summary of a Candid Discussion of Their Place in Higher Education*. Society for College and University Planning (Spring Conference).

BEER, S. 1975. On Heaping Our Science Together. In: R. Trappl and F. de P. Hanika (eds.), *Progress in Cybernetics and Systems Research*. Washington, D.C., Hemisphere Publications.

COLEMAN, J. S., *et al.* 1973. The Hopkins Games Program: Conclusions from Seven Years of Research. *Educational Researcher* (American Educational Research Association), August.

HERRERA, A. O., *et al.* 1976. *Catastrophe or New Society: A Latin American World Model*. Ottawa, International Development Research Centre (Box 8500, Ottawa, Canada K1G 3H9).

MIDDLETON, J.; ROOT, G.; BEAL, G.; JUSSAWALLA, M.; LIM, MEOW KHIM. 1979. *The Communication Planning Simulation Game*. 5 vols. Honolulu, Hawai, East–West Communication Institute.

ROOT, G.; SALAMATIAN, DJALI. 1976. A Dynamic Systems Model for Educational Television. (Unpublished paper available from the authors.)

WARFIELD, J. 1976. *Societal Systems*. New York, N.Y., Wiley Interscience.

Chapter 10

Cross-impact analysis

Dan J. Wedemeyer

Future events and trends do not operate in isolation, they interact and influence subsequent probabilities, timing and impacts of other developments. Cross-impact analysis is a method useful in addressing these interactions in a planning context. Cross-impact analysis shares the strengths and weaknesses of all modelling techniques. Although developed only a decade ago, cross-impact analysis is proving useful as a planning-simulation, communication and education tool. In addition, cross-impact gaming helps clarify and improve forecasts attained by other forecasting methods.

Definition

Cross-impact analysis is a systematic method in long-range planning for dealing with individual trend and event interactions. It is in the general family of dynamic models and useful in analysing the effects that can occur when one development affects another over time. A development is viewed as either a 'trend' or an 'event'. Here a trend measures change over time, while an event is the assumed 'catalyst' of changes. Cross-impact analysis is relatively easy to apply and is flexible, so it can be applied to a wide range of planning problems.

It makes use of a computer program to determine indirect consequences of combining selected developments over time. This assists in determining which developments should be inhibited or promoted to achieve specified planning goals. Finally, cross-impact analysis is a method that promotes communication and education among planners and therefore assists in analysis, understanding and decision-making.

Assumptions, history and main uses

Cross-impact analysis shares the general assumptions of all modelling techniques, namely that a satisfactory model of reality can be developed. It further assumes that trends and events do not operate in isolation. Rather, they are interdependent, and a change in one development has effect, directly or indirectly, on all other developments. It is assumed that: (a) many alternative future courses exist; (b) that some of these alternatives promote planning goals more dramatically than others; (c) that these alternative courses can be influenced in some way by human intervention. Finally, there is the implicit assumption that mathematical models provide greater insights into future consequences of planned action than less formal methods, thus justifying what may initially appear as a relatively higher cost.

Cross-impact analysis history is short. The concept was developed in the mid-1960s by Theodore J. Gordon and Olaf Helmer. Research literature on the technique did not appear until 1968. The basic concepts of cross-impact analysis were set out in 1970 by Helmer and Gordon in *Futures*, a game developed for Kaiser-Aluminum Corporation. It represented an effort to 'refine the forecasting' approach afforded by the Delphi technique (Helmer, 1973, p. 9). Presently, cross-impact analysis is widely used in *Futures* research and planning. It can be used with, or separately from, Delphi data. Many of these applications have modified[1] the basic form of the technique, but the intent of each approach is similar, i.e. to improve the exploration of alternatives and consequences in the planning decision-making process.

Cross-impact analysis has been applied to a host of long-range planning problems in communication, foreign relations, natural resources, food and education. Generally these applications of cross-impact analysis serve one or more of the following purposes:

Sensitivity studies. Where the effects of a change in one development affect other developments in the long term.

Scenario development. The generation of a few typical representative scenarios that can assist decision-making agencies in their planning efforts.

Comparative policy analysis. Testing various combinations of policies to provide insights into the most promising (Gray and Helmer, 1974, p. xii).

In each case the emphasis is on assisting in the decision-making process. The processes of considering the sensitivity of one development to another and the generation of representative scenarios suggest alternative planning options. The cross-impact technique provides insights regarding specific consequences of the various options available. Early in its development, Gordon pointed out (1972, p. 180) that, although cross-impact analysis has no general supporting theory, it

would *almost certainly permit the exploration of the side effects of decisions* under consideration . . . and might also be useful in illuminating less expensive means of attaining goals through investment in high payoff areas which initially seem to be unrelated or only weakly linked to the decision [emphasis added].

This perception generally proved to hold true. Three years later, Turoff viewed the technique more precisely within a policy, planning and management framework. He saw the utilization of the cross-impact technique as

---

1. Stovel and Gordon (1978, p. 320–3) describe at least six modifications of the basic concept of cross-impact analysis.

(1975, p. 338): (a) a modelling tool for the analyst; (b) a consistency analysis tool for the decision-maker; (c) a methodology for incorporating policy dependencies in large-scale simulations; (d) a structured Delphi conference for group analysis and discussion efforts; and (e) a component of a lateral and adaptive management information system.

Limits and cautions

Cross-impact analysis suffers from some of the same shortcomings of computer simulation models in general. More specifically, cross-impact analysis has been characterized as having the following weaknesses (Amara, 1975, p. 24):
Only interactions among event/trend pairs are considered.
Multiple accounting of probability assignments can occur because of inherent ambiguities in the nature of the interactions (i.e. one can, if not careful, double-count the impacts on one trend or event in the matrix A on B or B on A).
An adequate theoretical base for probability relationships does not exist.
At present, combinations of three or more event and trend impacts cannot be accounted for in the two-dimensional matrix. Even in a two-dimensional matrix it is difficult to avoid multiple accounting (for example, trend one's impact on trend five, and trend five's impact on trend one). These and other problems are also recognized by Helmer. He states (1976, p. 78–9):

A serious shortcoming of the method to date is the fact that only the interactions among pairs of developments are examined ... even with regard to merely two-dimensional cross impacts, there are still some unresolved technical problems. They have to do with: (1) the avoidance of double accounting; (2) the balancing, over time, of the impact of the occurrence of an event and the impact of its nonoccurrence; and (3) the nature of impacts on trends, specifically, whether they should be considered to be causing persistent shifts in their future course, or gradually declining shifts, or merely temporary blips.

Other techniques

As pointed out earlier, basic cross-impact analysis has been modified in various ways, producing some very useful techniques. One of the most promising is K S I M, which bridges the gap between detailed dynamic models and broader planning issues. K S I M utilizes a group technique and a mathematical forecasting model to focus communication on planning variables. It is most useful in needs identification, problem formulation and promoting dialogue. Other modifications expand or focus the basic cross-impact concepts to assist decision-makers in prioritizing or evaluating alternatives. The Q S I M technique is similar to K S I M, but uses a more subject-specific model formulation.

The early versions of cross-impact models only treated the effects of events on other events. To include trends it was necessary to define them in terms of events. The more recent cross-impact techniques include the impacts of events on other events and the impact of events on trends. K S I M and Q S I M only consider the impact of trends on trends; however, Lipinski and Tydeman (1979) have recently extended K S I M to include both trends and events.

Ideally, cross-impact analysis will produce a working model of the planning environment. The output of the model will assist in clarifying important interrelationships of key variables, promote further communication among planning participants and assist in moving towards desired planning goals. The results of a cross-impact gaming session will be in a quantitative format, expressing revised event probabilities or trend levels based upon the manipulated variables at the beginning of the 'run'. Finally, the mathematical shifts in trend and event values provide substance for discussion and scenario development.

Level of detail and level of confidence

Cross-impact analysis provides relatively precise numerical outputs. Trend outputs are reported within the imposed limits of the model, while event outputs are reported by the number of occurrences (based upon probability and Monte Carlo techniques) over the simulated future of x years.

Outputs of cross-impact analysis are not intended to be 'hard data', rather they are substance for discussing or clarifying problems and alternatives. Like all *Futures* research, results should not be over-believed or acted upon without support from other information sources. The outputs are only as good as the assumptions built into the model and the reliability of input forecasts.

Communicability and credibility of results

One of the strengths of cross-impact gaming is the ease of communicating the results. The output of each simulation 'run' facilitates communication and promotes subsequent exploration of strategies.

Cross-impact gaming is still relatively new and is therefore undergoing substantial development and testing. Many contend that its credibility lies in its ability to promote discussion among planners of different backgrounds and in its educational value.

Cross-impact analysis is a flexible technique which can be utilized for both short- and long-term planning. Usually the inputs, which can be the results of a Delphi exercise, limit cross-impact's utility as a planning method from one to thirty years.

Resources needed and procedures

The required resource for conducting cross-impact analysis includes access to a computer, a cross-impact computer program, a set of forecasts and an experienced monitor, and a project team representing various areas of expertise as required by the subject under evaluation. Setting up a simulation session requires less than a week once the required inputs are available. The estimated cost on one simulation varies, but is usually less than U.S.$5 in computer time.[1]

The procedures for conducting a cross-impact gaming session follow three general phases: a preliminary information/set up phase; a playing/simulation phase; and a results interpretation phase.

PHASE ONE: PRELIMINARY STAGE

Definition of problem boundaries.

Selection of problem team.

Listing a set of important developments (trends and events) with associated forecast levels and probabilities of occurrence (can be obtained by Delphi technique).

Development of a matrix of cross-impact factors describing the paired relationships of all selected developments (assessment of direction, strength etc. of one impact on another).

Input of trend levels, event probabilities and cross-impact factors to the computer—and subsequent calibration of the mathematical model to the forecasts.

PHASE TWO: SIMULATION STAGE

Selecting an event(s) or trend(s) and changing these levels in accordance with anticipated planning action.

Playing the matrix several times, testing various combinations of anticipated actions.

PHASE THREE: INTERPRETING THE RESULTS

Examining the outputs, i.e. the new trend levels and event occurrences, and determining which simulated future consequences are most in line with desired goals.

Case example

INTRODUCTION

This hypothetical example, an application of cross-impact analysis to a planning situation, involves developments in satellite communication over the next

---

1. Versions of cross-impact programs are available in Basic computer language. They can be obtained from the author of this chapter or from the Center for Futures Research, University of Southern California.

thirty years. The hypothetical organization employing this approach designs and manufactures communication satellites and earth stations. The future success of the organization requires that accurate forecasts be made concerning the international and domestic developments affecting communication satellites and related hardware. The issues involved are political, technological, economic, social, cultural and international in scope. The nature of the interaction of these issues was vital information which could be used to determine possible actions which might determine the future directions in this field. It was important, therefore, to develop plans which maximize the planning organization's status culturally, technologically, economically and socially. A team of three planners was formed for this analysis: one with a background in engineering and business, one in the area of communication planning and research, and one international economist with a background in public administration and policy. By balancing the team there was an opportunity to formulate equitable actions which not over emphasize any one approach. The planning group was charged with developing and recommending long-range guidelines and actions which would advance the overall position of the organization.

DEVELOPMENT INCLUDED IN THE ANALYSIS

The future of satellite communication was examined by identifying developments which could have a significant impact on the growth and usage of this mode of communication over the next thirty years. The developments and their estimated values are shown in Table 1. For the purpose of this example, seven events having a reasonable probability of occurring during this period were selected, three in the technological area (E3, E4 and E5), two from the business area (E2 and E6) and two from the international political area (E1 and E7). Nine trends were selected: four that described growth (T1, T2, T5 and T6), two dealing with cost factors (T3 and T4) and three that measured the percentages of certain uses of communication satellites compared with alternative delivery systems (T7, T8 and T9).

Since this study was concerned with forecasting growth, the events selected are the type that could cause significant changes in the field of satellite communication. For example, the ability to launch satellites from a space shuttle would allow them to be heavier and thus have more capacity and higher reliability. In addition, the space shuttle in combination with a space tug could provide the ability to repair and maintain the satellite in synchronous orbit, thus extending satellite lifetimes well beyond the present goal of seven years. Examples of two types of satellite systems operational today are international (Intelsat) and domestic (Anik in Canada and Westar in the United States). Two systems in the late planning stages are a digital-data system and a maritime system (e.g. Inmarsat). Although these two planned systems are not expected to be large with respect to Intelsat, they will represent new satellite services and ground/sea antennae stations, and have a high probability of occurring. The

TABLE 1. Forecasts concerning developments relevant to the future of satellite communication

Events	Estimate of the year by which the probability is			Trends	Estimate of the trend value in		
	10%	50%	90%		1975	1998	2005
E1 United Nations passes Direct Broadcast Satellite Act permitting reception on individual receivers (television), thus bypassing national authorities	80	10	N	T1 The number of transponders in use in communication satellites (present number = 100)	100	300	450
E2 Establishment of an international maritime communication system (separate from the Intelsat system)	76	78	85	T2 The number of Intelsat antennae in operation (present number = 105)	105	175	275
				T3 The cost of a minimum-size (8 m) ground station (transmit and receive) (present level = U.S.$0.5 million)	0.50	0.40	0.45
E3 The ability to repair communication satellites in orbit	87	92	00	T4 The lease cost/half circuit/month from Intelsat (present level = U.S.$705)	705	500	400
E4 The ability to launch communication satellites via the space shuttle	81	84	88	T5 The total number of countries holding membership in Intelsat (present level = 89)	89	115	135
E5 The ability to replenish station-keeping expendables in orbit	87	92	00	T6 The total number of countries and regions having domestic systems (present level = 3)	3	9	13
E6 The placing into operation of a digital-data communication-satellite system	79	82	85	T7 The percentage of total educational instruction, at all levels, delivered by satellite (real-time or delayed, international or domestic) (present value = 3 per cent)	3	15	25
E7 Large-scale participation in Intelsat (or a similar international consortium) by the communist-bloc countries	81	93	N	T8 The percentage of intercultural exchange taking place via satellite (present level = 5 per cent)	5	10	15
				T9 The percentage of business contact taking place via communication satellite links (versus face-to-face contact) (present level = 7 per cent)	7	15	30

United Nations issue (E1) deals with national sovereignty while the Intelsat-communist bloc issue (E7) deals with political ideology.

With regard to the trends, the number of transponders (nominally one television channel or 1,200 telephone circuits) in use is probably the best measure of the global magnitude of satellite communication. The international scope is also measured by the number of Intelsat signatories and the number of Intelsat antennae installed. In the next thirty years much of the growth in traffic will result from the development of domestic and regional systems. An important parameter in the growth curve is cost. Trend 4 (T4) is a measure of the operating cost and Trend 3 (T3) is a measure of the ground-segment capital cost for a large (but smaller than Intelsat) ground station. Trends 7, 8 and 9 (T7, T8 and T9) are measures of public and business uses of satellite communication. Trend 8 (T8) is concerned only with Intelsat or regional usage, whereas the other two include all systems, and the percentages are not comparable since the base values are different.

FORECASTS AS INPUTS

The establishment of the forecasts was done primarily by means of a two-round mini-Delphi-type inquiry. The event and trend-value estimates here should not be taken too seriously, although they reflect reasonable accuracy. Events 1 and 7 (E1 and E7), are political and thus may never have a 90 per cent probability of occurrence. Events 2 and 6 (E2 and E6) were assigned relatively high probabilities (near-term years) because they are currently being planned. Event 4 (E4) also has a high probability, since the space shuttle is NASA's priority programme, whereas Events 3 (E3) and 5 (E5) require additional system development.

CROSS-IMPACT MODEL CONSTRUCTION

Scene values

In this step the effects of interaction among the selected developments were investigated. The time horizon was thirty years and the time span was divided into ten (10) equal segments (scenes), each with a three-year length (see Table 2). In order to get the probability of events and the trend values for each scene, curves were constructed from the available data. For example, for Event 2 (E2), a curve was drawn using the three points: $t = 1976$, $p = 0.10$; $t = 1978$, $p = 0.50$; and $t = 1985$, $p = 0.90$. The scene probabilities were obtained by interpolating the curve for the cumulative probabilities, and then converting these values to scene probabilities. Two example curves for the scene probabilities and trend values are shown in Figures 1 and 2.

The determination of the scene trend values is simpler, as it involves only the construction of a curve and subsequent interpolations. For example, for Trend 5 (T5) the curve was sketched on the basis of three points ($t = 1975$,

TABLE 2. Selected trend values and event probabilities (The future of satellite communication) Number of scenes: ten. Time span: thirty years. Scene length: three years

		Scenes										
Description	I	2	3	4	5	6	7	8	9	IO	C
Events: Probabilities											
E1 United Nations Direct Broadcast Act	0.07	0.04	0.04	0.05	0.04	0.05	0.05	0.04	0.06	0.06	0.4
E2 Establishment of maritime system	0.50	0.48	0.50	0.46	0.50	0.33	0.50	0	0	0	0.7
E3 Ability to repair orbitous satellites	0.02	0.01	0.03	0.05	0.21	0.37	0.31	0.5	0.6	0.7	0.6
E4 Ability to launch from shuttle	0.02	0.08	0.44	0.70	0.73	0.50	0.50	0	0	0	-
E5 Ability to replenish expendables	0.02	0.01	0.03	0.05	0.21	0.37	0.31	0.5	0.6	0.7	0.6
E6 Placing of a digital data system	0.07	0.25	0.51	0.62	0.41	0.50	0.40	0.333	0.50	0	0.7
E7 Communist-bloc participation	0.04	0.06	0.11	0.13	0.16	0.15	0.22	0.25	0.44	0.68	0.2

		Scenes												
Description	I	2	3	4	5	6	7	8	9	IO	II	S	M	C
Trends: Values														
T1 Number of transponders	100	144	186	266	266	300	334	366	398	426	450	25	900	0.6
T2 Number of Intelsat antennae	105	117	131	148	160	175	196	218	237	258	275	20	550	0.5
T3 Ground-station cost	0.5	0.48	0.45	0.42	0.41	0.41	0.42	0.43	0.44	0.445	0.45	0.10	I	0.7
T4 Lease cost/half circuit/month	705	626	584	550	524	500	478	456	436	424	400	50	1410	0.6
T5 Intelsat membership	89	94	99	105	110	115	119	123	127	132	135	6	270	0.2
T6 Number of domestic/regional systems	3	3.8	5	6.4	8	9	9.8	11	11.8	12.7	13	2	26	0.3
T7 Percentage of education	3	5.6	8.2	10.6	13.0	15	16.8	19.4	21.4	23.2	25	4	100	0.6
T8 Percentage of intercultural exchange	5	6	7	8	9	10	11	12	13	14	15	3	100	0.4
T9 Percentage of business contact	7	8	9.3	10.8	12.8	15	18.1	21.3	24.2	27.3	30	4	100	0.6

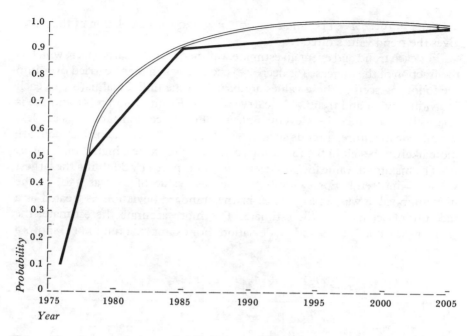

FIG. 1. Event 2: cumulative probability over time

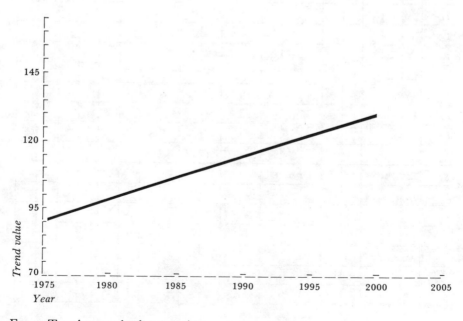

FIG. 2. Trend 5: trend value over time

$n = 89$; $t = 1990$, $n = 115$; and $t = 2005$, $n = 130$). Interpolation of the curve gives the trend values directly.

For each trend and event an estimate was made for the carry-over, which is the fraction of the increase (or decrease) occurring in a scene carried over into the following scene. These values are based on the individual nature of each individual event and trend. The carry-over for Events 1 and 7 (E1 and E7) is relatively small since these events reflect political decisions and thus are less cumulative in nature. Trends such as T1 which involve capital investment are more likely to be felt in the following scene and thus have a higher carry-over.

The maximum value for most trends was computed by doubling the largest value of the trend. For example, the largest value of T1 was 450, so the maximum value was set as 900. S, or the standard deviation, is treated as a measure of accuracy of the estimate. The more accurate the estimate, the smaller the value of the standard deviation. For example, Trend 1 (T1) shows a

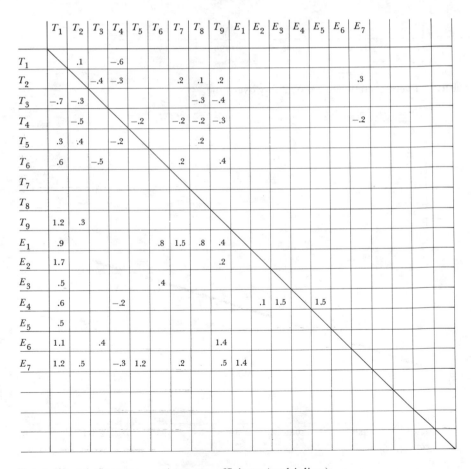

	T_1	T_2	T_3	T_4	T_5	T_6	T_7	T_8	T_9	E_1	E_2	E_3	E_4	E_5	E_6	E_7
T_1		.1		-.6												
T_2			-.4	-.3			.2	.1	.2						.3	
T_3	-.7	-.3					-.3	-.4								
T_4		-.5			-.2		-.2	-.2	-.3						-.2	
T_5	.3	.4		-.2				.2								
T_6	.6		-.5				.2		.4							
T_7																
T_8																
T_9	1.2	.3														
E_1	.9					.8	1.5	.8	.4							
E_2	1.7								.2							
E_3	.5					.4										
E_4	.6			-.2							.1	1.5		1.5		
E_5	.5															
E_6	1.1		.4						1.4							
E_7	1.2	.5		-.3	1.2		.2		.5	1.4						

FIG. 3. Trend of event cross-impact coefficients (multipliers)

standard deviation of 25 units. This can be interpreted as implying a 99.7 per cent probability that the value of the estimates for this trend is within + or − 75 units (3*sd*).

Constructing the cross-impact matrix

Also of concern is the interaction of trends and events on other trends and events. This cross impact requires that predictions be made concerning the movement of each trend or event in relation to movements in each other trend and event. This can be done by following a Delphi procedure of at least two rounds. Planners estimate the cross-impact values. The cross impacts are 'row-on-column', and are stated as the increases in the number of standard deviations in response to an increase of one standard deviation. The sign is negative if the developments move in the opposite direction. For example, the cross-impact of Trend 5 or Trend 2 (T5 and T2) is 0.4. This means that Trend 2 will move in the same direction as Trend 5 and for each standard deviation that Trend 5 moves, Trend 2 will move in the same direction by 0.4 standard deviations. The cross-impact matrix is shown in Figure 3. Two guidelines were followed in the construction of the matrix: (a) only direct effects were included (only A on B, not A on C on B); and (b) double-counting was avoided (although in a few cases A on B and B on A was legitimate and incorporated in the matrix).

The initial check-out run exposes some significant differences between the outcome of the simulation and the Delphi predictions, with the simulation results generally displaying higher values. After a review of the reasons for this, a number of the cross-impact values were decreased to more realistic numbers, and a subsequent 'basic' run reflected much closer agreement with the Delphi forecasts.

Computer model run: check-out and sensitivity simulation

Before proceeding with simulation, the model had to be verified. An initial run was made (ten passes) to check out the event occurrences, trend values and shape of the trend curves. The objective was to achieve reasonable correlation between these values and the values from Figure 2, and to have smooth curves. This initial run, labelled basic run, is shown in Table 3. Next, all the standard deviations and cross impacts were multiplied by 0.6[1] to see if the correlation improved. These results are not shown, because the differences from the basic run were slight. However, all the remaining runs were made with this 0.6 factor and were run ten times.

In order to check out further the internal consistency of the model, two

---

1. After analysis, the outputs were determined to be consistently inflated by the standard deviations and the cross-impact coefficients. The figure 0.6 was a multiplier arrived at by trial and error to deflate the estimates and make the model isomorphic with the experts' forecasts.

TABLE 3. Basic run

Events	Year of occurrence										Total
	1975	1978	1981	1984	1987	1990	1993	1996	1999	2002	
E1	0	1[a]	0	3	0	2	0	0	1	0	7
E2	6	1	1	1	0	0	0	0	0	0	9
E3	0	1	4	2	0	2	0	1	0	0	10
E4	3	1	2	3	1	0	0	0	0	0	10
E5	0	1	0	1	4	2	0	1	1	0	10
E6	1	4	4	1	0	0	0	0	0	0	10
E7	0	0	2	0	2	1	3	1	0	0	9

a. Cell numbers are the number of occurrences out of ten runs.

Trends	Trend value by scene/year										
	0 1975	Scene 1 1978	2 1981	3 1984	4 1987	5 1990	6 1993	7 1996	8 1999	9 2002	10 2005
T1	99.99[b]	156.94	221.29	261.67	295.16	345.71	360.12	395.54	409.24	454.36	484.99
T2	105.00	107.05	132.78	154.71	163.44	192.27	213.99	237.39	265.14	289.45	304.07
T3	0.50	0.47	0.48	0.44	0.44	0.43	0.43	0.41	0.44	0.41	0.42
T4	705.00	631.50	605.66	526.66	508.54	489.64	438.14	427.05	392.09	405.47	388.96
T5	89.00	95.47	101.05	106.13	110.97	120.08	121.78	125.45	128.31	132.79	134.67
T6	3.00	3.79	5.14	6.34	8.87	8.63	9.76	11.46	11.59	12.91	13.19
T7	3.00	5.62	8.04	10.36	14.48	16.77	19.95	20.31	23.10	24.59	26.81
T8	5.00	6.29	6.68	8.20	9.31	9.94	11.24	12.81	13.11	14.94	16.56
T9	7.00	9.19	10.67	11.25	15.18	16.83	20.35	22.59	27.88	32.04	33.69

b. Cell numbers are the average value over ten runs.

TABLE 4. First sensitivity run (0.6 SD; 0.6 XI; E4 in Scene 2).

Events	Year of occurrence										Total
	1975	1978	1981	1984	1987	1990	1993	1996	1999	2002	
E1	0	1	0	3	0	1	0	0	1	0	6
E2	6	1	1	1	0	0	1	0	0	0	10
E3	0	1	5	2	0	1	0	0	0	1	10
E4	3	7	0	0	0	0	0	0	0	0	10
E5	0	1	2	1	3	2	0	0	1	0	10
E6	1	4	4	1	0	0	0	0	0	0	10
E7	0	0	2	0	4	1	1	1	0	0	9

Trends	Trend value by scene/year										
	0 1975	Scene 1 1978	2 1981	3 1984	4 1987	5 1990	6 1993	7 1996	8 1999	9 2002	10 2005
T1	99.98	156.94	228.31	266.85	294.70	352.01	366.36	404.02	412.39	454.51	484.02
T2	105.01	107.05	132.76	156.42	166.73	196.86	222.50	243.93	267.17	291.33	303.81
T3	0.50	0.47	0.47	0.44	0.44	0.42	0.41	0.40	0.43	0.41	0.41
T4	705.00	631.54	599.25	510.95	498.96	470.33	414.33	414.65	378.94	402.89	386.52
T5	89.00	95.48	101.04	106.29	111.27	121.89	122.46	124.46	127.99	132.83	134.54
T6	3.00	3.79	5.14	6.30	8.81	8.64	9.51	11.35	11.40	12.74	13.21
T7	3.00	5.62	8.05	10.41	14.67	17.06	19.98	20.42	23.17	24.62	26.74
T8	5.00	6.29	6.68	8.23	9.40	10.03	11.36	13.03	13.16	14.96	16.52
T9	7.00	9.19	10.66	11.29	15.40	17.23	20.80	23.12	28.03	32.24	33.61

TABLE 5. Second sensitivity run

Events	1975	1978	1981	1984	1987	1990	1993	1996	1999	2002	Total
					Year of occurrence						
EI	0	I	0	3	0	I	0	0	I	0	6
E2	6	4	0	0	0	0	0	0	0	0	IO
E3	0	I	4	2	0	2	0	I	0	0	IO
E4	3	I	2	3	I	0	0	0	0	0	IO
E5	0	I	0	I	4	2	0	I	I	0	IO
E6	I	9	0	9	0	0	0	0	0	0	IO
E7	0	0	2	0	4	I	I	I	0	0	9

Trends	o 1975	Scene 1 1978	2 1981	3 1984	4 1987	5 1990	6 1993	7 1996	8 1999	9 2002	10 2005
					Trend value by scene/year						
TI	100.00	156.93	252.06	302.91	304.36	373.56	394.83	422.76	436.34	481.83	509.41
T2	105.00	107.06	132.78	162.08	175.15	209.33	230.65	254.62	279.20	302.64	317.00
T3	0.50	0.47	0.50	0.44	0.42	0.40	0.38	0.37	0.39	0.37	0.37
T4	705.00	631.47	605.67	477.39	449.10	451.77	383.88	378.55	352.41	367.85	349.22
T5	89.00	95.47	101.05	106.13	112.18	122.46	122.21	125.03	128.67	133.18	135.17
T6	3.00	3.79	5.14	6.34	8.87	8.63	9.60	11.41	11.57	12.90	13.18
T7	3.00	5.62	8.04	10.36	15.17	17.91	20.64	21.21	24.19	25.57	27.77
T8	5.00	6.29	6.68	8.11	9.63	10.44	11.61	13.33	13.58	15.36	16.99
T9	7.00	9.19	12.55	11.40	15.95	18.45	21.85	24.54	29.76	34.11	35.68

sensitivity runs were made. This was accomplished by causing a change in a parameter and observing the change in the results. The first sensitivity run shows the effect of the occurrence of Event 4 (E4), launch from shuttle, in Scene 2 and is shown in Table 4. The value of Event 4 (E4) increased from one in the basic run to seven in this run for Scene 2. Selecting an affected trend for observation, Trend I (TI), which has a cross impact of 0.6, increased from 221 in the basic run to 228 in Scene 2. The second sensitivity run (Table 5) shows the effect of decreasing Trend 4 (T4), lease cost per half circuit, by 100 units in both Scenes 3 and 4. The effect on Trend 2 was an increase from 155 (basic run) to 160 in Scene 4, second run (Table 5), which seems to agree with the direct cross impact of −0.5. These examinations and others led to the conclusions that the model appeared to be assembled and working correctly.

Action determination and simulation[1]

After a review of the Delphi developments three alternatives were selected as possible future actions to be evaluated using the cross-impact model. The descriptions and subsequent consequences are as follows.

1. Compare all action simulation runs to basic run (Table 3) to determine consequences of contemplated actions.

TABLE 6. Simulation of Action step one (0.6 SD; 0.6 XI; T4: − 100 in Scene 3, − 40 in Scene 4)

Events	Year of occurrence										Total
	1975	1978	1981	1984	1987	1990	1993	1996	1999	2002	
EI	0	I	0	2	0	I	0	0	I	0	5
E2	6	I	I	I	0	0	0	0	0	0	9
E3	0	0	3	I	I	2	0	2	0	I	10
E4	3	I	2	3	I	0	0	0	0	0	10
E5	0	I	0	I	3	2	0	I	2	0	10
E6	I	4	4	I	0	0	0	0	0	0	10
E7	0	0	I	I	4	I	I	I	0	0	9

Trends	Trend value by scene/year										
	0	Scene I	2	3	4	5	6	7	8	9	10
	1975	1978	1981	1984	1987	1990	1993	1996	1999	2002	2005
TI	99.98	151.05	200.97	242.00	285.95	327.99	347.27	376.05	392.54	427.73	451.04
TI	105.01	110.74	130.47	160.45	168.39	189.65	209.26	225.84	247.19	267.29	283.42
T3	0.50	0.47	0.46	0.43	0.41	0.42	0.42	0.41	0.44	0.44	0.45
T4	705.00	629.34	499.10	455.61	459.18	446.36	433.92	427.82	408.23	416.46	402.77
T5	89.00	94.89	100.24	106.66	111.09	119.20	121.09	123.52	127.29	131.64	133.99
T6	3.00	3.74	5.01	6.30	8.33	8.74	9.58	11.16	11.62	12.74	13.13
T7	3.00	5.60	8.08	10.75	14.04	16.18	18.54	19.42	21.55	22.89	24.76
T8	5.00	6.16	6.78	8.39	9.28	10.05	11.05	12.21	12.69	14.03	15.42
T9	7.00	8.66	10.04	11.67	14.61	16.35	19.45	21.31	25.04	28.27	30.07

TABLE 7. Simulation of Action step two

Events	Year of occurrence										Total
	1975	1978	1981	1984	1987	1990	1993	1996	1999	2002	
EI	0	I	0	2	0	I	0	0	I	0	5
E2	6	I	I	I	0	0	0	0	0	0	9
E3	0	0	3	I	I	2	0	2	0	I	10
E4	3	I	2	3	I	0	0	0	0	0	10
E5	0	I	0	I	3	2	0	I	2	0	10
E6	I	4	4	I	0	0	0	0	0	0	10
E7	0	0	I	I	3	I	2	I	0	0	9

Trends	Trend value by scene/year										
	0	Scene I	2	3	4	5	6	7	8	9	10
	1975	1978	1981	1984	1987	1990	1993	1996	1999	2002	2005
TI	99.99	151.06	211.47	265.67	302.96	334.35	349.85	378.67	394.37	428.94	452.01
T2	105.00	110.74	130.50	152.48	161.33	185.99	206.26	224.16	246.93	267.33	283.55
T3	0.50	0.47	0.41	0.37	0.38	0.40	0.40	0.41	0.44	0.43	0.45
T4	705.00	629.27	599.13	545.09	502.01	475.11	454.50	438.07	413.32	419.16	404.19
T5	89.00	94.88	100.25	105.20	110.60	118.97	120.92	123.85	127.39	131.68	134.01
T6	3.00	5.74	7.07	6.96	8.55	8.81	9.59	11.16	11.62	12.74	13.13
T7	3.00	5.60	8.51	10.90	13.87	16.06	18.42	19.32	21.50	22.89	24.77
T8	5.00	6.16	6.78	8.20	9.09	9.95	10.97	12.15	12.69	14.03	15.42
T9	7.00	8.66	10.70	12.02	14.64	16.30	19.35	21.25	25.01	28.28	30.10

Action step one involves front-end money for a feasibility study, an analysis and design supporting the maritime system and a digital-data satellite system. Both goals require analysis of traffic patterns, application experiments and the design and development of related hardware and software components. These basic activities have already been initiated, but by adopting this action a considerable organizational commitment (i.e. the expenditure of money and assignment of manpower) would be required. By such actions it is reasonable to expect that the establishment of a maritime satellite system (E2) and a digital-data satellite system (E6) would occur in Scene 2 (1978–80). A simulation run was made of this alternative (Table 6) and the following effects were observed:

The occurrence of E2 and E6 in 1978 had the effect of reducing the likelihood that E1 (United Nations direct broadcast) would occur.

There were subsequent increases in T1 (number of transponders) and in T2 (number of antennae). Slight increases were observed in T7, T8 and T9.

There were subsequent decreases in T3 (cost of earth stations) and T4 (least cost/half circuit).

No changes were observed in T5 and T6.

Action step two was concerned with advancing the total number of domestic and regional systems. Such an action would require increased marketing information and application efforts in potential countries/regions. This requires that additional money and personnel be concentrated on likely countries/regions in order that specific problems and applications would be client-centred. These efforts would require increasing familiarity with national and regional cultures, terrains and decision-makers in order that effective planning and decisions could be made. This action was simulated by increasing T6 by + 2.0 (one standard deviation) in Scenes 2 and 3. The subsequent effects on the total system are as shown in Table 7.

The following effects are observable:

Decrease in the probability of occurrence of E1; T3 (cost of ground stations), T4 (least/cost circuit), T7 (percentage of education), T8 (percentage of inter-cultural exchange) and T9 (percentage of business contact) all show decreases.

There is a smaller decrease in T1 (number of transponders) and T2 (number of antennae).

Trends 5 and 6 remained constant.

Action step three concerned the establishment of a privately/commercially owned digital-data system and the related development and construction of the ground segment to be leased to industrial and governmental customers. This would incur substantial investment costs in the near future on the part of the planning organization. This alternative was simulated by increasing T1 by 48 units (about two standard deviations) in Scenes 1 and 2 and effecting E6 in Scene 1, with the resulting effects as shown in Table 8.

TABLE 8. Simulation of Action step three

Events	Year of occurrence										Total
	1975	1978	1981	1984	1987	1990	1993	1996	1999	2002	
EI	0	1	0	2	0	0	1	0	0	0	4
E2	6	1	1	1	0	0	0	0	0	0	9
E3	0	1	4	2	0	2	0	1	0	0	10
E4	3	1	2	3	1	0	0	0	0	0	10
E5	0	1	0	1	4	2	0	1	1	0	10
E6	10	0	0	0	0	0	0	0	0	0	10
E7	0	0	3	2	2	0	1	1	0	0	9

Trends	Trend value by scene/year										
	0	Scene 1	2	3	4	5	6	7	8	9	10
	1975	1978	1981	1984	1987	1990	1993	1996	1999	2002	2005
TI	147.98	231.40	294.74	315.05	352.95	414.58	418.26	448.15	461.93	500.82	524.96
T2	105.01	111.92	161.49	189.43	202.35	230.77	252.24	271.05	292.41	315.15	327.72
T3	0.50	0.51	0.48	0.37	0.35	0.33	0.39	0.32	0.35	0.33	0.34
T4	705.00	529.30	482.55	398.37	400.41	379.42	337.65	350.92	326.67	338.66	329.76
T5	89.00	95.48	103.45	108.73	113.78	121.65	122.56	125.68	128.97	133.72	135.61
T6	3.00	3.79	5.14	6.34	8.71	8.59	9.41	11.51	11.60	12.72	13.11
T7	3.00	5.62	8.79	12.03	16.51	19.09	21.63	22.62	25.37	26.33	28.61
T8	5.00	6.29	7.01	9.04	10.45	11.06	12.19	14.02	14.10	15.78	17.48
T9	7.00	11.61	12.52	13.29	18.66	20.64	24.56	26.98	32.12	36.16	37.69

A decrease was observed in the likelihood that EI (United Nations direct broadcast) would occur. Trend decreases were observed in T3 (cost of ground station) and T4 (least cost/half circuit).

Increases occurred in TI (number of transponders) and T2 (number of antennae) and slight increases in T7, T8 and T9.

Conclusions of simulation runs

The alternatives have been simulated with the model. In reality, the final decisions would be made with the information provided by each simulation run augmented by other sources of information. Disregarding the costs of implementing any of the actions for the moment, the planning organization would probably select Action step three. The rationale for this choice over options one and two is as follows: Action step three has a stronger positive effect on TI (number of transponders) and T2 (number of antennae), which are two products that the organization manufactures. In addition, option three increases the trend values of T7 and T8 and T9 decreases the cost of ground stations and lease cost/channel, a benefit to the potential users.

The second choice would be Action step one. This has some of the positive outcomes of option three, but lacks the intensity in the desired effects. Option two is the least attractive of the three alternatives. It both decreases the trend values concerned with the organization's products and increases the costs of ground stations and lease costs to users. Option two effects dramatic changes of a positive nature in scenes directly following the policy decision, but does not have any positive long-term effect on the system and therefore is judged less desirable.

Conclusions and recommendations

The computer model appears to be reasonably well constructed and internally consistent. Once the model was 'run', the results confirmed that the developments which were selected were strongly biased towards growth. If the study was to be continued, the following changes might be made to introduce some negative developments: (a) combine E3 and E5 into a single event and replace E5 with, 'spacecraft stabilization problems arise, leading to doubts about raliability'; (b) add Trend 10, reading, 'the number of half-cricuits available in submarine cables for overseas communication'; (c) add additional cultural or social trends (indicators); and (d) add additional trends and events to increase the scope of the model.

Although the data used in this analysis are unrefined, cross-impact analysis appears to be applicable to this type of alternative simulation and planning. It can be concluded that as a supplement to other specific forecasting models, cross-impact gaming would greatly increase the reliability and effectiveness of the long-range planning activity.

Annotated bibliography

ALTER, S. 1976. *The Mathematics of Time-Dependent Cross Impact Modeling or Everything I Think I Know about This Topic*. Los Angeles, Calif., University of Southern California, Center for Futures Research. Alter details some of the underlying and internal workings of cross-impact gaming.

AMARA, R. 1975. *Some Methods of Futures Research*. Menlo Park, Calif., Institute for the Future. Overview of futures research methods with word discussion of cross-impact gaming strengths and weaknesses.

ENZER, S. 1975. *Cross-Impact Methods in Assessing Long-Term Oceanographic Changes*. Paper presented at the International Conference on Technological Assessment and reprinted by the Center for Futures Research, University of Southern California (Los Angeles, Calif.). General discussion of cross-impact analysis including its use and procedures as applied to oceanographic futures.

GORDON, T.J. 1972. The Current Methods of Futures Research. In: A. Toffler, *The Futurist*. New York, N.Y., Random House. Early discussion of interests of cross-impact analysis as well as procedures for conducting cross-impact analysis.

GRAY, P.; HELMER, O. 1974. *California Futures Study—Analysis of Impacts for Transportation Planning*. Los Angeles, Calif., University of Southern California, Center for Futures Research. Good description of an actual application of cross-impact gaming to planning.

HELMER, O. 1973. *Accomplishments and Prospects of Futures Research*. Los Angeles, Calif., University of Southern California, Center for Futures Research.

LIPINSKI, H.; TYDEMAN, J. 1978. Cross-Impact Analysis: Extended K S I M. *Futures*, Vol. 11, No. 2, p. 151–4. Latest version of K S I M description and its abilities to handle both trend and event cross-impact simulation.

STOVEL, J.G.; GORDON, T.J.; FOWLES, J. (eds.). 1978. Cross Impact Analysis. *Handbook of Futures Research*, p. 301–28.

WEDEMEYER, D.J. 1978. Cross Impact Analysis as a Methodology for Communication Policy and Planning. In: S.A. Rahim *et al.*, *Planning Methods, Models, and Organizations. A Review Study for Communication Policy Making and Planning*, p. 156–62. Honolulu, Hawaii, East–West Communication Institute. A chapter on the application of cross-impact analysis to communication planning problems. Included also is a discussion of the mathematical assumptions of cross-impact analysis and procedures for building a model.

Chapter 11

Input–output analysis

Meheroo Jussawalla

Marc U. Porat

Input–output analysis serves a major purpose of emphasizing the interrelatedness of the many decision-makers who comprise the economy of a country. Wassily Leontief (1961) claims that input–output as a method is applicable both to general equilibrium analysis, i.e. at the macro level, and industry-specific analysis at the micro level. Therefore, the effects of a micro-economic change, such as technical progress within one industry, can be traced across the entire economy. The essence of input–output analysis lies in its ability to bring out the intricate interrelationships between the various sectors or industries of an economy. Consider, for example, the repercussions of a 10 per cent increase in the output of the machine-goods sector. This means that there will be a 10 per cent increase in the production of all the outputs of machine goods which are used as inputs in the other productive sectors of the economy. It also means that, because each sector which supplies inputs to the machinery sector must expand its output, those supplying sectors will in turn require more inputs from other sectors. All these repercussions call for still further adjustments. The crucial point is that the degree of interrelatedness in an input–output matrix is such that a change in any one 'cell' or 'box' in the table will bring about a chain reaction on all the other cells and boxes, exemplifying the interrelatedness of economic activity.

Why is a knowledge of general equilibrium analysis important? Is an understanding of interrelationships between prices and sectors vital to planners and decision-makers who allocate resources? Up to a point, at least, such an understanding is an indispensable tool in evaluating the overall operation of the economy and specifically helps communication planners to focus on the sector producing information and communication goods and services. For example, if a policy change favours protective tariffs levied on Japanese television receiver sets and microprocessors, the immediate effect is to increase the price of the imported equipment and thereby increase the demand for American-made similar products. The result is that output and employment will rise in the American part of the communication industry related to television receiver sets and microprocessors. But this ignores the fact that Japanese incomes will decline as a result of their inability to sell in the

American market. With smaller incomes, the Japanese ability to buy American exports of machine tools or chemicals or some other exports may decline. The obvious initial increase in employment in America is offset, wholly or in part, by the indirect declines in other American export industries. Therefore, general equilibrium analysis reminds us that the extra resources which are shifted into the expanding communication industry must come from other industries.

Our interest in input–output analysis is not merely pedogogical, but is derived from the empirical measurement of the various interactions between sectors of the economy. These measurements are an instrument of economic forecasting and prediction. In a developing economy, input–output analysis enables planners to determine how realistic and feasible planned production targets are and how far adjustments can be made on an intersectoral basis within technological constraints and scarce resources.

The fact that imperfect competition generally exists in product and resource markets detracts from the price system's capacity to allocate resources efficiently. Input-output analysis provides a tool for focusing on interdependent sectors and their measurement. The perfect competition of the marketplace, and the operation of the 'invisible hand' meshing divergent economic activities, gets replaced by planning. It organizes and co-ordinates economic activities, and perfect competition is abandoned in favour of 'perfect computation by the bureaucrats' (Kohler, 1977, p. 409–15).

Definition

An input–output table shows the web of interrelationships in a hypothetical economy by listing the flows of various commodities and services between their suppliers and recipients. It is made up of columns and rows. The columns show sets of inputs during the period for which the table is drawn up. Each row contains information about how the output of a particular sector is allocated among the various recipients. Boulding (1966, p. 88) defines the analysis as 'a matrix which shows how much of the output of each sector becomes input for every other sector'. A simplified version may be presented as in Table 1.

TABLE 1. Input–output matrix

	Durables	Non-durables	Services	Construction	Total output
Durables	30	30	40	20	120
Non-durables	40	40	70	30	180
Services	40	80	100	10	230
Construction	10	30	20	10	70
TOTAL INPUT	120	180	230	70	600

Assumptions

In Table 1 we have assumed that input equals output for each sector. If this does not operate in this manner, there would be surplus accumulation of commodities, or unemployment or overemployment of services. It is also assumed that production takes place under constant returns to scale and that household demand is constant.

By far the most notorious assumption in the input—output methodology is the assumption of fixed coefficients. If a unit increase in input always produces the same increase of output, then we can calculate coefficients for each cell of the above matrix. Such coefficients show the quantities of inputs, required by the average producer in the industry, per unit of industry output. This assumption of fixed coefficients gives us room for price changes and technical substitution changes. Demand changes with a change in prices and/or a change in income. The problem of capturing these changes in the input—output table is difficult though not insurmountable. Technical coefficients represent the flow of physical goods and services translated into money (at producer's prices) by the use of unit prices. Experimental changes can be made in these coefficients and interpreted in useful ways. For example, we can ascertain the effect on prices of all goods and services of a sustained 10 per cent per year drop in the price of electronic components. Or we can measure the total output and impacts on labour of intensified use of computer and telecommunications resources in the manufacturing sector of the economy. The assumption we use is one of holding the requirement for computing capacity and/or telecommunication services constant so that total demand for all outputs will decrease in proportion to the drop in price.

History

In the eighteenth century (1758) the physiocrat economist François Quesnay first envisaged the Tableau Économique, which presented a circular flow of economic life. The central concern of classical political economy was accumulation; the neo-classics substituted general equilibrium in a stationary state. A century ago Leon Walras, the pioneer in mathematical economics, worked out a simple model of general equilibrium. He postulated that there are known methods of production of each commodity and that, in the market-place, the prices and output of all commodities can be arrived at by a process of bargaining (haggling). The equilibrium prices arrived at would be better than what any individual can do for himself. Economists after Walras realized that it is not possible to reach equilibrium price by trial and error, so they postulated the conditions necessary to ensure that at least one position of equilibrium exists (see Robinson and Eatwell, 1973, p. 183, 283-4).

Von Neuman (1953) described an economic model in which everything can be produced out of everything. All the fruits of production are ploughed back into the system for growth of more of the same output. This approach is particularly relevant for developing countries aspiring for balanced growth through a stream of inputs and outputs.

The first set of national accounts providing data on production relationships between industries was compiled by the Soviet Central Statistical Administration in the 1920s. Feldman's model related the influence of the composition of final output on the overall structure of production in the Soviet five-year plans. Leontief's first practical application of input–output economics came during the Second World War, when he investigated the dislocations that might occur as the United States shifted from a wartime to a peacetime economy. He constructed an inter-industry tableau like Quesnay's, using input-output tables (Leontief, 1951). As part of the price that Leontief had to pay to make Walras's general equilibrium empirically measurable, he was forced to make the technical assumption that all proportions of factors of production entering the table as inputs are technologically fixed or constant (see Samuelson, 1976, p. 754–5).

Over forty countries, developed and developing, free-market and centrally planned, have computed input–output tables as an amplification of their national income data and as a tool for developmental planning.

Theory

In theory, input–output analysis is a method of accounting for the cycle of production, as it repeats itself from year to year, to enable net output to be distinguished in physical as well as value terms. The input–output tables used in national accounting are made from the statistics of actual output. These are collected in the first instance in terms of money values (dollars, say). The statistics do not represent pure physical quantities and the values depend on the level of gross margins in the markets in which they are sold.

Piero Sraffa devised (1966) a model for studying the problem of profits in an actual economy. In its simplest form this model looks at the production of each commodity in a period of time, using a particular amount of labour time (assuming all workers are alike) and particular inputs of other commodities. At the beginning of each period, there are stocks of the inputs in existence. These stocks are entirely used up in the process of production and re-created by the same process. The excess of output over the replacement of necessary inputs is the net output of the period. These physical data do not tell us how the net output is divided between wages and profits. The point of Sraffa's theory was to show that the value of a stock of capital has no meaning independently of the distribution of net product between wages and profit.

The first general equilibrium models of Walras, Sraffa and others were purely theoretical treatments of an ideal economy and not empirically soluble. The usefulness of input–output analysis lies in the numerical solution it provides for a wide class of problems, with immediate policy-planning relevance. Figure 1 shows that inter-industry flows form the heart of the matrix. The transactions shown also include the flow to the final demand sectors and

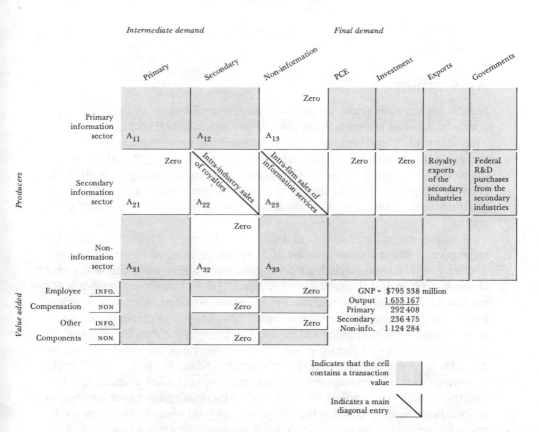

FIG. 1. Input–output schematic diagram showing the primary and secondary information sector

the value added generated by each industry. The figure provides a simplified overview showing primary and secondary sectors. To read the table the following points should be noted:

1. The output of each industry is distributed across the row to other firms (intermediate demand) and to final consumers.
2. The purchases, or inputs, of each firm are composed down the column of each industry in the intermediate sectors, including an input of value added.
3. The margins of the table are identical to the consolidated national income and products accounts of a country, i.e. total GNP is the sum of all final demand purchases (equal in the aggregate to value added).
4. The 'technical coefficients' show each industry's composition of inputs directly necessary to produce $1.00 of gross output.
5. If production occurs under constant returns to scale (let us assume it does) then Leontief provides the technique of matrix inversion to allow planners to calculate all effects of changes (direct and indirect) generated by a $1.00 increase in final demand. Since all industries are interdependent, a change

225

in demand for one industry's output generates a 'ripple' throughout the economy.

Applications

Input–output method can be used for several applications in predicting and planning. Central planners might look at this year's GNP and might not like what they find. They might prefer to have more capital equipment or increase the stockpiles of corn by 20 million tons per year. They might wish to reduce payments for imports to zero. The plan document incorporating all these changes would be worked into a new input–output matrix to represent a picture of desired future economic activity. It is therefore a useful tool for goal-setting.

Another useful application of this method lies in predicting the consequences of technological change. If a particular technology increases productivity of a resource (such as fibre optics for television) this will cause changes in price and demand for television. These changes can be explicitly modelled by changing the technical coefficients. Similarly a change in factor prices, such as wage rates or interest rates, can change the prices of output. A wage change in a particular occupation can change the output prices of all goods and services in the economy. If wage increases are compensated by productivity increases, then the net inflationary impact would be zero. Supply conditions can be investigated by changing the technical coefficients. For example, if office automation is introduced by increasing computer inputs and terminal equipment, reducing the compensation paid to clerical support workers, what would be the total effect on prices, employment and output? (Yan, 1969, p. 73–5).

Another useful application of input–output analysis for development planners is in the area of balanced-growth strategic planning. In the face of labour, capital, natural resources and skills limitations, planning for balanced growth is necessary in order to avoid bottlenecks. Analysis to counteract bottlenecks extends input–output techniques to include linear programming. This involves projections of alternative final-demand objectives as constrained by factor limitations or capacity bottlenecks (Cameron, 1968, p. 46–61, 69–81). For example, planning rural home telephone services may face a bottleneck if there is a small or non-existent electronics-component industry or an inadequate supply of technical workers. Any industry's growth can be hampered by bottlenecks in some remote part of the economy. Conversely, any industry may itself become a bottleneck in the expansion of some other remotely linked sector. Balanced-growth analysis, then, is a technique for identifying the bottlenecks in the economy and determining which policy will carry the economy forward on the development path.

Procedures for the use of input–output tables in communication planning

The most significant use of the input–output (I–O) matrix for a developing country is comparative structural analysis, which is a qualitative I–O technique identifying a country's stage of technological development. National planners can devise specific plans to move a country in a chosen direction (Leontief, 1963). Two methods are used for such analysis: (1) triangulating the technology matrix; (2) developing self-sufficiency or 'skyline' charts.

1. The technology matrix is a complete picture of the structural relationships of an economy at a given time. Industries are arranged by an arbitrary census classification code. Figure 2 shows a completely hierarchical structure. The shaded cells represent linkages between industries. Industry 1, at the top, is structurally the deepest on the input side because any change in the final demand for the output of Industry 1 would spark a round of purchases by Industry 1 for the outputs of all other industries. By contrast, Industry 5 is the shallowest because changes in the demand for its products have no effect on other industries. If there is structural depth on the input side, the planner knows which industries are candidates for development.

On the other hand, Industry 5 is structurally deep on the output side, since it sells most of its output to intermediate demand and almost none to final demand. Since all other industries depend on Industry 5, a critical failure (e.g. mismanagement, poor productivity, destruction by strike or war) will severely

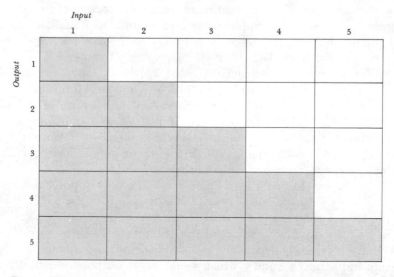

FIG. 2. Triangularized input–output matrix: hierarchical structure

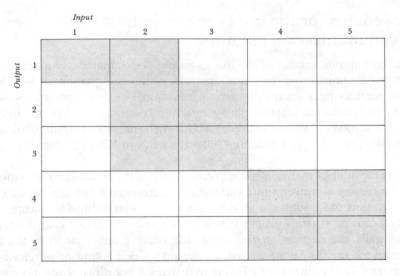

Fig. 3. Triangularized input–output matrix: block independence

damage the whole economy. Conversely, if Industry 1 is wiped out, the rest of the economy will not lack for supplies, but it will suffer a serious loss in demand. In less-developed economies, a high-technology industry typically enters the economy either as a direct investment by a foreign multinational or as a project financed by an international capital fund. A specific example is a computer-terminal assembly factory. Industries of this sort are often structurally shallow on the input side (e.g. Industry 5), since they make very little demand on the endemic and often more traditional sectors of the economy. Explosive growth in the employment and output of a shallow industry, through mass hiring and a large contribution to the exports ledger of final demand, does not ripple back through the economy to any great extent, and general development is not materially aided. However, the traditional industries (e.g. Industry 1) may be technically obsolete, and large infusions of capital may not yield long-run development either. A planning problem frequently posed is to take a middle industry, such as Industry 3, and 'build' it into a deep sector by investing in the prior industries in the input chain. Balanced development is achieved by encouraging growth in an entire production sequence that involves the greatest number of already existing sectors.

The top sector (Industry 1) in Figure 3 is an isolate—it purchases nothing from any other industry, and only sells its output to Industry 2. If this sector also produces a small amount of final demand or income, it plays a very small role in the economy. If, on the other hand, it represents a large share of GNP, the country is critically dependent on its well-being, and should develop the 'missing' industries (3, 4 and 5) which would buy its output domestically. Here is an example of a policy to develop structural depth on the output side. The industries of the second block (2 and 3) are independent on the output side, since they only sell the goods internal to the block. They are mildly independent on the input side, although Industry 3 purchases goods from the third block. The last group is completely decoupled on the input side, and only makes contact with Industry 3 through intermediate sales.

These block dependencies and independencies reveal weaknesses in a country's development. A mature economy, in which balanced growth has occured, typically shows no block independence—all cells of the matrix either are full or are triangularized hierarchically. As economies develop, blocks become smaller and smaller. There is more 'circularity' in the economy, with industries trading among themselves. Once a methodologically tractable scheme is developed, it can be applied to the economies of many other countries.

2. A useful method of comparing the I–O structures of several countries is by building 'skyline charts' of the sectoral blocks. A skyline chart summarizes the importance of these sectors in relation to other sectors, and shows whether the block is self-sufficient. Figure 4 shows the skyline charts for a developed economy and a less-developed economy. A quick qualitative survey reveals that: (a) the developed economy has a fairly level profile, with most industries producing between 80 and 120 per cent of the economy's domestic requirements, whereas the less-developed economy has a very jagged skyline, with industries producing from 20 to 250 per cent of the economy's internal requirements; (b) the developed economy's blocks are roughly the same width, indicating that their share of GNP is nearly equal, whereas some industries in the less-developed economy are clearly dominant, others almost non-existent.

The two skylines in Figure 4 condense a great deal of information useful for national planning. For example, assume that the less-developed country has decided (for whatever reason) to shape its technical development after the developed country shown in Figure 4. An analyst would quickly point out that almost every pattern is inconsistent: Whereas the DC skyline shows Industries 1, 2, 4 and 5 as slightly more than self-sufficient, the LDC skyline shows that Industries 1 and 4 are highly dependent on imports, and Industry 2 is over-invested in terms of its output capacity. Whether resources can be shifted out of Industry 2 and into Industry 4 is problematic. Similarly, resources should be shifted out of Industry 5 and moved into the ailing Industries 1 and 4 to achieve a less jagged skyline. Industry 2 in the less-developed country is suspect, since it seems to produce much more output than is required internally, but generates negligible GNP. The industry is probably shallow structurally, and not particularly worthy of development. A balanced-growth programme for the less-developed country would by necessity involve harmonizing changes in one sector with the impacts on all other sectors. It is conceivable that, after all aspects are considered, the LDC will reject the development profile suggested by the DC skyline, and look for a different model.

The developed country is more mature. It is not 'suffering' dependencies

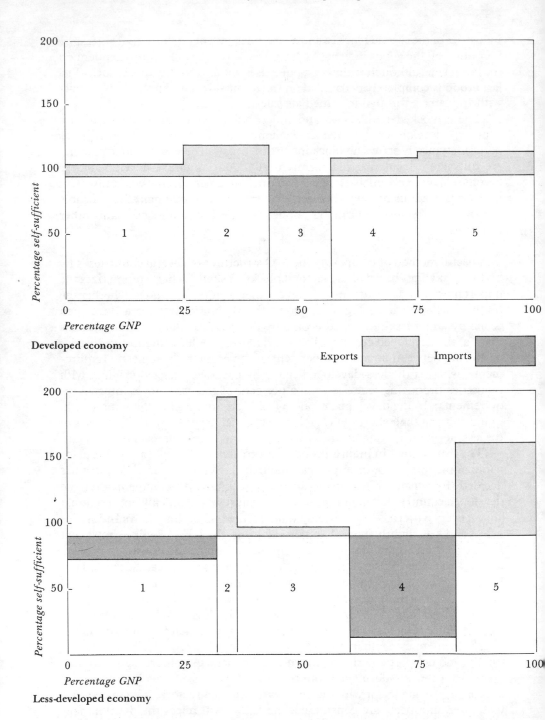

FIG. 4. Model skyline charts of a developed and less-developed economy

on either the import or the export side. Therefore, a trade embargo or a loss of trading partners would not severely hamper its internal stability. There is no economic presumption against total specialization by one industry other than a political distaste for vulnerability. The less-developed country may be perfectly rational in keeping Industry 4 heavily dependent on imports if there are no strategic uncertainties about supply and if the country has no comparative advantage in producing the goods. By symmetry, the developed country's GNP could rise if it allowed itself to enter into more dependencies. These are issues that can be investigated using the I–O matrix.

Case example: a compensated defence cut

In 1961, Leontief published a now classic application of input–output analysis. Porat followed his experiment to illustrate the use of the primary information matrix.

The 'arms race' and its economic impact on the United States entered the public consciousness during the late 1950s. President Eisenhower, whose loyalty to both the military and the private industry was resolute, ended his term in 1960 with a surprise warning that the 'military-industrial complex' was a creature to be restrained. Casual evidence persuaded many people that corporate interests were so finely enmeshed with military expansion that arms build-ups began to carry an imperative independent of stated public policy. Could the United States, as a nation, afford *not* to engage in stockpiling increasingly expensive and sophisticated war machines? This question was tackled by Leontief and Hoffenberg, and brought to the public attention in a *Scientific American* article published in 1961. The authors concluded that the economic effects of disarmament might not be as severe as the most fearful suspected. In equilibrium, revenues lost as a result of cuts in defence spending would be reallocated to other final-demand sectors. Certain industries would indeed be hard hit: the ordnance industry would suffer (in 1958) a 19.2 per cent drop in employment given an $8,000 million (or 20 per cent) defence cut; the aircraft industry would experience a 17.9 per cent unemployment rate; and the ships and boats industry would lose 11 per cent of its employees. But other industries would gain, especially those selling to personal consumption and to the non-defence portions of government. The net impact on 1959 employment of a 20 per cent compensated defence cut would be a mild 0.2 per cent increase in unemployment for the total economy. The experiment is now even more relevant, as advanced communication and computing technologies are an integral part of the American defence arsenal. One might expect a strong argument against defence cuts from the industries which supply information goods and services.

Porat reproduced the Leontief experiment for the 1967 economy using somewhat different assumptions. Leontief allocated the money saved by disarmament on a pro rata basis to all other final-demand categories. The experiment reported in this section returns the defence cut in the form of a 3 per cent

TABLE 2. Total net output of a compensated defence spending cut ($ millions, 1967)

Selected industries	Information industries	Non-information industries
Gainers		
69 Wholesale and retail trade, net		2 778
14 Food and kindred products		2 255
71 Real estate and rental, net		2 101
70* Finance and insurance components	1 065	
1 Livestock and products		759
2 Other agriculture products		607
18 Apparel		580
77 Medical, education services and non-profit organizations		580
68 Electrical, gas, sanitary services		564
77* Medical, educational, non-profit	435	
59 Motor vehicles and equipment		407
71* Real estate: fees, royalties and office rent	386	
69* Trade margins on information goods	383	
16 Fabrics, yarn and thread mills		265
29 Drugs, cleaning, toilet preparations		253
73* Repair: radio and television equipment	253	
66* Telecommunications, excluding radio and television	199	
15 Tobacco manufacturers		196
31 Petroleum refining and related industries		176
79 State and local-government enterprises		135
24 Paper, allied products excluding containers, net		132
8 Crude petroleum and natural gas		119
34 Footwear and other leather products		113
54 Household appliances		101
Losers		
60 Aircraft and parts		−2 228
13 Ordnance and accessories		−1 437
56* Radio, television, communication equipment	−1 112	
57* Electronic components	−447	
37 Primary iron and steel manufacturing		−335
38 Primary non-ferrous metal manufacturing		−313
80 Imports		−296
27 Chemicals and products, net		−184
11 New construction, net		−176
62* Mechanical measuring and control instruments	−145	
53 Electrical industrial equipment and apparatus, net		−142
65 Transportation and warehousing		−126
50 Machine-shop products		−114
49 General industrial machines and equipment		−101
TOTAL NET IMPACT	1 267	7 294

*The two-digit input–output industries marked with an asterisk are the reaggregated information industries. All non-information components were 'removed' at the six-digit level.

TABLE 3. Net impact on output and employment of a 20 per cent compensated cut in defence spending

Industries	Output ($ millions, 1967)			Employment (thousands of jobs, 1967)		
	Total	Direct	Indirect	Total	Direct	Indirect
Total	*+ 8 563*	*5 658*	*2 905*	*+ 598*	*447*	*151*
Information	1 268	628	640	121	92	29
Non-information	7 295	5 030	2 265	477	355	122

reduction of individual income taxes in 1976. Hence, the entire amount saved by the defence cutback is 'spent' experimentally by households in the form of personal consumption.

SUMMARY OF CASE EXAMPLE

A 20 per cent cut and a corresponding rise in personal consumption expenditures leads to a slight *increase* in output and employment, as summarized in Table 3. A reduction of $14,266 million in defence spending, matched by a compensating rise in household expenditures, resulted in a net *gain* of $8,600 million in output and 598,000 jobs. The information industries as a group gained about $1,300 million in output, and increased their labour requirements by 121,000 jobs; the non-information industries enjoyed a $7,300 million gain in output, and 'hired' 477,000 workers. (Note that these results are based on 1976 technology, using naïve assumptions regarding defence cutbacks, price movements and consumers' income elasticities of demand.) Table 3 shows the detailed output effects on selected industries. Labour-force changes can similarly be decomposed into total, direct and indirect impacts. It can be seen from Table 2 that input–output analysis can enable communication planners to identify major related changes in the economy—such as simultaneous growth in finance and insurance components (70) and the non-broadcasting telecommunications (66) which serve them—with profound implications for the planning of communication systems.

Annotated bibliography

BOULDING, K. E. 1966. *Economic Analysis*.Vol. II, *Macroeconomics*, New York, N.Y., Harper & Row.

CAMERON, B. 1968. *Input–Output Analysis and Resource Allocation*. Cambridge, Cambridge University Press.

KOHLER, H. 1977. *Scarcity and Freedom*. Lexington, Mass., D. C. Heath.

LEONTIEF, W. 1941. *The Structure of the American Economy: An Empirical Application of Equilibrium Analysis*. Cambridge, Mass., Harvard University Press.

——. 1951. *The Structure of the American Economy 1919–1939*. 2nd edn. Fair Lawn, N.J., Oxford University Press. In his quest for a model of a real world economy Leontief used large input–output tables based on the U.S. Department of Labor Statistics figures and covering hundreds of industries. These input–output tables are meant to show the relationship between sectors of the economy when the products that are outputs of firms in one sector become inputs of another sector. These tables first constructed for the U.S. economy by Leontief are adopted for gross national product accounts and development planning in France, India, the United Kingdom and other countries. Leontief rendered general equilibrium empirically measurable. In order to do this he made the technical assumption that all factor proportions to each other and to the total output are technologically fixed or constant. In this input–output model, Leontief keeps the demand sector outside the production economy. The planner uses such a table to forecast the effects of changing consumption requirements.

——. 1963. The Structure of Development. *Scientific American*, September, p. 148.

NEUMAN, J. VON; MORGENSTERN, D. 1953. *The Theory of Games and Economic Behavior*. 3rd ed. Princeton, N.J., Princeton University Press.

ROBINSON, J.; EATWELL, J. 1973. *Introduction to Modern Economics*. Maidenhead, McGraw-Hill. The book is a simple analysis of doctrines, methodology and modern problems for those who have no previous training in economics. It deals succinctly with the operation of capitalist economies. A simplified model is used to discuss effective demand, the short-peroid distribution of income between wages and profits, and technical progress. The parameters of the model are gradually relaxed as the discussion grows more complex. Book 2 in the same volume introduces some theoretical problems of planning under a controlled, centralized system. Since economic relationships do not lend themselves easily to smooth mathematical functions, the authors have constructed numerical examples and diagrams to enlighten the lay reader. The book explains problems of policy-making, in its concluding section.

SAMUELSON, P.A. 1971. *Economics*. 10th ed. New York, N.Y., McGraw-Hill

SRAFFA, P. 1960. *The Production of Commodities by Means of Commodities*. Cambridge, Cambridge University Press. In this book Sraffa uses an input/output method to arrive at a unique standard ratio which is such that the ratio of outputs in every sector is the same as the ratio of inputs. It is a system similar to von Neuman's except that in the Sraffa work there emerges a surplus which enters the consumption stream, so that there is no growth. Unlike von Neuman's system, in which the rate of profits equals the rate of growth, Sraffa does not permit growth because the entire surplus is consumed. No portion of the surplus is saved and invested. He describes the distribution of labour in the input-output matrix in terms of a process multiplier.

In the Sraffa model in its simplest from, the production of each commodity in a given period of time (say one year) requires a particular amount of labour time and particular inputs of commodities. At the beginning of each period there are stocks in existence of the inputs required for a particular rate of output. When the economy is in a stationary state, reproducing itself from period to period, there is no net investment and all net profits are consumed. The physical data cannot tell us how the net output is divided between wages and profits. The point of Sraffa's argument was to show that the 'value of the stock of capital', in general, has no meaning independently of the distribution of net product between wages and profits. There is no meaning in the concept that the rate of profit is determined by the marginal product of capital.

YAN, C. 1969. *Introduction to Input–Output Economics*. New York, N.Y., Holt, Rinehart & Winston.

Chapter 12

Compact policy assessment (Compass)

Barclay M. Hudson

Compact policy assessment (Compass) is a workshop format designed to summarize succinctly the pros and cons of policy proposals. It can be used to crystallize immediate decisions, specify short-term research agendas or provide a forum for wide participation in policy design. Compass offers a structured procedure for rapidly pooling a diversity of informed opinion. It can also be applied to validation of forecasts, or for exploring policy implications of completed research. The time span is variable, from a minimum session of one hour to follow-up actions running into weeks.

Compass can be used by itself or as a complement to other methods. Its main advantages are that it is low in cost, easily organized and carried out, involves no analytical skills apart from the role of moderator, thrives on diversity among participants, emphasizes conciseness in reporting results and maintains a strong focus on practical policy implications.

Definition

Compass is a specialized tool for compact policy assessment:[1] a brief structured conference of diverse participants, guided by a moderator, to elicit pros and cons on a policy proposal. Key points of debate are recorded on long sheets of paper for immediate decision or investigative follow-up. Debate may be orientated towards formulating new policies, or alternatively to evaluate ongoing programmes, validate research findings or design information systems for future monitoring of uncertainties. The final written product is a concise summary of points ranged on each side of a policy debate, specifying areas of

---

1. Compact policy assessment consists of various procedures for intensive short-term formative evaluation of programmes and proposals, stressing: (a) diversity of analytical methods and data sources (using informed judgement as well as quantitative information previously available); (b) early specification of concrete action possibilities (even if hypothetical); (c) use of composite (cross-disciplinary and cross-jurisdictional) task-force investigation teams detached from their normal institutional setting; (d) succinct iterative reporting schedules, for incorporation of critical reactions by diverse interested parties; and (e) explicit recognition of insoluble issues, to maintain focus on productive investigation.

consensus and disagreement, key assumptions and an action agenda for research on critical uncertainties.

Assumption, history and main uses

Compass relies on pooling judgements to yield answers where 'hard data' are not immediately available, or where raw facts and numbers fail to capture qualitative subtleties of policy choice. Judgements are assumed to incorporate objective evidence, but they also reflect participants' personal experience, training and intuitions. Compass recognizes that consensus is not always possible in policy debate; nor is it always desirable, given the possibilities of choice between alternative futures. It emphasizes independent thinking by participants, and it assumes that paper-and-pencil questionnaires limit the range of policy debate, distracting people from drawing most fully on their own experiences and perceptions and restricting the creative tensions of face-to-face dialogue.

To protect against the imposition of views by 'authority figures' and to preserve independent critical thinking, Compass relies on a number of devices:
Systematic confrontation of all statements with exploratory counter-statements.
Clear separation of the workshop phase—where issues are raised—from subsequent task-force operations to resolve them.
Use of a written graphic display (usually on butcher's paper) to record statements, providing a clear frame of reference for second thoughts and the raising of alternative assumptions.
Emphasis on diversity among participants.
Compass invites representatives from a range of problem perspectives—programme insiders as well as outside experts, practitioners as well as theoreticians, intended programme beneficiaries as well as programme suppliers, sponsors as well as implementors, politically sensitive observers as well as technical staff. Choice of participants follows no rigid formula. This assumes (and experience bears out) that participants can speak for parties not directly represented, often with flair and imagination.

Compass originated during the early 1970s at the University of California, Los Angeles, Urban Planning Program, in the work of Barclay Hudson and others, chiefly in application to analysis of public services. An early version called 'dialectical scanning' was discussed in the *Journal of the American Institute of Planners* (July 1974) in relation to analysing local impacts of transportation plans (Hudson, Wachs and Schofer, 1974). Further evolution reflected overseas applications of the method to urban and regional development planning, educational-systems evaluation and other sectoral studies. Compass has increasingly moved beyond academic and government sector studies to community and political debate on policy issues. It is finding increasing application as a private-sector tool for task-force management and decision-making on programmes with complex outcomes and heavy demands on co-ordination.

Specific applications include: evaluative research design; design of questionnaires on policy issues; feasibility analysis and formative evaluation of innovative programmes, including anticipatory assessment of social and environmental impacts; design of monitoring systems for long-range programme side-effects; formulation of planning goals incorporating succinct recording of diverse viewpoints in the context of public hearings; and management of professional conferences, particularly in the organization of workshops for creative thinking. In organizational settings, Compass is applied in the drafting of funding proposals, helping in the anticipation of key issues and design of appropriate research strategies. It also serves as a way of streamlining management through a shift towards task-force operations, in place of permanent divisional units. Because Compass dispenses with the questionnaire format, it has good potential for application to crisis management, including training under simulated conditions. This would apply to such issues as nuclear safety, energy problems, labour negotiations or disaster preparedness.

Limits and cautions, other techniques and products

Compass cannot deal with abstract or general speculations. It can answer questions such as 'What will the future be like?' or 'What should we do?', but only after some specific proposal or hypothesis has been offered for reactions, criticism and suggested modifications. It has to start with a concrete idea.

Compass requires openness to unexpected findings: it cannot be limited to *a priori* categories of outcomes of pre-specified linkages. The logic of debate is open-ended, and becomes structured by the evolution of statements and counter-statements listed in the graphic display. Compass is designed for participants to move quickly from one point to the next, resisting polarization of opinion by preventing discussion from becoming bogged down in any one point of debate. By the same token, however, it does not allow discussion to focus in depth on specific issues within the workshop session itself. Resolution of disagreement is kept for a later, separate research agenda, defined in the course of writing up findings from the graphic display.

Results can be biased by the choice of participants, who are not chosen for shared expertise so much as diversity of viewpoints. Qualifications for inclusion are therefore not rigid, but remain a matter of wise judgement, reflecting the substance of the matter under discussion and the intended uses of results.

Compass draws on elements of Delphi, cross-impact analysis, goals-achievement analysis, the logical framework, scenario writing, synectics, dialectical strategy planning and other forms of compact policy assessment. It is probably closest to Delphi, but draws on broader participation than a panel of 'experts', dispenses with questionnaires and statistical summaries, usually has only one iteration and relies on a different set of group dynamics to preserve independent thinking (for a systematic comparison of Compass and Delphi, see Hudson, 1979).

Products of Compass are as follows:

The workshop graphic display, serving as an immediate overview of issues raised (one to twohours).

An immediate follow-up report, providing opportunity for immediate feedback and revisions (twelve to thirty-six hours). In subsequent drafts, minority opinions and technical appendices may be added for support on positions expressed.

A written agenda for high-yield research, focusing on remaining areas of uncertainty and disagreement that directly affect policy. It defines special areas of expertise and appropriate combinations of techniques needed to triangulate on findings.

Results can be written up to dovetail into traditional management and planning formats, such as technical reports, legislative analysis or implementation guidelines.

A structured but open-ended procedure for communication and mutual understanding among members of a highly diversified group jointly concerned with solving a shared concrete problem or exploring a specific scenario.

Level of detail and level of confidence

Compass is primarily designed for covering issues in breadth rather than depth. It sketches out a landscape rather than exploring small areas in depth. Meanwhile, it provides an overall context for identifying priority items for subsequent detailed investigation.

Results are based on pooling informed opinion rather than on objective data. Nevertheless, each statement is systematically exposed to counter-arguments that help to establish its validity. This helps define conditions that would make statements plausible or dubious. Compass also provides a specific agenda for follow-up investigation on points of key uncertainty. Special distinctions are made between issues that might be resolved by subsequent scientific investigation, versus those (such as value conflicts) which have no means of objective resolution. Dissenting opinions are preserved in the write-up of results. In short, confidence in results might be judged 'low' if the expectation is consensus, or if conventional standards of scientific investigation are applied. Conversely, confidence can be judged high in terms of the exposure of tacit assumptions underlying conclusions, and of systematic aligning, supporting and challenging statements.

The *communicability of results* is fairly straightforward. Written products are structured around substantive issues raised by the participants themselves. There is built-in provision for concise, immediate reporting aimed at soliciting commentary, supporting evidence or dissenting views. No quantitative methods, computer methods, questionnaires or esoteric analytic concepts are involved. The significance and emotional content of some issues raised by Compass are partially lost in the succinct reporting format normally used to summarize results. Subsequent drafts, however, can incorporate invited comments by persons holding strongly felt views. The original graphic display helps writers recapture the original context of remarks and the spirit of the moment in which they were made. The graphic display can also serve as an 'index' to locate material in simultaneous tape or video recordings.

The *span of forecasts* is unlimited. Compass can be used to validate short- and mid-range projections by a systematic critique of underlying assumptions and cause–effect linkages. It can also be used to explore long-range forecasts from a broad range of normative and technical perspectives simultaneously considered in a single forum.

With regard to *data needs*, the moderator (or project manager) should provide participants with a brief statement of the scenario (forecast, policy proposal or design plan) to be debated. Participants are encouraged to support statements with verbal reference to specific data sources if they exist, and to follow up with written source references or available data if requested. The follow-up report normally specifies data needs and appropriate methodologies for resolving key issues raised in the discussion.

Personnel, skills and time needed

The procedure requires a moderator. Usually this is a role for an outsider, because part of the job is to reveal tacit assumptions that are difficult for an organization's own members to expose. As in all such procedures, the personality of the moderator makes a difference. Someone with a sense of humour, for example, can encourage people to take 'risks' in their thinking, or empathize with arguments from another's perspective. A very rigid moderator, however, can make participants feel manipulated and inhibited. The ground rules for Compass are simple and palatable, but they cannot substitute for an instinctive understanding of the group dynamics that facilitate creative thinking. Some moderators possess this understanding naturally or by experience, others by training.

The Compass workshop itself can be as short as half an hour for a simple canvass of pros and cons. Generally, however, the session takes the good part of a morning or afternoon, allowing participants to review the results and identify key points of agreement and contradiction. They may also want to push further on one or more new lines of thinking opened up in the course of debate. Preparation for the session takes no time, except in lining up participants and the moderator. In cases where no concrete proposal, forecast, scenario or action plan already exists, the moderator would need roughly a day to construct a suitable hypothesis for debate, drawn up in consultation with the project manager and selected staff or based on a reading of selected background materials.

Follow-up reporting takes twelve to thirty-six hours, depending on the moderator's editorial assistance, logistic support and personal stamina. Beyond this, two days a week might be spent in canvassing reactions to the preliminary draft, adding dissenting opinions and technical appendices, and undertaking short-term intensive research on critical issues. (See earlier footnote on compact policy assessment.)

Cost

No hardware is involved: the main cost is the moderator. Logistic support is needed in the preparation of reports. There are implicit or real costs in bringing workshop participants together. Compass is designed to shorten policy research through closer focus on resolvable issues having a direct bearing on decisions. To this extent, the costs of the workshop are fully recouped from savings in the follow-up stage of investigation into critical issues raised in the workshop debate.

Case example: Planning a neighbourhood communications system

BACKGROUND

A large planning and engineering firm, GenCo, has been awarded a neighbourhood renewal contract, largely for physical design and construction, but calling for social planning as well. Among the social plan elements required are: (a) revitalization programmes to reflect the special needs of disadvantaged groups—particularly low-income elderly and women family heads; (b) pilot development of a co-operative system of marketing and provision of household services; and (c) maximum feasible participation of local residents both in planning and operating the revitalization programmes contemplated. Through past experience and consultation with local leaders, GenCo staff are aware of difficulties of such a project: questionnaires to assess resident views are cumbersome, often met with suspicion or resentment, rarely successful for stimulating creative ideas about the future and inherently biased towards individualistic rather than collective efforts at self-improvement. Unstructured interviews have many of the same disadvantages. Public hearings are tedious in their procedure, seemingly limited in their accommodation of dissenting or highly creative opinions, and blandly legalistic in reporting results.

Through informal discussions with residents, local leadership and a consultant on communications planning, certain tentative conclusions are reached: (a) the communications system developed to plan the renewal programme should also be designed to serve the evolving needs of the community in the more distant future; (b) specific proposals should be developed in order to attract interest and concrete reactions from the community, avoiding the kind of abstract discussions which would alienate residents from the planning process; (c) the initial proposal presented to the community should be clearly labelled as 'disposable'—something designed to provoke thinking in search of other, better suggestions from the community; and (d) follow-up response to the community should be fast, concrete and explicitly linked to comments raised by residents.

GenCo decides to run a Compass on one of the proposals suggested; namely, a community weekly news-sheet, dealing with planning designs in progress and providing an information clearing-house on goods and services that are needed or offered within the community (12,000 residents), as well as public and private services already available for the elderly and unemployed, day-care information for working mothers, and other issues directly related to the redevelopment mandate. Short editorials or essays may be included on self-help opportunities or referring to lessons of experience from other communities. Questions of funding, editorial control and staffing remain open to discussion.

PRINCIPAL RESPONSIBILITIES

In order to run a Compass session, the project manager (in this case from GenCo's staff, but a community official or local leader could serve as well), has these reposibilities:

1. The project manager needs to commit a small but definite budget of time and staff resources to the effort—perhaps 1 to 5 per cent of the total resources devoted to the social-planning element. It means asking staff to devote a few hours or days to a very intensive and quite unorthodox form of policy research. If participants from outside the community are to be included, a list of names must be prepared and invitations made.
2. The meeting must be publicized to residents by public notice and contact with local organizations and leaders, emphasizing the concrete nature of the proposal and the major issues at stake.
3. The project manager needs both the authority and mental flexibility to modify research priorities and reassign tasks based on results of the Compass session. Otherwise the effort is relatively pointless.

The moderator has these functions:

1. He/she must help crystallize the proposal for discussion. The proposal can be a 'straw man', or a serious working hypothesis or it might represent the outcome of an earlier study needing critical review. (Experience suggests that the moderator can often suggest a concrete proposal for debate more easily than a project manager: the moderator is not as inhibited about making naïve and premature suggestions, and not as defensive about free-wheeling criticism of proposals offered.)
2. The moderator manages the Compass session itself. Pros and cons are summarized on a graphic display. A large (3 ft × 15 ft/1 m × 5 m) piece of butcher's paper works well: it is big enough to keep the entire discussion in view, but it can be removed and preserved, or cut up and sorted out in the process of editing a summary report on the session.

3. The moderator edits the graphic display into a seven- to ten- page pre-liminary report on findings, delivered within twelve to thirty-six hours. Editing mainly consists of: (a) clustering pros and cons around points of consensus or debate, identifying the grounds of disagreement (factual un-certainty, value conflicts, cause–effect assumptions?); (b) highlighting key issues based on a subjective 'sense of the meeting' or straw vote at the session's conclusion; and (c) specifying short-term lines of attack on those issues which seem objectively resolvable, and directly bearing on practical policy choices.

4. The moderator is responsible for surveying reactions to the preliminary draft, in preparation for a revised version incorporating refinements, dis-senting opinions and relevant supporting data.

5. The moderator should also be prepared to work with the project manager and staff to set up 'compact' forms of follow-up investigation into key issues, including design of task-force roles, collaboration with outside agen-cies and a comparative case review of historical precedents for policies under consideration.

GROUND RULES AND GROUP DYNAMICS

Compass is a simple process, though quality control takes experience and know how. The moderator needs tact in applying the ground rules. He/she needs to synthesize commentary into highly concise summary phrases for the graphic display. At some point, he/she will need to request clarification on how a new statement relates to earlier ones. In the first moments of a session, participants usually need reminding to state their conclusions first: 'I'm pro [I support the conclusion] because. . . .' Or, 'I'm against, because I take issue with Statement 5' (each statement is numbered consecutively for later reference). Participants usually adapt quickly, however. Their statements become shorter, more ex-plicit about policy implications, more specific about whether they support earlier points or depart from them. They learn to put the punchline first.

A session of one hour will bring out perhaps fifty statements. For the graphic display, each is reduced to a short phrase, perhaps a half dozen words, sometimes a pictograph, sometimes place-names evocative of lessons from past experience. The moderator plays a key role in rendering these summaries, at least initially. In most cases, participants fall into using the same style, and the moderator can turn over the felt-tipped pen to someone else for summarizing ideas and writing up the display. The moderator has other functions: to loosen the reins when creative energies are flowing, to draw them in when discussion rambles. He/she needs to keep pro and con statements in rough balance: 'So far, you've only said negative things about the proposal. Are there any pluses?' Or, 'You've only said positive things. But if it's so good, why aren't people already doing it? What practical problems are we forgetting? What would it take to get action on it?'

The process is designed to allow people to drop out of the discussion mentally to mull over ideas and then jump back in. The graphic display gives everyone random access back to all points raised earlier. The moderator can help make these bridges: 'Are you referring back to that earlier point—where was it?—point 17? OK, do you want to reinforce it, or are you suggesting an entirely different alternative to the co-operative-newspaper idea?' Or, 'How does that relate to helping disadvantaged groups you have chosen to speak for? Can you give an example of benefits that they get any more than other groups?' Or, 'That's an interesting idea—maybe unique. Have you heard of something like that being tried? Did it work? Can I get a reference to anything written on it after this meeting?' The moderator has to keep debate from getting bogged down or polarizing around sub-issues. For example, an objection might surface: 'I'm against the newspaper idea. It'll become a political tool.' From another participant, 'That's a pro! Nothing's going to get done until people get politically mobilized.' 'But who's going to control it? Whose politics are going to manipulate who?' If such discussions go on for long without resolution or constructive development, or without including more than a couple of people talking, the moderator needs to step in. Resolvable issues need to be sorted out from hopeless dilemmas. It has to be seen whether anything will change people's minds, or whether the positions on each side have solidified and must be simply acknowledged, recorded and moved beyond. 'OK, let's look at some real examples of community-owned public services. Are they always manipulated?' Or how were they ever protected from it?' One participant suggests a solution—giving equal newsprint space to opposing factions in the community. Another replies, 'The problem isn't political manipulation, it's financial rip-offs. Why, I knew a co-operative laundry facility that got swindled by its own managers.' And so on. Each of the statements adds to the list of pros and cons. The moderator's role is to see that policy implications are also drawn out. Each statement is a potential design requirement: how to preserve the opportunities presented, how to mitigate the anticipated threats. Sometimes the design requirements are well met by the original proposal. Usually, significant modifications are suggested, along with some focused research into some key uncertainties that bear on the proposal's feasibility and acceptability. Sometimes it is necessary to start again from scratch with an entirely different proposal. But the next round will not have to start from scratch in communications with the local residents. The community has spoken, and the write-up from the first round should demonstrate that they have been heard, making them more confident in the planner's ability to take their ideas seriously. Follow-up actions have been specified. Participants have a better sense of themselves as a community, both in terms of diversity and potential alliances They can begin to translate individual concerns into collective expression, based on shared experiences and values.

Compass is not a good method for controlling opinion. If community participation is intended to be purely pro forma, the result may go beyond that. The outcome may be a stronger sense of the threats as well as opportunities posed by new development plans. Advocacy groups might congeal, developing an action agenda of their own that departs from planners' preconceived notions. It may become increasingly difficult to impose solutions when participants find their own voice to define problems. But these are dangers inherent in any genuinely democratically structured communication system.

Annotated bibliography

The Compass technique stems from two considerations. One is a question of practicality, which calls for low-cost, fast-track approaches to planning and project evaluation. The other consideration is related to the problem of epistemology—how to define valid knowledge bases for a shared understanding of planning problems among people with highly diverse values, technical backgrounds and belief systems. The first group of references below deals with the practical issues; the second group with the question of establishing valid knowledge based on interplay between diversified viewpoints, information sources and expertise.

COMPASS IN RESPONSE TO THE NEED
FOR PRACTICAL PLANNING TECHNIQUES

HUDSON, B. 1978. Forecasting Educational Futures: Resolving Uncertainties and Disagreements through Compact Policy Assessment. *World Future Society/University of Houston Conference on Educational Futures, Houston, Texas, 20–22 October 1978.* (Paper.) Explains Compass, comparing it with Delphi, and illustrates its use applied to the evaluation of a scenario of educational futures and policy needs for the year 2000.

——. 1979. Comparison of Current Planning Theories: Counterparts and Contradictions. *Journal of the American Planning Association,* Vol. 45, No. 4, October, p. 387–98. Suggests an application of Compass as a short-term, intensive 'prelude' phase of planning that allows clients to compare and experience alternative planning styles in a 'dry run' exercise. The article compares five planning styles or traditions: synoptic; incremental; transactive; advocacy; and radical. The five approaches are contrasted in terms of their view of the public interest, feasibility of application, potential for generating action, theoretical bases for interpreting social processes, degree of concern for the humanistic impacts of social policy choices and openness to critical analysis of underlying assumptions. Argues that fast-track approaches are vital for permitting real comparison and choice between planning approaches.

HUDSON, B.; SIEMBAB, W.; SOJA, E. 1978. *A Formative Evaluation of ACCESS—The Alternative Comprehensive Community Environment Study System.* Los Angeles, Calif., UCLA Planning Program. (Final Report to the US Office of Environmental Education.) Discusses problems of generating community interest in region-wide planning issues. Suggests means for planning to serve as a process of public learning, through visual thinking and rapid review of concrete historical experience illustrating prototypical solutions to community problems. Little explicit reference to Compass, but explains the importance of concrete images, public input and fast-track methodology, which are major ingredients of the Compass method.

HUDSON, B.; WACHS, M.; SCHOFER, J. 1974. Local Impact Evaluation: Ingredients for Network Design. *Journal of the American Institute of Planners,* Vol. 40, No. 4, July, p. 255–66. Discusses an early version of Compass, called 'dialectical scanning', along with strategies for dealing with conflicts based on value issues that cannot be resolved through scientific methods of inquiry.

WHOLEY, J.S. 1979. *Evaluation: Promise and Performance.* Washington, D.C., The Urban Institute. Based on long experience in evaluating Federal Government programmes, Wholey suggests a reformed approach to programme evaluation whose rationale is substantially the same as for Compass: the need for 'evaluability assessment' (a fast, preliminary scan of a programme's objectives, the plausibility of its operating assumptions and intended uses of evaluation information); 'rapid feedback evaluation' (selection of a set of measurements and data analyses which are cost-feasible and likely to be useful); and 'sequential purchasing of information' (carrying-out of analyses in successive increments, rather than withholding analytical results until a final conclusion is reached).

COMPASS IN RESPONSE TO ISSUES EPISTEMOLOGY:
VALIDATION OF PLANNING INFORMATION

HUDSON, B. 1975. [Review article on] Morris Hill, *Planning for Multiple Objectives* (Philadelphia Pa, Regional Science Research Institute, 1973). *Transportation*, Vol. 4, No. 2, June, p. 187–90. Develops another tenet of Compass—that 'soft' dimensions of programme impacts (intangibles, symbolically important elements, local perceptions and experience) can be treated rigorously and systematically without being reduced to quantitative measurements or monetary-value equivalents.

——. 1977. Domains of Evaluation. *Social Policy*, Vol. 6, No. 3, September, p. 79–89. Develops a central tenet of the Compass method—that programme objectives cannot be deduced from *a priori* goals, only from diverse reactions to concrete alternatives.

——. 1979 (rev.). *Compact Policy Assessment and the Compass Method. Practical Application of Dialectical Theory to Educational Planning and Forecasting.* Cambridge, Mass., Harvard University Center for Studies in Education and Development. (Paper.) Discusses various interpretations of 'dialectical' methods of inquiry, in contrast to the highly formalistic application of social science to social-policy analysis. Explicitly relates Compass methodology to the dialectical bases of social science, including historical analysis, acknowledgement of multiple perspectives, evolution of institutional bases for action and mutating systems of cause and effect.

——. 1980. Varieties of Science: Not by Rationalism Alone [and] Dialectical Science: Epistemology for Evolutionary Systems. Santa Monica, Calif. (Manuscript chapters for book in progress on social-policy evaluation and fast-track methods of participatory planning.) Refines the ideas presented in the previous reference, suggesting major flaws in social-science methodology which has improperly adapted the techniques of natural science to study of man-made social and political processes. Suggests why 'quick and dirty' methods may often be not only faster than the traditional, expensive and ponderous planning traditions but also more valid for defining actions and estimating their impacts.

HUDSON, B.; DAVIS, R.G. 1980. *Knowledge Networks for Educational Planning. Issues and Strategies*. Paris, International Institute for Educational Planning. Discusses several elements of planning method underlying the design of Compass: the use of creative conflict to generate policy; the simultaneous use of 'bottom up' and 'top down' planning; the choice of planning method to reflect underlying 'philosophies of development'.

IV

Methods
for decision

Introduction

All planning requires decisions, whether formal or informal, and whether planning is structurally separated from decision-making or is part of a fully integrated planning and decision-making process. In this part we present four formal methods for creating and organizing information about choices.

Information is one of two key aspects of decision-making. The other is composed of sets of criteria (or standards for choice). These criteria incorporate the values of planners and decision-makers, and reflect the prevailing social image of the society in which planning takes place. A central criterion in most societies is cost. A second is expected benefit. Thus most decision methods explicitly take both costs and benefits of alternatives into account. Some methods also enable decision-makers to bring other criteria, such as the probabilities associated with various outcomes, to bear in the decision process. And methods are increasingly incorporating other values as criteria in open and explicit ways. Use of formal decision methods focuses attention on the criteria and calls for explicit comparison of alternatives. This tends to push for rather technical processes of decision-making. However, as all planners will recognize, technical choices are always subject to political review. Power is required to implement decisions, and power considerations are never far from the heart of decision processes. Formal decision methods, nevertheless, at least provide a reasoned analysis as a significant input into the decision process.

Methods presented

Four formal decision methods are presented in this section: decision analysis; cost–benefit analysis; zero-based budgeting; and goal-achievement matrix.

DECISION ANALYSIS

Planning requires intimacy with uncertainty. Even in the most stable and certain environments, projections of future courses of action involve a degree of error and risk. Statistical decision analysis provides a framework through which these uncertainties can be explicitly incorporated into decision-making.

The method enables the decision-maker simultaneously to consider costs, expected benefits and the probabilities of success for different strategy elements.

The method itself is relatively simple to apply once planners master the various steps involved, although users with a background in statistics and probability theory will find the method easier to master. The challenge lies in the estimation of probabilities for various strategy outcomes. The apparent difficulty of using the method has probably tended to restrict its use to rational/comprehensive planning approaches. However, the flexibility of the method in incorporating probabilities of strategy outcomes recommends it to all planning situations. The potential of the method for participatory planning lies primarily in the estimation of probabilities, which can involve both technical and non-technical persons.

COST – BENEFIT ANALYSIS

Cost–benefit analysis is probably the central decision-making method in all planning. It is central to a full economic analysis of strategy alternatives, enabling planners to estimate the economic pay-off of alternative strategies, taking into account (with discounting techniques) the present value of future benefits and costs. True application of cost–benefit analysis requires the translation of the benefits of strategies into monetary terms. Because this is often difficult, if not impossible, to do in many types of planning, the related techniques of cost-effectiveness and cost–output analysis have been developed. The former accepts non-monetary measures of the impact of strategies; the latter uses even simpler measures of output. These alternatives are discussed in the presentation of cost–benefit analysis that follows.

The method requires considerable data and skill resources, and is therefore found primarily in its full form in rational/comprehensive planning. However, informal application of the principles underlying cost–benefit analysis is found in planning under incremental, allocative and transactive planning. Because of the complexity of the method, there is little scope for non-technical participation in its use.

ZERO-BASED BUDGETING

Decision-makers are constantly confronted with choices in the allocation of budget resources. Zero-based budgeting is one of a cluster of methods (including programme planning and budgeting) which organize information about costs and expected outcomes of alternative strategies, to facilitate decision-making. A key feature of this method is its ability to portray the effects of incremental budget reductions or increases in terms of likely effects on expected output. The method requires relatively little information beyond the budgets for alternative strategies and estimations of strategy effects. It is therefore useful under most planning approaches, although by its very nature it fits most closely with allocative planning. The capability of the method to depict clearly the probable effects of alternative choices makes it an excellent method for obtaining public participation in the decision-making process.

GOAL-ACHIEVEMENT MATRIX

The goal-achievement matrix is a decision-making tool which seeks to blend values, costs, benefits and the concept of differing value to different groups in society. The method presents decision-makers with explicit choices among different goals and strategies, together with information about the relative costs and benefits of each alternative for different groups within society. The method can be applied at different levels of complexity, through computer models or through hand calculation, making it useful under all planning approaches. The method has particular potential for public participation, and would be particularly useful for transactive planning.

Other uses of presented methods

Decision methods are largely restricted to the decision element of planning. However, the results of a decision analysis can be used as a partial basis for monitoring programme implementation.

Other methods for decision

Various methods useful in strategy development contribute directly to decision analysis, notably scenarios,[1] simulations/games[1] and cross-impact analysis.[1] Typically, however, these methods create information which is then further organized by a decision method.

1. Methods presented in other sections of this book.

Chapter 13

Decision analysis

J. K. Satia

Statistical decision analysis is the name given to techniques of making decisions which involve choices among alternative courses of action with uncertain outcomes. In this chapter, we discuss decision-matrix and decision-tree analysis, which aid the decision-maker in one-time and sequential decisions respectively. These techniques share the strengths and weaknesses of other formal analytical techniques. The use of these techniques helps in identifying and gathering needed information, stimulating creative generation of alternatives and communicating the rationale for the decision to others, and leads to scrutiny of the problem as a whole. However, the analysis using these techniques may lead to over-simplification of the problem. Although these techniques were first developed by statisticians, they are increasingly used in other fields for analysis of decisions.

Definition and assumptions

Statistical decision analysis is a set of analytical techniques which aid in making choices among alternative courses of action with uncertain outcomes. These techniques involve: estimating the outcomes, and their probabilities, associated with each course of action; reducing them to the equivalent outcome values in terms of a selected criterion of decision-making; and comparing the decisions using equivalent outcome values. The analysis procedure is rather basic in nature and, therefore, can be applied to a wide variety of decision-making problems.

Several assumptions are made in using statistical decision analysis:
The alternatives identified are feasible and mutually exclusive.
All feasible alternatives have been identified.
The outcome of a decision depends upon the alternative chosen and the state of the nature. The states may be defined using many variables. We assume that there are only a finite number of states, and that they are collectively exhaustive, mutually exclusive, independent of the alternative chosen and not certain.
The decision-maker uses a well-specified criterion for evaluating decisions, and all outcomes can be assigned in terms of this.

History and main uses

The use of statistical decision analysis was developed by H. Raiffa and R. Schlaifer in the mid-1950s, although statisticians had used these techniques earlier. Since then the interest in these techniques has grown rapidly, and they are now included in almost all the curriculums of management education.

Statistical decision analysis has been applied to many fields of human endeavour including business, government and personal decisions. Because of the inherent nature of the decisions, additional complexities arise in estimating the outcome of communication strategies. It is usually better to consider explicitly the effects of uncertainty, with attendant difficulties, rather than ignore them. The utility of applying statistical decision analysis is a matter of judgement affected by the expense and significance of the communication effort under consideration.

Limits and cautions

Decision analysis is only a part of the decision process, which includes organizational issues such as the role of the decision-maker and affected parties, and the process of implementation of the decision. Attention needs to be paid to these issues if a better quality of decision is to result. Several complications may arise in applying statistical decision analysis. These includes:

The number of decisions and possible outcomes may be numerous and simplifications may be required to keep the analysis manageable.

An extensive analysis of environment may be required to estimate probabilities of outcomes.

In many situations, multiple outcomes may simultaneously result with conflicting desirabilities, and it may be difficult to assign single values to these outcomes.

Procedures

ONE-TIME DECISIONS: DECISION-MATRIX ANALYSIS

The decision situation is characterized by four elements:

1. States of nature (S), the different states of environment such as receptivity of environment, possible reach of media and so on.
2. Feasible alternatives (A), the possible alternatives which are feasible to implement given the constraints on cultural environment, media availability, budgets and so on.
3. Outcomes (O_{AS}), the results of a particular state (S) and an alternative (A).
4. Value of outcome $V(O_{AS})$, the measure of effectiveness for a particular outcome O_{AS}, usually gains or benefits-costs measured over the planning-horizon time period and reduced to a single number.

The general symbolism of the matrix decision model which incorporates the

254

TABLE 1. Matrix decision model

Alternative	State			
	S_1	S_2	$S_3, \ldots$	S_N
A_1	$V(O_{11})$	$V(O_{12})$	$V(O_{13}), \ldots$	$V(O_{1N})$
A_2	$V(O_{21})$	$V(O_{22})$	$V(O_{23}), \ldots$	$V(O_{2N})$
$\vdots$	$\vdots$			
A_M	$V(O_{M1})$	$V(O_{M2})$	$V(O_{M3}), \ldots$	$V(O_{MN})$

above-mentioned four elements is given in Table 1. Once a decision situation has been represented in the matrix format, a decision criterion is used to compare the alternatives. There is no widespread agreement on the criterion to be used when the outcomes are uncertain. The literature on decision analysis has identified serveral criteria which may be used for making choices. Table 2 shows these criteria, their shortcomings and decision situations where they are generally appropriate.

ONE-TIME DECISIONS: CASE EXAMPLE

Planners face the need to evaluate alternative communication strategies to improve the acceptance of immunizations in a group of rural villages. After reviewing past experience with similar campaigns, they identified three strategy alternatives and estimated the cost of each:

Strategy A_1: radio campaign only (R): cost, 20 units.

Strategy A_2: radio campaign plus intensive home visiting (R + IHV): cost, 50 units.

Strategy A_3: radio campaign, intensive home visiting plus discussion group meetings in the villages (R + IHV + DGM): cost, 100 units.

Planners also recognized that the level of immunization coverage achieved would also depend on the receptivity of villager audiences, and identified three probable states of receptivity: high (H), medium (M) and low (L). Then, percentages of coverage were estimated for all combinations of alternatives and states. This information was then combined as shown in Table 3.

Past experience enabled the planners to estimate the *benefits* of each strategy/state combination as equal to two units of value for each percentage point of coverage. The *outcome value* of each strategy/state combination was then calculated as: Value outcome = Benefits − Cost. For alternative A_1 and state H, for example, the value outcome was calculated as: Benefits (2×50) − Cost $(20) = 80$. Values for each of the alternative strategy/state combinations were calculated in the same way. Finally, the planners estimated the probabilities of each of the three receptivity states occurring as 0.4, 0.3 and 0.3 for states H, M and L respectively. The final decision matrix is given in

TABLE 2. Decision criteria

Decision criteria	Procedure for application	Shortcomings	Appropriate decision situation
A. These criteria do not require probabilities of various outcomes:			
1. Maximin	Select the alternative so as to maximize the minimum possible value of the outcome. Formally select alternative k such that $\max_i \min_j V(O_{ij}) = \min_k V(O_{kj})$ for all alternatives i and states j.	1. Ignores other possible outcomes for decisions. 2. Pessimistic but avoids very bad outcomes.	Where any bad outcome would be disastrous.
2. Maximax	Select the alternative so as to maximize the maximum possible value of the outcome. Formally select alternative k such that $\max_i \min_j V(O_{ij}) = \max_k V(O_{kj})$ for all alternatives i and state j.	1. Ignores other possible outcomes for decisions. 2. Is optimistic and very bad outcomes are possible.	Where bad outcomes are tolerable but there is a need to do as well as possible.
3. Coefficient of optimism	Select an index of optimism L on a scale from 0 to 1. For each alternative calculate $L(\max_j V(O_{ij})) + (1 \cdot L)(\min_j V_j(O_{ij}))$. Select the alternative which has the highest such value.	1. Ignores intermediate outcome values. 2. Need arbitrarily to select value of coefficient of optimism.	Where all possible outcomes are within tolerable range.
4. Minimax regret	For each state, calculate the regret value for each alternative by subtracting the outcome value from the highest outcome value for any alternative for that state. Select the alternative so as to minimize the maximum regret.	1. Same as that of maximin principle.	Where decision-maker is competing with several decision-makers facing identical situation.
5. Laplace principle	Calculate expected gain for each alternative i, $E(A)_i = 1/M \cdot jV(O_{ij})$ where M is the number of states. Select the alternative which has the highest expected gain.	1. Assigns equal likelihood to all states. 2. Ignores the variation in outcome values.	Where all states may be approximately equally likely.

B. These criteria require that probabilities be assigned to outcomes :

6. Expected gain	Select the alternative which has the highest expected gain, where the expected gain for an alternative i, $E(A_i)$, is calculated by summing the values for the outcomes weighted by their probabilities, for all states. Formally, $E(A_i) = \Sigma_j P_j V(O_{ij})$ where P_j is the probability of state j.	1. Ignores the variation in outcomes.	Where decision-maker may face such situations repetitively.
7. Expected gain-variance	Select the alternative which has the highest value for expected gain, $k \sqrt{}$(variance of the gain), where k has a specified positive value and variance of the gain for alternative i is given by $\text{Var}(A_i) = \Sigma_j P_j (V(O_{ij}) \cdot E(A_i))^2$	1. Ignores distributions of outcomes. 2. Need to assign an arbitrary trade-off between expected value and variance of gain.	Where risk considerations are important.
8. Expected utility	Select the decision which has the highest expected utility; values are assigned to each of the outcomes.	1. Need to assign utility values.	Where decision-maker is clearly identifiable and risk considerations are important.
9. Aspiration level	Select the alternative which has the highest probability of achieving a desired gain.	1. Ignores range of outcomes.	Where it is important to achieve at least a certain level of performance such as winning majority vote in an election.

257

TABLE 3. Percentage immunization coverage

State			Receptivity	
Alternatives	Cost	H	M	L
A_1 R	20	50	20	15
A_2 R + IHV	50	70	40	25
A_3 R + IHV + DGM	100	80	60	50

TABLE 4. Decision matrix for the illustrative example

	Probability		
	0.4	0.3	0.3
	State		
Alternative	H	M	L
A_1	80	20	10
A_2	90	30	0
A_3	60	20	0

Table 4. The three alternatives are compared using nine different decision critieria in Table 5.

SEQUENTIAL DECISIONS: DECISION-TREE ANALYSIS

A serious limitation of one-time decision-making procedures discussed so far is that they ignore consequences of future decisions which would depend upon the outcomes of the present decisions. Indeed, sequential decision-making would be the rule rather than exception in the real world. There are many reasons, however, why one-time decision making is used. The decision-maker may not have any involvement in the future decisions and may be accountable for only a short horizon. The dependence between the future and present decisions may not be identifiable or significant. For instance, the communication strategy for health a few years hence may depend upon the then prevailing critical health problems, economic development, changes in technologies and so on. The inclusion of such considerations may lead to additional complexity without adding significantly to better choices now. Whenever it is safe to assume that the consideration of future decisions will not affect the present decisions, it is better to limit the analysis to one-time decisions. If the possible future decisions should have a significant influence upon present choices, sequential-decision analysis procedures should be used. In this analysis, it will be assumed that the decision-maker would use the expected gain criterion.

TABLE 5. Comparison of alternatives

Criteria	Value	Alternatives			Discussion
		A_1	A_2	A_3	
1. Maximin	Minimum gain	10	0	0	A_1 has the highest value.
2. Maximax	Maximum gain	80	90	60	A_2 has the highest value.
3. Coefficient of optimism	$L = 0.5$, value	$0.5(80) + 0.5(10) = 45$	$0.5(90) + 0.5(0) = 45$	$0.5(60) + 0.5(0) = 30$	Either A_1 or A_2 may be selected.
4. Minimax regret	Maximum regret	10	10	30	Either A_1 or A_2 may be selected.
5. Laplace	Expected gain	$\frac{1}{3}(80 + 20 + 10) = \frac{110}{3}$	$\frac{1}{3}(90 + 30 + 0) = \frac{120}{3}$	$\frac{1}{3}(60 + 20 + 0) = \frac{80}{3}$	A_2 has the highest value.
6. Expected gain	Expected gain	$0.4(80) + 0.3(20) + 0.3(10)$ $= 41$	$0.4(90) + 0.3(30) + 0.3(0)$ $= 45$	$0.4(60) + 0.3(20) + 0.3(0)$ $= 30$	A_2 has the highest value expected gain.
7. Expected gain-variance	$k = 0.05$, value	-10.45	-29.25	-3.0	A_3 has the highest value.
8. Expected utility					The decision will depend upon utility values assigned to outcomes.
9. Aspiration level	Aspiration level = 30, probability of gain of 30 or more	0.4	0.7	0.4	A_2 has the highest probability of meeting aspiration level of 30.

The steps in analysing a sequential-decision problem are as follows:
1. Exhibit the anatomy of the problem in terms of a decision tree.
2. Evaluate the consequences and then assign values for the outcomes.
3. Assign probabilities to the branches of chance forks.
4. Determine the optimal strategy by averaging and folding back.

FORMAL REPRESENTATION OF A DECISION TREE

The decision tree represents a sequence of decisions, possible outcomes, subsequent decisions, possible outcomes and so on. The probabilities of outcomes and values of the outcomes are also indicated. The following notation is used:

$\triangledown$ = a decision point, labelled as $D_1, D_2, \ldots i^{th}$ decision point.

$\triangledown\!\!-$ = a branch emanating from decision point, alternative to be chosen.

$\bigcirc$ = a node in the tree where chance events influence the outcomes.

$\bigcirc\!\!-$ = a branch representing a probabilistic outcome with probabilities marked.

V = a value associated with a particular outcome.

P = a probability of outcome.

A symbolic decision tree for a simple sequential decision is presented in Figure 1. The sequential decision problem depicted involves two decision points D_1 and D_2. If alternative A_1 is chosen, it can have two probable outcomes O_1 and O_2. If O_1 occurs, then a decision D_2 is required. Two alternatives $A_{1\,1}$ and $A_{1\,2}$ are available at that point, which again lead to probabilistic outcomes. The ultimate question to be answered is which alternative to choose at D_1.

ANALYSIS OF THE DECISION TREE

The fundamental process in analysing a decision tree is to find out the expected gain of the initial decision by starting from the highest decision point (the point farthest away from the base of the tree), working back by a process known as 'averaging and folding back' to end at the first decision point. To do this, we apply the principle of *expected gain* (E) to determine the probable maximum gain for each decision alternative. It will be recalled that expected gain is calculated as follows:

$$E\,(A_i) = \sum_j P_j V(O_{ij})$$

and that value in our example is calculated as the percentage of coverage of a given strategy alternative multiplied by 2, minus cost.

In the decision tree example in Figure 1, decision point 2 has two alternative strategies. These are $A_{1\,1}$ and $A_{1\,2}$. Expected gains for each of these alternatives are calculated. Then decision point D_2 is given the expected gain value equal to the highest expected gain of the two alternatives $A_{1\,1}$ and $A_{1\,2}$. At this point in the analysis, we would have expected gain values for D_2, V_1 and V_2. The values for D_2 and V_1 would be weighted by their probabilities ($O_1 P_1$)

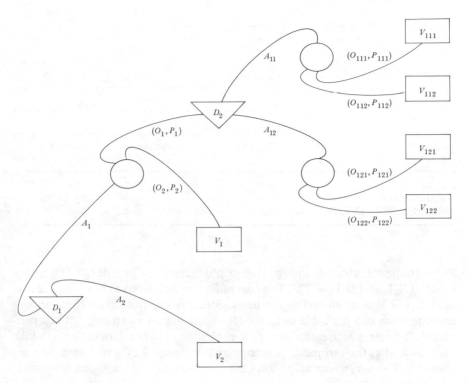

FIG. 1. A symbolic decision tree

and $(O_2 P_2)$. The highest value of the two would be assigned to alternative A_1, and the result compared with A_2 for final decision.

SEQUENTIAL DECISION ANALYSIS: CASE EXAMPLE

Earlier in the chapter we considered a one-time decision for a communication strategy. The data, with some numbers changed for illustrative purposes, are given in Table 6. To begin the decision analysis, planners decide that, if the coverage of any of these three alternatives (called 'stage one' alternatives) and state combinations is less than 50 per cent, additional strategy alternatives must be added and evaluated. These are called 'stage two' strategies. In this way it will be possible to compare the initially strongest stage one strategies with other combinations of stage one and stage two alternatives. As shown in Table 6, alternative A_3 achieves at least 50 per cent coverage for all three states. In addition, strategies A_1 and A_2 achieve the 50 per cent criterion in the high-receptivity state (H). Thus stage-two strategy alternatives will need to be added to the analysis for stage-one alternatives A_1 and A_2 under state conditions of medium (M) and low (L) receptivity, as shown in the bracketed area in Table 6. Two stage-two strategy alternatives are identified: (a) addition of

TABLE 6. Data for stage one of the illustrative example

Stage-one alternative		Cost	Probability					
			0.4		0.3		0.3	
			State					
			H		M		L	
			Coverage (%)	Gain	Coverage (%)	Gain	Coverage (%)	Gain
A_1	R	20	50	80	20	20	15	10
A_2	R + IHV	50	60	70	40	30	25	0
A_3	R + IHV + DGM	100	90	80	60	20	50	0

leaflets to be distributed; and (b) leaflets plus television broadcasts. These are labelled B_1L and B_2L + TV. The cost of B_1L is estimated as 60 units; the cost of B_2L + TV is estimated as 110 units. Strategy experts advise the planners that there are two probable outcomes for each stage-two strategy. They provide the planners with estimates of the probability that each outcome will take place as well as the estimated percentage of coverage for each. These data are shown in Table 7, which also shows the combinations of stage-one and stage-two alternatives.

The planners decide to apply the decision criterion of expected gain. To do this, they construct a decision tree representing the sequence of decisions among the stage-one and stage-two alternatives, as shown in Figure 2. They then calculate the expected gain for each branch of the tree by first computing the value of the coverage (coverage × 2) and then applying the formula for expected gain for each branch, taking into account the probabilities of each end point and the cost of the branch. Expected-gain values are shown in Table 7, and to the far right in Figure 2. As shown in Figure 2, the planners face four decision points (D_2) regarding the combination of stage-one and stage-two alternatives. At each decision point they will choose the stage-two alternative which provides maximum gain. For strategy A_1, for example, there are two stage-two decisions. The first represents a choice between a branch (B_1L) which has an expected gain of 30, and a branch $(B_2L$ + TV$)$ which has an expected gain of 38. The branch with an expected gain of 38 is chosen, and its expected gain assigned to the decision point. The process is repeated for all stage-two decisions.

The reduced decision tree is shown in Figure 3. Now the situation is similar to a one-time decision. The planner calculates the expected gain of each of the alternatives A_1, A_2 and A_3 by multiplying the value of each branch by its probability. For alternative A_1, for example, expected gain is calculated as:

$$E(A_1) = 0.4(80) + 0.3(38) + 0.3(18) = 48.8.$$

TABLE 7. Probabilities, coverage and expected gain for stage-two alternatives

Selected alternative	State	Coverage (%)	Alternatives	Cost	Outcome 1 Probability	Outcome 1 Coverage (%)	Outcome 2 Probability	Outcome 2 Coverage (%)	Expected gain ($EG = P(VO)$)
A_1 Radio (R)	M	20	$B_1 L$	60	0.5	40	0.5	50	$0.5(80) + 0.5(100) - 60 = 30$
			$B_2 L + TV$	110	0.3	60	0.7	80	$0.3(120) + 0.7(160) - 110 = 38$
	L	15	$B_1 L$	60	0.4	30	0.6	40	$0.4(60) + 0.6(80) - 60 = 12$
			$B_2 L + TV$	110	0.3	50	0.7	70	$0.3(100) + 0.7(140) - 110 = 18$
A_2 Radio +IHV	M	40	$B_1 L$	60	0.5	45	0.5	65	$0.5(90) + 0.5(130) - 60 = 50$
			$B_2 L + TV$	110	0.3	45	0.7	65	$0.3(90) + 0.7(130) - 110 = 8$
	L	25	$B_1 L$	60	0.4	35	0.6	55	$0.4(70) + 0.6(110) - 60 = 34$
			$B_2 L + TV$	110	0.3	45	0.7	65	$0.3(90) + 0.7(130) - 110 = 8$

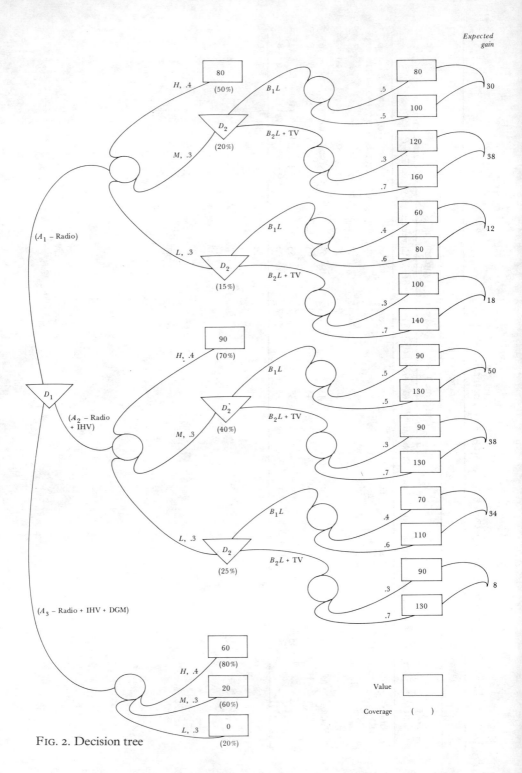

FIG. 2. Decision tree

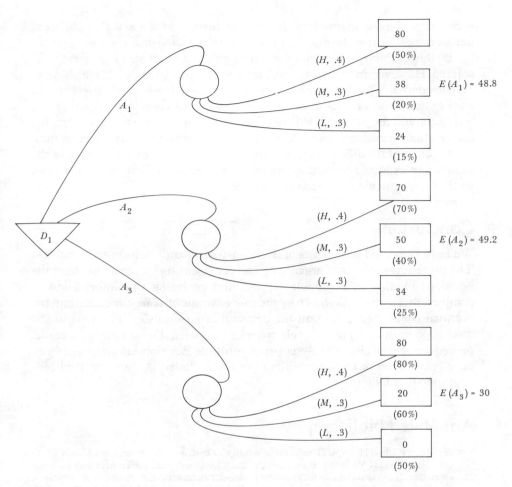

FIG. 3. Folded decision tree

Now the planners are ready to make decisions. It can be seen that, given the way the planners have combined the strategies and made their estimates, strategy A_2 is the best initial choice, with an expected gain of 49.2. Once planners implement strategy A_2 with radio and intensive home visiting, they evaluate actual coverage achieved. If they achieve 70 per cent or more, no further strategies are needed. They will find themselves in the high receptivity state with an expected gain of 90. If, however, coverage is only 40 per cent, then strategy B_1L is still the best stage-two strategy with an expected gain of 34. Thus, while this analysis helps the planner evaluate a number of future courses of action, the commitment is initially only for the first decision (here, for A_2). As the decision is implemented and new information becomes available, further strategies may be chosen. Also, as implementation proceeds, new strategies may suggest themselves, leading to further analysis with a different decision tree. This is the essence of sequential decision-making.

In this example, only two decision points (stages of strategy) were considered. However, in real-world problems several decision points may have to be considered. This would result in increased complexity. Planners would have to decide on a trade-off between the additional complexity of using this technique and the potential benefits. The quality of decisions is affected by the information available about the states. In this example the coverage and probabilities of the different states were estimated. Other methods, such as the sample survey, could be used to gather more precise information of this kind, further strengthening the decision analysis.

Conclusion

We have presented techniques of decision-matrix and decision-tree analysis. The procedures consist of organizing and representing information about the decision situation in a suitable format, and analysing this information to compare alternatives. As shown by the case example of a one-time decision, the eventual choice depends upon the decision criterion used. Throughout the discussion in this chapter, a single criterion was used. During the last decade, procedures for decision analysis using multiple decision criteria have been developed. References to such literature are included in the annotated bibliography that follows.

Annotated bibliography

KEENEY, R.L.; RAIFFA, H. 1976. *Decisions with Multiple Objectives: Preferences and Values Trade Offs*. New York, N.Y., Wiley. Presents techniques for quantifying preferences over multiple objectives. It discusses single-attribute and multi-attribute utility theory and its applications. The issues related to preferences over time and aggregation of individual preferences are also discussed. This book, unlike most of the earlier literature on decision analysis, does not emphasize an uncertainty analysis. Much has been written on uncertainty analysis— statistical validation of a model, use of data for inference, the codification of judgemental estimation by the decision-maker and by expert groups. This book attempts to improve the balance by focusing on preference analysis.

MOORE, P.G.; THOMAS, H. 1976. *The Anatomy of Decisions*. Harmondsworth, Penguin Books. MOORE, P.G.; THOMAS, H.; BURNS, D.W.; HAMPTON, J.M. 1976. *Case Studies in Decision Analysis*. Harmondsworth, Penguin Books. These two paperbacks present the material on decision analysis in a readable format for popular use. The first book discusses decision analysis. The second book presents applications of decision analysis to many business decisions such as new product launch, investment decisions, evaluation of research and development projects, and bidding.

RAIFFA, H. 1968. *Decision Analysis: Introductory Lectures on Choices under Uncertainty*. Reading, Mass., Addison-Wesley. Discusses statistical decision analysis with mathematical requirements kept to a minimum. It introduces decision analysis and discusses decision-tree technique, utility theory, economics of sampling and risk sharing. It emphasizes foundations of the subject and also discusses some controversial issues.

RAIFFA, H,; SCHLAIFER, R.A. 1961. *Applied Statistical Decision Theory*. Boston, Mass., Division of Research, Graduate School of Business Administration, Harvard University. Presents decision analysis in a formal mathematical style using calculus and matrix analysis. It discusses prior and posterior distributions at length and presents many results on sampling distributions.

SCHLAIFER, R.A. 1969. *Analysis of Decisions under Uncertainty*. New York, N.Y., McGraw-Hill. An introduction to logical analysis of problems of decisions under uncertainty that does not use mathematics beyond high-school algebra. It shows in great detail how one can structure apparently realistic problems and how one can elicit responsible judgemental inputs from the decision-maker. This book is written to be used for a graduate course in business administration.

Chapter 14
Cost–benefit analysis

Meheroo Jussawalla

Chee-wah Cheah

Cost–benefit analysis involves an assessment of the economic desirability of a project which yields its return over a period of years or over the economic life of an investment. It is one of several planning methods that caters to the need for systematic processes of decision-making that concern the rate and pattern of economic growth. Cost–benefit analysis is used by planners who require a holistic and integrated approach to resource allocation. It covers the spectrum of economic, social and institutional costs and benefits and is relevant at all levels of decision-making, including assessment of alternative strategies in national or macro planning as well as appraisal of specific micro projects and the various decision levels in between. Used in the public sector, cost–benefit analysis is analogous to profitability analysis in the private sector.

Cost–benefit analysis entails quantification of programme inputs and outputs into monetary figures. However, the monetary estimation of benefits is not possible in some social programmes. For instance, the imputation of benefits stemming from a fertility-control programme requires one to place a value on human life in order fully to monetize programme benefits. For this reason, cost-effectiveness analysis is deemed more appropriate. Such analysis only requires that programme costs be quantified, while allowing outputs or benefits to be expressed in terms of the actual substantive programme outcomes rather than in monetary values. In this respect, the efficacy of a programme in attaining given goals is assessed in relation to the monetary value of the resources or costs put into the programme.

The impacts of most social projects do not occur instantaneously. That is, programme costs and benefits are usually dispersed over time. For example, how should a communication planner support research on fibre optics as a substitute for transmarine cables, a source of intercontinental communication that is likely to be available by the end of the twentieth century? Should India and Malaysia be connected by sharing transponders on Intelsat V or should they have their telecommunication service through the use of fibre-optics technology? The benefits and costs of both these communication technologies span the future. How should the decision-maker choose between these two technologies? Alternatively, take the example of television studios in a developing country being constructed by the private industry as against those constructed by the government department of information and broadcasting. To render such a selection realistic, future benefits and costs of both projects must be translated into *present values*. This involves the technique known as discounting, which adjusts costs and benefits over time to a common base for comparison. To put it simply, the opportunity cost of resources withdrawn from the private sector should be measured in terms of the *present value* of private consumption forgone. Therefore, the evaluation of a given programme and the comparison of alternatives requires that interest be reckoned to determine the present value of future benefits and costs. The stream of benefits and costs must be discounted back to the present to render comparisons more real.

Communication planners are aware of the difficulty in searching for alternative strategies that meet national objectives because physical and financial resources are limited. It becomes crucial for them to assess the long-term social costs and benefits of a given communication programme in order to justify the allocation of scarce resources.

Definition

Cost–benefit analysis is a conscious assessment and quantification of any given programme's effects. Once specified, the social costs and benefits of the programme are translated into a common monetary unit, so that benefit–cost comparisons can then be made. It is designed to provide decision-relevant information inasmuch as it seeks to maximize the present value of all benefits less costs of a proposed programme (within certain constraints). For certain programmes in which benefits cannot be measured in pecuniary terms, programme assessment can be conducted via a cost-effectiveness analysis. Such an analysis also allows for comparison and ranking of choices among potential alternatives according to the magnitudes of their effects relative to their costs. Note that the comparison here is stated in terms of units of effectiveness for achieving particular programme outcomes. In cost–benefit analysis, present values are arrived at by the technique of discounting. This technique essentially reduces the stream of programme costs and/or benefits to a single denomination via the method of compound interest.

Interest rate and discount rate are different names for what is arithmetically the same thing, but the two terms are used in different contexts (Pearce, 1971). The discount rate provides an indicator for the opportunity cost of waiting for a benefit. For example, suppose you have the opportunity to lend money for one year at an 8 per cent rate of interest. You are then trading one today's dollar for one dollar and eight cents a year from now. You will refuse to lend at 4 per cent when 8 per cent is available, other things being equal. The opportunity cost of money is thus 8 per cent. In general, then, one dollar invested today at r per cent for n years will be worth $\$1 \times (1 + r)^n$. The *present value* of one dollar payable in n years would be

$$\$1 \times \frac{1}{(1 + r)^n}$$

The *present value* of a project of which the investment R yields an income stream over n years would be

$$PV = \frac{R_1}{1 + i} + \frac{R_2}{(1 + i)^2} + \frac{R_3}{(1 + i)^3} \cdots \frac{R_n}{(1 + i)^n}$$

By definition we can treat a present value calculated over future time exactly as if it were a payment occurring at that time. The discount rate at which the present value of a project becomes zero is known as its *internal rate of return*.

In communication planning, the production and dissemination of information requires an investment of time, talent and equipment, because information is not free. Therefore, many interrelated activities have to be carefully analysed. A cost can be thought of as a negative benefit and a benefit as a negative cost. The 'homo economicus' of textbook notoriety is not ubiquitous (Stokey and Zeckhauser, 1978). Cost–benefit analysis is a means of converting inputs into intermediate outputs by a systematic examination of costs, effects and risks involved.

Assumptions

During the process of planning very few decision-makers use economic information to help them make trade-offs among alternative objectives and projects. They seldom ask 'Is it better to spend an additional $50,000 in locating public-telephone call offices in certain villages or provide CB radios to development workers in those same villages?' They are more likely to ask questions about the increased pay-off (benefits) that could be expected from increased allocations (costs) in a particular project. For example, given the objective of increased farm productivity and output, what additional improvements in per acre yields can be had with a given increase in investment? In such a case the planner needs to find data on the relative economic and social effectiveness of alternative approaches. The planner will perform a cost–benefit analysis.

The following assumptions are relevant to this exercise:

1. Individuals within one nation or within a single task environment constitute society with respect to calculation of social costs and benefits.
2. Only individuals comprising present society are considered, on the assumption that preferences of future generations are subject to change.
3. The benefits and costs accounted for in the analysis refer to changes, deriving from a programme or project, in the well-being of individuals within society. A positive change is considered a benefit whereas a negative change is considered a cost.
4. Social well-being or welfare is obtained as a matter of adding together the gains obtained by the totality of individuals.

The conceptual problem in discounting is straightforward, but the practical application presents difficulties. There are many caveats in using the rate of interest as a measure of appropriate discount in the public sector. Studies of observed consumer behaviour in the purchase of consumer durables have shown that individuals use a discount rate much higher than the interest rate when making a decision on which particular durable commodity to purchase. For example, consumers in the United States are willing to pay an interest rate of 18 per cent to finance durables while the interest on their time deposits is only 5.5 per cent. Any individual, corporation or public enterprise that is making positive savings at present should use a discount rate equal to the rate of interest received over time. But when investment is financed from borrowing then the discount rate is higher than the current rate of interest. The divergence between an individual discount rate and the social discount rate can be narrowed by policies of tax subsidies or tax credit (Hausman, 1979), such as the one given for home insulation on American energy legislation and the investment-tax credit given on the purchase price of equipment to manufacturers. Some important assumptions in using the discount rate are as follows:

1. We assume that financial markets are competitive because, if they are not, then the rate of change in buying public communication goods and services like postal services may be lower than incremental return on private investments. To put it simply, in order to determine the future stream of benefits in the public sector we need to know the rate at which capital would grow in the private sector. If financial markets are not assumed as competitive, then the problem would emerge of which rate of interest is appropriate as a measure of discount in the public sector.

2. Another important assumption is that the market rate of interest is closely related to the marginal productivity of investment and time preference, i.e. the degree of preference to spend in the present rather than postpone consumption to the future (Margolin, 1963). Marginal productivity is the measure of additional output per every unit of investment.

3. In the public sector, the convention is followed of assuming that all payments are made at the end of the year. Therefore, the term 'now' is misleading and may mean one year from now. The assumption is that the first payment is made one year from now, the last payment being made n years from now. While this terminology is confusing, there is no other way but to use it.

Finally, there remains the question of operational assumptions in conducting a cost–benefit analysis. It is assumed that valid and reliable data on costs, effects or benefits over the life span of the project can be gathered. This presupposes *a priori* knowledge of the physical quantities of inputs used by the project as well as the physical quantities of the project's outputs. Reliable estimates of the annual stream of costs and benefits thus depend on the attachment of realistic prices to these physical quantities.

History

The first time that an evaluation using the cost–benefit technique found expression was in the Flood Control Act of 1963 in the United States. Later, in 1950, the Federal Inter-Agency River Basin Committee produced a book of rules, called the Green Book, to help uniform implementation of cost–benefit analysis. However, pioneering work in this planning method came with the publication of Otto Eckstein's book *Water Resource Development* in 1958. A further detailed statement was published by the Harvard Water Resource Program in 1962.

In less-developed countries, cost–benefit analysis is widely used for the appraisal of hydroelectric projects, irrigation and transportation programmes. For such areas, Little and Mirrlees have published a manual of industrial project analysis in developing countries (Little and Mirrlees, 1969).

The application of cost-effectiveness as an evaluative technique has not been very extensive, compared with cost–benefit analysis. The cost-effectiveness method was developed primarily by military analysts in their evaluations of weapon systems. This method arises from the difficulties of constructing cost–benefit calculations for the horrors of war. Thus, military analysts modified the cost–benefit framework in the area of national defence by placing emphasis on the achievement of particular objectives at minimal cost. For example, an objective may be the destruction of enemy targets with effectiveness being assessed according to the portion of the specific target likely to be destroyed by various combinations of strategies, like manned bombers versus missiles (Hitch and McKean, 1960).

Despite the relatively undeveloped status of cost-effectiveness analysis as an evaluation tool, it often provides a more appropriate approach to evaluating policy-orientated experiments or quasi-experiments. This is because many social programmes generate outcomes which cannot be converted into monetary measures. Since data on effectiveness are easier to gather, cost-effectiveness analysis can provide useful information on the impacts of alternative programmes. To the extent that programme effects can be translated into monetary values, a cost-effectiveness analysis can be extended into a cost–benefit analysis.

The history of using the discount rate is tied in with the development of cost–benefit analysis and has evolved from the early thirties in the United States. Its application was widely divergent but focused mainly on projects of river-basin and water-resource development, and emerged from the theory of the time value of money or the general tendency of consumers to exercise a time preference between spending now and spending in the future. The higher the social time preference to spend now, the higher would be the discount rate on investment to induce postponement of current expenditure and to reduce future income into present value.

Irving Fisher in the early 1930s distinguished between the market rate of interest and the real rate. Real interest is measured in terms of satisfaction forgone or in terms of the goods given up when interest is paid. In other words, it is a measure of the opportunity cost of capital. This real rate, in the long run, establishes an equilibrium towards which the economy automatically tends when prices are stable. Historically the discount rate approximates to this real rate of interest.

Theory

The available resources within a society at any one point in time are limited. Society must choose among various courses of action so as to bring about the most efficient utilization of the scarce resources. Cost—benefit analysis is an appropriate method for evaluating the relative attractiveness of alternative uses of resources, particularly when such resource-allocation decisions must be made outside the market system. The theory-of-choice framework in economics provides some foundations for such an analysis.

Economics is the study of the allocation of scarce resources among competing uses in the satisfaction of human wants. It deals with questions regarding choice, subject to constraints. Given the fact of existing technology, available resources and consumption preferences of society, economists resort to welfare economics in deciding how resources ought to be allocated to maximize social well-being (Arrow and Scitovsky, 1969). Welfare economics provides certain criteria by which decision-makers can judge whether society has been made better or worse off as a result of an economic change, e.g. what are the impacts on rural residents' state of well-being when telephone services are provided there? It is assumed that individuals themselves are rational, that is, they know what is good for them and are better judges of their own welfare than a benevolent dictator. Change in an individual's state of well-being is deemed measurable in terms of his/her consumer's surplus. The activity of consumption is taken as means to an end, namely, want-gratification. Thus, consumer's surplus is interpreted as an indicator of satisfaction gain or loss consequent on the act of consumption in the satisfaction of human wants. The principle underlying consumer's surplus as an indicator of welfare is willingness to pay, or demand backed by purchasing power (Anderson and Settle, 1976). A rational individual expresses his or her preference for a good or service in terms of his or her demand measured by his or her willingness to pay for that good or service. Given the specific amount of goods or services bought, consumer's surplus is the difference between the maximum amount an individual is willing to pay and the amount he/she actually pays. For example, if the cost of a telephone connection to an existing network is $20, and if a prospective user is willing to pay $25 rather than not be connected, his consumer's surplus is $5. Thus, the individual experiences a satisfaction gain and is said to have reaped a benefit of $5 by being allowed access to the existing telephone network. In principle, consumer's surplus for each individual connected to the network can be aggregated to yield a measure of social benefits stemming from the provision of telephone services. It is important to note that this is only valid on the assumption of constant marginal utility of income. This assumption implies that an additional dollar yields the same amount of satisfaction to all individuals, irrespective of an individual's wealth.

The preceding example demonstrates how a project's benefits can be valued when the good or service is sold in the market-place. In many cases, the output of a public programme or project cannot be valued on the basis of the willingness-to-pay principle, for two main reasons. First, prices are or cannot be fixed for some publicly produced goods or services either because they are not traded or sold in the market-place or because of some wider objectives of public policy (e.g. national defence). Second, the effects of a public project can be very widespread, such that a more than routine consideration of direct impacts is required. For instance, the social benefits of education transcend those which accrue to the individual being educated. While it may be possible to measure private benefits in terms of what students are willing to pay for their education (in terms of tuition fees etc.), such measures will necessarily underestimate the magnitude of benefits accruing to society as a whole. Under such circumstances, planners need to derive more realistic imputations of benefits by careful examination of the overall effects of a public project on all parties consuming or who are affected by that project's outcome.

Whether or not a particular change in economic circumstances induced by a public programme or project is worth while may be judged on the basis of the Pareto criterion. The nineteenth-century economist, Vilfredo Pareto, established the criterion of efficient resource allocation being accomplished when there is no possibility of rearranging the existing pattern of resource use such that at least one person can be made better off with no one being made worse off. This simply means that any economic action or change must be judged by its effects on the happiness/satisfaction of all those affected by the change. A resource allocation is efficient so long as someone is made happier and no one is made less happy. For example, a rural electrification project may be considered Pareto-optimal if it raises the well-being of all residents in the rural area. Unfortunately, it is a fact of life that most changes in economic circumstances will 'hurt' at least someone. It is plausible that electric generators will pollute the air, thereby 'hurting' those rural residents living near by. Thus, reliance on the Pareto criterion would prevent any public-sector project from being undertaken at all.

The fundamental feature of cost–benefit analysis still remains that, for any activity, the gains must be compared with the losses. Hicks and Kaldor devised a compensation principle whereby those who gain from an economic change can compensate (hypothetically) the losers and still be better off than before the change. In this context, those who gain from a communication project would be willing to pay some maximum amount for the change induced by the project and still be no better or worse off than before. Similarly, those who lose require some minimum compensation in order to accept the change. If the former exceeds the latter, the economic activity is warranted on the basis of the compensation principle. Note that these compensations are hypothetical, although the criterion does include instances which require actual compensation being made. In this respect, it is important to identify the actual incidence of a project's impact on society. That is, we need to identify gainers and losers as well as consider the distributional aspects of the project's costs and benefits. The distributional aspects of benefits and costs are important because the marginal utility of income is not the same for all persons. For example, an additional ten dollars may not have the same utility for an affluent person as it has for a poor person, because ten dollars may stand between the poor person and starvation. Consequently, willingness to pay for identical goods or services may vary.

In traditional economic theory the distributional effects of cost—benefit analysis are ignored. But if they are to be measured, then a social-welfare function can be evolved on the basis of the following formula:

$$SW = a_1 \cdot B_1 + a_2 \cdot B_2 + \ldots a_n \cdot B_n$$

in which B_1 to B_n are benefits to individuals '1' to 'n' and a_1 to a_n are the weights assigned to each individual. In other words, each person's gains or losses are assigned equitably. Such a social-welfare function is based on the hypothesis that the size of the economic pie and its division may not be the only factor of concern to the community. The method of slicing the pie may also be relevant (Maass, 1962). The incidence of benefits and costs across income and class groups needs consideration. The problem is translating the hypothetical gain into money values in order to determine compensation. Cost—benefit analysis makes allowances for the existence of welfare losses arising from projects in order to distribute income more equitably. It brings these objectives to bear on production decisions.

Social cost—benefit analysis differs from that conducted in the private sector in two important aspects. First of all, prices used in social analysis may be shadow prices and not actual prices paid or received in practice. Second, spill-over effects are included in social analysis whereas a private firm would not be interested in them. Such effects, known as externalities, are also valued in terms of shadow prices. Shadow or accounting prices are simply prices attributed to a good or service or a factor of production on the premise that they are better reflections of true scarcity values. Shadow prices are also attributed to project outputs which are 'unpriced', that is, non-traded outputs. An example of shadow pricing is that the cost of employing an extra worker must be valued at its opportunity cost to society. In the presence of minimum-wage laws and high unemployment, the cost of hiring a previously unemployed person is often mistakenly valued at the minimum wage. It is important to understand that since this worker did not previously engage himself/herself in any productive activity, the opportunity cost of hiring him/her is zero. That is, the shadow price of this worker should be zero since society did not give up any output in return for hiring him/her.

As another example, consider the case where funds used in a public project are borrowed at an interest rate fixed by regulation. The opportunity cost of these funds is the interest forgone by the bank if it had lent the money to someone else for other purposes. Thus, the shadow price of borrowing money should reflect its true scarcity value, that is, the interest rate these funds would have commanded in an unregulated financial market. The use of shadow prices is essentially an attempt to measure the real costs of inputs or real benefits of outputs to society. This is what makes social cost–benefits analysis different from discounted-cash-flow methods of investment appraisal. However, the mode of obtaining present values, via discounting, remains the same. In discounting the future streams of project costs and benefits, we have to be very careful not to confuse the discount rate used in cost–benefit analysis with the discount rate which the federal reserve system in the United States charges to its member banks for money borrowed. The member bank pays interest when the loan is negotiated rather than when it is repaid. Commercial banks are discouraged in normal times from using the federal 'discount window'.

In theory the use of the discount rate in calculating the present value of future benefits is highly sensitive. Different discount rates yield different present values when we use the formula explained in the section on definition (Musgrave and Musgrave, 1976):

Projects	X	Y	Z
Costs ($)	10 380	10 380	10 380
Number of of years	5	15	25
Annual benefits ($)	2 397	1 000	736
		Present value of benefit stream ($)	
Discount rate (%):			
3	10 978	11 938	12 816
5	10 380	10 380	10 380
8	9 571	8 559	7 857

In the above table of three different investments X, Y and Z, with equal cost and income flows spread over five, fifteen and twenty-five years, the present values of benefits remain the same at a 5 per cent rate of discount. As we reduce the discount rate to 3 per cent, Z becomes the best investment and X the worst. Reducing the discount rate increases the present value more if the period of benefits is longer. But when we increase the discount rate to 8 per cent, project X becomes more attractive because a higher rate favours short-term investment. Such ranking of investments is important and useful to the decision-maker.

When cost–benefit analysis is used by communication planners, it is important to remember that information production and use are not free. There are interdependent activities in communication planning such as the use of mobile vans to carry health workers to target audiences under a family-planning programme. Under those circumstances, the theory of cost–benefit must be used to sub-optimize the output of individual agencies within a system. Such an agency calculates its own internal benefits and costs in respect of alternatives elsewhere. Often there are spill-over effects from one communication subsystem to another. These sub-optimization exercises have to be coordinated for macro-level planning and forecasting.

Main uses

Assuming that the tangible and intangible benefits and costs are known, then planning of a specific project becomes economically feasible and declared viable. The key to the optimization of resource allocation is found in a comparison of marginal costs and marginal benefits, after which it becomes necessary to calculate the rate of depreciation in the service value of a project, its maintenance and operational costs (Jussawalla, 1969). Net benefits will be maximum when marginal benefits are equal to marginal costs, i.e. the optimal scope of the activity will be obtained when the benefit—cost ratio is unity. This is shown in Figure 1.

Marginal benefit (cost) is defined as the change in total benefit (cost) per unit change in the quantity of output. For instance, when output is at three units, total benefits are valued at $73,000. As output increases to four units, total benefits are now valued at $94,000. Thus, the additional benefits (or marginal benefits) resulting from a unit increment in output are $94,000 — $73,000, or $21,000. Marginal benefits for the range of quantity produced are depicted in the bottom diagram. Marginal costs are obtained in a similar manner. Note that when the difference between total benefits and total costs is at its maximum, marginal cost is equal to marginal benefit.

Assume four different communication projects involving different forms of media: A. Newspapers and journals; B. Radio; C. Interpersonal communication; and D. Television. The cost increases from A to D. In Table 1, column (4) measures the marginal benefit—cost ratio by dividing the increase in costs encountered by moving up from a less expensive to a more expensive medium. For example, radio costs $5 million more than newspapers and yields $15 million more in benefits. The marginal benefit—cost ratio is 3 : 1.

In many cases, decisions relating to one policy may affect the operations of another. There may also be some degree of complementarity. Optimization would be more meaningful if such interdependencies are also evaluated, i.e. the benefits of the school system depend partly on the availability of library services. Greater centralization of decision-making authority results from the technology of processing large amounts of data.

A second use of cost—benefit analysis is in helping macro-level planners to narrow down objectives for specific implementation. Many objectives of national policy are not, in the first instance, meaningful in operational terms. They appear in plan documents in very general terms like 'better educational opportunity' or 'higher productivity of farm lands' (United Nations Centre for Development Planning, 1976). For these to be achieved through direct policy action, they require *ex ante* evaluation of the cost—benefit type, i.e. an evaluation prior to programme or project implementation. It helps in establishing

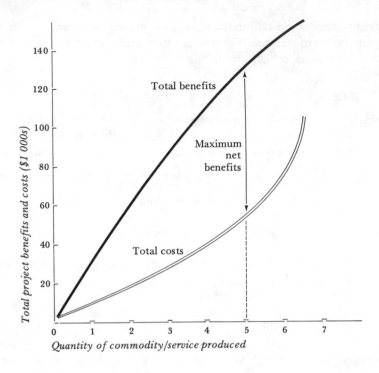

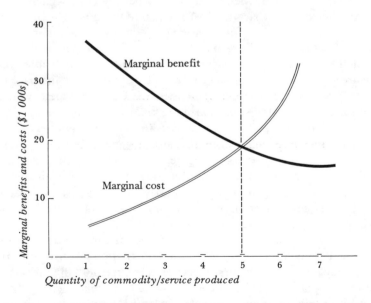

FIG. 1. Maximum net benefits in relation to total benefits/costs and marginal cost/benefit

TABLE 1. Marginal benefit–cost ratios in four communication projects

Policy	(1) Total cost ($ million)	(2) Total benefit ($ million)	(3) Benefit–cost ratio	(4) Marginal ratio
A Newspaper	5	50	10 : 1	10 : 1
B Radio	10	65	6.5 : 1	15/5 = 3 : 1
C Interpersonal	15	71	4.73 : 1	6/5 = 1.2 : 1
D Television	20	75	3.75 : 1	4/5 = 0.8 : 1

performance targets and offers insights, such as the response of consumers to changes in telephone tariffs or of schools to audio-visual aids, especially where the target group is large and heterogeneous. If the objectives are over-optimistic then targets can be redefined.

A third use of cost–benefit analysis is at the micro level, not only before the selection and operational decisions are made, but during and after project implementation. This is because original cost estimates may escalate as new expenditures arise, unexpected externalities may appear and some predicted results may not materialize. Net benefits may not be the same *ex post* as in the original forecast.

A fourth use of cost–benefit analysis is that it can be used as a sub-set in a performance budgeting exercise or in a programme, planning and budgeting system (PPBS). In a government decision-making process, cost–benefit analysis helps in the selection of a specific programme among alternative means of accomplishing given ends. If objectives are clearly defined, the analysis gives specific assistance in ascertaining the decisions that are most advantageous in terms of the objectives accepted. It helps to make implicit judgements more explicit and helps to eliminate the worst projects (Due and Friedlander, 1973).

A fifth use of this planning method is that it considers different approaches to measuring and fixing a trade-off point in situations that call for wide-ranging impacts beyond the scope of the project. For example, an educational television programme viewed by rural women may raise the nutritional value of family meals, increase agricultural output, decrease the birth rate, lower the infant mortality rate. An evaluation that helps to choose a programme that reinforces other goal areas can maximize the payoff in the use of scarce resources.

Limits and cautions

In comparing programmes with different objectives, cost–benefit analysis is of limited usefulness because it does not solve the problem of optimal outputs of social goods. Another limitation is that it does not help in prioritizing various programmes, such as, for example, NASA versus training of skills or Satellite

Business Systems versus highways. Quantification of social benefits and selection of an appropriate social rate of discount pose many difficulties in the way of accurate cost–benefit analysis. The technique tends to overemphasize those benefits and costs that can be quantified compared with those that cannot. While it aids in measuring the distributional effects of alternative programmes, it does not contribute to the establishment of a social-welfare function. It should not be used for providing society's answer to the relative desirability of various patterns of income distribution (Weisbrod, 1968).

The calculation of accounting prices and shadow wages is difficult and complicated, so that less accurate, simpler analysis may be called for. One of the major difficulties in the estimation of accounting prices is to decide whether an output is traded, non-traded or a mixture of the two (Mirrfees, 1978). For instance, an appropriate discount rate for a developing economy depends on prevailing conditions in the labour market. Where labour is in excess supply and where unemployment is high, wages are not counted as economic cost and are not deducted from the gross benefit stemming from investment in the project. Again, in less-developed countries a zero shadow wage of labour is assumed on the basis that productivity of unskilled labour is low or near zero wages. In such a case, the social yield on capital is measured only in terms of the rate of return on capital, and the output of the project would be attributable only to capital and land.

Procedures

Cost–benefit analysis is a tool in the evaluation of programmes or projects for which economic considerations are important and benefits can be quantified in monetary terms. It starts with the specification or identification of the project's inputs and outputs. Expected programme outputs are then quantified via accounting prices to arrive at the anticipated flow of benefits over time from the inception to the economic demise of the project. Benefits and costs are then compared and combined into a measure of social profitability. Cost–benefit

TABLE 2. Framework of cost–benefit/effectiveness analysis

Costs	(compared with)	Effects	(or) Benefits	(to arrive at)	Measures of social profitability
1. Direct capital, administration, operational etc.) 2. Indirect		1. Quantified outputs 2. Other measures	1. Outputs valued in monetary units		1. Benefit–cost ratio 2. Net benefits 3. Internal rate of return 4. Cost-effectiveness ratio

comparison involves the technique of discounting, which reduces future flow of benefits and costs into present values. In general, the well-being of society or residents within a task-environment is said to have increased as a result of a programme if benefits exceed costs. Cost–benefit analysis also provides a criterion for choice among alternative programmes. In those social programmes where expected benefits are impossible to quantify, a cost-effectiveness analysis can be used. A cost-effectiveness analysis allows for comparison and ranking of choices among alternative programmes according to the magnitude of non-quantifiable outcomes relative to their costs. The framework of cost–benefit/effectiveness analysis is illustrated in Table 2. Five stages in completing a cost–benefit analysis are listed below.

1. *Statement of objectives.* What does the activity seek to attain within the framework of overall social welfare? The goal may be quite specific, like the use of an educational and communication satellite to reduce the birth rate through family planning and expand agricultural output through the diffusion of improved farm practices. There may be other long-range related goals, such as the improved health of the rural population, an increase in the country's food supply and the building of buffer stocks of food grains. But the first stage for cost–benefit analysis is to find a definition of the objectives so that it can be used for decision-making. It is also important that the project's objective be clearly defined so that the anticipated effects of the project can be measured more precisely.

2. *Evaluation of alternatives.* There may be alternative ways of attaining the given objectives; there can be different locations for earth stations and different timings for relaying the information to farmers and housewives; and programme designs and contents may vary to produce the maximum impact on the target audience. Cost–benefit analysis cannot consider all alternatives because information production itself is expensive. Only major alternatives are considered and arranged in order of priority based on selected explicit criteria. One must note that, although selection of alternatives is a matter of value judgement, the selected alternatives must be potentially viable and operational to allow for estimation of costs and benefits. For instance, what are the relative values of an extra earth station and an additional subsidy to an agricultural experimentation centre? Benefits and costs of both alternatives have to be measured in monetary units to avoid the problem of adding apples and oranges. In economics the assumption is that consumers prefer present gratification to future receipt of benefits. If the frame of reference for the project is fertilizer technology for farming, then the analysis proceeds to assess the present value of the future stream of benefits.

3. *Calculation of costs.* The costs of a programme refer to those inputs or resources that are required, directly or indirectly, to conduct the programme. Normally, the costs of any particular programme are presumed to be equi-

valent to the financial outlay associated with that programme. These direct expenditures, sometimes called accounting costs, are, however, only a partial measure of the total programme costs. One must realize that the change, if any, in the well-being of individuals stemming from one particular use of resources (i.e. the programme under consideration) must be compared with alternative uses of the same resources (i.e. other programmes) because of economic scarcity. This implies that an appropriate measure of programme costs is the value of opportunities forgone. For example, the cost to an individual participating in a vocational training programme may be his forgone earnings from a regular job while receiving the training. The concept of cost as the value of opportunities forgone is the economist's notion of opportunity cost.

The cost components associated with a particular programme can be usefully categorized as direct and indirect costs. Direct costs include all those explicit programme expenditures for personnel, administration, equipment, facilities, supplies and any other labour and operating costs incurred. In addition to these explicit expenditures, implementation of a particular programme may incur implicit or indirect costs which are normally reflected in forgone opportunities. Such indirect costs may include forgone earnings or output consequent on the use of resources in a particular programme instead of for other uses and 'hidden' inputs which are not reflected in the budgeted costs of programmes, e.g. value of volunteer services in child-care programmes, value of time spent waiting for service in public-health centre etc. In short, the estimation of total programme costs requires the determination and valuation of (a) direct and specific resources used by the programme and (b) indirect inputs not included in programme budgets.

After an exhaustive identification and valuation of programme costs, the time factor has to be considered, so as to enable comparisons of costs accruing in the future to those occurring in the present. That is, the flow of programme costs over time must be discounted to arrive at present value. As an example, we will consider a study conducted by Martin Carnoy on educational-television projects in Third World countries (Carnoy, 1975). Detailed data on the investment costs and the operating costs for the educational television (ETV) project in El Salvador were obtained from a comprehensive study by Richard Speagle (1971) and are reported in Table 2 of Carnoy's paper. We shall use these data to illustrate how to discount the flow of future costs to arrive at the present value of the project's cost. Before we do so, however, we need to make some assumptions. The data available are for the period 1966–73, with the major investment in the project (transmission equipments) occurring in 1971. Because the life of transmission equipments is estimated at ten years, we need to make assumptions concerning the project costs from 1973 to 1980. We make the following assumptions:

1. The scrap value of transmission equipments at the end of ten years is zero.
2. Reception equipments have a life of five years, i.e. subject to a rate of depreciation of 20 per cent per year. The scrap value of reception equipments is equal to the purchase value minus depreciation.

TABLE 3. The cost of ETV in El Salvador (in million colones)

Year	Investment						
	Transmission equipment	Reception equipment	Building and air conditioning	Remodelling of classrooms	Start-up costs	Operating costs	Total
1967	0	0	0	0	0.2	0	0.20
1968	0.1	0	0	2.3	0.8	0	3.20
1969	0.6	0.1	0	0	0.8	0.7	2.20
1970	0.1	0	0.6	0	0.6	0.9	2.20
1971	3.9	0.3	0.3	0	0.5	1.1	6.10
1972	0	0.3	0.2	0	0.5	1.2	2.20
1973	0	0.3	0	0	0.5	1.2	2.00
1974	0	0	0	0	0	1.32	1.32
1975	0	0	0	0	0	1.45	1.45
1976	0	0	0	0	0	1.60	1.60
1977	0	0.3	0	0	0	1.76	2.06
1978	0	0.3	0	0	0	1.93	2.23
1979	0	0.3	0	0	0	2.13	2.43
1980	0	0	0	0	0	2.34	2.34

The data on the cost of ETV in El Salvador under these assumptions are reported in Table 3.

It would be simple to add up these costs and conclude that the cost of the project (not including start-up costs) is 31.53 million colones. But this is wrong, for a colón which must be paid this year is worth more than that to be paid ten years from now. If the interest rate is 15 per cent per year, depositing 25 colones in a bank this year only the account will have 100 colones ten years from now. Thus, to meet a 100 colones expenditure this year will require spending 100 colones, while meeting a 100-colón expenditure ten years from now requires only a present expenditure of 25 colones. Put in more technical terms, the *discounted value* or present value of 100 colones due in ten years is only 25 colones, if the *discount rate* (i.e. the interest rate) is 15 per cent per year.

Using a discount rate of 15 per cent, which given our assumption of a 10 per cent rate of inflation implies 5 per cent real interest, we can calculate the present value of the ETV project as follows:

$$P = \sum_{i=0}^{13} \frac{C_i}{(1+r)^i} - \frac{S}{(1+r)^{14}}$$

where P is the present value of the flow of expenditures as of 1967; i is the year number, starting with 0 for 1967 when the project started and ending with 13 for 1980; C_i is the project's costs in year i, and S is the scrap value of the reception equipments, which are to be purchased during 1978–79 to replace those purchased earlier (1970–73). The reason the scrap value is discounted for fourteen years is that we assume that these equipments will be sold at the end of

TABLE 4. Discounted expenditures (at 15 per cent discount rate)

Year	Expenditure (C_i)	Discounted expenditure $(C_i/(1 + r)^i)$	Year	Expenditure (C_i)	Discounted expenditure $(C_i/(1 + r)^i)$
1967	0.20	0.20	1975	1.45	0.47
1968	3.20	2.78	1976	1.60	0.45
1969	2.20	1.66	1977	2.06	0.51
1970	2.20	1.45	1978	2.23	0.48
1971	6.10	3.49	1979	2.43	0.45
1972	2.20	1.09	1980	2.34	0.38
1973	2.00	0.86	1981	0.59	− 0.08
1974	1.32	0.50			

1980. The proceeds from selling these equipments at the purchase cost less depreciation is:

$$S = 0.3(1 - 0.20)^3 + 0.3(1 - 0.20)^2 + 0.3(1 - 0.20) = 0.586$$

We entered this number with a negative sign in 1981, for it represents a revenue for that year as opposed to the expenditures in the years 1967–80 in Table 4. Thus, at the start of the project, 1967, the present value of costs over the life of the project is 14.69 million colones, less than half the figure obtained by simply summing the totals of Table 3. The meaning of this figure of 14.69 million colones is quite simple. To undertake a communications project with the expenditures pattern of E T V, all that is needed is an initial deposit of 14.69 million colones at interest rate of 15 per cent. The annual expenditures on the project are met by withdrawing the required amount from the account.

4. *Calculation of benefits.* The effects of a project can be categorized as having direct impacts only on social well-being or as impacting on total welfare so that no single person is rendered worse off by the investment (Mishan, 1975). The former category is also known as a partial equilibrium approach which only considers direct programme effects, whereas the latter category is the general equilibrium approach that takes into account both direct and secondary programme effects.

Figure 2 illustrates in a simplistic and synoptic way two aspects of the effects that influence the decision-making process, particularly as it relates to the public sector. The effects tree indicates that for a general approach all the effect flows would have to be assessed, i.e. all the outputs of a project that positively or negatively affect people's welfare. The problem is to include them in a meaningful way. In the effects tree, increased output that stems from the increased output of a project is a secondary tangible benefit. But from the assessment point of view all 'stemming from' benefits, if included in an assessment, would result in a gross overstatement. For example, it would be

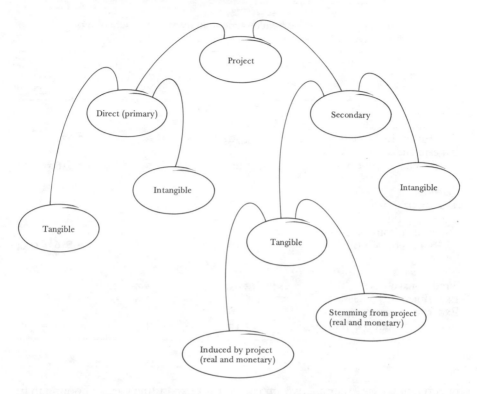

FIG. 2. Direct and secondary influences on decision-making

tantamount to calculating the value of bread as stemming from the establishment of a public-telephone call office that helps the farmer to market his wheat at competitive prices.

Tangible benefits can be direct and indirect. The direct benefits can be easily identified and measured in economic terms. For instance, the extension of telephones to rural areas would reduce the need for farmers to spend money on travelling to markets for price and demand information. Telephone networks are less expensive than travel by bus or railway and do not cause air and noise pollution. The by-products of the telephone system such as communication for emergency medical relief, or for fire and flood emergencies, are externalities or indirect benefits. In like manner, foreign aid for communication-technology transfer may entail a mutually beneficial increase in trade that can be quantified as a direct benefit. But a reduction in the risk of war would be an indirect benefit and economic analysis cannot quantify the 'worth' of averting a war.

Where benefits are not quantifiable in monetary units, project evaluation may proceed on the basis of measuring the project's cost-effectiveness. The following example from Martin Carnoy's study demonstrates the cost-

TABLE 5. Summary results of cost-effectiveness analysis (basic schooling alternatives, El Salvador)

Subject	Gain, February to October	Gain over traditional	Cost-effectiveness ratios
Mathematics			
Traditional classes	1.95		
Experiment ETV class	5.70	3.7	3.7/$22 = 0.17
Experiment control group			
(reform but no ETV)	5.20	3.2	3.2/$16 = 0.20
Science			
Traditional classes	1.34		
Experiment ETV class	4.20	2.9	2.9/$22 = 0.13
Experiment control group			
(reform but no ETV)	5.10	3.8	3.8/$16 = 0.24
Social studies			
Traditional classes	2.61		
Experiment ETV class	6.40	3.8	3.8/$22 = 0.17
Experiment control group			
(reform but no ETV)	3.10	1.5	1.5/$16 = 0.10

effectiveness assessment of two alternatives for expanding basic schooling in El Salvador (Carnoy, 1975). The choice to be made was between the establishment of ETV and an educational-reform programme involving expanded curriculum and materials and retrained teachers. Both programmes were designed to serve the same number of students with the objective of expanding basic schooling. Programme benefits were interpreted as educational gains measured by means of standard achievement tests administered at the beginning and at the end of the school year in 1972. Actual annual costs for both programmes were calculated to be $16 and $22 per student for the reform programme and ETV respectively. Table 5 summarizes the results of the cost-effectiveness analysis. Since the cost-effectiveness ratio for ETV is generally larger than that for the reform programme (with the exception of social studies), Carnoy argues for investing in the curriculum and teaching reforms instead of installing ETV.

Cost–benefit analysis differs from cost-effectiveness analysis in that the former approach requires quantification of benefits in money terms. The basic problem is to determine the appropriate value to be attached to the programme's output. If the output produced is sold, market prices could be used to estimate the benefits of this output. This is only valid subject to the condition that the market is perfectly competitive. Otherwise, market prices are said to be distorted and do not reflect the true scarcity value of the output. For example, some governments practise rationing by imposing a price ceiling on essential goods or services. To the extent that such goods or services may command a higher price in an unregulated market, the use of the regulated market price may underestimate the true value of benefits to society. In this instance, the 'correct' price for accounting benefits should be the unregulated market price.

In many cases, the programme's output is not sold or traded in the market. For such non-traded outputs, planners need to impute shadow prices that will reflect the estimated value of benefits resulting from these outputs. For instance, the value of an irrigation project could be measured in terms of the consequent reduction in flood damage and the increased crop production associated with the availability of irrigation. Suppose the irrigation project reduces the probability of a flood from 1/20 to 1/100 and that losses from flooding at any time are estimated at $10 million. In the absence of the irrigation project, expected losses are 1/20 × $10 million, or $500,000. When the project is implemented, expected losses are reduced to $100,000 (i.e. 1/100 × $10 million). The expected benefits of the irrigation project in terms of flood damage averted are $400,000. Suppose further that crop production increased from 10,000 tons to 20,000 tons and that a ton of crop output can be sold at a competitive price of $2. The benefits of increased crop production are thus $20,000 (i.e. 20,000 − 10,000 tons × $2/ton). In this example, the total estimated benefits of the irrigation project are $420,000, out of which benefits worth $400,000 derive from a non-traded output, namely reduction in flood damage.

In some cases, an estimate of the value of a non-traded or unpriced programme output can be obtained by determining how much individuals would be willing to pay for an equivalent service. For example, the benefits derived from using a community television set in a village may be imputed from the cost of privately owned sets, and the numbers used. Or the value to society of public education may be estimated on the basis of tuition fees changed by private institutions. Estimating the benefits of a project would have to cover the stream of benefits over a number of years and this would mean making allowance for uncertainty of future conditions (*Business Week*, 1979). Because of the time preference of society, present benefits are considered more important than future benefits. In order to make present and future benefits comparable, future benefits must be adjusted on the basis for the year in which they actually occur, via the technique of discounting. The application of discounting as applied to benefits is conceptually similar to that in the case of costs (see section 3 above).

5. *Comparison and use in decision-making.* The basic problem in comparing a programme's costs and benefits is the commensurability problem. That is to say, benefits and costs are usually not directly comparable, because they occur at different points in time. For instance, the costs of a vocational-training programme are borne during the training phase, whereas the benefits will presumably span over the working life of the trainees. This is the main reason

why discounting is performed, in order to put all costs and benefits on the same time basis.

One major issue in discounting is the choice of an appropriate discount rate. There are three major theories of deriving the social discount rate, each of which reflects different underlying assumptions for discounting.

Theory One: The social time preference must be reflected in the discount rate. This theory stems from the fact that if money is not spent but invested, it earns interest. When the money gets used for a communication project, it loses interest but future benefits flow from it. The future has to be discounted in terms of the present. The social time preference rate is an elusive concept inasmuch as the desire of society as a whole to spend in the present has to be estimated. Next, we have to measure the rate at which society can be induced to postpone present consumption and to invest in future consumption. Such a social time preference rate would equal the marginal productivity of capital in the private sector if investment were made in a riskless society. Since this is not realistic the only substitute is to use the current government bond rate, which reflects riskless investment. If people are willing to buy bonds at 7 per cent this rate reflects society's time preference. The bond rate may not be a true reflection of social time preference, but it is the closest approximation.

Theory Two: For public projects the social rate of discount should reflect the rate of return forgone if the same investment had been made in the private sector. This is known as the opportunity-cost rate. In general, one dollar invested today at y per cent rate of interest for n years will be worth $\$1 \cdot (1 + r)^n$. Its present value is $\$1 \cdot [1/(1 + r)^n]$. If the rate of interest is 8 per cent then the value of every dollar invested for two years is $(1.08) \cdot (1.08) = \$1.166$ and the present value of every dollar due for repayment two years hence is $(1.00/1.08) \cdot 2 = 0.857$. Therefore, a project of which the benefits occur over n years will generate a present value of

$$B = \frac{b_0}{1} + \frac{b_1}{(1 + r)} + \frac{b_2}{(1 + r)^2} + \cdots \frac{b_n}{(1 + r)^n}$$

where r is the rate of discount and b_1 is the dollar amount of benefits generated in the first year and so on till n years.

Theory Three: The selection of the actual rate of discount should consider the possibility that the social time preference rate (bond rate) is generally lower than the opportunity-cost rate (marginal productivity of capital). This relationship has an important implication for the projects that would be selected when high discount rates are used. Projects with a long gestation lag would receive low priority if a high rate of discount is used, because the ratio of value added would have to be high to warrant selection of the project for investment. For instance, in 1979 the United States Government commissioned cost–benefit experts to assess whether the investment made by the US Army Corps of Engineers on waterways is worth the taxpayer's money. While the corps has justified its projects over decades using cost–benefits analysis, it is under attack for the rate of discount used and overstatement of benefits. The rate of discount is criticized as being unrealistically low (*Business Week*, 1979). High discount rates tend to lower benefits while low rates raise benefits.

It is apparent that the results of a cost–benefit analysis are sensitive to the choice of discount rate. One way of resolving the complex and sometimes controversial issue of whether the appropriate discount rate has been used is by conducting 'sensitivity' analyses. Such an approach only requires that discounting calculations be made based on several different but plausible rates of discount. Another resolution to the sometimes arbitrary use of discount rate(s) is made by the calculation of the programme's anticipated rate of return. A programme's rate of return is that discount rate which would equate the present value of programme benefits to programme costs.

The final step in a cost–benefit study consists of comparing costs with benefits stemming from each alternative under consideration. The same discount rate should be applied to each set of calculations to ensure comparability of results across projects. One common approach directly compares programme costs with benefits to ascertain net benefits. That is, benefits less costs or net benefits are computed over the life span of the programme and then discounted to the present. The sum of these discounted net benefits reflects the present value of the project. Alternatives can thus be ranked according to the magnitude of this present value, thereby providing a basis for choice among alternatives. This approach is particularly useful in *ex ante* studies.

Another criterion for choice is the benefit–cost ratio. This ratio is obtained by dividing the sum of discounted benefits by the sum of discounted costs. The benefit–cost ratio is an indicator of the average pay-off per dollar spent on the programme. Hence the larger the ratio the greater would be the expected pay-off of the programme in question. The benefit–cost ratio is particularly useful in assessing the social profitability of a particular use of resources. Its main weakness is that it does not provide decision-makers with information regarding the magnitude of expected net benefits deriving from a programme.

Finally, choice among alternatives can be made on the basis of each alternative's anticipated rate of return. As mentioned earlier, the rate of return is that discount rate that would equate the present value of benefits to the present value of costs. Since the flow of benefits usually occurs after costs have been borne, it would require a higher discount rate to equate discounted benefits to discounted costs when the flow of benefits is higher relative to the flow of costs. In other words, a high rate of return implies that programme benefits exceed costs. As in the case of the benefit–cost ratio, the rate of return does not provide information on the size of programme net benefits.

It is important to realize that cost–benefit analysis is not a rigid technique with a specific set of rules and routines. Given the diversity of nuances and caveats inherent in public programmes, this evaluative technique should be used with wisdom and caution. Because of the lack of standard guidelines, it is foreseeable that particular cost components or programme outputs may be omitted, or that the wrong discount rate may be selected, or that the wrong method for cost estimation and benefits quantification has been used. All these represent areas where different judgements may appreciably alter the benefit–cost ratings of alternatives (Williams, 1973).

The analyst in particular should be obligated to provide decision-makers with data and results that are germane to the undertaking of rational public choices. Assumptions regarding cost and output quantification should be spelt out clearly. Reliability of such estimates as well as the likely effects that alternative assumptions would have on findings should be indicated. Decision-makers should recognize that conclusions of cost–benefit studies do not define policy actions. Rather, such conclusions should serve as useful sources of information that must be considered within a wider socio-economic framework.

Case example

Samuel Paul conducted a study of a two-year postgraduate programme in management education at the Indian Institute of Management in Ahmedabad (Paul, 1972). This study involves calculation of both private and social returns of the training programme. Using Paul's approach, we will conduct an *ex post* cost–benefit analysis of a similar but hypothetical programme in country X.

Country X implemented a three-year postgraduate management-education programme in 1977. The objective of this government-run programme is to augment and upgrade the supply of managerial workers as a means towards improving the production and distribution of goods and services within the country. Available data from the graduating classes of 1978, 1979 and 1980 indicated a post-training average starting salary of 1,000 pesos. Data for those who had worked prior to entering the programme showed an average pre-training monthly pay of 650 pesos. The typical employed graduate also receives an annual year-end bonus of 10 per cent of annual salary.

From the individual standpoint, the benefits of entering the programme are the expected improvements in earnings upon graduating. These benefits will presumably span the remaining period of an individual's working life. The expected earning improvement in the first year after graduation is 12 months $\times$ (1,000 − 650) $\times$ 1.1 = 4,620 pesos. After adjustments for the associated increase in personal income taxes, the estimated incremental earnings are 4,200 pesos. To calculate the future stream of benefits, two assumptions are required: (a) the programme graduate will maintain a constant earning differential of 4,200 pesos per year throughout his/her working career; (b) the typical graduate will have a post-training working career of thirty years. The private costs of entering the programme include both direct and indirect costs. The former category refers to tuition fees, books, travel and other incidental expenses. The indirect costs are earnings forgone by the potential trainee during the three-year training period. Direct and indirect costs are estimated to be 8,500 pesos for the initial year and 8,000 pesos for the second and third year. Benefits and costs are discounted to obtain measures of private returns. On average, an individual could have earned 10 per cent on his/her capital in alter-

TABLE 6. Net benefits

	Year 1	2	3	4–33	At $i = 10\%$
Benefits	0	0	4 200	4 200	$PV_B = 32\,902.36$
Costs	8 500	8 000	8 000	0	$PV_C = 20\,349.36$
NET BENEFITS	− 8 500	− 8 000	− 3 800	4 200	12 553

native uses. That is, the private opportunity rate of interest is 10 per cent. This serves as a good approximation for the discount rate. The present value of benefits (PV_B) is calculated by the formula:

$$PV_B = \sum_{n=1}^{33} \frac{B_n}{(1 + i)^n}$$

$$= \frac{0}{(1.1)} + \frac{0}{(1.1)^2} + \ldots + \frac{4\,200}{(1.1)^4} + \ldots + \frac{4\,200}{(1.1)^{33}}$$

where: B_n = benefits occurring at year n; i = rate of discount; and n = index of time. Similarly, the present value of costs (PV_C) is calculated by the formula:

$$PV_C = \sum_{n=1}^{3} \frac{C_n}{(1 + i)^n}$$

$$= \frac{8\,500}{(1.1)} + \frac{8\,000}{(1.1)^2} + \frac{8\,000}{(1.1)^3}$$

where C_n = costs incurred at year n. Note that the costs stream is only discounted over three years, since the individual incurred these costs during his/her training period.

The summary measures of private profitability are shown in Table 6. The present value of net benefits (or net present value) is simply the difference between PV_B and PV_C. At a discount rate of 10 per cent, the undertaking of management education is worth 12,553 pesos to the individual at the time he/she enters the programme. The benefit–cost ratio, obtained as PV_B/PV_C, is 1.6 : 1. This ratio can be interpreted as a pay-off of 1.6 pesos for every one peso 'invested' by the individual in terms of his/her out-of-pocket expenses and earnings forgone. Finally, the implicit rate of return is estimated to be 16.8 per cent. From the potential trainee's standpoint, it would pay him/her to undergo management education as long as his/her opportunity rate of interest is less than 16.8 per cent.

In order to estimate social benefits and costs, we must recall that the programme's objective is to increase the supply of trained managers available to country X's economy. As a result of earnings improvements, individuals will have to pay higher taxes. From the social standpoint, this increase in tax revenues represents an increase in the economy's resources and thus should be counted as social benefits. Moreover, trained managers are expected to contribute to increasing the economy's output of goods and services. These benefits may be estimated as that share of indirect taxes falling on the additional output as a result of the use of trained managers. Such an estimate may be based on the ratio of excise duties to value added of joint stock companies.

Besides earnings improvement, there are also substantial savings from indigenous training over what it would have cost to be trained elsewhere. These benefits may be estimated by comparing the cost of indigenous training with that of a likely alternative in the United States. Suppose that management training in the United States cost $10,000 per year. At an official exchange rate of 12 pesos per dollar, the cost of foreign training is 120,000 pesos compared with 20,000 pesos for similar training domestically. These costs include tuition fees and incidental expenses but exclude forgone earnings since this would be the same irrespective of where training is obtained. The estimated savings per graduate per year is thus 120,000 − 20,000 = 100,000 pesos. Because of import subsidization or other government policies, it may be more appropriate to use a shadow exchange rate. If the shadow exchange rate is 15 pesos per dollar, the cost savings would be 130,000 pesos. A variety of shadow rates may be used to test the sensitivity of estimated cost savings to various assumptions.

The quantification of earnings improvements and increases in personal taxes requires actual and/or projected figures for trainees graduating from the programme. This, in turn, requires a careful analysis of the demand for trained managers within the economy. Having established the demand for graduates, it would be possible to estimate the number of potential students entering the domestic programme rather than going overseas. The magnitude of cost savings can then be calculated on the basis of such an estimate.

In addition to those monetary benefits listed above, there are other external benefits which are not quantifiable. For example, education tends to generate an external benefit by improving the quality of social life. Moreover, there is a social value associated with the presence of assembled faculty resources to the extent that faculty members are available for consultation on local and national problems. A complete statement of social benefits must include these external benefits. Since they cannot be quantified, they will be disregarded. For this reason, decision-makers should be aware of the possible underestimation of social benefits stemming from the programme.

Social costs include fixed investment and operating and maintenance costs. Fixed investments refer to outlays on physical facilities like land, building, libraries, equipment etc. There is also a component of start-up costs in terms of training programmes for the faculty and the hiring of foreign advisers for curriculum development. Operating costs are salaries and wages of teaching and administrative staff, costs of ancillary services and supplies and routine maintenance. Finally, social costs must include earnings forgone by individuals who enter the programme. It is important to note that the amount of

TABLE 7. Hypothetical example of present values (in thousand pesos)[1]

Social benefits		Social costs	
Increase in direct personal taxes	750	Fixed investment	500
Increase in indirect taxes	800	Operating and maintenance costs	3 600
Cost savings	3 000	Earnings forgone	900
Earnings improvement	1 500		
		TOTAL COSTS	5 000
TOTAL BENEFITS	6 050		

1. From this example, the benefit–cost ratio is 1.2:1, implying a social pay-off of 1.2 pesos for every peso invested. Net present value is approximately 1.05 million pesos.

operating costs and forgone earnings depend on the actual and/or projected size of the student population.

The social profitability of the management education programme can now be estimated by making some reasonable assumptions about the social discount rate and length of the project's life. Alternatively, a variety of assumptions may be made to illustrate the programme's social profitability over a range of scenarios. Table 7 presents a hypothetical set of present values of programme costs and benefits.

Annotated bibliography

ANDERSON, A.; SETTLE, B. 1976. *Benefit–Cost Analysis. A Practical Guide.* Lexington, Mass., D.C. Heath. The authors explain the use of this evaluation method and its limitations. The work gives a step-by-step procedure for using benefit–cost analysis, dealing more with its practical implications than its theory.

ARROW, M.J.; SCITOVSKY, T. (eds.). 1969. *Readings in Welfare Economics.* London, Allen & Unwin.

Business Week. 1979. Cost–Benefit Trips up the Corps. 12 February.

CARNOY, M. 1975. The Economic Costs of Returns to Educational Television. *Economic Development and Cultural Change,* Vol. 23. No. 2, January, p. 207–48.

DUE, J.R.; FRIEDLANDER, A. 1973. *Government Finance: Economics of the Public Sector.* Homewood, Ill., Irwin.

HAUSMAN, J.A. 1979. Individual Discount Rates and the Purchase and Utilization of Energy-using Durables. *The Bell Journal of Economics,* Vol. 10, No. 1, Spring.

HITCH, C.J.; McKEAN, R.N. 1960. *The Economics of Defense in the Nuclear Age.* Cambridge, Mass., Harvard University Press.

JUSSAWALLA, M.F. 1969. *Evaluation of the Benefits of Nizamsafar Irrigation Project.* New Delhi, Planning Commission, Government of India.

LITTLE, J.; MIRRLEES, J.A. 1969. *Social Cost–Benefit Analysis.* Paris, OECD. (Manual of Industrial Project Analysis in Developing Countries, Vol. II.)

MAASS, A. (ed.). 1962. *Design for Water Resource Systems.* New York, N.Y., Macmillan.

MARGOLIN, A. 1963. The Social Rate of Discount. *Quarterly Journal of Economics,* Vol. 77, February.

MIRRLEES, J.A. 1978. Social Benefit–Cost Analysis and the Distribution of Income. *World Development,* Vol. 6, No. 2. This journal article supports the work done by Mirrlees and Little in using benefit–cost analysis in the Third World. The author emphasizes the difficulties of measuring social benefits and costs as distinct from economic ones.

MISHAN, E. 1975. *Cost–Benefit Analysis.* London, Allen & Unwin. The author has given every conceivable detail regarding the theory, rationale and practice of this method of project evaluation. It is a classic covering every aspect of the merits and drawbacks of using the method.

MUSGRAVE, R.A.; MUSGRAVE, P.B. 1976. *Public Finance in Theory and Practice.* New York, N.Y., McGraw-Hill. A well-worn textbook on the theory of government finance that serves as a handy guidebook for benefit–cost equations and discounting technique (see table on discount rates).

PAUL, S. 1972. An Application of Cost–Benefit Analysis to Management Education. *Journal of Political Economy*, Vol. 80, No. 2, p. 328–46.

PEARCE, D.W. 1971. *Cost–Benefit Analysis.* London, Macmillan.

SPEAGLE, R.E. 1971. *Educational Reform and Instructional TV in El Salvador: Payoffs and Benefits.* Washington, D.C., AED.

STOKEY, E.; ZECKHAUSER, R. 1978. *A Primer for Policy Analysis.* New York, N.Y., W.W. Norton. This book covers different methods used by economists in evaluating development projects. It includes econometric and economic methods and describes each method in detail.

UNITED NATIONS CENTRE FOR DEVELOPMENT PLANNING. 1976. Evaluation in Planning and Policy Making. *Economic Bulletin for Asia and the Pacific*, Vol. XXVII, No. 1, June.

WEISBROD, B.A. 1968. Income Redistribution Effects and Benefit Cost Analysis. In: S.B. Chase (ed,), *Problems in Public Expenditure Analysis.* Washington, D.C., Brookings Institution.

WILLIAMS, A. 1973. Cost–Benefit Analysis: Bastard Science and/or Insidious Poison in the Body Politick? In: W.A. Niskanen *et al.* (eds.), *Benefit–Cost and Policy Analysis.* Chicago, Ill., Aldine.

Chapter 15

Zero-based budgeting

Gerald E. Moriarty

Zero-based budgeting (ZBB) is a highly structured, systematic planning and budgeting process that has as its underlying need the requirement to search for and analyse alternative ways and levels of activity for all operational functions or projects. When used for planning recurring operational budgets, it precludes the practice of simply adding and justifying a fixed increase on the previous year's budget. It requires managers to:

Begin planning and budgeting exercises assuming they will have a near 'zero-budget' base. (The name of the technique can lead to unfortunate and incorrect connotations. It is not generally possible, or expected, to go right to zero base.)

Analyse all proposed uses of resources.

Justify complete plans and budgets from the ground up.

Hence, the ZBB process encourages the identification of functions and duties that have become inefficient and need to be reduced in priority or eliminated. It helps management allocate resources away from ineffective functions and make those resources available to more efficient functions. The method enables each competing request for funds to be compared and analysed against the limited financial resources available.

Definition

ZBB is a planning and budgeting technique that involves managers at all levels of an institution. It requires each manager to:

Establish operational objectives for his or her function, preferably derived from the overall institutional goals and strategies.

Define alternative methods of achieving each of those operational objectives.

Evaluate all advantages and disadvantages of each alternative and select the most appropriate to achieve the operational objective. Frequently the evaluation of alternatives will involve more than financial considerations, and it may not be possible satisfactorily to evaluate all promising alternatives fully within the time frame of the ZBB process. In this case, such alternatives should be identified for extensive consideration before the next planning and budgeting period.

Break up the chosen alternative into incremental levels of effort.

Prepare and rank, in order of priority, decision packages (see definition below) for each incremental level.

Decision packages are then reranked by successively higher levels of management, and those above a predefined level of affordability or decision point (set by previously approved expenditure guidelines) are approved and funded while others are deferred.

ZBB has developed well beyond the simple financial budgeting method its name tends to imply, to an overall planning and resource allocation technique. Accordingly, zero-based budgeting and planning, or zero-based planning, are more appropriate titles for the technique to be described in this chapter. Throughout, the following terms will be used and are usefully defined at this point:

Decision package is defined as 'an identification of a discrete function or operation in a definitive manner for management evaluation and comparison to other functions' (Phyr, 1970).

Decision-package set is a group of decision packages.

Decision unit is made up of one or more decision package sets and encompasses a whole and complete result-area for an organization. It is a cluster of activities for which a given manager can be held responsible, and for which we can define an input (or cost) and output (or benefit).

Assumptions

The fundamental requirement for performing ZBB is to have clearly understood objectives for using the technique. There are a number of uses ZBB can be put to, but unless the goals are clearly understood the implementation may fall short of expectation. Ultimately the success of ZBB requires an ability for innovative and analytical thinking by managers at all levels. ZBB assumes that in preparing decision packages for ranking, all functions, and the different levels of activity for achieving those functions, can be evaluated using a common measure—generally a monetary one.

History

ZBB was first used by the United States Department of Agriculture in the early 1960s and then abandoned shortly after. Its first widely known successful application was by Peter A. Phyr, who initiated its use in the late 1960s at Texas Instrument Corporation. This success prompted the newly elected Governor of the State of Georgia, Jimmy Carter, to introduce it to the Georgia State Department in the early 1970s. In 1977, shortly after his election to the Presidency of the United States, Carter ordered the establishment of ZBB through the United States Federal Government.

TABLE I. Most significant reasons for implementing ZBB

Purpose	Number	Percentage
To allocate resources better	17	30
To improve decision-making	14	25
To facilitate planning	11	20
To reduce costs/personnel	7	12
To reorganize	–	–
Miscellaneous	7	13
TOTAL	56	100

Source: Austin, 1977.

The popularity of ZBB is growing rapidly as its usefulness as a planning and resource allocation technique is appreciated. A 1977 survey by the American Management Association revealed the reasons given by a number of users for installing and operating this method (see Table I).

Main uses

The application of ZBB in communication planning is most likely to be seen as an operational planning and budgeting method by institutions involved in carrying out communication planning work. However, the systematic nature and approach of the method can be useful for planning and budgeting of resource allocation within specific communication projects themselves. ZBB is an excellent technique for relating detailed planning and budgeting to overall goals and strategies.

Within an institution, its main application is for use in the planning and budgeting of ongoing or recurring activities; for example, overhead operations such as finance and accounting, personnel, marketing, management services and engineering research. The technique or its general characteristics can be put to a range of other uses, for example:

Planning and budgeting for capital budgeting programmes.

Relating long-range strategies to reliable and achievable long-range plans.

Conducting a cost-reduction exercise on staff overheads.

Diagnosing specific operations within an institution so as to refine policy or set long-term strategies.

Allocating staff overheads on a more equitable basis.

Auditing the effectiveness of staff programmes.

Providing a data base to restructure an entire institution.

Although ZBB is a process by which goals and strategies are consolidated into specific operational plans and budgets, the method also provides the basis for modifying goals and strategies to recognize realities discovered during both planning and implementation.

Limits and caution

ZBB works best in an organization of participatory-management style. For optimum results, it requires managers who can be innovative and creative even under the pressures of budgeting and forward operational planning (which is often a tightly scheduled, tension-producing experience).

For most applications, the starting-point is a coherent set of overall institutional goals and strategies which must be made available to lower levels of management. In some situations, such as those in which competitive marketing organizations may find themselves, this may cause difficulties in risking the inadvertent disclosure of proprietary information as more and more people have access to that information. The time and paperwork to perform ZBB may be greater than for other planning and budgeting techniques—particularly 'incremental' techniques. This additional time and effort is most likely to be experienced in the first year of ZBB use. However, both time and paperwork will decrease considerably as the ZBB processes become more refined and staff become more familiar with them. It is probable that the time required to establish goals, strategies and operational objectives and to formalize the planning processes which are prerequisites for the success of ZBB should be employed whether zero-based budgeting or 'incremental' systems are used.

Short cuts and gamesmanship can develop and may detract from the success of the system and lead to possible failure. The politics or some other behavioural characteristics of institutions may also limit the benefits available from the technique. As with most methods, the success of ZBB will be dependent on the care and effort put into its introduction, implementation and follow-up.

Other techniques

Zero-based budgeting and planning as described in this chapter includes concepts similar to those of the programme, planning and budgeting system (PPBS). The overall ZBB operation draws on a number of other well-known managerial techniques. For example, in formulating specific operational objectives and analysing alternative methods to achieve those objectives, managers draw heavily on the techniques of management by objectives (MBO). Those institutions that already successfully use an MBO system find ZBB a valuable adjunct for translating broader institutional goals and strategies into specific operational objectives, and then for measuring and controlling the achievement of such objectives within available resources.

In ranking decision packages, the ZBB process requires the use of cost–benefit analysis and often the discounting technique. In choosing between decision packages, the use of techniques such as decision matrices and forced-choice matrices is extremely desirable if not essential.

Brainstorming is a very useful technique for developing alternative methods and breaking methods up into different incremental units.

Programme evaluation and review technique (PERT) and critical path method (CPM) are both excellent tools for analysing the implementation detail of plans. Often a PERT or CPM plan of a particular project will be useful in identifying all of the project components and their interrelationships over time prior to preparing decision packages.

Product or results

The end product or outcome of ZBB varies to some extent, depending on the use to which the process is being put. However, in all cases the specific result represents an integration of planning and budgeting. When used for operational or capital development planning and budgeting throughout an institution, the specific products will typically be the following:

Decision packages which identify discrete operations or projects, with their costs and benefits, to best achieve the specific institutional goals and strategies within an approved budget limit.

A ranking table which shows which decision packages will and will not be funded and the priority of packages so that adjustments during the year can easily be made.

Specific operational or capital development plans for each section or unit of the institution.

An overall consolidated institutional budget, which generally will be subdivided to include an individual budget for each section or project area.

Identification of alternative operational methods which require more intensive evaluation some time in the future.

Level of detail and level of confidence

One of the main reasons for the success of ZBB as a planning and budgeting tool is that it requires a very high level of detail to be produced throughout its process. The work involved in generating this extensive detail is widely distributed throughout the institution. In this way, precise information is produced by managers at all levels who are most familiar with the operations that are being evaluated.

As with all forward-planning techniques, the confidence managers can have in plans and budgets developed through ZBB is dependent on the levels of realism and detail in the supporting data on which costs are assessed (i.e. expected inflation levels, wage and material increases, effect of competition etc.). An advantage of the ZBB process stems from the way that operations are broken down into individual functions which are cost–benefit analysed in detail by those managers who understand them best and who will be responsible for implementing plans within those budgets. These analyses are then combined and scrutinized by higher and higher levels of management. Unlike many other budgeting and planning techniques, conducted by a very small number of persons in an institution, this process provides some safeguards against the probability of largely incorrect assumptions passing undetected.

An additional advantage of the participatory nature of ZBB is that it provides both an educational experience for younger, lower-level managers and an opportunity for higher-level managers to test the validity of their perceptions and values. The credibility (confidence-level) of the final budgets and plans is also dependent upon the consistency and care taken by all managers in evaluating and ranking alternatives throughout the process.

Communicability of results and span of forecasts

The ZBB process in itself generates a high level of communication among managers and staff at all levels. Indeed, one of the great advantages is that it helps managers clearly understand the operations for which they are responsible. The specific products of the process, i.e. specific operational objectives and plans, decision packages and consolidated budget reports, are all generally easily communicable within the organization.

ZBB is often used for short-term (one year) and medium-term (three to five years) planning and budgeting. Additionally, the ZBB principles can be usefully employed to translate long-range (ten to twenty years) goals and strategies into meaningful action programmes by the managers responsible for their implementation. This is necessarily an iterative process, as decision packages may well have to be added or cut to facilitate achievement of goals, and goals and strategies may need to be modified according to the detailed analysis of the decision packages.

Resources needed

Resources required to operate zero-based budgeting can be broadly classified as follows:

Goals and future-orientated forecasts. For overall operational and capital development planning and budgeting, an institution must have a set of overall goals and strategies as a starting-point for use of ZBB.

Managers must have access to costing information and forward-range forecasts (i.e. social needs, labour conditions and costs, new technologies, markets etc.), to allow them to evaluate alternative methods fully and to prepare cost–benefit analyses of different levels of activities.

Human-specialist assistance. ZBB distributes responsibility for the planning process and requires a broad participation while retaining centralized final authority. This means that many more people become involved in planning and budgeting, some for the first time. This can require significant investment in training programmes and possibly the use of consultants during initial setting-up and introduction. Within the institution, assistance is necessary to all managers from finance-department staff and purchasing agents in preparing cost information.

Procedural assistance. As well as adequately trained staff, successful implementation of ZBB requires: (a) carefully structured procedures—initially these will take time to plan and implement and possibly will require the assistance of a consultant; (b) well-developed forms—these should be prepared in such a way as to provoke managers' thinking throughout the exercise (well-developed forms can help minimize the time and cost required by the zero-based budgeting process).

Procedures

Identify decision units (see Fig. 1, circle 1). To perform ZBB, an institution must be divided up into 'Decision units', e.g. tangible activities or groups of activities for which a single manager has responsibility. Decision units may conveniently be based on traditional budget cost centres, which is often particularly useful when introducing ZBB for the first time. A decision unit may be identified as a section of the institution, for example staff training, accounting, sales and marketing etc. A research and development project or a particular service provided may also be considered a decision unit. For capital development planning, capital projects can form individual decision units, or a cluster of capital projects could form one decision unit.

When identifying decision units, the managers responsible for those units will also be identified. At higher levels in the institutional hierarchy, group or divisional managers, for example, will be responsible for a number of decision units. Section supervisors, on the other hand, are more likely to be responsible for individual decision units.

Define objectives (see Fig. 1, circles 2 and 3). The implementation of ZBB is an iterative process which 'ripples through' the institution in all directions. The institutional relationships at upper levels of management are shown in Figure 1. Similar relationships exist down through the institution. The diagram shows how the overall institutional goals and expenditure guidelines are developed into overall strategies which are translated by managers at each level of the hierarchy into local operational strategies. Decision units are divided into discrete operational functions for which specific operational objectives are defined. In many cases, and this is true once ZBB has been established in an organization, these objectives will exist in an agreed and written form. In this case, they should be reviewed to ensure that they are consistent with the updated organizational strategies. This should produce a clear statement of the operational objectives which will be related to the overall goals and strategies of the institution.

Identify and choose alternative methods (see Fig. 1, circles 4, 5 and 6). This step in the ZBB process requires a good deal of time, creativity and co-operation between managers and their superiors and managers and their staff. Alternative methods of undertaking each operational function must be identified and evaluated. Brainstorming sessions among groups of staff can

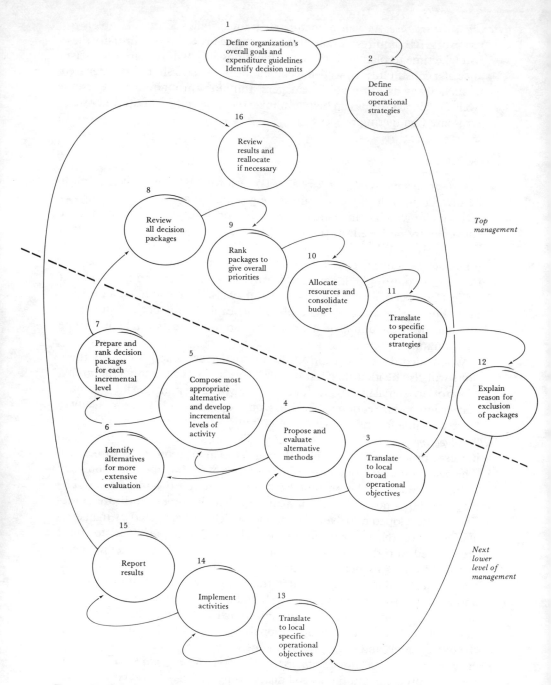

FIG. 1. ZBB organizational relationship at upper management levels (similar relationships continue down through the organization)

be of great use here. Old traditions must be questioned, new technologies investigated, different staffing patterns considered and the use of external versus internal expertise explored.

When practical options have been identified, their relative advantages must be evaluated. This requires not only relative financial cost–benefit analysis, but also a broad cost–benefit analysis taking into consideration non-financial advantages and disadvantages, i.e. public relations, community service, training implications, political sensitivity, social costs, staff morale, specialist availability etc. The final evaluation and weighing of all cost–benefit values is generally done by managers in consultation with their immediate superiors or, in some cases, supervisors at even higher levels. The reasons supporting the final choice of alternative method must be well documented and generally are required to be included on later decision-package forms so that they can be reviewed during the ranking process.

In some cases, a number of alternative methods can be developed as decision-package sets and their financial cost–benefit relationships formally evaluated through the ranking system. This is not the normal approach, since preparation and ranking of decision packages is a time-consuming process. Normally, the most appropriate alternative method of achieving each operational function is chosen before development of decision packages takes place.

As indicated previously, it may not be possible, because of lack of time or necessary data, to evaluate some alternatives fully and these should therefore be identified for more intensive evaluation by the manager concerned or by a specific planning section at a later date. In this way potentially good ideas are prevented from being lost.

Prepare decision packages (see Fig. 1, circle 7). Having chosen the most suitable method of achieving a given function, the chosen method is broken into incremental levels of activity. Such activity levels are additive, from a minimum level that can stand alone, to activity levels well above any current operations. In practice, three to five activity levels are used. Minimum activity levels should generally describe a level of service well below that currently being provided.

Decision packages are prepared for each incremental level. These are best produced on standard forms for the purpose and should generally include the following detail: description of the function; the goal(s) or objective(s) of the function; specific measures of performance; the benefits to be derived from its funding; the consequences to result from non-funding; the projected costs of the packages; and alternative ways of performing the same activity (Pattello, 1977).

Conduct ranking and resource allocation (see Fig. 1, circles 7 to 13). Decision packages are ranked after preparation by the decision unit manager. Some useful ranking techniques are described later in this section. Ranking is in order of decreasing benefit to the institution. The ranking order allows the manager to test the expenditure-level guidelines and identify the advantages gained by that particular level of funding and the disadvantages of not approving decision packages that fall below the proposed 'cut-off' point. Once ranked by decision unit managers, packages are forwarded to the next higher level of the institution, where they are grouped with other comparable-level packages for review and reranking. Reranking reflects a broader view of the institution's goals at that management level. It is usual for this reranking to be done by a committee of managers whose packages are concerned, including at least one person from the higher institutional level (usually the committee chairman).

The process 'ripples up' through the organization until, finally, decision packages are reviewed at the top management level. Because of the large number of packages at this point, and at some lower levels, it is normal for the ranking manager or committee simply to review and pass the upper 75 per cent (for example) and rerank only the lower 25 per cent. It is those closest to the cut-off point that compete for the available funding that require the greatest scrutiny. When top management has reviewed and reranked the packages, the final overall expenditure-level 'cut-off' point can be fixed. This decision determines what will go into the operating budget and resource allocation plan.

The final operation of compiling the budget report is a simple mechanical function of collating the expenditure information from the individual decision-package forms and final ranking table. Thus the final budget report can be prepared in any format desirable. The approved decision packages can then also be used to expand the original broad operational strategies into specific operational strategies or plans. This can be done at a corporate and individual operating level. An important aspect of successful ZBB operation is the need to provide feedback to managers on why their packages were or were not included in the final plan.

Establish review process (see Fig. 1, circles 14, 15 and 16). Once resources have been allocated and the work of implementation has begun, the ZBB process should incorporate a systematic monitoring and review procedure so that the validity of the assessed benefits and the actual costs of decision packages can be monitored. This review process, together with changing institutional circumstances, may indicate to management a need to reallocate resources during the planned period. The reporting and review information provide excellent data on which to base decision packages and ranking decisions in subsequent years.

Decision techniques

Ranking can be done by a system of committee voting which desirably should include the use of one of a number of decision-making aids, such as decision matrices or forced-choice matrices. (For a more complete treatment of ranking techniques, see Cheek, 1977). A decision matrix (see Fig. 2) is generated by

		Member A	Member B	Member C	Member D	Total
Decision packages	1					
	2					
	3					
	4					
	5					
	6					

FIG. 2. Decision matrix

Compared to

		2	3	4	5	6	Total	Rank
Decision packages	1	1	0	1	1	1	4	2
	2		0	0	0	0	0	6
	3			1	1	1	5	1
	4				1	1	3	3
	5					1	2	4
	6						1	5
Column totals		0	2	1	1	1		

FIG. 3. Forced-choice matrix

listing all the packages in a column which the voting members assess in a row. Each voting member is given 100 points to divide up among the decision packages according to his/her assessment of the relative priorities. When voting is complete, the totals for each package can be determined. Large discrepancies between members' allocations can be discussed and, if necessary, the voting repeated to move closer to a consensus opinion.

Paired-comparison ranking can be conducted using a forced-choice matrix. This technique forces a comparison of packages two at a time to produce a numerical expression of relative priority. Generally it is easier to choose between two options than a greater number. Figure 3 shows a typical forced-choice matrix. This is produced by comparing the first decision package to the second and deciding which is the more important. If package 1 is more important than 2 (as it is in this case) a 1 is written in row 1, column 2; if package 2 is more important than 1, 0 is written in this same space. Next, package 1 is compared with package 3 and a 1 or 0 is written in row 1, column 3. In the same manner package 1 is compared with other packages up to 6, and the cross-comparison is then repeated with packages 2 to 6 to fill out the matrix. Now all the 0s appearing in each 'Compared to' column are added, and this sum is written in the individual column's 'Total' space. Finally, all the numbers across each row are added and this number is unserted in the Total column. The order of the totals gives the order of ranking. Equal numbers in the Total column indicate inconsistency in the comparisons and the process should be repeated.

Experience suggests this is a useful technique up to approximately fifty packages.

Case example

The case example describes the use of ZBB within a hypothetical radio-broadcasting organization adapted from 'real life' to serve the purpose of this chapter. The organization is assumed to be a public corporation, operating both commercial-radio stations and non-commercial networks throughout its country. The corporation is directed by a government-appointed board of directors and has an administrative executive known as the general manager. Funding for the radio corporation is from commercial revenue and from a listener licence fee. Separate budgets and plans are produced within the organization for recurring operational expenditure and capital-project ex-penditure. A dynamic interrelationship exists between the two:

The capital-development programme covers project-equipment costs. Operational costs of planning, supervising and implementing capital pro-jects are included initially in the operational budget and those costs that can be directly related to specific projects during the year are 'capitalized' at the completion of the project. Thus the capital-development programme must be prepared before the operational budget and plan.

New and extended capital facilities can have a significant effect on the pattern and cost of operation of radio stations and service sections. Therefore, it must be known which capital projects have been approved before oper-ational budgets can be consolidated.

Justification for capital expenditure is largely based on such things as return on investment, operational-cost reduction, cost-effectiveness and improved operational efficiency. Hence such operational information must be de-termined as part of the capital planning and budgeting process.

Operational and capital planning is done annually and provides not only a firm budget and plan for the next financial year but projected plans for the following two years as well. Budgeting for the commercial service is done separately from that of the non-commercial. ZBB is used within each commercial station, which is budgeted 'autonomously'. Head-office service sections are planned and budgeted as a single group, and this is the main focus of this example.

Organizational goals

The case study describes part of the planning and budgeting process for the 1981–84 period. The following is an extract of some of the corporate goals as reviewed for the three-year period:

Maintain and increase profitable operation of all commercial stations. Target for overall commercial-operation surplus as follows: $2.5 million, 1981/82; $3 million, 1982/83; $3.2 million, 1983/84.

Continue to fund non-commercial services from licence fee.

Limit operating-cost increases for non-commercial networks to 10 per cent per year.

Pool commercial surplus and balance of licence fee for capital development and plan initially for capital-development funding of: $3.2 million, 1981/82; $3.5 million, 1982/83; $4 million, 1983/84.

Complete primary technical coverage of country by main non-commercial network by 1984 and extend coverage of serious music network to one provincial area per year.

Extend ethnic broadcasts.

Promote regional programming on non-commercial networks.

Develop educational broadcasts.

Organizational strategies

Each corporate goal is translated by the general manager and his senior executives into a set of broad corporate strategies, and in some cases strategy options, for each year of the forward-planning period. For example, objective one: 'Maintain and increase profitable operation of all commercial stations etc.' could produce the following broad strategies:

Maintain staff reduction policy—maximum of 5 per cent overall reduction over three-year period.

Introduce commissioned sales staff.

Maintain commercial content at 14 minutes/hour.

Increase advertising rate bi-annually.

Increase network sales volume.

Limit head-office overhead costs to commercial stations.

Maintain community service at present level.

Seek extension of broadcast time on all commercial stations.

Allow for 18 per cent wage benefits inflation/year.

Decision units, engineering services and operational objectives

Each head-office section (for example, staff services, engineering, finance etc.) has been identified as an individual decision unit. The case study follows the sequence of alternative evaluation, decision-package development and ranking for one decision unit, the engineering services section of head office.

The engineering services section has the chief engineer as its decision-unit manager and is split into two separate functions: technical operations and engineering planning and development. All the corporate-strategy statements are examined and those most relevant to engineering services are extracted for special consideration in preparing the engineering services budgets and plans and in reviewing the specific objectives of the services' functions.

In the light of the updated corporate strategies, the broad operational objectives of the two functions of engineering services are reviewed. The updated objectives for the engineering planning and development function are stated as follows:

To execute all equipment projects within the approved capital development programme.

To undertake engineering research in areas of technological application unique to the country and organization as approved in the capital programme.

To undertake forward planning of projects for subsequent planning periods.

To assess and introduce new labour-saving equipment to assist corporate strategies of cost containment and maintenance of community services.

To introduce new and more efficient equipment-installation techniques.

Alternatives

The alternative methods considered for achieving the operational objectives for the planning and development function are:

1. Continue with the present decentralized in-house engineering operation (i.e. engineering staff located at selected radio stations throughout the country).
2. Revert to centralized in-house engineering operation (i.e. all engineering staff located in one centre).
3. Contract all engineering work to outside consultants and manufacturers.
4. Continue with decentralized in-house operation but increased use of outside resources.

To evaluate the four options, a detailed analysis was made of the costs of engineering developments over the past two-year period during which a decentralized in-house operation had existed. A similar exercise was conducted to assess the cost of implementing the same work-load using a centralized staff. Finally, an attempt was made to assess the costs of using outside consultants and manufacturers. The latter study was difficult as little experience was available on which to determine the quality and costs of outside resources. The financial information from the above studies was then combined with a list of non-financial advantages and disadvantages of each alternative. After extensive discussion between the chief engineer and his senior staff, alternative number 4 was selected. A summary of the final considerations is as follows:

1. The existing decentralized operation has achieved most of the objectives desired when instituting it only three years earlier (i.e. engineering designs more related to their end purpose, engineering staff more closely involved in day-to-day broadcasting, better scope for technical staff advancement, higher technical-staff morale etc.).
2. Although marginally less expensive to operate, centralized operation would not easily achieve the benefits in 1, as had been shown by past centralized operations.
3. The assumed costs of complete inside consultancy and manufacture suggest this to be the most expensive alternative.
4. The study of outside resources indicates that some areas of work could be more cheaply implemented by outsiders. Additionally, it was agreed desirable to assess the use of outside resources in a limited area in order to develop more accurate costing information and evaluate quality of performance.
5. The use of selected outside resources for short-term or specialized functions would allow the regular engineering work-load to proceed with the possibility of a small decrease in permanent staff which would be in accord with corporate staffing strategies.

Decision packages

Much of the information for the preparation of decision packages comes from the preliminary detailed planning of projects to be executed. As indicated previously, decision packages are additive. In this case they are prepared for the following:

1. Decentralized operation with twenty in-house staff and no outside resources (lower level of activity than currently provided with twenty-four in-house staff).
2. Additional three in-house staff and 2,000 hours of outside labour (i.e. a cumulative total of twenty-three staff and 2,000 hours of outside resource, which is approximately equivalent to the current activity level).
3. Additional one in-house staff and 2,000 hours of outside labour (i.e. a cumulative total of twenty-four staff and 4,000 hours of outside resource).
4. Additional two in-house staff and 2,000 hours of outside labour (i.e. a cumulative total of twenty-six staff and 6,000 hours of outside resource).

Decision packages for activity levels 1 and 2 above are shown in Figures 4 and 5. In this exercise, the above activity levels are proposed to continue for the three-year planning period. These might well have changed in a year's time when the planning and budgeting process was conducted for the 1982–85 period.

Description of forms

The left-hand section of the decision-package forms is mostly self-explanatory

Section	Function		Package	Ranking		Funded	
					Corporate approved	Yes	No
Engineering services	Planning and development		1 of 4	Sectional 1			

Description of broad objectives of function	Code	Expenditure item	Budget for current year	F.Y. 1981/82	F.Y. 1982/83	F.Y. 1983/84
1. To execute equipment projects within approved capital development programme. 2. To undertake engineering research projects as approved in capital development programme. 3. To undertake forward planning of projects for subsequent planning periods. 4. To assess and introduce new labour-saving equipment. 5. To introduce new and more efficient installation techniques.	101	Salaries	$288 000	$283 200	$334 176	$394 327
	102	Overtime	11 000	10 541	12 122	13 941
	103	Welfare subsidies	2 880	2 832	3 341	3 943
	104	Outside contractors	–	–	–	–
Description of specific work funded by the package 1. Completion of projects: A, B, D, E. 2. Partial completion of projects: C, F, G, H, I, J. 3. Completion of research activities: M, N. 4. Partial completion of research activities: O, P, Q, R. 5. Provision of 1 000 hours of forward-planning time. 6. Partial completion of assessment of new labour-saving equipment.	105	Telephone and tolls	3 800	4 025	4 628	5 323
	106	Printing	600	690	790	912
	107	Travel	25 000	24 000	27 600	31 740
	108	Freight	330	322	370	425
	109	Insurance	2 000	2 300	2 645	3 041
Specific means of implementing work Employ twenty decentralized in-house staff and no outside resources. (Provides lower level of service than with current twenty-four in-house staff.)	110	Professional fees	300	322	370	425
	111	Routine maintenance	1 800	2 070	2 380	2 737
	112	Office furniture	1 200	1 380	1 587	1 825
Alternative methods: reasons for rejection 1. Revert to centralized operation—centralized staff proved in past to be remote from day-to-day broadcast operation, equipment and systems designs were not well related to user requirements, low technical staff morale and high staff turnover, limited scope for advancement of majority. 2. Contract all work outside—much more expensive and would lose in-house expertise. 3. Mix existing decentralized operation with some outside resources. (See other packages.)	113	Literature	700	805	925	1 064
	TOTAL GROSS EXPENDITURE		$337 610	$332 487	$390 934	$459 703
	Estimated capitalized expenditure		$253 207	$249 365	$293 200	$344 777
	TOTAL NET OPERATING EXPENDITURE		$84 403	$83 122	$97 734	$114 926

Benefits of funding package		Performance measure				
1. Completion of urgent projects A, B, D, E. These will produce $54 000/year cost savings for stations concerned. Partial completion of extended coverage project C. 2. Completion of research activity M and partial assessment of new labour-saving equipment will prepare for introduction of new efficient systems in future.	Total project time required (hours)		Current year objective	1981/82	1982/83	1983/84
			44 000	46 760	56 560	66 360
Consequences of not funding package 1. No expenditure available for the execution of capital development programme. 2. Twenty staff redundant. 3. Loss of in-house engineering expertise. 4. Cost-savings on radio stations not achieved if new equipment not provided. 5. Extension of coverage delayed leading to high audience and political pressure.	Manpower hours funded by this package	In-house	42 240	35 200	35 200	35 200
		Outside	–	–	–	–
	Cumulative manpower funded by packages: 1	In-house	42 240	35 200	35 200	35 200
		Outside	–	–	–	–
	Work delayed to next year		1 760	11 560	21 360	31 160
Prepared by A. Jones	**Date** 1 November 1979	Percentage of required work completed	By this package		75%	62%	53%
			Cumulative packages: 1	96%	75%	62%	53%

FIG. 4. Decision package form for activity level 1

and contains much of the information described so far in the case study. It shows to the ranking managers what work is being funded by the package (projects A, B, C etc. refer to projects in the capital programme), the broad objectives of the unit's function, the specific means of implementing the work, alternative methods considered and reasons for not selecting them and implications of funding or not funding the package.

The right upper section of the forms records detailed expenditures for each

Section	Function	Package	Ranking		Funded	
				Corporate	Yes	No
Engineering services	Planning and development	2 of 4	Sectional 3	approved		

Description of broad objectives of function			Budget for current year	F.Y. 1981/82	F.Y. 1982/83	F.Y. 1983/84
1. To execute equipment projects within approved capital development programme.	Code	Expenditure item				
2. To undertake engineering research projects as approved in capital development programme.	101	Salaries	$288 000	$42 480	$48 852	$57 645
3. To undertake forward planning of projects for subsequent planning periods.	102	Overtime	11 000	1 581	1 818	2 091
4. To assess and introduce new labour-saving equipment.	103	Welfare subsidies	2 880	424	488	576
5. To introduce new and more efficient installation techniques.	104	Outside contractors	–	20 000	23 000	26 450
	105	Telephone and tolls	3 800	200	230	264
Description of specific work funded by the package	106	Printing	600	–	–	–
1. Completion of projects: A, B, C, D, E, F.	107	Travel	25 000	3 593	4 132	4 752
2. Partial completion of projects: G, H, I, J.	108	Freight	330	–	–	–
3. Completion of research activities: M, N, O.						
4. Partial completion of research activities: P, Q, R.	109	Insurance	2 000	–	–	–
5. Provision of 1 000 hours of forward-planning time.	110	Professional fees	300	–	–	–
6. Partial completion of assessment of new labour-saving equipment.	111	Routine maintenance	1 800	–	–	–
Specific means of implementing work	112	Office furniture	1 200	100	115	132
Employ three decentralized in-house staff and 2 000 hours outside labour. (Together with package 1 this provides a	113	Literature	700	–	–	–
total of twenty-three in-house staff and 2 000 hours outside labour—approximately equivalent to existing service.)	TOTAL GROSS EXPENDITURE		$337 610	$68 378	$78 635	$91 910
Alternative methods: reasons for rejection	Estimated capitalized expenditure		$253 207	$51 283	$58 976	$68 932
1. Revert to centralized operation—centralized staff proved in past to be remote from day-to-day broadcast operation, equipment and systems designs were not well related to user requirements, low technical staff morale and high staff turnover, limited scope for advancement of majority.	TOTAL NET OPERATING EXPENDITURE		$84 403	$17 115	$19 659	$22 978
2. Contract all work outside—much more expensive and would lose in-house expertise.	Performance measure					

Benefits of funding package			Current year objective	1981/82	1982/83	1983/84
1. Completion of urgent project C as well as project F. This represents completion of stage I of coverage extension.						
2. Completion of research activities N and O and completion of the assessment of new labour-saving equipment will allow new efficient systems to be introduced immediately.	Total project time required (hours)		44 000	46 760	49 280	51 800
	Manpower hours funded by this package	In-house	42 240	5 280	5 280	5 280
Consequences of not funding package		Outside	–	2 000	2 000	2 000
1. Three staff redundant.	Cumulative manpower funded by packages: 1+2	In-house	42 240	40 480	40 480	40 480
2. High public and political reaction owing to delay in extending coverage.		Outside	–	2 000	2 000	2 000
3. Introduction of new systems as a result of research activities and the assessment of labour-saving equipment delayed.	Work delayed to next year		1 760	4 280	6 800	9 320

Prepared by	Date						
		Percentage of required work completed	By this package		15.5%	14.7%	14%
A. Jones	1 November 1979		Cumulative packages: 1+2	96%	90.5%	86%	82%

FIG. 5. Decision package form for activity level 2

year of the planning period as well as the approved budget for the current year. This is the expenditure directly related to the decision package alone and not the cumulative total of the package and any previous ones. As indicated earlier, those costs which can be directly related to particular projects are recorded during the year and 'capitalized' at the end of the project. Thus the net operational budget is given by the gross costs, minus the 'capitalized' costs (see bottom of expenditure section).

In the right lower section, the performance measure is shown. This is based on the number of hours of project work to be completed each year. The level of performance achieved by the particular package is shown as well as the cumulative total of the package and any previous ones. The differences between the 'total project time required' and the 'cumulative manpower' available is work which will not be completed in the year. This is regarded as 'work delayed to next year' and is added to the base project time required in the next year. It can be seen that in the current year it is expected to complete 96 per cent of the work on hand. Activity level 1 will achieve only 75 per cent completion of the required work in 1981/82. This means a high level of work delayed into subsequent years. The performance measure shows the effect of maintaining the manpower resource constant during these later years: the percentage of the work-load completed falls to 62 per cent in 1982/83 and 53 per cent in 1983/84. Activity level 2 provides for a cumulative (i.e. packages 1 and 2) completion of 90.5 per cent of the work-load in 1981/82. Although decision packages are not shown for activity levels 3 and 4, cumulatively they would provide for completion of 99 per cent and 111 per cent of the total work-load in the 1981/82 year. Thus activity level 4, if approved, would provide a margin for new and unexpected work, which inevitably occurs during the year.

Ranking

The four decision packages are grouped with those for the technical operations function, and all are ranked by the chief engineer. His ranking order is shown on the sectional ranking table (Fig. 6). This form shows the costs of each package and the progressive summation of packages (i.e. cumulative total) for the 1981/82 year. Separate ranking forms are produced for each year of the planning period. At the top of the form, the current year's budget for the decision unit is recorded so that it can be compared with the progressive cumulative total for the new financial year.

Once the ranking table has been completed, the ranking manager can easily test the effect of setting the cut-off expenditure at particular levels. For example, the corporate-expenditure guidelines indicate that engineering expenditure should be confined to a maximum increase of 18 per cent above the previous year. This would put the cut-off point between ranks 5 and 6 (as indicated by the arrow). The chief engineer has, however, decided that the cut-off point should preferably be between items 6 and 7. To achieve this he knows he must have an extremely persuasive argument to support his packages at the corporate ranking committee. Accordingly, he produces more detailed information on costs of delaying projects, documented information of audience reaction to further delays in radio coverage and possible political implications. This information expands on that contained in summary on the decision-package forms, particularly for levels 2 and 3.

Final ranking involves 120 packages from ten head-office service sections (i.e. decision units). All are first inspected by the director of finance and most of

Decision unit:	Ranking form
Engineering services	

Functions within unit:	Budget for current year
1. Engineering planning and development	$84 403 (Total net)
2. Technical operations	$158 600
3.	
4.	

TOTAL DECISION UNIT BUDGET: $243 003

Rank	Decision package	Increment No.	Cost of package 1981/82	Cumulative 1981/82
1	Planning and development	1 of 4	$83 122	$83 122
2	Technical operations	1 of 4	148 500	231 622
3	Planning and development	2 of 4	17 115	248 737
4	Technical operations	2 of 4	12 100	260 837
5	Technical operations	3 of 4	8 900	269 737
6	Planning and development	3 of 4	10 040	279 777
7	Planning and development	4 of 4	13 580	293 357
8	Technical operations	4 of 4	5 600	298 957
9				
10				
11				
12				

FIG. 6. Sectional ranking form

the higher-priority packages from each unit are passed. A total of seventy packages are passed in this way, including the top four ranked of engineering services. Some decision-package sets have already been through several ranking sessions by this time, i.e. the packages of the different programme-supply sections are first ranked by section managers, then the programme supply manager, and the head of programme services. The general manager's ranking committee finally considers fifty packages in detail. These represent packages for activity levels between approximately 85 per cent and 110 per cent of the expenditure guidelines for each unit. From this point, separate consideration and ranking is given to each year of the three-year period, with greatest emphasis being placed on the 1981/82 year. Separate meetings are held to conduct final ranking of each year's packages and a separate ranking form produced for each year. This is the most difficult task in completing the ZBB process, as packages represent the many different service functions within the organization. The committee reviews all the packages in detail and unanimously approves ten and declares another twelve as clearly beyond the scope of current resources. The remaining twenty-eight are ranked using a forced-choice matrix, generated by subjecting the comparison of each pair of packages to committee vote. These represent the twenty-eight packages around the expected level of affordability.

On the final-ranking table, a number of trial cut-off points are identified. The effect of setting head-office costs as each of these points is assessed by feeding these different expenditure levels into the corporate income and expenditure analysis computer program, which 'apportions' head-office costs to both commercial and non-commercial operations according to previously defined formulae. The computer analysis is supplied with the ZBB budget results from the commercial stations and non-commercial networks together with all revenue projections. After detailed consideration of the different income and expenditure analyses and some minor trimming of a few decision packages, the final budget levels are fixed for all areas.

With the final budget prepared and the knowledge obtained of which decision packages will be funded, the broad corporate strategies and broad operational objectives for each function are consolidated and developed into specific strategies and plans. The final budget has included three of the four engineering planning-development packages. From these, the detailed objectives of the unit for the 1981/82 year are written, and PERT and CPM diagrams prepared for the section as a whole and for individual projects.

Conclusions

Although the case study illustrates well the basic ZBB process, the planning of capital project equipment and labour separately in the different planning and budgeting areas (i.e. capital and operating) tends to create difficulty in the ranking of packages. The example demonstrates well the advice given by Logan M. Cheek (Cheek, 1977):

Don't waste time arguing over priorities. Programs ranked high, whether for legal, economic, or other merits, are going to be approved and funded. The same principle applies, in reverse, to low priority programs. Zero-based budgeting is, above all, a *decision-making tool*. Thus, the review process should focus on those dozen or so programs above or below the decision point or affordability level.

Annotated bibliography

AUSTIN, L.A. 1977. *Zero-Base Budgeting: Organizational Impact and Effects*. New York, N.Y., AMACOM (a division of the American Management Association) (AMA survey report). Presents the results of a 1977 survey of 481 enterprises that had been using ZBB and/or had attended ZBB seminars conducted by the American Management Association. To quote from the report itself: 'Section 2 traces the development of zero-based budgeting from its inception to current applications and contrasts the method with other budgeting methods. Section 3 presents the characteristics and responses of organizations implementing zero-based budgeting. Section 4 discusses special needs and considerations in implementing zero-based budgeting, and Section 5 discusses some benefits and limitations of the process.' The report proper is followed by the appendix, references and bibliography.

AUSTIN, L.A.; CHEEK, L.M. 1979. *Zero-Base Budgeting: A Decision Package Manual*. New York, N.Y., AMACOM (a division of the American Management Assoication). Presents sample decision packages and ranking sheets from many organizations both public and private to illustrate what is happening in the field. The book is introduced with a description of the basic concepts of ZBB and provides detailed step-by-step discussions on how to develop and rank decision packages. Also included is a section on conducting a post-installation ZBB performance audit which many organizations have found, after several years' experience with ZBB, to be a natural complement to the ZBB process.

CHEEK, L.M. 1977. *Zero-Base Budgeting Comes of Age. What It Is and What It Takes to Make It Work*. New York, N.Y., AMACOM (a division of the American Management Association). This book is intended to share the author's experiences as well as those of several progressive organizations that have enjoyed success with ZBB. The ZBB concept, the need for carefully designed forms, procedures and approaches to ranking of budget proposals are described in detail. A clear link is established between ZBB and long-range planning. A variety of persuasion techniques critically needed for initiating the process, and the role of top management, are discussed.

PATILLO, J.W. 1977. *Zero-Based Budgeting: A Planning Resource Allocation and Control Tool*. New York, N.Y., National Association of Accountants. The monograph describes the basics of ZBB—the planning-system design and implementation. Benefits and limitations of the process are presented and the organizational relationship analysed.

PHYR, P.A. 1970. *Zero-Base Budgeting. Harvard Business Review*, November–December.

——. 1973. *Zero-Base Budgeting: A Practical Management Tool for Evaluating Expenses*. New York, N.Y., John Wiley & Sons. The author is one of the first successful users of ZBB and in his book he describes the method in detail. He discusses implementation problems and benefits of ZBB and analyses the differences between the ZBB and programme, planning and budgeting systems. This leads to a description of merging the two techniques. The author shows how ZBB meets management's divergent needs for centralized co-ordination and direction, with decentralized operations and all that this includes. In an appendix, the author presents a sample ZBB manual directed at managers who will be involved in the ZBB process, particularly in developing decision packages.

SARANT, P.C. 1978. *Zero-Base Budgeting in the Public Sector: A Pragmatic Approach*. Reading, Mass., Addison-Wesley. The text is designed as a training aid for government officials involved in applying ZBB in the public sector in the United States. It describes a link with a new planning, budgeting and review system, and other public-sector reforms. It describes in detail the different requirements and stages of the ZBB process within the 'real world' of the United States Federal Government, and presents factors involved in automating the overall process.

STONICH, P.J., et al. 1977. *Zero-Base Planning and Budgeting: Improved Cost Control and Resource Allocation*. Homewood, Ill., Dow Jones–Irwin. Relates ZBB to the total planning and control process based on the author's experiences in designing and implementing ZBB systems in over seventy-five organizations in the United States, Canada and Mexico. The book identifies specific functional areas of the organizations in which zero-based planning and budgeting applies, and suggests design and implementation practices that are particularly well suited to those areas. It presents summaries of five cases, with a matrix that indexes various points with special interest in the cases for the reader. The complete cases, with a sixth teaching case, are included in an appendix. Towards the beginning, the book presents a step-by-step explanation of the process, and at the end this approach is repeated, emphasizing the psychological and mechanical problems that are frequently encountered in implementation of ZBB.

WHOLEY, J.S. 1978. *Zero-Base Budgeting and Program Evaluation*. Lexington, Mass., Lexington Book. The book presents a 'simplified' version of ZBB in which managers prepare and rank decision packages for their lowest-priority activities and functions as well as for extension of existing programmes or new programme initiatives. These are discussed in face-to-face dialogue between policy-makers and managers of major organizational units as part of the decision-making process. The principal points of the process are established from case studies of ZBB and programme evaluation efforts in U.S. local government and in regional and federal agencies.

Chapter 16

Goal-achievement matrix

Bruce McKenzie

The 'goal-achievement techniques' of planning were originally intended to be specific aids to the decision-maker in choosing the most appropriate method for resource utilization. The early development of these techniques followed similar lines to other evaluative techniques of cost–benefit analysis and balance-sheet planning. However, planners soon discovered that the adoption of goal-achievement analysis as the approach to evaluation created a number of new opportunities for the total planning process. These opportunities related to the greater guidance given to a planning project by the incorporation of 'measurable' objective statements, and identification of 'affected' community groups in the planning report. From this vantage point the planning process emphasizes the generation of alternatives that give decision-makers a 'real' choice, each alternative being consistent with the predetermined goals and their nominated priorities. Further, the goal-achievement approach is particularly appropriate to emerging dimensions of planning where terminology, concepts and theory in the area for which planning is to be done are in an early stage of development. Communication is such a developing area.

Goal-achievement techniques, in common with all other approaches to planning, can be simple or complex according to the number of variables and amount of detail they are expected to process. Several students of regional science have developed elaborate and extremely complex cybernetic models of goal-achievement analysis while the mere goal-achievement check-list represents extreme simplicity. The process outlined, and the case example presented here, seek to take a middle course indicating the basis for greater complexity, but also highlighting ways in which the communication planner, with limited resources, can effectively utilize the simple technique. The profile of the technique discussed in this chapter is shown in diagrammatic form in Figure 1.

Definition

The concept underpinning the goal-achievement method in planning is that public planning and decision-making has many different goals and clients, and

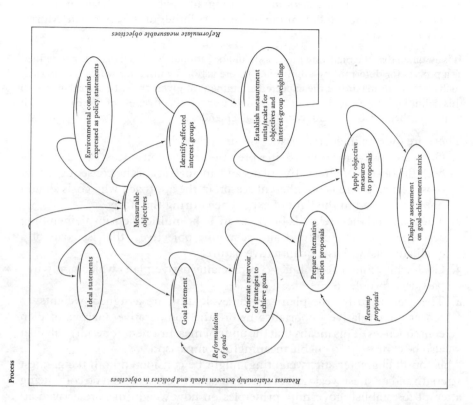

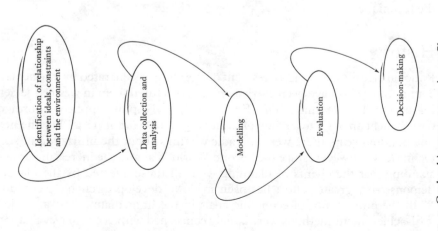

FIG. 1. Goal-achievement matrix profile

that rational action is dependent upon adequate consideration of all. While the approach is primarily focused on evaluating alternative proposals, it has the effect of shaping the total planning process. As father of the approach, Morris Hill (1973, p. xiii) wrote:

It is assumed that the planning process should be rational. Rational planning is defined as a process for determining appropriate future action by utilizing scarce resources in such a way as to maximize the expected attainment of given ends. In accordance with this definition, the evaluation of plans should test the effectiveness of these plans with respect to their probable achievement of given ends.

There are four main characteristics of the approach:
1. Goals are always formulated (in a preliminary fashion at least) in advance of both the design of alternative plans and an analysis of the consequences of those plans. There is no inherent reason in the approach why goals should not be modified in the light of experience during the study.
2. The goals and their related objectives are to be multidimensional, including aesthetic, political, cultural and economic objectives, that is, goals of a qualitative as well as a quantitative nature.
3. Goal-achievement techniques compare alternative plans which apply to a particular problem.
4. The goals used for the plan and the evaluation are assigned 'weights' to reflect their relative importance before the comparative analysis of plan consequences. This means that the units of measurement for each goal must also be expressed to enable meaningful comparison.

This fourth characteristic (weighting) might be considered both the greatest strength and greatest weakness of the approach. There has been no convincing attempt to establish governing principles on how weightings are arrived at; thus, very little theoretical justification of the approach is available. On the other hand, different groups of planners have been free to choose the principles by which the weightings should be arrived at, enabling ready indigenization of the technique.

History

Rational planning and the assessment of alternatives generated by it to achieve community goals have been carried on in a structured form in western society for a considerable time. The Frenchman, J. Dupuit, applied a form of cost–benefit analysis to a study of utility of public work in 1844. For the next one hundred years there were sporadic writings about the utilization of such techniques. However, since the Second World War and the increasing understanding that the clients of planning were all those affected by the plans, a demonstrably greater effort has been made to develop a reliable technique. With the prominence of economic goals in the immediate post-war period, goal-achievement methods were largely concerned with economic evaluation. Some specific highlights of this era in the United States were:

The publication in May 1950 by the Federal Interagency Committee on River Basin Planning of the 'Green Book'—proposed practices for economic analysis of river-basin projects.

The Rand Corporation's sustained attention to the application of rational approaches to decision-making in the field of national defence.

President Johnson's adoption of a planning-programming-budgeting approach with goal-analysis techniques for the whole federal system.

The application of the technique by Litchfield, Margolis, Rothenberg, Weisbrod, Fein and Flarman to transportation–land-use studies, urban planning and the education and health fields.

Morris Hill's formation of the goal-achievement matrix is, then, a logical extension of benefit–cost and cost-effectiveness analysis. The advance offered by Hill's theory was that the goal-achievement approach accommodates multiple goals, whereas cost–benefit analysis places emphasis on single goals of economic efficiency. In the main, the goal-achievement matrix has largely been used by land-use planners in the field of transport planning, as they endeavoured to decide among alternative plans which impinged upon many different community groups holding different ideals/goals about the role of transportation. Hill's initial work with the approach was in evaluating alternative plans for the development of transportation facilities in Cambridge, England. However, with the emergence of participatory planning, the goal achievement approach has become a useful analytical tool in many other fields, including communication planning.

Other techniques

Two broad categories of goal-achievement techniques can be identified by using the criteria of measurement sophistication. In one group, there are those involving a simple ranking of plans according to the number of the given goals they are likely to achieve. In the other, there are those techniques that use performance measures to assess the extent to which plans are likely to achieve the stated goals.

The most simple use of a goal-achievement approach involves only a statement of goal objectives, with no indication of their relative importance. The probable or perceived effectiveness of alternatives in achieving the goal objectives is expressed by the planner on only a four-point scale: a significant positive effect $(++)$; a partial or marginal effect $(+)$; a significant negative effect $(-)$; or no apparent relationship (0). The preferred option is chosen on the basis of a simple sum of these ratings. There is considerable variety within the category of goal-achievement approaches. One popular method uses numerical weights to reflect the differential importance of the objectives. For example, three of a set of objectives may be considered twice as important as all others in the study and thus be given weights of 2, while others are weighted 1. Each performance measure is used to indicate the extent of objective achievement. The plans are then ranked on an ordinal basis according to their particular performance score. The preferred plan is selected by a simple summation of rank scores multiplied by the objective weights, which give an overall weighted score to each alternative.

Advantages

The primary advantages of the goal-achievement techniques of planning are their capacities to consider multiple objectives in a pluralistic environment. Transportation-systems planning was the most obvious focus for the technique in the 1960s and 1970s. The characteristic of a transportation system which attracted planners to the goal-achievement approach was the multitude of expectations and impacts such a system evokes and has on groups within a given society. This same characteristic (which has been dormant in many other areas of public planning) is now becoming increasingly important, especially with the emergence of public participation in the planning process. The goal-achievement approach structure has two important advantages for the planner in such situations:

1. The public is able to focus its contribution on clearly stated and measurable objectives (dealing with concrete issues).
2. The various special-interest groups that are generated by public participation can see the impact of a proposal on them, compared with the impact on other groups. That is, the technique provides feedback to participants as an integral part of the process.

With the rapid expansion of the 'electronic and cybernetic' effect of information processing, and the resultant increased sensitivity and public awareness of the potential for communication to make an impact on the community, more communication planners are beginning to use this approach. In sum, the technique is increasingly used in planning issues incorporating one or more of the following: multiple objectives; public participation; communal controversy.

Limits and cautions

As the critics of the approach have rightfully emphasized, there is a fundamental dependence on the planner's institution having a clearly enunciated set of ideals from which goals for a given issue can be generated. That is, since the technique operates only when units of value can be assigned to the achievement of each objective, values or ideals which determine the horizons of achievement are essential. Further, the approach involves the total institution's ideals as well as sectoral goals; evidence supporting such ideals is often difficult to elicit. While the goal-achievement matrix is intended to help determine which planning proposal is in the 'public best interest', the approach does not specify the nature of the public interest, thus leaving such definition to the planner and so allowing opportunity for hidden bias. The formulation of equity weights is the responsibility of decision-makers, since the weights reflect ethical and political judgements and this needs to be completed in advance of an estimate of distributional effects. Litchfield (1975), in discussing this important aspect of the goal-achievement matrix, refers to the work of Hill in his comment:

It will be noticed that Hill advocates that if possible objectives should be set, and the relative values of achieving different objectives established, in advance of any analysis of plan consequences, and that equity weights are introduced before the incidence of gains and losses from different groups has been indicated. . . . Hill recognizes that in practice, the prior identification of objectives, their relative values and equity weights may present severe difficulties . . . he has stressed that they may all be modified as a result of subsequent analysis of plan consequences and liaison with decision takers.

Product or result

Ideally, goal-achievement analysis will produce a comparative-impact statement of various proposals on a given community in the achievement of predetermined goals. That is, alternatives are compared and ranked according to the perceptions and beliefs of planners and decision-makers but they are not tested for their absolute desirability. The process will indicate relationships between variables in a form that enables decision-makers to apply their value weightings to assist in making value judgements. The matrix, once established, is a useful ongoing tool to support further planning and monitoring of an implemented proposal. Finally, the matrix is an excellent tool for communicating the consequences of planning to the public at large and hence for assisting in the stimulation of public awareness of planning activity. The following then, is the final product of every plan:

1. The set of goals and the relative value to be attached to each goal are established.
2. The objectives are defined operationally, rather than in abstract terms.
3. The consequences of each alternative course of action are determined for each objective.
4. The incidence of the benefit and cost for each course of action, measured in terms of the achievement of the goal, is established for each goal.
5. The relative weight to be attached to each group affected is also established.

The goal-achievement matrix is shown diagrammatically in Table 1. In the table, α, β, and γ are the descriptions of goals. Each goal has a weight (2, 3, 5) as has been previously determined. Various groups (a, b, c, d) are identified as affected by the course of action, and a relative weight for each goal is determined for each group. The letters A, B etc. are the costs and benefits, which may be defined in monetary or non-monetary units or in terms of qualitative states. Costs and benefits are recorded for each objective according to the parties that are affected. A dash (–) in a cell implies that no cost or benefit that is related to that objective would accrue to that party if that plan were implemented. A particular party may suffer both costs and benefits with respect to a particular objective. For certain goals, an underlining (as for α) indicates that summation of the costs and benefits is meaningful and useful. For each action proposal a table similar to this is produced.

TABLE I. Goal-achievement matrix

Goal description				α			β			γ		
Relative weight of goal				2			3			5		
Incidence		Relative weight of group	Cost	Benefit	Relative weight of group	Cost	Benefit	Relative weight of group	Cost	Benefit		
Group a	I		A	D	4	E	R	2	Q		
Group b	3		H	–	3	–	–	I	S		
Group c	I		L	J	2	–	S	2	2		
Group d	2		–	–	I	U	–	I	–		
			Σ	Σ								

Level of detail

INPUT

As discussed earlier, the goal-achievement approach allows for different levels of detail. However, the proponents of the goal-achievement matrix agree that one should use the highest-order measurement scales practicable (see definitions below). Listed by ascending order of complexity, restriction of initial premises and range of applicable measurement, the major classes of measurement scales and their basic empirical operation are:

1. Nominal scale—which classifies and numbers entities.
2. Ordinal scale—which ranks entities.
3. Interval scale—which provides equal intervals between entities and indicates the difference or distances of entities from some arbitrary origin.
4. Ratio scale—which provides equal intervals between entities and indicates the differences or distances of entities from some non-arbitrary origin.

The scales may be mixed with a goal-achievement matrix, but this limits the summations possible.

OUTPUT

The matrix will reflect the level of input detail and, where common scales have been used, concise mathematical formulations of goal-achievement analysis can be displayed. However, it is more normal to represent the results of A, B etc. for a particular set of data.

Level of confidence, span of relevance and resources needed

The output of the goal-achievement matrix should represent the best analysis possible within the constraints of comparative measuring devices. While in theory all the institution's goals have been taken into consideration, it is found in practice that only a relatively small number of goals are relevant or significant in the particular planning process. Usually functional, institutional, legal, financial and jurisdictional constraints tend to limit the amount of judgement available to planners and decision-makers. Thus, time and care invested in presenting these critical goals in the goal-achievement matrix will enhance confidence in the outcome. However, it must also be borne in mind that institutional goals change over time. Since the approach is based on pre-determined goals, its validity to the institution only holds as long as those goals remain viable.

As indicated above, the method's relevance is dependent on the relevance of the basic ideals it refers to. Further, any rational determination requires the evaluation of anticipated consequences while allowing for the possibility of unanticipated consequences. The approach usually treats uncertainty by using conservative estimates on the measurement scale. The validity of the plan and the evaluation over time is directly related to the accuracy of the probability formulations and the sensitivity of the objectives to variations in the external environment.

No special physical resources are required to operate a goal-achievement approach to planning. Large charts are useful in communicating the outcomes of planning to decision-makers.

Process

The procedure for utilizing the goal-achievement matrix in planning has five stages: identifying and ranking goals, designing alternative courses of action, evaluating alternatives, selecting the 'best' alternative and monitoring implemented action.

STAGE I: THE IDENTIFICATION OF GOALS AND THEIR RANKING IN TERMS OF THEIR RELATIVE IMPORTANCE

The purpose of planning is the 'attainment of ends', the ends being the goals of clients (defined as those groups or individuals affected by the planning proposal); the goals are established at the outset of the process. Where more than one goal is to be pursued and conflict may exist, ranking of goals is necessary. This stage may be obvious in many planning situations, however, it is essential that it occurs before planning commences, although subsequent planning activity may lead to modification of initial statements.

STAGE II: THE DESIGN OF ALTERNATIVE RELEVANT COURSES OF ACTION TO ATTAIN DESIRED GOALS

Utilizing his own techniques, the planner generates and formally details a number of courses of action (strategies) that are based on goal attainment.

323

STAGE III: COMPARATIVE EVALUATION
OF ALTERNATIVE COURSES OF ACTION

1. The planner determines the costs and benefits for each alternative course of action. Depending on the definition of the goals (Stage I), the costs and benefits are expressed as: (a) tangible costs and benefits expressed in monetary terms; (b) tangible costs and benefits which cannot be expressed in monetary terms but can be expressed quantitatively, usually in terms derived from the definition of the goal (e.g. number of persons on welfare); (c) intangible costs and benefits (e.g. goodwill, beauty). For each goal and for each alternative course of action, costs and benefits are compared, aggregated where possible and reported separately.
2. The weightings which reflect the community's valuation of each of the various objectives, and the community's valuation of appropriate incidence of benefits and costs, are then introduced to the analysis. The planner therefore identifies those sections of the public—considered by income group, occupation, location or any other preferred criterion—who are affected by the consequences of a course of action. The incidence of favourable and unfavourable consequences, accruing to sections of the public, can then be assessed. (The aggregated set of incidence weights applying to all the objectives can be considered as representing the community's conception of 'equity'.)

STAGE IV: SELECTIONS OF THE 'BEST' COURSE
OF ACTION BY DECISION-MAKERS

This involves the selection of that course of action whose probable consequences, in terms of the goal-achievement matrix completed in Stage III, are preferable in realization of the goals

STAGE V: MONITORING THE IMPLEMENTATION
OF THE SELECTED COURSE OF ACTION

The goal-achievement matrix established in Stage III is utilized as an ongoing monitor of goal achievement and means of testing the impact of changing external factors on the consequences already expected from the course of action.

In practice the procedure is not a simple linear function as described here, but moves backwards and forwards between stages as the data and decisions at one stage are seen to have ramifications for each of the other stages.

Case example

INTRODUCTION

This imaginary case is an application of goal-achievement matrix to a communication-planning situation. The context of the case is based on a real world task confronting a university engaged in distance education. The use of the goal-achievement matrix in this example is illustrative rather than exhaustive and the reader will no doubt perceive many extensions that would be made in practice.

CONTEXT

The university has been discussing among its council, academics and students, the value, quality and cost of its distance-teaching programme. From these discussions three general directions for the programme have emerged. These statements in general represent the position of the three key interest groups in the discussions:
1. University council: through the quality and growth of the distance teaching programme, the university will enhance its status as a major tertiary teaching institution in the country.
2. University finance committee: through increased enrolments in its distance-teaching programme, the university will achieve higher levels of fiscal efficiency.
3. University external-students committee: through more effective communication with existing students, the university will improve the results of its external students and its reputation and attractiveness of this mode of teaching to potential students.

All participants in the discussion agreed that their statements concern ideals for the university such as the following: (a) equal opportunity for higher education no matter where an individual is residing; (b) improved quality of higher education; (c) effective communication between teaching staff and students; (d) increased student choice of learning mode; and (e) sufficient resources for all students.

PROCESS

The university council established a committee from the interested groups to recommend a number of functional (instrumental) goals or objectives that would form the basis for action to move the university towards the ideals. The committee, as its first stop, moved intuitively to list the type of objectives which would be either furthered or thwarted by changes in the distance-education programme. A measurement devised for each objective was suggested to ensure the functional nature of each objective proposed. The following list of objectives illustrates the committee's work (records for each measure are kept over time):
1. To increase the number of participants in the university's distance-teaching programmes (measured by enrolment statistics).
2. To increase availability/use of cassette mode of programme teaching (measured by number of cassette transactions).
3. To increase availability/use of broadcast mode of programme teaching

(measured by the number of students completing broadcast-mode requirements).
4. To improve the clarity and comprehensiveness of distributed information (measured by enrolment in all available courses).
5. To decrease the drop-out rate from programmes (measured by withdrawals and non-presentation of assignments).
6. To increase participation by external students in voluntary face-to-face weekend schools (measured by attendance at schools).
7. To establish the university as a primary focus for external study (measured by proportion enrolling at the university against total enrolment in all available courses).
8. To increase ease of access to reference material supporting external programmes (measured by borrowing of reference materials).
9. To maintain consistency between internal and external programmes (measured by assessment criteria and results).
10. To operate the university with a minimum of external resources (measured by costing external resources as a percentage of total costs).
11. To achieve equality of internal/external student costs (measured by comparing internal/external costs).
12. To enhance professional standing of teaching staff in distance education (measured by external recognition of teaching staff).

The committee, as its second step, identified the policies of both the university and the wider community that could influence the actions which could be taken to achieve these objectives. The following are some of the policy areas identified.

Policy areas

1. *Modes of communication.* The production of booklets, audio/video cassettes, radio/television broadcasts, tele-tutorial, computer interactive packages, other.
2. *Internal–external student services.* Minimum levels of services: resources, staff, facilities, other.
3. *Faculty entrance.* Minimum academic standards.
4. *Course selection.* Vocational and professional requirements.
5. *Academic assignments/examinations.* Minimum levels of competence, time constraints, resource utilization experiences.
6. *Course accreditation and design.* Government-regulating authority requirements; level (degree of difficulty) of content; quality of communicating information; clear and concise requirements, other.
7. *Teaching staff.* Qualifications, experience, ratio to student numbers, other.
8. *Production of material.* Technical standards for public distribution.
9. *Charges.* All types of financial costs which accrue to the student who uses the external form of learning, or costs which accrue to the institution providing the programme to the student.

10. *Financing.* Policies on aspects such as use of federal and state grants.
11. *Legal.* Copyright laws on materials and other legal restrictions that may apply to distribution of materials through post, radio, television or telephone.
12. *Other.*

The committee also identified two requisites (values which are not specific goals for the plans but which set limits to objectives—they are generally conditions that must be satisfied in order that the plans be acceptable alternatives for evaluation).

Requisites

1. *Feasibility.* Capable of being implemented within existing community constraints.
2. *Immediacy.* Capable of being implemented as a high priority in current programme of development.

The committee completed its work by identifying relationships between policies and objectives—and objectives and ideals—in a matrix form, as shown in Figure 2. The policies at the lower left of the matrix are represented as inputs intended to achieve a set of objectives, while in the matrix at the upper right, these same objectives are represented as a set of inputs for the achievement of a set of ideals. The relationship between each type of policy and each objective, and each objective and each ideal, is considered in turn. The symbol 1 in a cell means a positive effect is thought to exist, while a 0 means that no particular relationship occurs. It must be stressed that the use of the symbol 1 does not represent a judgement about the degree of relationship that exists between ideals, objectives and policies.

Decision to generate alternative course of action

From the distance-education goal matrix the university council made three groupings of the objectives. In each grouping were objectives which primarily affected a particular sector of the distance-education programme. It was acknowledged that objectives would usually affect more than one sector but they were grouped in terms of primary effect. The groupings were as follows:

1. *Communication between teachers and external students*: Increase cassette mode of teaching. Increase broadcast mode of teaching. Increase clarity and comprehensiveness of distributed data. Increase face-to-face participation. Increase ease of access to reference material.

2. *Financial viability of the university*: Operate with minimum external resources. Maintain current capital/recurrent cost rates in total budget. Achieve level of cost per student equal to or less than internal programme.

Policy areas / *Objectives*	Increased number of external students	Increased cassette model of teaching	Increased broadcast mode of teaching	Increased clarity and comprehensiveness of materials	Decrease 'drop-out' rate	Increase numbers in face-to-face weekend programmes	Establish university as focus for 'distance' teaching	Increased access to references	Consistency between internal/external programmes	Minimum external resources	Fiscal efficiency, internal programmes	Professional enhancement
Modes of communication	1	1	1	0	1	1	0	1	0	1	0	1
Student services	1	0	0	0	1	1	1	0	0	1	1	0
Faculty entrance	1	0	0	0	1	0	0	0	1	0	0	1
Course selection	1	0	0	0	1	0	0	1	0	1	0	1
Assignments	1	1	1	1	1	1	0	0	1	1	0	1
Course design standard	1	1	1	1	1	1	1	1	1	0	1	1
Teaching staff	1	1	1	1	1	1	1	0	1	1	1	1
Production of materials	1	1	1	1	1	0	1	1	0	1	1	1
Charges	1	1	1	0	1	1	1	1	0	0	1	0
Financing	0	1	1	0	0	1	1	1	0	1	0	0
Legal	0	1	1	0	0	0	0	1	1	1	0	0
Other												

Objectives / *Ideals*	Opportunity	Quality education	Communication	Choice of mode	Resources	Other
Increased number of external students	1	1	1	0	1	
Increased cassette model of teaching	1	0	1	1	1	
Increased broadcast mode of teaching	1	0	1	1	1	
Increased clarity and comprehensiveness of materials	0	1	1	0	1	
Decrease 'drop-out' rate	1	0	0	0	1	
Increase numbers in face-to-face weekend programmes	0	1	1	1	1	
Establish university as focus for 'distance' teaching	0	1	0	0	1	
Increased access to references	1	1	1	0	1	
Consistency between internal/external programmes	1	1	0	0	0	
Minimum external resources	0	1	1	0	1	
Fiscal efficiency, internal programmes	1	0	0	0	1	
Professional enhancement	0	1	1	0	0	

Requisites:
Feasibility
Immediacy

FIG. 2. University distance-education goal matrix

3. *Academic status of the university*: Increase student enrolments. Decrease drop-out rate. Focus for external studies. Consistency between internal and external programmes. Maintain and enhance professional standing of teaching staff.

The university then established three planning teams to generate alternative proposals for each set of objectives. This case is specifically concerned with the communication-planning team which considered the objectives grouped under the heading, 'Communication between teachers and external students'.

EXPLORATION OF COMMUNICATION OBJECTIVES AND GENERATION OF ALTERNATIVES

The team examined the objectives that would affect communication changes. The implications of communication changes were explored for each objective.

Alternative communication policies for enhancing the achievement of the objectives were suggested. Finally, for each objective the circumstances which would tend to emphasize or de-emphasize the objective were considered. Full details of this aspect of the planning process are well covered in the literature. It is sufficient to say that, from a brainstorming session, a number of specific activities were considered for weaving into a plan of action. A sample of these activities is given in the following list.

Strategies

Record audio/video all internal lectures.
Exchange-cassette service.
Place cassette playback equipment in key area.
Hire out playback equipment.
Arrange discount purchasing of playback equipment.
Place reference material in regional libraries.
Place reference material in mobile libraries.
Provide 24-hour problem-answering service by telephone.
Provide computer-based self-learning packages.
Place telephone computer terminals in key areas.
Conduct telephone tutorials.
Place tutorial phones in key areas.
Install technically capable broadcast recording facilities.
Appoint technically competent staff.
Create teams of academic/editor/technician in each programme area.
Subsidize cost associated with face-to-face programme.
Move staff to students as well as students to staff.
Relate face-to-face session to student problems.
Provide talkback radio sessions in CB/FM/AM.
Utilize word-processing printer.
Test student for language-ability level.
Other.

Two alternative courses of action

The communication-planning team drafted two proposals which had different foci. Plan A was structured around a decentralized-location model of communication while Plan B was structured around a centralized-location model of communication. Both plans met the requisites. Brief outlines of the plans and their primary resource utilization are set out here, together with a simplified map (Fig. 3) showing some of the environmental factors taken into consideration by the planning team.

Plan A (decentralized model)

Conduct recruitment and enrolment session in regional centres.
Establish regional centres: (a) with a radius of half an hour driving time (25 miles rural,

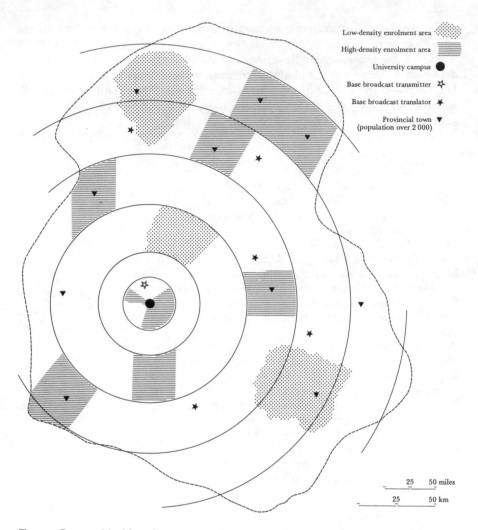

FIG. 3. Geographical location

15 miles urban) in high-density enrolment areas (5 students/course); and (b) with a radius of one-hour driving time (50 miles rural, 30 miles urban) in low-density enrolment areas (5 students/course).

Centres in high-density areas to have library of: internal lectures on cassette; recommended further-reading references. Facilities to include: audio playback equipment; cassette-copying equipment; tele-tutorial phone.

Additional services: one face-to-face four-hour session for semester programme; four tele-tutorial sessions per semester course; twice weekly availability of video playback equipment with course material on cassette.

Course notes mailed to each student to concentrate on: guiding the student on how to use references and cassette resources; setting out programme and associated assign-

330

ment requirements plus guidelines on methods to complete required tasks; annotated bibliography of programme resources.

Teaching staff requirements: brief course notes; detailed assignment notes; four 45-minute tele-tutorials per centre per semester course; one for-hour seminar per centre per semester course; recording of internal lectures; annotated bibliography of resources; select reference materials for regional centres; notes on use of regional-centre reference material.

Technical equipment: audio-cassette player/centre; video-cassette player for six centres; tele-tutorial phone/centre; cassette per lecturer/semester course/centre.

Technical staff: technical; printer; librarian (external-student services).

Other resources: multiple copies of printed reference material.

Special note: These centres would be established using existing facilities and personnel (e.g. public libraries) and would only need limited modification and costs to provide required services.

Plan B (centralized model)

Produce course publicity brochure/enrol by mail.

Produce four broadcast standard half-hour programmes for radio for each semester programme.

Produce two broadcast standard quarter-hour programmes for television for each semester programme.

Broadcast programmes through available networks, plus have available multiple copies in central lending library for borrowing.

Conduct weekend face-to-face seminar in university with subsidized accommodation for students in college residential halls.

Course notes to contain: detailed exposition of course material, designed to accompany a primary course text; some reference material by other authorities, to be attached; annotated bibliography of course resources; course assignment requirements, plus guidelines on methods to complete required tasks; multiple copies of references in central library.

Teaching staff requirements: detailed course exposition; detailed assignment notes; annotated bibliography of resources; four half-hour radio scripts; two quarter-hour television scripts; six broadcast recording sessions; one weekend seminar per semester course; select course text.

Technical requirements: broadcast production and recording facilities; word processor and offset multicolour printing equipment; multiple copies of cassettes.

Technician staff: qualified producer; technician; printer; word-processor operator; part-time supervisor/librarian per centre.

Other resources: multiple copies of printed reference material.

Goal-achievement matrix

The planning team next evaluated the two alternatives utilizing the objectives and the measuring devices established prior to generating the alternatives. Some parts of this process are discussed to illustrate the stages, and the results are displayed on a goal-achievement matrix (see Table 2) to show the form—for information purposes—that was used to aid the university council

TABLE 2. Distant-education goal-achievement matrix

Sectoral interest groups	Communication-planning objectives											
	Increase cassette mode of teaching		Increase broadcast mode of teaching		Increase clarity and comprehensiveness of data distributed		Increase face-to-face participation		Increase ease of access to reference materials		Equality between internal and external student costs to the university	
	Plan A	Plan B	Plan A	Plan B	Plan A	Plan B	Plan A	Plan B	Plan A	Plan B	Plan A	Plan B
Students within twenty-five mile radius of the university	+	=	=	+	=	+	=	=	=	=	=	−
Students in high-density enrolment areas	+	=	=	+	+	=	+	=	+	=	=	+
Students in low-density enrolment areas	=	+	=	+	+	+	=	=	+	=	−	=
Students in social-science courses	=	+	=	+	+	=	=	=	+	=	I	I
Students in physical-science courses	+	=	=	+	+	+	I	NC	+	=	I	I
Students living more than fifty miles from university.	=	=	=	+	+	=	+	=	+	=	−	+
SUMMATION, ALL SECTORS	A > B		A < B		A > B		A > B		A > B		A < B	

KEY

Symbol	Interpretation	Symbol	Interpretation	Symbol	Interpretation
A	Plan A	−	Decrease, relative to secular change	I	No clear outcome
B	Plan B	NA	Not applicable	NC	No change
=	The same, subject to normal change over time (secular change)	A > B	A is superior to B with respect to goal achievement	E	Considered elsewhere
+	Increase, relative to secular change	A = B	A is equivalent to B		
		A < B	A is inferior to B		

332

in its decision-making. There was interest in knowing how the proposals might affect certain sectors or groups within the academic community. A sample of the possible groupings is shown on the goal-achievement matrix. (It should be noted that this might lead to double-counting but it certainly sheds additional light on the analysis.) The symbols and letters employed in the analysis are shown in Table 2.

Looking at each goal in turn, we find the following:

Increase cassette mode of teaching. Plan A envisages a large number of cassettes available locally to students, while Plan B has a limited number of 'quality' cassettes available centrally, as is the current practice. The lower-quality lecturer tapes may require some interpretation; where there is a high concentration of students this is not seen as a major problem. Similarly, with the physical sciences, facts can be checked from texts. On the other hand, 'lecture'-quality cassettes are unlikely to capture the discussion/debate nature of social-science content. A positive change is therefore anticipated in cassette borrowings in both plans, with A being the superior.

Increase broadcast mode of teaching. Only Plan B contributes to this goal, since the financial-feasibility requisites require some rationalization of resources between broadcast and staff travel, the two major cost areas in the proposals. Plan B is therefore unquestionably superior, causing a positive change in all sectors.

Increase clarity and comprehensiveness of distributed data. Experience has shown that very few inquiries follow face-to-face information exchanges and, further, that there is a positive relationship between length and frequency of contact. While it is expected that minor gains can be made with professionally produced material for mailing, such change would not be significant without face-to-face support, or where face-to-face support has never been a possibility. Plan B is therefore seen to make a positive change in three sectors. Plan A will make a positive change in five sectors, with the sixth sector already enjoying the conditions proposed in A.

Increase face-to-face voluntary participation course seminars. Plan B does not propose any changes and, while there may be some heightened motivation because of the broadcasts, there may also be less need for the information usually transmitted at such seminars. Plan A, however, brings the opportunity to participate at a much lower cost (time, money etc.) to the student (a much higher cost to the university), to the point where students in high-density enrolment areas will enjoy the same opportunity as those within twenty-five miles of the university campus. This latter group has always had a much higher percentage of participants and so it is expected a positive change will result for Plan A.

Increase ease of access to reference materials. While Plan B provides for increased quality of reference material, it does not propose changes to access. However, Plan A, in decentralizing resources, allows students to utilize their local network to facilitate borrowings. A positive change is therefore anticipated.

Achieve equality between internal and external student costs to the university. Plan A costs are likely to increase with increasing enrolments through greater resources being required at each decentralized centre, although there will be some sub-threshold expansion areas. However, the initial cost will be fairly high. Plan B represents reasonably fixed costs, and an increasing enrolment will therefore quickly reduce the cost per student. So while both plans have an initial negative effect, Plan B, it is anticipated, could lead to positive changes in the future. No such prediction is advanced for Plan A.

DECISION-MAKING

The goal-achievement matrix was studied by the university council and various relative values were attached to the objectives to ascertain the overall significance of each proposal's consequences. As with all decision-making, the outcome was political and reflected the value judgements of the majority of the university-council members. Plan B was implemented.

Bibliography

BOULDING, K.E. 1966. *Economic Analysis.* Vol. II, *Macroeconomics*, p. 88. New York, N.Y., Harper & Row.

CAMERON, B. 1968. *Input–Output Analysis and Resource Allocation*, p. 46–61, 69–81. Cambridge, Cambridge University Press,.

KOHLER, H. 1977. *Scarcity and Freedom*, p. 409–15. Lexington, Mass., D. C. Heath.

LEONTIEF, W. 1941. *The Structure of the American Economy. An Empirical Application of Equilibrium Analysis.* Cambridge, Mass., Harvard University Press.

——. 1951. *The Structure of the American Economy 1919–1939.* 2nd ed. Fair Lawn, N.J., Oxford University Press.

——. 1963. The Structure of Development. *Scientific American*, September, p. 148.

NEUMAN, J. von; MORGENSTERN, D. 1953. *The Theory of Games and Economic Behavior.* 3rd ed. Princeton, N.J., Princeton University Press.

ROBINSON, J.; EATWELL, J. 1973. *Introduction to Modern Economics*, p. 183, 283–4. London, McGraw-Hill.

SAMUELSON, P.A. 1971. *Economics*, p. 754–5. 10th ed. New York, N.Y., McGraw-Hill.

SRAFFA, P. 1960. *The Production of Commodities by Means of Commodities.* Cambridge, Cambridge University Press.

YAN, C. 1969. *Introduction to Input–Output Economics*, p. 73–5. New York, N.Y., Holt, Rinehart & Winston.

V

Methods
for action

Introduction

The test of planning comes through action. In large systems, planning is often separated from action. Plans are developed, decisions made and implementation turned over to various 'implementing agencies'. In smaller systems, planning and action are often integrated, particularly under incremental approaches. In either case, planning for action takes place, requiring the use of methods for the creation and organization of information for co-ordination, control and monitoring. Planning for the accomplishment of these three key tasks calls on methods drawn from organizational and management sciences. These methods enable planners/implementors to take the process of translating strategy into action, begun in the strategy element of planning, to the fine level of detail necessary for successful implementation. Methods useful in this element of planning tend to focus on the relationships among systems and on the relationship between action and time. These two relationships are central to effective implementation.

Methods presented

Four methods are presented here: inter-organizational co-ordination; planners' workshop; programme-evaluation review technique; and flow charting.

INTER-ORGANIZATIONAL CO-ORDINATION

Most communication planning (and action) involves a number of organizations which are expected to work together in order to accomplish goals. The adaptation strategy of any single system is thus dependent on the performance of other systems. Clearly this creates a situation in which planners must give careful attention to the problem of co-ordination. Inter-organizational co-ordination is rather more than a planning method: it is a methodology for rational approach to the problems of co-ordination, incorporating a set of principles and procedures which can increase the probability of successful co-ordination. To the extent that multiple organizations are involved in different elements of the planning process, inter-organizational co-ordination procedures can be applied throughout. The methodology is not particularly complex. It does not require large amounts of information. Consequently, it may profitably be used under all planning approaches. By its very nature the methodology is participatory, at least at the planning and decision-making level for sets of co-ordinated institutions.

PLANNERS' WORKSHOP

Co-ordination problems occur not only between organizations, but also within the work of a single system. The process of translating strategy into action often stops before it is decided 'what is to be done and who is to do it' (in the words of the authors of this method chapter).

A number of management techniques have been developed to help in the process of work planning. Perhaps best known among recent methods is management by objectives. In the chapter on planners' workshop, the authors build from the basic principles of this method to develop a methodology for planning specific tasks for implementation, assignment of staff and monitoring of work. Developed from direct field experience in communication planning, this methodology is relatively simple to apply. The high level of detailed information it calls for makes it most useful for planning within single systems, most probably at the level of organizational units. It can be used under any planning approach. A strong feature of the methodology is participation of the staff, who are required to carry out planned tasks.

PROGRAM EVALUATION REVIEW TECHNIQUE

The scheduling and monitoring of complex sequential activities is a common challenge to communication systems. Programme evaluation review technique (PERT) is a widely used method which enables managers to identify the interrelations between sequential tasks and to establish realistic time frames for task accomplishment. The method provides a flexible tool for constant monitoring of progress and revision of plans.

PERT can be used at different levels of complexity. In its full application, it requires the use of relatively simple statistical analysis to estimate probabilities of task accomplishment within specified time frames. Simpler versions require only the development of a task 'network' against a time line, enabling the manager to estimate task completion dates and to monitor progress. PERT can be used under any planning approach. Simpler versions of the method have successfully been used with relatively untrained rural-planning and community groups, demonstrating its potential for participatory planning.

FLOW CHARTING

The creation of a graphic display of the elements of a planned process is quite possibly the most universal planning method. Flow charts are perhaps the most widely used type of graphic for this purpose. The method involves the use of standard symbols to display the flow and sequence of activities. It is widely used in depicting the results of a systems analysis. Flow-charting techniques are easily mastered and applied, and the method is useful in all planning approaches. As a technique for displaying clearly the structure of planned action, flow charting is quite useful in participatory planning.

Other uses of presented methods

PERT and flow charts are widely used to plan for the processes of analysis, strategy development, decision-making and learning as well as for action. Thus these are generally useful methods in planning for planning.

Other methods for action

There are many management methods and techniques which are useful in planning for action other than the selected examples presented here. Of considerable importance are management information systems, which can provide regular and accurate information on implementation. These can be complex computer-based systems, or they can be based on routine reporting from implementation units, supplemented by periodic conferences and meetings.

Chapter 17

Inter-organizational co-ordination

George Beal
Victor T. Valbuena

Most planning has to take into account a number of existing or newly created organizational units in the planning, organizing, implementing or evaluating processes. Planners often have to make decisions about whether or not to, or how to, involve these organizations in some type of inter-organizational co-ordination relation in their plan. To make these decisions, planners need to understand what can be co-ordinated, the types or forms of inter-organizational co-ordination relations, the dimensions of co-ordination, the probable costs and benefits from co-ordination and the procedures available to attempt to secure inter-organizational co-ordination. This chapter attempts to provide that understanding.

Method

DEFINITION

Inter-organizational co-ordination is a process engaged in by two or more organizations (or relatively independent units in an organization) to increase the availability of scarce resources and/or improve the impact of activities to reach organizational or programme goals more effectively and/or efficiently.

PHILOSOPHY AND ASSUMPTIONS

There are different philosophical orientations regarding inter-organizational co-ordination. There are those who believe there is something intrinsically 'good' about co-ordination, e.g. that co-ordination and co-operation are intrinsically better than competition, contest or conflict. Others appear to have a basic belief that co-ordination will 'automatically' lead to more efficient use of resources and more effective programmes. A more common orientation is that in certain situations an analysis of the existing environment, or what can realistically be projected as a potential changed or new environment, may lead to the conclusion that organizations possess needed resources that if mobilized and combined would probably result in more efficient and/or effective programme-goal attainment. Further, if co-ordination is to be undertaken, the analysis of the situation should indicate the needed co-ordination that could probably be obtained, recognizing there will be both costs and benefits in the co-ordination process and resulting activity—but that benefits will outweigh costs.

There are a number of explicit and implicit assumptions in this last orientation towards inter-organizational co-ordination. The following appear to be among the more important assumptions:

Resources are needed for planning and implementation of programmes, projects and activities—including the communication components.

Resources are often found in existing organizations—or existing organizations represent a viable alternative for creating or mobilizing existing resources.

Roles and resource bases of organizations are difficult to change, e.g. it is often very difficult to reallocate resources from one organization to another, or create a new organization to perform a function or closely related function presently being performed by an existing organization.

Co-ordinating the resources and activities of various organizations often represents the potential for (a) assembling the critical mass of needed resources, (b) the efficient use of those resources and (c) a resulting greater programme impact.

Inter-organizational co-ordination represents only one alternative. Its use or non-use should be based on an assessment of the costs and benefits of co-ordination.[1]

HISTORY

As societies become more complex, the problems of individuals, groups and categories of people, communities and other social systems become more complex. The government and private sector tend to respond by providing greater opportunity for citizen involvement and communication and providing information, education and services through the creation of new programmes and activities. These are administered through new agencies and organizations or by adding new functions and responsibilities to the roles of existing institutions and agencies. The social organizational world becomes more complex, formalized and fragmented. Resources are limited and scarce. When planners, including communication planners, analyse the environment and diagnose problems, they are usually struck by the large numbers of organizations directly or potentially related to the problem and/or which represent resources for its possible solution. Thus, organizations—their leaders, members, resources, supporters, clients—are often important units of analysis in problem definition, resource analysis and programme implementation.

1. For example, it may be argued that the cost of time and energy to create and maintain co-ordination will outweigh benefits in efficiency and/or impact. Or some might argue that 'duplicate' organizations competing for the same client system may result in more effective programming than a co-ordinated programme.

Parallel with the development of complex societal organization has come the development of a body of knowledge about organizational (intra- or within-organization) management. One of the main concepts of many management models is co-ordination. However, it was observed that the principles and techniques of intra(within)-organizational co-ordination often were not applicable to inter (among)-group co-ordination. It was at this time (the early 1960s) that there began to develop an interest in conceptualizing and conducting studies to understand better, explain and in some cases prescribe principles and strategies of inter-organizational co-ordination. Among the early contributors to the field were Aiken (Aiken and Hage, 1968), Levine (Levine and White, 1961), Litwalk (Litwalk and Hylton, 1962), Reid (1969), Warren (1967) and White (1974).

There is not a well-developed, agreed-upon theory or set of propositions on inter-organizational co-ordination. There are a number of different perspectives. However, there are concepts, propositions and insights, and strategies and training materials have emerged that have proven valuable to many policy-makers, planners, programme directors and implementors. Some of these will be presented in the discussion that follows.

MAIN USE

The use of inter-organizational co-ordination is not necessarily limited to any one of the planning functions. The planner may want to involve a number of organizations in the data-gathering, problem-analysis and goal-setting processes. Thus, the planners themselves may be actively engaged in inter-organizational co-ordination to secure this type of involvement. In developing general plans, planners may decide that the most feasible plan is for existing and/or new organizations to co-ordinate their resources and other activities to reach programme or project goals. Thus, inter-organizational co-ordination may be encouraged, suggested or required in the plan developed. In developing operational plans for programme implementation, more specific inter-organizational plans such as the type of co-ordination, resources to be exchanged, time sequence, duration etc. may be specified. Or inter-organizational co-ordination for evaluation and feedback might be specified. Some planning methods may be most appropriate for specific planning functions. The reader should be aware that the inter-organizational co-ordination method may have potential for several functions.

The co-ordination process

It is evident that inter-organizational co-ordination emphasizes processes. It will become obvious that many processes are involved, e.g. analysis, communication, decision-making, planning, negotiating, exchange, co-ordination, commitment, formalization and evaluation.

Organization. In inter-organizational co-ordination, i.e. among organizations, the unit of analysis emphasized is the organization. It is recognized that co-ordination of roles, functions and resources *within* organizations (intra-organizational co-ordination) is important (in fact it may be a prerequisite to effective inter-organizational co-ordination). Within formal or bureaucratic organizations there tend to be: well-defined roles and authority and responsibility patterns, well-understood sanctions (rewards and punishments) for performance; effective communication networks; well-understood decision-making processes. In this case intra-organizational principles apply. However, here we emphasize co-ordination between and among organizations. It is assumed that the organizations have a relatively high degree of autonomy—they have major control over their own goals, programmes, resources, personnel. A given organization (or administrator) does not have authority over other organizations. Our definition does allow for an exception to the general rule of organizational autonomy. Many organizations are large, complex and have many subdivisions within them. They may be complex vertically, e.g. central government, ministries, divisions, agencies, regions, provinces, districts, centres, municipalities, barrios. They may be complex horizontally, e.g. many different divisions or agencies (even within a ministry), many barrios, many local clinics etc. In some cases, because of this complexity, or lack of strong administrators or poor administrative skills, sub-units (for example within a ministry) develop their own power base and become relatively autonomous—even though organizationally they are under the authority of a central administrator. In some of these cases, principles and strategies of inter-organizational co-ordination (rather than intra-organizational co-ordination) appear to be appropriate if co-ordination is to be accomplished.

What can be co-ordinated. Our definition emphasizes the co-ordination of 'resources'. When people see the term 'resources', they often think only of 'tangible' resources. As a communication planner, you may think of inter-organizational co-ordination as a potential for obtaining tangible resource needs as inputs into the programme of activities you are planning: resources such as money, equipment, educational materials, physical facilities, services, research and evaluation information, staff, para-professionals, volunteers, clients, consultants. But there are obviously many other 'things' (instruments)[1] that can be co-ordinated—many of which could be highly relevant to communication planners. Some of these could be valuable as inputs into the development of the plan; others may be relevant for specification in the developed plan. For example, there can be involvement of two or more organizations in the communication-planning process itself—inter-organizational co-ordination in planning. Plans can be made for co-ordinating

1. Instrument is a more general term than resources; definition: 'a means by which something is done.' For our purpose, 'an input or activity used (or that could be used) by an organization to accomplish its goals'.

344

programmes, projects and activities (existing or newly developed) of existing or newly formed organizations. This co-ordination could deal with many different instruments, e.g.: materials development; materials production; message consistency or complementarity; recommendations; media mix; timing and scheduling of programme increments; differentiation, combination or complementarity of services or client systems; policies and procedures. There could be inter-organizational co-ordination of other major activities or facilities such as research, evaluation, libraries and data banks, client records, training. Additional potential areas for inter-organizational co-ordinated activities might be directed towards, legislators, policy-makers, specific constituencies, publics.

Types. There are several types of inter-organizational co-ordination structures. One of the major variables which distinguishes these types is the location and amount of authority a given person or organization can exercise over other organizations. An understanding of the types of inter-organizational co-ordination and the environment in which communication plans are created and carried out should aid communication planners in determining the feasibility of inter-organizational co-ordination and which type offers the greatest potential for success.

The first type is *co-ordination by existing authority*. In our previous discussion, we noted that in some cases in complex organizations sub-units developed their own power base and relative autonomy even though there is an authority structure. In these cases, the plan may call for plans and/or suggestions that the existing authority structure be made operative—that existing authority be used for coordination. It may be necessary to use inter-organizational co-ordination principles and steps to accomplish this end. In other cases, a person or 'committee, council, or board' is appointed by a higher authority and given the authority and responsibility to co-ordinate. Under either of these conditions we can illustrate co-ordination diagrammatically as in Figure 1. The solid lines indicate a high degree of authority or control. The arrows on the lines go down to indicate co-ordination by superiors of subordinates.

The second type of co-ordination is *co-ordination by negotiated authority* (Fig. 2). In this case, relative, autonomous or independent organizations agree to give up (delegate) a portion of their authority to a co-ordinator or a co-ordinating body which has has the designated authority to co-ordinate specified resources and activities of each of the organizations. The differences between this diagram and the previous diagram are that: (a) the lines show arrows going both ways, indicating that authority is given to the co-ordinating unit as well as the co-ordinating unit having designated authority over the co-operating units; and (b) the line is shown as broken, to indicate that each organization can choose to withdraw from the co-ordination agreement, usually under specified conditions that include prior notice of withdrawal.

The third type is *non-authority, negotiated co-ordination: standardization or*

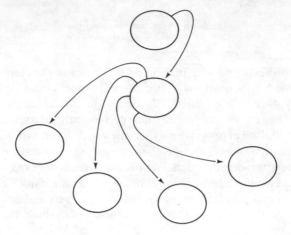

FIG. 1. Co-ordination by existing authority

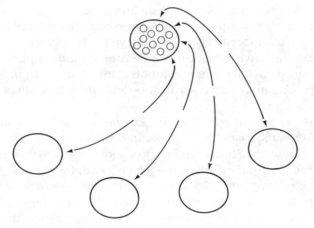

FIG. 2. Co-ordination by negotiated authority

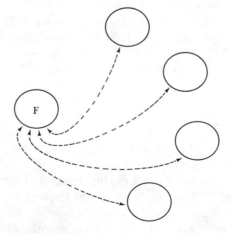

FIG. 3. Non-authority negotiated co-ordination: standardization or plan (dyadic)

plan. Again, we assume relatively autonomous or independent organizations and no pre-existing or negotiated delegation of authority. However, through communication and negotiations, two or more organizations (or units or individuals within organizations) agree to perform certain roles, deliver or exchange specified resources, provide certain services, co-ordinate certain activities, serve certain clients. Co-ordination is negotiated; these commitments and the specific types and amounts of resources or activities are clearly spelt out, usually in writing, with time sequence, direction, communication and feedback specified. Thus, the title of co-ordination by standardization and/or plan is derived.

In the case of *co-ordination by standardization or plan*, co-ordination may be among peer organizations—that is, organizations with relatively equal resource bases, power and prestige. Co-ordination may also be among organizations with highly different resources, power, and prestige. In either case, often (though not always) one organization takes the leadership in exploring the potential for co-ordination. In Figure 3, we will assume there is one organization (F, for focal or central organization) taking the leadership initiative. It is shown on the 'side' not on 'top' as in the authority types. The broken lines indicate that no formal authority exists between the initiating co-ordination organization (focal organization) and other organizations. The double arrows indicate that co-ordination is negotiated between the organizations. The term 'dyadic', given in the caption to Figure 3, is used by people in the field of inter-organizational co-ordination to indicate 'two units regarded as a pair'. Thus the relationship and agreements are between the one 'focal' organization and every other organization. No relationships are shown among the other organizations.

Another type of negotiated co-ordination is labelled 'system' co-ordination. In its 'ideal type' (pure, extreme form) this 'system'-type of negotiated co-ordination could be shown diagrammatically as in Figure 4. In the 'system' type of co-ordination, each organization has a negotiated relationship with each other organization. Thus, there are double arrows from each organization to each other organization, indicating two-way negotiated agreements. The arrows are broken, indicating that either organization can withdraw from the relations at its own discretion. The system type is more complex to negotiate. However, there is a high probability that this type of co-ordination would be stronger because of the interlocking nature and commitment of a 'closed system' of agreements. Obviously, there can be different degrees of relationships among organizations between the extremes of dyadic and system.

The fourth type of co-ordination is *mutual-adjustment co-ordination* (Fig. 5). In this case, relatively autonomous organizations are assumed, but co-ordination is less formal, less specified, less binding and more flexible. It is often based on informal communication and personal relations. Organizations have a considerable degree of freedom to make 'mutual adjustments', to anticipated or actual behaviour of other organizations and the environment.

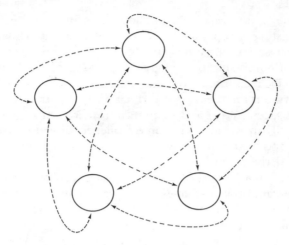

FIG. 4. Non-authority-negotiated co-ordination: standardization or plan (system)

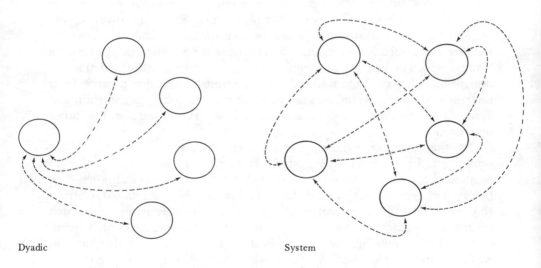

Dyadic   System

FIG. 5. Non-authority-negotiated co-ordination: mutual adjustment

The last type of co-ordination to be discussed is *facilitative co-ordination* (Fig. 6). The key component of this type of co-ordination is information exchange among organizations. This may provide a basis for co-ordination but there are no agreements to co-ordinate. The decision to change organizational behaviour based on the information exchanged is completely up to each organization. This type of 'co-ordination' is typical of many informal and formal co-ordinating bodies. For example, regular monthly 'co-ordinating'

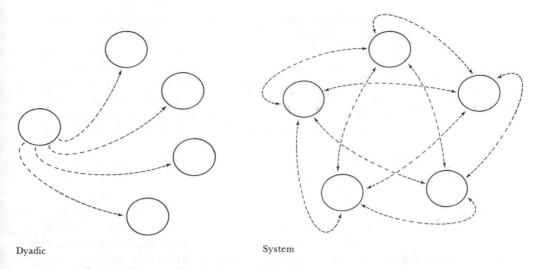

Dyadic   System

FIG. 6. Non-authority-negotiated co-ordination: facilitative

meetings may be held at which each organization may report on its programmes, activities, staff changes, goal achievement (performance successes) and
problems. However, no mutual attempt is made to reach agreements on co-
ordination. Each organization is left free to go 'back home' and make any
adjustments it desires. There are no mutual agreements on the adjustments to
be made. The lines in Figure 6 are shown as very light lines, representing a very
low and tenuous level of co-ordination. They are also shown as frequently
broken lines to indicate no commitment beyond information exchange.

In terms of formal agreements, authority, and commitment, facilitative co-
ordination is the weakest type of co-ordination. However, its value should not
be overlooked. Facilitative co-ordination may be an important input into
inter-organizational co-ordination, helping all organizations involved to
understand their own and other organizations better: (a) goals, programmes,
projects and activities; (b) operating procedures; (c) client systems; and (d)
resource bases etc. It may provide a basis for and lead to organizations reformulating their goals; activating existing goals; adjusting existing programmes, developing new means for more effective programme performance; and,
reallocating their resources. Also, it may be a first step towards more formalized co-ordination activities.

Dimensions of co-ordination. It is obvious from the above discussion that there
are a number of important conceptual dimensions running through the various
types of inter-organizational co-ordination. For the planner, each of these
concepts represents an important analytical tool and also a decision-making
point in developing and operationalizing communication plans. On each of
these dimensions the planner should determine what exists in the environment

and what would be ideal from a planning and implementation point of view and then temper that with what is potentially possible, feasible and benefit–cost effective. Some of the more important dimensions will be discussed below. The *location and degree of authority* is a major dimension that was noted in the various types of co-ordination discussed above—varying from existing authority, through negotiated authority to no authority or agreements to co-ordinate, and facilitative co-ordination. What exists? What would be ideal? What is feasible? These are important analytical and decision points for communication planners.

A second dimension is *formalization of inter-organizational co-ordination structures*. Formalization of structure involves the degree to which those to be involved, their roles, their responsibilities, their authority and the scope of their activity are clearly defined, formally stated and understood. Structures may vary from very formal, well-defined structures to very informal, casual structures. Varying degrees of formalization of structure may be appropriate and feasible depending on the environment, organizations involved and goals of what is being planned by communication planners, and may change over time as the environment and the relations among organizations change.

A third dimension is *formalization of agreements*. This is the degree to which there is an attempt to reach agreements regarding inter-organizational co-ordination between/among organizations and to which those agreements are given formal observable, official recognition, and the degree to which sanctions (rewards and punishments) for compliance with the agreement are formalized. Formal agreements are usually in written form. They specify relations among organizations; instruments to be co-ordinated; responsibilities and authorities; time sequence of exchanges or activities; continuity and duration of agreement; and basis for continuation or termination. At the other extreme, the agreement may be very informal, casual, general and usually verbal and open-ended.

A fourth dimension, *standardization*, may be regarded as a subconcept under formalization of agreement. It does represent a decision point for communication planners. Standardization refers to the degree to which the units of resources and instruments to be delivered or exchanged are clearly defined, their quality and quantity stated and time dimensions specified. For example, if an organization is providing a staff member for a project, is it stated as 'staff member will be furnished' or, at the other extreme, is it 'standardized' in terms of staff title, role, training, experience, number of days, time available, amount of compensation, who will compensate, who will provide what supporting services etc. all being specified?

A fifth dimension is *scope*. This deals with the number, breadth, diversity, complexity and size of the resources, and of other instruments which offer potential and then may be regarded as feasible for inter-organization co-ordination. For example, does the scope of co-ordination include exchanging money, personnel, equipment and all activities during the year or just the co-ordination of the applications for funding?

The last dimension is *intra-organizational commitment*. Since inter-organizational co-ordination assumes participation from organizations (or units or individuals within organizations) it is important to determine the existing or potential commitment of the organizations considered for involvement.

There are two important types of commitment that need to be determined or planned. One is *commitment to the need or problem*, often called commitment to the focal field. How high a priority does an organization place (or can it be influenced to place) on the problem or need that is the focus of co-ordination planning? The second relevant type of *intra-organizational commitment* is *to inter-organizational co-ordination* as an acceptable, viable means or method for problem solution. Even when there is agreement among organizations as to the high significance and priority of the problem, if the potential of inter-organizational co-ordination is to be objectively and effectively explored and carried out, there must be a high degree (or high potential) for *intra-organizational* commitment to the idea that inter-organizational co-ordination represents a realistic alternative means for problem solution.

Costs and benefits. As discussed, different people give different reasons for inter-organizational co-ordination and these reasons suggest different bases for making decisions regarding planning for inter-organizational co-ordination. Exchange theory—the exchange of instruments between and among organizations—is one framework within which to discuss inter-organizational co-ordination. The exchange approach suggests a major consideration of costs and benefits of the exchanges—especially in those cases where there is no well-defined authority structure which has the power to dictate exchanges.

In considering costs and benefits of inter-organizational co-ordination in the communication planning or implementation processes, an important question for planners to ask is, 'Costs and benefits to whom?' Costs and benefits may differ depending on whether the referent is you or your planning unit, different organizations you are considering as having potential for co-ordination, different individuals, sub-units or larger units within each of the organization, the programme, project or activity for which planning is being done, or the ultimate clients, users or recipients.

Each situation is unique as to costs and benefits of inter-organizational co-ordination. However, a listing of some of the costs and benefits as developed by planners, administrators and those implementing programmes may help you to stimulate thinking and the development of criteria along these lines. Benefits are often evaluated in terms of maximizing or optimizing the use of resources such as money, equipment, supplies, physical facilities, materials produced, services, staff, para-professionals, volunteers, knowledge, skills, access to clients. Additional benefits may come in the form of: reducing overlap or reducing duplication of activities; more effective programmes—greater impact; reaching new client groups; enlarging programme scope; delineating gaps in programmes or client systems; standardization of procedures, policies, forms, records etc.; eliminating mistrust, competition, conflict; creating more positive programme images; obtaining greater constituency support; more direct programme involvement, commitment and delivery of resources.

On the cost or limitation side, inter-organizational co-ordination will involve time, energy and other resources to set up and maintain co-ordination. There will probably be some loss of organizational autonomy; there is a possibility of one organization co-opting another organization or portions of its programme. It may be difficult to determine or 'sort out' an organization's contribution—e.g. did inter-organizational co-ordination lead to more efficiency or impact, and if so, which organizations contributed to it? Success is diffused—can credit for success be allocated and rewards be made observable? Because of inter-organizational communication and knowledge, there may be cases where innovative ideas and methods are 'borrowed' by other organizations or internal organizational weaknesses exposed.

It should be easily recognized that some of the ideas mentioned can be either costs or benefits, or both, and in many cases what is a cost to one 'unit' may be a benefit to another.

Domain. One additional important concept often used in inter-organizational co-ordination analysis and planning is domain. It is used to describe the sphere of operation of an organization. The description of domain might include such dimensions as: goals and objectives; programmes, activities or services provided; territory of operation; client system(s) served; authority and responsibilities. Domain consensus is a term used to describe the degree of agreement between or among organizations regarding the role, function, territory etc. of an organization. It is often expanded to include an analysis of domain consensus: degree of agreement among organizations regarding the role and function of a number of individual organizations or of a network of organizations. Some of the greatest deterrents to effective inter-organizational coordination are: (a) lack of clear domain definition; (b) lack of knowledge of domain interface and interrelations; (c) domain overlap; (d) domain gap; (e) domain conflict; and (f) lack of domain consensus. On the positive side the resolution of these problems, sometimes through inter-organizational co-ordination, can be important positive inputs into effective communication planning and implementation.

Steps in inter-organizational co-ordination

Determining the need and potential for inter-organizational co-ordination, securing organizational commitment and agreement and carrying out agreed-upon co-ordinated activities are a complex process. There will probably be great variation from situation to situation. Thus, it is difficult to be highly specific in detailing how to use the method. However, an extensive review of the literature in the field, the theory, research and generalization, indicates there is a potential for developing guidelines and procedures for accomplishing inter-organizational co-ordination. These may be heuristically conceptualized as ten steps. When these steps are successfully negotiated, this appears to result in beneficial co-ordination among organizations. To place these steps in context, the following points may be made. The steps are presented from the point of view of an organization (sub-unit, small informal group or individual(s)) which is exploring the potential of inter-organizational co-ordination, deciding at each step to proceed further, and in the end carrying out and evaluating inter-organizational co-ordination. For example, as a communication planner, you may decide you want to explore the potential of involvement of a number of organizations in the planning process—these steps should aid you in this process. Or, in developing a general communication plan, you may be faced with deciding whether to plan for inter-organizational co-ordination or to propose independent organizational actions—these steps should be useful as a tool for analysis and decision. It may also help decide what types of co-ordination to specify or recommend in your plan. Also if the general communication plan calls for inter-organizational co-ordination, these steps may be valuable for developing the operational plan.

Planning steps one to three may be regarded as *orientation steps* at which organizations attempt to analyse the reasons for and potential of the proposed co-ordination and the task environment in which it would have to occur. Planning steps four and five may be seen as the *intra-organizational evaluation stage*, at which organizations tentatively determine whether to participate, and instruments should be considered for exchange. Steps six to eight may be seen as the *legitimation stage* at which organizations attempt to agree on inter-organization co-ordination goals, means and domain concerns and their role(s) in the co-ordination activity. The plan is defined as legitimate and acceptable and is formalized. Last comes the *implementation stage*—carrying out and evaluating the co-ordination activities. In summary, the stages and steps are as follows:

Orientation stage:
Step 1. Definition of the problem
Step 2. Specification of the territory
Step 3. Identification of relevant organizations: preliminary organizational set
Intra-organizational evaluation stage:
Step 4. Intra-organizational commitment to the problem
Step 5. Intra-organizational commitment to co-ordination within the focal field
Legitimation:
Step 6. Inter-organizational agreement on goals within the focal field
Step 7. Inter-organizational agreement and commitment on the means to be used to accomplish the goals
Step 8. Formalization of the negotiated agreement
Implementation:
Step 9. Implementation
Step 10. Evaluation

A more detailed description of each of the ten steps is as follows.

ORIENTATION STAGE

Step 1: Definition of the problem. In this step, the need for inter-organizational co-ordination is examined. This starts with a conceptualization and definition of a problem (e.g. lack of resources, poorly integrated communication, difficulty of audience penetration, overlapping functions, and programmes). Second, it involves an analysis of what is needed, what alternatives might be developed, to help alleviate or solve the problem. The third step involves an analysis of the potential of inter-organizational co-ordination as a potential contributor to problem alleviation or solution.

Step 2: Specification of the territory. In this step, an attempt is made at least tentatively to define and clarify the geographical boundaries of, and location(s) for, the proposed co-ordination activity. The territoriality of the proposed co-ordinated activity could be national, province, district, county, municipality, community, neighbourhood etc. If the proposed activity is of national scope but ultimate impact is to be on local client systems broadly distributed in the nation, it is important to think through clearly, at least on a tentative basis, how the co-ordination will be carried out vertically within organizations and re-inforced by horizontal co-ordination at relevant levels (locations).

Step 3: Identification of relevant organizations: preliminary organizational set. In the third step, an analysis of the task environment should identify the most relevant organizations (and groups or individuals) that have potential for inclusion in the potential inter-organizational co-ordination activity—the preliminary organizational set. It may be noted that '(and groups or individuals)' were added to organizations above. There may be cases where informal groups as informal structures or power élites and individuals who do not necessarily derive their influence from formal organizations may also be highly relevant. The criteria for relevancy may vary from activity to activity, by geographic area and from time to time. At a general level we can specify criteria such as:

Actually or potentially having a high degree of organizational involvement or commitment to the purpose of the potential inter-organizational co-ordination activity—similar or complementary goals, activities, prestige in the field, clients etc.

Representing a potential of needed resources.

Those organizations to which your organization represents a potential of resources needed by them.

Representatives of or access to client systems to be served by the proposed inter-organizational co-ordination activity.

Potential sources of legitimation or prestige.

At this step a preliminary determination is made. However, events in later steps may indicate that some organizations judged as relevant are not as relevant as presently believed and/or other organizations should be added to the relevant organizational set.

Several general comments may be made about these first three steps, the 'orientation' stage, before moving to the second stage, intra-organizational evaluation. These first three steps have been written from the orientation of an initiating organization—an organization or individuals in an organization have taken the initiative. If the individuals in one organization are highly informed, these three steps could be (though not necessarily) completed without contacts with other organizations. In the majority of the cases studied, this is what happens. Or if contacts with other organizations are made, they are on an informal, low-profile basis. In some cases, a small number of people from a small number of organizations may go through these three steps working together on an informal basis. There are infrequent examples of large numbers of organizations initially going through these three steps together. However, in almost all cases, these three steps are repeated with each new organization.

The following steps assume increasing degrees of communication among organizations, and these may move from informal to more formal communication and interaction.

INTRA-ORGANIZATIONAL EVALUATION STAGE

The next two steps are presented as distinct steps because each step involves an important element in the decision-making process either to engage or not to engage in co-ordination. There is supporting evidence that they should probably be approached in the order given. However, in the real world of application these steps often are highly interrelated and in some cases are integrated into one more general step.

Step 4: Intra-organizational commitment to the problem. At this step an attempt is made to determine the degree of commitment each organization in the organizational set has to the problem defined. Put another way, how important does each organization believe the proposed problem or activity is? What is the priority of the proposed problem or activity when compared with other projects and activities of the organization now in operation, or other alternatives that might be considered? It is important to determine who in the organization is committed, how widely the commitment is shared and if the people with influence and/or authority have this commitment. The determination of intra-organizational commitment to the problem at this step is at a general, pre-dispositional level. The final determination of each organization will probably depend partly on the more specific resources required from each organization and their judgement of potential organizational and/or programme benefits from the co-ordination activity.

Step 5: Intra-organizational commitment to co-ordination within the focal field. Step five deals with the intra-organizational commitment to organizations working together (inter-organizational co-ordination) as a viable alternative to be considered in solving the problem. Put another way, assuming commitment to the importance of the problem to be attacked, is inter-organizational co-ordination an acceptable and preferably a high-priority means that can be used to attempt to solve the problem? As in step four, the determination of the degree of commitment to inter-organizational co-ordination as an acceptable means at this step will be at a general, predispositional level. The final determination of each organization will probably be made when serious, more specific negotiations occur in the following steps.

LEGITIMATION

Step 6: Inter-organizational agreement on goals within the focal field. At this step 'serious' negotiation begins. Inter-organizational co-ordination is typically viewed by participating organizations as a strategy for the resolution of a problem. Agreement and acceptance among organizations of a common definition of the problem and appropriate goals for the solution of the problem appear to be important conditions for further organizational participation in the proposed co-ordinated activity. This step usually involves a more detailed analysis of the problem, specification of goals and attempts to secure agreement on both. Specification of outcomes, impacts or criteria which would be accepted for evaluation of successful progress towards problem solution also occur here.

Step 7: Inter-organizational agreement and commitment on the means to be used to accomplish the goals. Means is used here as a general inclusive term. Though it may vary from proposed activity to activity, it usually will include such things as general strategies and actions to be taken, resources needed, who will provide these resources, the time sequence and schedule of providing resources and carrying out activities, the structural organization form within which co-ordination will be carried out and budgeting and evaluation procedures. This will probably be one of the most difficult steps to negotiate. It is at this stage that many of the ideas previously discussed in this method get their crucial test. You are beyond the general thinking and talking stage and down to the concrete negotiation stage. Attempts are being made to secure agreements and commitments on the specification, standardization and exchange of scarce resources. Domain consensus among organizations is put to the test of reality. Each organization is faced with the reality of specifying and evaluating the costs and benefits to it as an organization of entering into the co-ordinated activity. Compromises will probably have to be made to attain agreement and commitment among organizations.

Step 8: Formalization of the negotiated agreement. Many successful co-ordination activities are carried out on a relatively informal basis (mutual adjustment). However, there is evidence that in many cases major problems (including failures) arise in co-ordination because of lack of a formalized, written agreement specifying the goals and means agreed upon. Poor communication, real or convenient lapses in memory, changes in programme priority, changes in personnel etc. can each and all contribute to co-ordination failures. Serious consideration should be given to formalizing agreements reached, including a specification of the time sequence for providing resources and carrying out activities. If the time sequence is developed into a 'plan of work', it usually helps greatly in the implementation stage.

IMPLEMENTATION

Step 9: Implementation. Under this step, the negotiated agreements are carried out. In one sense, if the previous steps have been thoroughly and successfully negotiated with clear understandings and commitments, this can be a relatively simple, though high resource-consuming step. However, if the previous steps have not been well carried out, many problems will probably arise. To the extent that negotiations on goals and means were realistic, thorough and complete, and there is a well-designed and agreed-upon plan of work, and there is an adequate co-ordinating structure that includes effective means of communication and feedback and continuous reinforcement, the probability of successful implementation is increased.

Step 10: Evaluation. The placing of evaluation as the final step may or may not appear appropriate. We recognize (in fact assume) that there has been constant evaluation throughout the entire series of steps. In fact, to emphasize that point an evaluation step could have been inserted between each of the steps presented. The importance of this type of evaluation is recognized and recommended.

Several points may be made regarding evaluation (step ten). One of the items suggested for negotiation under step seven was 'evaluation procedures'. The most obvious interpretation of that item is to agree upon the criteria upon which the co-ordinated activity is to be evaluated, and acceptable measures and analysis of the data based on these criteria—project success, outcome criteria. However, there may be other types of evaluation, especially in the case of inter-organizational co-ordination activity or recommended in operationalized communication plans. There should probably also be evaluations of other dimensions such as: (a) the processes used in securing co-ordination; (b) the organizational-co-ordination structure set-up; (c) the adequacy of individual organization performance within the negotiated agreements; (d) an assessment of the costs and benefits actually accruing to each organization; (e) the adequacy of the organizational set involved in the co-ordinated activity; (f) the potential for additional co-ordinated activities; (g) alternative domain definitions of individual organizations; and (h) logical next steps in new or expanded project or programme areas. These, and other areas you may desire to add, should be considered for possible areas to include in evaluation.

As we have indicated many times before, most co-ordination activities involve costs to individual organizations. They must have feedback if they are to make decisions regarding continuing present, or engaging in future, co-ordination activities. Lack of adequate feedback to organizations as to benefits appears to be especially frequent in those cases where one organization is the focal co-ordination organization (resources are channelled through that organization), or where the ultimate clients served are not close to a usual client system or the organization contributing resources. Continuous evaluation and feedback can (if positive) be a strong reinforcing motivation to continued and additional co-ordination activity.

It is believed that adequate evaluation procedures and feedback to organizations can be one of the most important inputs into standardization (institutionalizing, or developing continuity) of inter-organizational co-ordination.

This series of stages and steps for inter-organizational co-ordination is only one way of conceptualizing the functions and time sequence for attempting inter-organizational co-ordination (or suggested operational plans for it). Its adequacy for your planning environment, organization and persons involved and programme goals will have to be evaluated by you and adapted (or new 'constructs' created) for your future communication planning.

Case example: a view of co-ordination at field level, Quezon Province, Philippines[1]

This case discusses the implementation of an inter-organizational co-ordination scheme designed to maximize the delivery of family-planning information–education–communication (IEC) and clinic services in selected localities in Quezon Province, Philippines. It describes how three previously competitive family planning agencies, namely, the Ministry of Health (MOH), the Institute of Maternal and Child Health (IMCH), and the Provincial Population Office (PPO), resolved some of their differences and pooled their resources to intensify their family planning IEC and clinic-service delivery activities.

BACKGROUND

From October 1977 to February 1979, the Cooperative Research Program of the Population Center Foundation implemented a family-planning research project in six municipalities and twelve barangays in the Province of Quezon. The scheme sought: (a) to determine the extent to which selected programme factors like comprehensive family-planning services, intensity of IEC exposure and use of commercial resources for contraceptive resupply affect family planning acceptance and continuation; and (b) to identify results useful for policy-making and programme planning at the national level. One of the

1. By Victor T. Valbuena.

research strategies—that of intensified IEC and clinic-service delivery—called for four specific tactics: the strengthening of comprehensive family-planning services; the establishment of satellite clinics; the organization of case-finding networks; and the setting-up of co-ordination bodies for family planning activities.

As envisioned by the project, the Cooperative Research Program will follow up the establishment and active operation of co-ordinating committees or task forces for planning at the municipal and barangay levels. These bodies will adhere closely to the provisions of the Ministry of Local Governments and Community Development regarding their establishment and composition. These committees will meet once a month to discuss common areas of concern and thresh out problems in implementing and co-ordinating their activities. As a Cooperative Research Program input, these committees will be assisted in drafting specific guidelines for co-ordination.

DEFINITION OF CO-ORDINATION PROBLEMS

During the different orientation and skills-training programmes, the various service-agency participants were asked to articulate issues relative to their difficulties in co-ordinating family-planning activities among themselves. These co-ordination issues included the initial dispensing of contraceptive pills by the PPO's Full-Time Outreach Workers (FTOW), duplication of sources of supply, non-visitation of remote areas by both clinic personnel and FTOWs, duplication of visits, faulty referral system, use of imported itinerant sterilization teams from Manila, lack of formal linkages and vague performance indicators for agencies doing similar work. It was clear that, for the project to succeed, harmonious working relationships among agencies would have to be developed.

When the subject of co-ordinating bodies was brought up, these agency workers said that since co-ordinating councils and committees have already been set up at provincial, municipal and barangay levels under a presidential directive, and since most of them were already members, another body would only duplicate these decreed councils and committees.

AGREEMENT AND LEGITIMATION

A consensus was reached that a set of co-ordination guidelines addressing the above issues would be more beneficial as this would clarify, among others, the roles and functions of each agency, the expectations of each other and areas of co-operation among agencies. A set of specific co-ordination guidelines became the main output of each of the different training programmes conducted prior to the launching of the Cooperative Research Program's project. The respective personnel of the Rural Health Units (RHU) of the MOH, the IMCH affiliate clinics and the FTOWs in the project municipalities and barangays, working as three separate groups, developed co-ordination guidelines outlining what they felt each agency and their field personnel should do in respect to family-planning I E C and service-delivery activities.

In a workshop attended by all these agency personnel from the R H Us, the I M C H clinics and the local population office, the three sets of guidelines were presented for discussion and consolidation into one synthesized set of co-ordination guidelines. Surprisingly, there was general agreement on most of the activity areas covered by the guidelines. There was initial disagreement and much argumentation and debate on the issue of pill dispensing by the F T O Ws, however. A policy of the Commission on Population (P O P C O M), the central co-ordinating agency for population and family-planning activities, allowed the population outreach workers to prescribe contraceptive pills with the use of a check-list. This policy was opposed by the clinic-based workers of the M O H and I M C H, who felt very strongly that women opting for the pill should undergo a thorough physical/internal examination. After much argument and counter-argument, the population outreach workers agreed to modify implementation of the policy, namely, to dispense initial supplies of contraceptive pills only in areas where the client might not have had ready access to a clinic or health centre. In other areas, the clinic personnel were to dispense the initial supply and thereafter refer the client to the F T O Ws for resupply.

The synthesized guidelines were then presented by the field personnel, as a group, to provincial, municipal and national representatives of participating agencies in Quezon Province as well as central P O P C O M officials. These representatives, including agency directors, reacted to and ratified the co-ordination guidelines proposed by the field-workers. On the whole, the group found the guidelines acceptable and not in conflict with their individual agency's organizational goals. Everyone expressed commitment to implement the guidelines. The formalized set of co-ordination guidelines, in effect, became the framework for a *standardized co-ordination plan*. It included sixteen items on R H U–I M C H–F T O W co-ordination activities and two on R H U–I M C H activities (See Appendix for details of these guidelines. Figure 7 illustrates the inter-agency linkages as defined by the guidelines.) These co-ordination guidelines, the agency representatives felt, would be a better mechanism than a simple co-ordination committee to ensure co-operation among the agencies participating in the project.

IMPLEMENTATION

Data based on observation and from interviews with field participants seem to indicate that the guidelines have, to some extent, improved the working relationship between the various participating agencies and their representatives at field level. The following incidents illustrate this.

Co-ordination in sterilization campaigns. Prior to the project, the R H Us, the I M C H clinics, and the P P O went about their own individual ways in pursu-

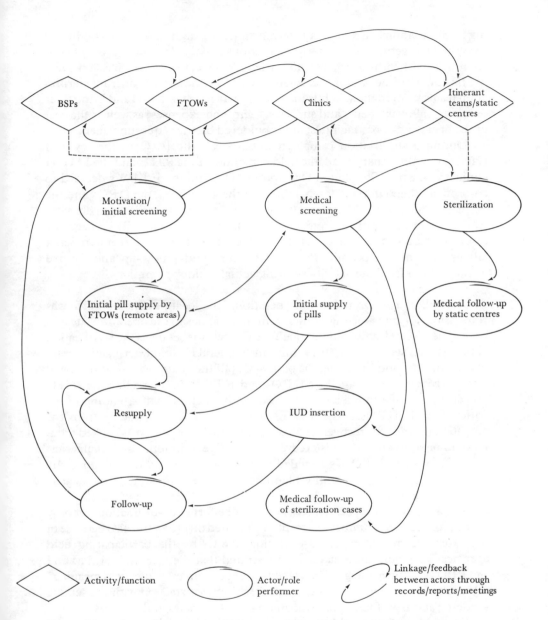

FIG. 7. Flow chart of inter-agency linkages as defined by the guidelines

ing family-planning activities. In sterilization campaigns, they each conducted separate IEC activities and service operations and tried to outdo each other in coming up with the most clients. This was, of course, very expensive, considering that on many occasions each agency would be importing itinerant sterilization teams from Manila. While these teams pay for their travel and bring their own surgical instruments and supplies, their food expenses, as well as the cost of the operating-room facilities, are shouldered by the requesting agency.

During a sterilization campaign initiated by the PPO in the town of Candelaria in February 1978, the field personnel of the RHU and the IMCH clinic, the District Population Officers (DPOs) and the FTPWs decided to co-ordinate their efforts. Closely following the guidelines, the DPOs and the FTOWs informed the clinic staff about the projected sterilization activity, which the local population office called Operation Tuldok. Together they discussed the advantages of conducting a joint activity, set the target number of clients, assigned responsibility for IEC work and follow-up and formed committees to facilitate activities during actual Tuldok operations.

Resource allocation. On the day of operations, the local population office was responsible for transporting clients from their homes to the operation site and back. The IMCH-affiliated Puericulture Center was set up as the sterilization clinic, with its staff assisting the Philippine General Hospital sterilization team in interviewing and screening the patients. Half the centre was also converted into a recovery ward staffed by DPOs and FTOWS. The adjoining RHU was also converted into a recovery ward, with its clinic staff attending to the patients. Male DPOs and FTOWs undertook to carry patients from the operating room to the recovery wards. Their female counterparts cooked food, served hot soup and administered post-operative antibiotics and analgesics. Other DPOs and FTOWs attended to waiting clients and their relatives by showing a series of family-planning feature films at the nearby library–museum building.

The activity may be described a successful effort at co-ordination not only because of the sheer number of accepters operated on (107), but also because of the extent of the extent of co-operation shown by the participating field agencies. The joint undertaking demonstrated that the local MOH, IMCH and PPO staff, by pooling efforts, facilities and resources, could yield meaningful results: more clients at less cost, greater client satisfaction with the service rendered and new-found goodwill among local agencies and workers.

On 11 May 1978, the Mary Johnston Hospital itinerant sterilization team performed operations at the Dona Marta Emergency Hospital in the town of Atimonan. The activity was initiated by the family-planning nurse-practitioner of the IMCH–affiliated Puericulture Center. At the start, she was apprehensive about approaching the other agencies in the area, fearing that they might think she wanted credit for herself and IMCH alone. In keeping with the guidelines, however, she informed the RHU staff and the FTOWs about the sterilization campaign and asked them to help her in motivating clients to undergo the operation. She explained that Mary Johnston Hospital would be credited with the actual delivery of service, but that each of the local clinics and FTOWs would be rightfully credited with the number of clients they brought to the operation. The local-agency participants not only joined her in recruiting clients, but also assisted in attending to the patients before and after their operation. Again, this demonstrates that local agencies are willing to co-operate with each other as long as due credit is given to their contributions.

Co-ordination in clinic services. There were certain alternate days in the week when practically all the staff of either the RHU or IMCH clinic in Tayabas town would be out in the field. This presented a problem to family-planning clients who happened to visit the town and wanted to have a check-up or contraceptive resupplies on these days.

In keeping with the spirit of the guidelines, both clinics agreed that whenever one was closed, the clinic that was open would attend to the other's clients. Any service rendered would be entered in the clinic's log-book but the client would still remain an accepter in the other's records. If, for example, an IMCH clinic staff worker attended to an RHU acceptor and resupplied her with a three-cycle pack of pills, this was noted down in the IMCH clinic as 'service rendered'. The information was later passed on to the RHU, and duly noted by the MOH clinic. The supply given by the IMCH clinic was then replaced by the RHU. Such an arrangement demonstrated that client-grabbing can be overcome when agencies openly discuss the problem and try to recognize and properly credit the complementary services they can provide to family-planning clients.

Co-ordination through meetings/dialogues. There were some guidelines, however, with which the field participants were not able to comply faithfully. For instance, they failed to operationalize the guidelines pertaining to monthly meetings to discuss activities, problems and achievements, and the guidelines on FTOW participation in zone conferences of RHU personnel and district meetings of IMCH staff. However, the participants met and discussed their problematic activities as the occasion demanded. The following incident will illustrate this.

Sometime in January 1979, one of the midwives of the Tayabas RHU met with the town's DPO to inform him that the FTOW under his supervision had not yet come to see her regarding the clients she asked him to follow up in another barangay. The DPO promised to have the FTOW see the midwife the first chance he met him. On the same occasion, the DPO attempted to discuss with the midwife the recent POPCOM instructions on recording and reporting. The midwife suggested that he present it instead during the weekly staff meeting of the RHU. This would afford the other clinic personnel the chance to have their questions aired and doubts clarified. The DPO heeded the suggestion.

On another occasion, the FTOW also initiated a meeting between the clinic staff and the DPO in the town of Sampaloc. The staff of the Sampaloc RHU used to be extremely prejudiced against the FTOW assigned in the area. They regarded the outreach worker as somebody who came to the clinic only to collect reports at the end of every month. Since they did not fully understand what the FTOW reports were for, they were under the impression that the outreach worker would turn them in with clinic performance included as his. Since the FTOW realized that earning the goodwill of the RHU staff was essential to his work, he requested his DPO to intercede in his behalf. The DPO met with the clinic staff, discussed the situation and explained in particular that the FTOW does not merely copy the reports of the clinic and turn them in as his own. The FTOW, he said, only collects the reports from all the family-planning agencies, consolidates them and turns them in to POPCOM. The reports, and the performance indicators therein, are properly annotated as referring to the RHU or some other family-planning agency. This meeting seemed to have cleared the doubts of the RHU staff about the role of the FTOW and even resulted in a co-operative campaign for sterilization. In accordance with the guidelines, the RHU personnel and a task force composed of the FTOW and several other outreach workers from neighbouring towns joined hands in conducting a house-to-house motivational campaign. This joint effort netted twenty sterilization accepters.

PROBLEMS IN IMPLEMENTATION

From the experience of the project in Quezon, the co-ordination of various local family-planning agencies through the use of guidelines appears to be feasible and effective. This has motivated the various offices to work harder at increasing the number of sterilization acceptors, not only in the project sites, but also in other outlying areas. It has also eliminated to a large extent the rough edges in day-to-day interaction among the different family-planning personnel. Optimism is high among field personnel that this co-ordination mechanism will remain effective.

Bias for one method. Successful coordination, however, has been achieved mostly in activities relating to sterilization campaigns. There has been little effort to co-ordinate IEC as well as service-delivery activities with regard to other contraceptive methods like the IUD. There seems to have been no initiative at all on the part of the FTOWs to motivate and refer clients for the IUD, despite the presence of skilled medical and nurse-midwife practitioners in the project sites. There are, for instance, in each of the RHU and IMCH clinics in Candelaria one doctor and one nurse highly trained in IUD insertion. The RHU nurse even opens the centre on Sunday for clients who may not have time to come on regular working days. And yet the FTOWs do not seem to encourage some of their clients to try this method. They seem predisposed to push sterilization only.

Problems in pill resupply. In terms of pill dispensing, the clinic personnel and outreach workers have agreed, as per the guidelines, that the former will hand out the initial prescription and the latter will attend to resupply. In view of the Cooperative Research project scheme to utilize *sari-sari* stores to resupply clients with pills and condoms, however, the F T O Ws have not had much opportunity to perform this function. The clinic staff, as a matter of course, just refer the pill or condom clients to the stores for resupply. The F T O Ws became resuppliers of the stores. There were instances when this arrangement was disrupted owing to non-coordination. One F T O W assigned in Sampaloc, for example, in his desire to come up with the P O P C O M-required number of Barangay Supply Points (BSPs), established one right opposite a barangay *sari-sari* store already serving as a contraceptive outlet. To all intents and purposes, this store was already efficiently functioning as a B S P. There was also the decision of the Family Planning Organization of the Philippines (F P O P) to set up a B S P in Barangay Dapdap, Tayabas, despite the presence of two supply sources, resulting in unnecessary competition and duplication of effects. There was little the D P O and F T O Ws, and the R H U and I M C H clinic personnel, could do about the situation. F P O P was not a participant in the project and in the formulation of the co-ordination guidelines. Also, its B S P in Dapdap was being supervised by an F P O P chapter outside Tayabas.

SUMMARY

To an appreciable extent, co-operation among three field agencies in Quezon Province has been accomplished, particularly in the area of sterilization campaigns. It has led to improved working as well as social relationships among their personnel. Looking back on the implementation of the project, the design and utilization of a common set of formal co-ordination guidelines prepared by field-based workers may have been responsible for the improved relationships among field personnel.

The process of drafting the guidelines has enabled the field participants to conduct dialogues with one another, clarify their roles and articulate their expectations of each other. Also, the process of actual co-ordination among the participating agencies during the operationalization of certain particular activities has enabled them to institutionalize a face-to-face feedback system in which immediate response to perceived problems is possible. The interface during the conduct of specific activities has led to the institutionalization of credit-assignment systems and task-assignment procedures that have facilitated work implementation.

Appendix

Guidelines for co-ordinating family-planning activities

Re IMCH–RHU–FTOW activities

1. The IMCH clinic and RHU personnel, particularly the nurses and midwives, will assist the DPOs and/or FTOWs in the initial prescription and dispensing of contraceptive pills. They will then refer the clients to the FTOWs for resupply.
2. FTOWs will motivate clients to accept family-planning methods in general; but before they dispense the initial supply of pills to pill acceptors, the clients will be referred to the RHU or IMCH clinic (whichever is nearest for assessment and physical examination). The initial supply of pills may come from either the FTOWs or the clinics.
3. In distant areas where it may not be practical for pill clients to go to clinics for their initial supply, FTOWs will dispense pills with the use of a check-list. Thereafter, the FTOWs will report to the clinics the names and addresses of the clients given pills and ask the clinic personnel to visit the clients for confirmation of the assessment and physical examination done with the check-list. The visits may be done by clinic personnel during their barrio trips.
4. FTOWs will, as a matter of SOP, refer clients for methods other than condoms to the nearest RHU or IMCH clinic for service.
5. In the event that RHUs and IMCH clinics run out of contraceptive supplies, the DPOs or FTOWs may be called upon to provide them the needed stock, and vice versa.
6. The IMCH clinic and RHU personnel in charge of family-planning client records will provide the DPOs and/or FTOWs with a complete list of clients enrolled in the clinic. The list will also include such other information as method used, date of acceptance and status of client, i.e. defaulter needing follow-up, resupply or clinic check-up.
7. Using the list provided by the IMCH clinic and the RHU, FTOWs will visit clients who need resupplying in terms of condoms and pills. They will either resupply the clients themselves or direct them to the FTOW-initiated barrio resupply points.
8. Using the same list, FTOWs will also visit clients who have defaulted on their clinic appointments for check-up or other similar activities and persuade them to return to the centre.
9. To ensure compliance with this request, the Provincial Health Officer will issue a memorandum to all Municipal Health Officers to assist the DPOs and FTOWs in this regard. Likewise, the Project Director of IMCH will issue a similar memorandum to IMCH-affiliated clinics in the Cooperative Research Program sites.
10. Once a month, the IMCH clinic and/or rural-health personnel will initiate meetings with DPOs and FTOWs to discuss common activities, problems and achievements. These meetings will coincide with the schedule for preparation of reports so that workers can cross-check their report entries for duplication and inaccuracies.
11. To facilitate feedback on joint FTOW–RHU or FTOW–IMCH activities to the provincial heads of agencies, DPOs and FTOWs will seek participation in zone conferences of the Provincial Health Office and RHUs, as well as in district conferences of personnel of the IMCH family-planning project.
12. Whenever possible, the IMCH clinic and RHU personnel will take along the FTOWs during the former's barrio visits and introduce them to local community leaders, orientate them on community activities and assist them in related barrio outreach work, particularly during the first months of the FTOWs on the job.
13. FTOWs will request the IMCH clinic or RHU to provide them with a schedule of their barrio visits and other family-planning activities so that they can plan on joining them, whenever possible, to assist in and/or ride on their activities.
14. On the other hand, the DPOs and/or FTOWs will inform the IMCH clinic and RHU personnel of their activities to facilitate the latter's extending their assistance. The DPOs and/or FTOWs will provide the IMCH clinic and RHU personnel a schedule of their activities to ensure dovetailing of common or supporting inputs.
15. During community assemblies which may be initiated by the DPOs/FTOWs or the RHU/IMCH personnel (or even by other agencies), the personnel will join hands and divide the activities among them. The Municipal Health Officer may give the lecture on family-

planning methods; the FTOW may discuss the cultural aspects of family-planning practice etc.

16. DPOs and FTOWs will take the initiative of introducing themselves to the personnel of RHU and IMCH family-planning clinics and offer their assistance to motivate, refer, follow up and remotivate clients for these clinics or to initiate community assemblies.

Re RHU–IMCH activities

1. The family-planning personnel of both RHU and IMCH will exchange a list of their acceptors for cross-checking duplications. The lists will also contain entries for the client's date of acceptance and method used. The date of acceptance may help determine to which clinic the client should really be listed; the method entries may help determine if the client is on just one method or two. If only on one, it is possible she is having excess supplies, if both clinics give her a three-cycle pack of pills every clinic visit. If on two, it is possible she is receiving condoms from one clinic and another contraceptive from another.

2. RHU and IMCH personnel will use standardized material for premarital/family-planning counselling. The material, written by IMCH in English, will be translated by the Provincial Health Office into Tagalog.

Bibliography

AIKEN, M.; HAGE, J. 1968. Organizational Interdependence and Interorganizational Structure. *American Sociological Review*, Vol. 33, p. 212–308.

ALDRICH, H. 1980. Organizational Sets, Action Sets, and Networks: Making the Most of Simplicity. In: Paul C. Nystrom and William H. Starbuck, (eds.), *Handbook of Organizational Design*. New York, N.Y., Oxford University Press.

BEAL G.M.; MIDDLETON, J. 1975. *Organizational Communication and Cooperation in Family Planning Programs. A Professional Development Module*. Honolulu, Hawaii, East–West Communication Institute, East–West Center. (1. Module Text, 2. Workbook, 3. Manager's Guide.).

EVAN, W.M. (ed.). 1976. *Interorganizational Relations: Selected Readings*. Harmondsworth, Penguin Books.

LEVINE, S.; WHITE, P.E. 1961. Exchange as a Conceptual Framework for the Study of Interorganizational Relationships. *Administrative Science Quarterly*, Vol. 3, p. 583–601.

LITWAK, E.; HYLTON, L.F. 1962. Interorganizational Analysis. A Hypothesis on Coordinating Agencies. *Administrative Science Quarterly*, Vol. 6, p. 395–420.

MULFORD, C.L.; KLONGLAN, G.E. 1979. *Creating Coordination among Organizations. An Orientation and Planning Guide*. Ames, Iowa, Cooperative Extension Service, Iowa State University. (North Central Extension Publ. 80.)

NEGANDHI, A.R. 1975. *Interorganizational Theory*. Kent, Ohio, Kent State University Press.

REID, W.J. 1969. Inter-Organizational Coordination in Social Welfare: A Theoretical Approach to Analysis and Intervention. In: Ralph M. Kramer and Harry Spect (eds.), *Readings in Community Organization Practice*, p. 188–200. Cliffs, N.J., Prentice-Hall.

SCHERMERHORN, J.R., Jr. 1975. Determinants of Interorganizational Cooperation. *Academy of Management Journal*, Vol. 18, No. 4, December; p. 846–56.

TUITE, M.; CHISOLM R.; RADNOR, M. (eds.). 1972. *Interorganizational Decision-Making*. Chicago, Ill., Aldine Press.

WARREN, R.L. 1967. The Interorganizational Field as a Focus of Investigation. *Administrative Science Quarterly*, Vol. 13, p. 396–419.

WHITE, P.E. 1974. Intra- and Inter-Organizational Studies: Do They Require Separate Conceptualization? *Administration and Society*, Vol. 6, p. 107–51.

Chapter 18

Planners' workshop

Jim Herm

Lertlack Burusphat

Many of the functional problems of organizations are due to the fact that there is little direct attention paid to the process of deciding what is to be done and how to do it. Most organizations just do the work—'the activity trap'. Work-planning workshops try to draw direct attention to the process of planning, implementing and monitoring/evaluating the work of an organization for all staff. Staff participation in this process is essential and this helps eliminate other functional problems in the organization.

This chapter describes a method for work planning which the authors have developed and used successfully in a variety of communication-planning situations.

Definition

A work-planning workshop is a group planning activity involving the staff of an organization or a section of an organization. The overall purpose of this workshop is to achieve optimum results by the organization or section. The specific purposes are to:

Improve the planning knowledge and skills of all staff.

Produce agreements among staff on the process and procedures of work planning and, to some extent, implementation and evaluation. These agreements will produce the framework for the procedures and style of the organization's management.

Produce an intermediate-term (three to six months) detailed work-plan. This might also be referred to as a microplan or strategic/logistical-level plan.

Assumptions

The assumptions are numerous and important; the following are in rough order of priority:

People will be more positively motivated to do their work when they have some say in what that work is and how it is done. People can also do better work when they understand how their work relates to the work of others in the organization. The workshop makes everyone's work explicit, and it clarifies the overall context in which the individual's work is a part.

The manager(s) must be committed to the process of changing the management system.

The manager(s) of the organization must be willing to delegate authority and responsibility.

National policies/plans and sector (ministry) plans must be realistic and reasonably specific, because the work-plans (the lowest and last level of planning before implementation) are based on these higher-level plans.

This workshop will be the main or only planning activity for the organization/section; therefore, it must be repeated every three to six months.

The work of organization cannot be totally experimental as, for example, in research organizations. If it is, it will be difficult to define realistic objectives. Also, there must be some predictability of the types of tasks involved and the amounts of time involved in completing these tasks.

Use of this technique must be given higher-level clearance if necessary. Part of that clearance decision must be an analysis of whether this approach to work planning (and overall management) will conflict with the approach used by other sections or related organizations. If this approach conflicts too much, it is probably unworkable overall.

History

This activity is based in part on 'management by objectives' (MBO), a planning/management approach started by Peter Drucker in the early 1950s. The practice of MBO through the 1960s was basically a management system based on setting clear objectives, implementation rigorously focusing on their achievement and evaluation based on objective fulfilment. Evaluation should also consider whether the objectives were the right ones or defined realistically. This approach still had higher-level managers making the decisions about the objectives, controlling their achievement and evaluating results (although Drucker did not intend it that way). In the early 1970s, MBO consultants and practitioners started to write about the need for more staff involvement in MBO:

The biggest gap in current MBO implementation is the lack of use of the work unit or team to facilitate the change. Most MBO implementations are based on a one-to-one design, where a superior speaks to each of his subordinates in turn. Virtually no MBO technique even tries to get the full team together—to work out effectiveness areas, objectives, and improvement plan as a group. [Reddin, 1971]

This activity finds the other part of its basis in 'organizational development'. This field started in the mid-1960s and could briefly be defined as the practice of consciously diagnosing organization's structure, function and environment and then making consciously planned changes in the organization to reduce

TABLE I. Subsystems that influence organizations (from Johnston, 1979)

	Internal subsystems				External subsystems	
Individual subsystem	+ Social subsystem	+ Operation subsystem	+ Administration subsystem	+	Client or demand subsystem	= Whole organization system
Attitudes	Climate	Work flow	Policy		Customer satisfaction	Output variables
Self-image	Status role	Equipment	Wage-salary		Service to and reactions of users	Profit/loss service
Skills: social, technical	Decision-making management style	Location: physical environment	Promotions Fringe benefits		Constraints-taxes	Costs attendance
Life values	Values	Material	Hiring-firing		Law and regulations	Turnover
Behaviour	Communication	Work arrangements	Rises		Competition	Commitment
Goals: job, career	Work-team goals	Schedules	Budgets Reporting		Mass media and publics Labour	Involvement Motivation
Self-appraisal	Progress review		Auditing		Government (state, local, federal) Internal factors	Quality

TABLE 2. Two kinds of change in organization subsystems

Subsystem	Directly change	Indirectly change/influence
Individual subsystem	Skills: Technical: planning skills Social: working in groups	Attitudes Self-image Behaviour Self-appraisal
Social subsystem	Decision-making management style Communication Work-team goals Progress review	Climate Status role Values
Operational subsystem	Work flow Work arrangements Schedules	To the extent that the workshop redefines these, they may be influenced: Equipment Location/environment Materials
Administration subsystem		Budgets Reporting
Client or demand subsystem	Customer satisfaction Service to and reactions of users	Competition
Whole organization	Output variables Profit/loss service	Costs attendance Commitment Involvement Motivation Quality

organizational problems. This is opposed to the past practice of allowing organizational changes to 'evolve'.

The influence of these two fields/practices will become clear in later sections (see 'Procedures' and 'Case example').

The history of this particular type of workshop started in the spring of 1978 when our colleague, Jim French, developed some of the basic aspects and tried it out with the Office of the Rubber Replanting Aid Fund of Thailand. We made a number of modifications, and since then the approach has gone into action in Nepal, Bangladesh and other projects in Thailand.

Main uses

Workplanning workshops are used to change organizations. Table 1 shows the subsystems that are functioning in any organization. The work-planning workshop is used to change these subsystems either directly or indirectly. As shown in Table 2, certain elements of subsystems can be changed directly; while others can usually only be indirectly changed or influenced.

371

Limits and cautions

1. The workshop is best organized and conducted by a person or group outside the organization the first time or first few times. This is so that initial problems can be 'blamed' on the outsiders. What is more important, outsiders provide the 'excuse' for the manager (in front of all staff) to make these changes.
2. The workshop should not be tried at a time when the manager and/or the staff are deeply involved in some other activity or issue, e.g. annual budget submissions.
3. The top manager and all other relevant managers should be given complete orientation on the real impact this workshop approach could have. They must all agree with the basics of the approach or it will not work.
4. It must be made clear to everyone that the system must be given a chance (about one year) in order to determine objectively whether it is suitable for their organization.
5. One of the reasons why item 4 above is true is that the staff's planning skills will probably not be highly developed. Therefore, the first workshop especially should emphasize skill-building and be less concerned with the actual plans.
6. The plan period should probably be no longer than three months for the first one or two workshops. This is because of 5 above. The plan period should probably be no longer than six months, no matter how good planning skills become.
7. Because this activity is done in a short period (two to four days), the first time it is done there is usually no time to apply any other techniques of decision validation for planning purposes. These techniques might otherwise include cost–benefit analysis, cross-impact analysis etc.
8. The mix of participants in the workshop is important. At a minimum, all technical and professional staff of the organization should be involved. Whether clerical and other support staff are involved is optional.
9. If only one section of an organization uses this planning approach, it may be initially more difficult to co-ordinate work between sections (when that is necessary). This is because the section using the approach will be far better planned than any other. Ideally, this situation would only be temporary. Either other sections should adopt this approach also, or patterns of co-operation would need to shift so that they were viewed by everyone as less problematic.

Other techniques

One-on-one management by objectives.
Management training, especially focusing on planning.
Organizational development exercises usually conducted or led by a consultant.

Job analysis.
Programme evaluation review technique (PERT).

Product or result

An agreed approach among all staff of the organization/section for planning at
  this level.
Work-plans—one or more plan form for each objective.
Master plan—for the top manager to plot major activities against time.
Individual work-plans—one for each person of the organization.
Monitoring forms—to be filled in during implementation (see Table 3).
Improved planning skills and possibly knowledge of staff and managers.
Clarification/agreements of ongoing planning roles and other management
  responsibilities.

Level of detail and level of confidence

The thrust of the workshop is to get the planning to such a level of detail that
the human resources are 'time-budgeted' down to estimates in working days, or
even parts of days. Each person's individual work-plan will show what they are
to do on every day of the plan period. As the human resources are the most
crucial resource in all but highly automated/high-technology organizations, it
is most important to plan their use accurately. Objectives are broken into
activities, and activities are broken into tasks of sufficient detail so that they can
be given estimates of completion time in person/days. Other levels of detail are
somewhat optional, especially during the first few workshops. It is helpful, of
course, to use this activity to specify other resources (finance, equipment,
supplies, facilities) at this level of detail.

  With this particular planning approach the level of confidence can be
examined in two perspectives. First, there is a level of confidence in this
planning approach itself by the managers and the staff. This, initially, has little
to do with the actual plans produced. Later, after several plan/implementation
periods, the plans and their utility in implementation can reinforce confidence
in the overall approach. However, if the entire organization is not initially

TABLE 3. Monitoring form: a specimen format

No.	Task No.	Was it done on time?			How was it done?			
		Yes	No	If not, why?	Well	Averagely	Poorly	Reasons why
.....	....	....	....	....	......	....	......	....
.....	....	....	....	....	......	....	......	....
.....	....	....	....	....	......	....	......	....

confident that this approach will make their work easier or better in some way, it is of little use to go further. Everyone will make sure that it does not work!

Second, there is a consideration of level of confidence in the plans themselves. In a scientific sense, we would be asking, 'At a given point in time (the day the plans are finished), how accurate are these plans in relation to what is actually implemented?' If that were the issue, then we could say that during the first six to eighteen months the level of confidence would be rather low for most organizations. It will take some time for most organizations to develop the predictive knowledge and skills required. It will also take some time for the organization to begin to have more control of the environment in which it operates. This should happen in most situations through the most aggressive management of planning and implementation that this approach requires.

After this initial developmental period (six to eighteen months), an organization should be able to plan with 75 per cent accuracy. This could, of course, be measured in a variety of ways, namely: (a) achievement of objectives; (b) conformity to schedules; (c) for objectives that were set, the accuracy and validity of the detailed plans. For an estimate of 75 per cent accuracy, we are referring to the third type of measurement. This is the only fair and realistic measurement for this type of planning, especially for social-science work. Given that certain objectives are agreed upon, then the process is as shown in Figure 1.

The ability to do this process accurately is the main capability that one could measure. We have no evidence that our 75 per cent figure is realistic, but for now, with our experience in the workshop, we feel this is an achievable standard. With many of the beginning planners we have observed, breaking down activities to the correct number and type of tasks and accurately predicting amounts of time is a major problem.

Communicability and credibility of results

The paper results of this planning workshop by themselves would not communicate the essence of the whole planning approach. It would only appear as if an organization/section had gone through a systematic, detailed planning exercise. However, people outside the organization/section have no need to look at these papers unless the entire approach is being explained to them or aspects that pertain to working relationships are being negotiated. The non-paper results (see section above on 'Product or result') of the workshops themselves have never failed to get communicated to all the staff involved. This is documented in the feedback we have received both during initial workshops and strongly reinforced in subsequent workshops.

The issue of credibility of results here is 'Credible to whom?' For us the primary issue of credibility is to the organizations/sections that we suggest use this approach. If it works for them, it is credible. We feel we have gone beyond the issue of general credibility—'Does it work at all?' It does work! The only issue is whether a particular group of people think it will work for

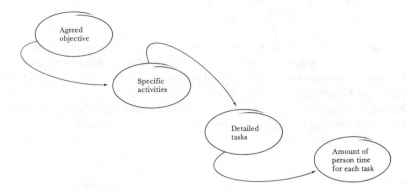

FIG. 1. Planning process

them. That decision is always up to them (and it is based primarily on their attitude—not on technical feasibility).

It is noteworthy that we have never done this workshop in exactly the same way. There are a few basics that must be done in order for the approach to work, but many formats and procedures are left up to the organization to decide what best suits their needs.

Span of forecasts. As mentioned above, we feel for this level of planning it is not feasible to plan more than six months at one time. It is not very cost-effective to take several days of all staff's time for planning if the plan period is anything less than three months.

Resources needed

1. All staff of an organization or section or, as a minimum, all technical and professional staff.
2. For the first one or two workshops, it is preferable to have an outside consultant or consultants to help lead the workshop with the top manager.
3. Set(s) of national and sector goals and objectives that relate to the work of the organization/section.
4. Some type of visual display, e.g. overhead projector, newsprint pads/felt pens, blackboard.
5. Examples of other work-plans.
6. Possibly, blank planning forms (although it is best in the first workshop to have the group design the type of information required and the format themselves).

Procedures

The procedures can be grouped into three phases:

PHASE ONE

This phase, which is only done once, comprises the preliminary organizational analysis (formal or informal) and decision to go ahead with the workshop.
1. Discussions by management, usually with outside consultant, about problems and needs of the organization.
2. Fact-finding about organizational structure and actual functioning.
3. Decision-making about whether and when to conduct the first work-planning workshop.

PHASE TWO

1. Collecting all resources required (see above) and making all logistical arrangements.
2. Clarifying the purpose of the workshop to all participants.
3. Giving participants a questionnaire to establish a baseline on their planning knowledge, experience and attitudes.
4. Clarifying/discussing the national and sector policies and objectives which relate to the work of the organization/section.
5. Formulating the programme objectives (the services the organization expects to develop/deliver for their clients).
6. Prioritizing these objectives especially with the plan period (three to six months) in mind.
7. Defining activities that will be required to achieve the objectives.
8. Breaking the activities down into tasks and assigning each task an amount of time (not dates).
9. Assigning specific staff to each task.
10. Doing preliminary scheduling—assigning specific dates to each task. Optional: the group can also give each activity a general range of time.
11. Defining other resources (equipment, supplies, finance, facilities) and location for each task. Some of these, including the location, may not be seen as needed, especially the first few workshops. These should be left for the organization to decide.
12. Formulating the organizational objectives. The organization must spend some time improving and maintaining itself so that it can better achieve its programme objectives. These objectives would involve activities like: changing the organizational structure, changing/improving management and supervisory practices, staff-training, facility and equipment development, and research and evaluation. These objectives should be clearly defined and planned; therefore, steps 6 to 11 should be repeated for the organizational objectives.
13. Preparing individual work-plans for each person in the organization involved in the workshop. At this point some scheduling may need to be adjusted. Frequently in previous planning steps the same person may have been scheduled to do more than one thing at the same time.

14. Defining the monitoring and evaluation procedures including the type of information to be collected and in what format. These will be maintained during implementation.
15. Preparing a master plan by first deciding on a master-plan format and then filling it in from the objective-based work-plan forms.
16. Defining the planning activities that were not completed during the workshop and assigning staff to complete them.
17. Formally and/or informally evaluating the workshop itself and closing it.

These steps define the first workshop. During the second and all subsequent workshops steps 2 and 3 could be dropped and 4 could be de-emphasized. Later on (nine to eighteen months later) the questionnaire (with some modification) in step 3 should be given again to compare knowledge, experiences and attitudes more objectively. Steps 2, 3, and 4 would be replaced in later workshops by a step reviewing the implementation during the past plan period. This would be done by reviewing planning forms with monitoring/evaluation forms and facts brought out in discussion.

PHASE THREE: IMPLEMENTATION/MONITORING/EVALUATION

1. Begin implementation of tasks as planned.
2. Maintain monitoring/evaluation information.
3. Make adjustments in plans as conditions change. This could mean even changing some objectives and doing some significant replanning.
4. Plan and schedule the next work-planning workshop.

Case example

Title: Work-planning staff meeting for the Information, Education Motivation (IEM) unit, Population Control and Family Planning Ministry, Bangladesh.
Dates: 2–5 May 1979 (four half-day sessions).
Location: Dacca, Bangladesh.
Project: Strengthening (IEM) and Training in the Population Control and Family Planning Directorate (PCFPD).
Report compiled by: James R. Herm, Training Specialist, United Nations Development Training/Communication Planning Office (DTCPO).

I. PARTICIPANTS/RESOURCE PERSONS

Participants: The eighteen staff have the responsibilities of planning, implementing and evaluating PCFPD's communication activities. These include conducting communication training, producing and distributing materials for field-worker training and use with clients, and preparing materials for mass media.
Resource persons: The IEM Director, the Unesco Regional Population

Communication Programme Officer and a DTCPO Training Specialist acted as resource persons.

II. BACKGROUND INFORMATION

The meeting was held at the suggestion of DTCPO and on the decision of the Government and concurrence of the United Nations Fund for Population Activities (UNFPA) Co-ordinator. It was intended to specify exactly what the unit would do in total for the rest of 1979 and what would be achieved on a UNFPA-assisted project specifically.

Reason: change in procedures. *Type:* in-service.

Decision-makers: 1. Whether or not meeting will be held: Joint Secretary, PEFP; Director, IEM; UNFPA Co-ordinator.
2. How workshop will be conducted: Director, IEM; Deputy Director, IEM; DTCPO Training Consultant.

III. OBJECTIVES

Overall: 1. To develop a system for IEM detailed planning and management.
2. To produce a detailed work-plan for at least the rest of 1979 (possibly for twelve months).
Formulated by: Planning Committee, co-ordinator/resource persons, supervisor(s) of participants.

Specific: At the end of the meeting the IEM staff will have or be able to:

1. Define at least three PCFP goals and discuss their relation to national goals.
2. Define and prioritize IEM programme objectives for the rest of 1979: (a) define at least three major audience groups; (b) develop at least three programme objectives for each audience group.
3. Definine: the activities to achieve each programme objective; the tasks to achieve each activity; the amount of person/time required for each task; who, specifically, will be responsible and/or involved in each task; the specific time that each task will be started/completed; the location(s) of each task.
4. Define and prioritize IEM organizational objectives for the rest of 1979. These objectives will usually fall into four categories: management; staff development/staff training; communication/media capacity; research and evaluation.
5. Define: the activities to achieve each organizational objective; the tasks to achieve each activity; the amount of person/time required for each task; the specific person to be responsible and/or involved in each task; and the specific time that each task will be started/completed, as well as the location(s) of each task.
6. Define planning tasks that remain at the end of the meeting and determine who will complete them.

378

7. Evaluate the meeting with reference to overall objectives and specific objectives.

IV. CONTENTS

How to develop a logical planning system.
How to write unit objectives.
The differences between programme objectives and organizational objectives.
How to set objective priorities.
How to formulate and reconcile detailed work-plan: types of information required, the order to define information, the way to estimate and compare with reality.

V. METHODOLOGY

The meeting spent most of the time working in three or four small groups trying to complete the planning task. Planning methods were discussed and agreed before each planning exercise. The results of each group were discussed by the whole group.
Methodology: case study, group discussion, group exercise.

VI. TRAINING MATERIALS

A hand-out was given to the participants on the objectives, methods, time and products of the meeting. The groups were also given a planning exercise form for detailed planning and blank overhead transparencies to complete/present their objectives. Charts of the overall planning process and of potential audiences were also developed.
Materials: hand-outs, workbook/exercises. *Aids:* charts.

VII. EVALUATION

The participants seemed very enthusiastic about this type of involement in and organization of their work. Participation was genuine and complete with one or two exceptions. The real evaluation will be the unit's ability to make the plans operational. This does not mean that every task and timing should be carried out as planned, rather that everyone is working and that changes in the plan are made on a logical management basis. Major deviations from the plan should be documented. Another evaluation of the meeting will be the official approval of the product, the detailed work-plan, by the PCFPD Division Managers. See Appendix A for the informal comments of the participants during the concluding oral session.
Evaluation: oral sessions (informal). (See also Appendix A.)

VIII. PRODUCTS (see Appendix B)

1. Detailed work-plan sheets (one set from each of the four groups).
2. Detailed organizational chart of I E M.
3. List of potential audiences.
4. List of remaining planning tasks.

IX. RECOMMENDATIONS

1. The remaining planning tasks be approved within ten days.
2. This same activity be repeated in three to four months and continue to be done every three to six months depending on implementation experience.

X. WHAT THE RESOURCE PEOPLE LEARNED

1. Do an analysis of the unit's manpower first. Develop a total number of person/days to be planned during the period to be planned.
2. After setting priorities, do not suggest the consideration of other secondary priorities until the top priorities have been planned in detail.

XI. COST

Government: staff time, all donated after hours; materials, (TK100 =) $7; refreshments, (TK1,500=) $97; petrol, (TK375=) $24. *Unesco:* staff time, $1,000; travel/PD, $674. *D T C P O:* staff time, $1,034; travel/PD $404. TOTAL: $3,240.

Appendix A Comments on workshop

1. It was very good and very useful for the I E M unit.
2. This was a first-time event! First time we have done *anything* together! First-time participatory planning, we'll now take pride in the *results*, and now take commitment to implement what we have planned. We learned that top people saw need to include lower staff in planning.
3. Before, planning was top down—imposing this, changing that. This can show us what bottlenecks we can expect and we can plan to prevent them.
4. This should be done in future and we can improve our planning when we do it next time.
5. Planning can be good, but implementation will be poor if we cannot improve staff morale. It is low now because we are not getting staff rewards [salary increments etc.].
6. [In response to 5.] We have to make the plan taking into account staff morale. We have to budget more staff time for each task than if we had high-morale, hard-working staff.
7. We need to have another planning session in three months.
8. We all became clear on what the whole unit is doing. It has become clear in terms of general activities and specific tasks.
9. We still need to define what other resources are needed (besides staff) like equipment, supplies, outside resources, finance.

Appendix B

1. Work-plan

Project:
Objective: Increase the level of knowledge and skill of the FPAs, FWAs, FWVs and other extension workers

Group I: Sunil, Nasir, Jim, Z. Alan and S. Alam
Estimated funds required:
Staff:
Travel:
Equipment/material:
Miscellaneous:
Total:

Activity	Time frame	Tasks	Dates	Persons involved	Time required (in days)	Location
Planning of manual	Mid-May to end-May	1. Collect and analyse existing motivation manuals. Brief Director (IEM).	14 May 18 May 19 May	A.R. Z.U. A.R., Z.U., J.H.	4 4 1 each	I/P.M.
		2. Discuss with PCFP training unit.	21 May	J.H.	2	I/P.M.
		3. Prepare outline of manual including objectives.	22–23 May	Z.U., P.R., J.B., N.U.	2 each	
Preparation and production of manual	End May to early October	1. Drafting full script and art pool.	24 May 5 June	K.A.C., B.B. Z.U. T.H.	10 each 10	
		2. Designing and illustration of manual including photography.	5 June to 28 June	S.B.P., R.S., N.U., M.A., A.S.	20 each	
		3. Editing.	28 June to 30 June	A.A., Z.U., P.R.	3 each	
		4. Prepare dummy copy/copies.	2–9 July	S.B.P., N.U. R.S., P.R.	7 each	

(Contd)

2. Work-plan form: an example

From another project (February 1980)

Objective: .... Programme: X Organizational: VI
What (action verb plus object): Develop a systematic approach to planning, implementation, evaluation of supervisory training
Why (in order to ...): Because ORRAF requires retraining of supervisors to implement their new organizational changes
Who (people affected and people doing): For ORRAF mid-level supervisors, by ORRAF Training Section, DTCPO, Thai CSC

Where (general location/s): DTCPO, Bangkok; Villa Navin, Pattaya
When (target date): May/June 1979
How (general approach): Teamwork in planning and implementation
How well (quantity, quality, rate/time etc.): So that 80 per cent of supervisors can perform at or above job standards in four months after training

Totals
Staff days: 48
Finance: $1,500
Equipment: mimeo, OHP
Supplies: OHT paper

Activity	Task	Time required (in days)	Persons involved	Specific dates	Location	Equipment, supplies and/or facilities	Finance
A. Planning the course (excluding job analysis and trainee analysis which has been done earlier)	1. Set objectives based on trainee analysis (overall objectives)	1	S.N., C.S., K.K., J.F.	10 May	DTCP	No specific equipment/supplies other than paper, pens/pencils	None
	2. Group meeting to discuss and revise objectives	$\frac{1}{2}$	S.N., C.S., K.K., J.F., J.H., M.V.	11 May (p.m.)	DTCP		
	3. Set specific objectives for each topic	5		14–18 May	Hat Yai		Trip to Hat Yai paid under another objective

Task	No.	Responsible	Dates	Location/Org.	Materials	Cost
4. Select and organize content scope		C.S. (work individually and discuss in evening with M.V., J.F., S.N.)				
5. Select methods and techniques						
6. Select materials (hand-outs and aids) and design						
7. Select and design evaluation procedures and tools						
8. Select training location (maximum daily cost of $200)	1	P.J., Ubol	14–18 May	Up-country		
B. Preparation of detailed course						
1. Write lesson plans	14	C.S.	21 May 6 June	DTCPO ORRAF CSC	Overhead transparencies	$1,500 for training materials
2. Produce materials	10	P.P.	27 May 14 June		Transparency marker Mimeograph paper	
3. Produce evaluation tools (to be elaborated)	3	M.V.	27 May 6 June			
4. Group meeting to discuss and revise lesson plans, materials, evaluation tools	Not more than ½ day each meeting	The above plus J.H., J.F.	27 May 3 June	DTCPO	Graphic arts equipment and facilities	

3. Individual work-plan: an example

(from another project)

Name: ....
Month: February

Tasks and task numbers

Day		Analysis of ORRAF training evaluation (ORRAF) IV.D.3	Discussion with new Indonesian project (DTCP) IX.B.2	Preparation for management training (ORRAF) IV.G.4	Observe staff job performance S. Thailand VI.A.3	Final arrangements and set-up for management training (DTCP) IV.H.3	Conduct/ observe management training (DTCP) IV.I.1
1	Friday	Task completed (X)					
2	Saturday	Task work confirmed (line across all columns)					
3	Sunday	Task work confirmed (line across all columns)					
4	Monday		Task completed (X)				
5	Tuesday		Task work confirmed				
6	Wednesday		Task work confirmed				
7	Thursday			Task work confirmed			
8	Friday			Task work confirmed			
9	Saturday	Task work confirmed (line across all columns)					
10	Sunday	Task work confirmed (line across all columns)					
11	Monday			Task work confirmed			
12	Tuesday			Task work confirmed			
13	Wednesday			Task work confirmed			
14	Thursday			Task work confirmed			
15	Friday			Task work confirmed			
16	Saturday	Task work confirmed (line across all columns)					
17	Sunday	Task work confirmed (line across all columns)					
18	Monday				Task work probable (dashed)		
19	Tuesday				Task work probable (dashed)		
20	Wednesday				Task work probable (dashed)		
21	Thursday					Task work confirmed	
22	Friday					Task work confirmed	
23	Saturday	Task work confirmed (line across all columns)					
24	Sunday	Task work confirmed (line across all columns)					
25	Monday						Task work confirmed
26	Tuesday						Task work confirmed
27	Wednesday						Task work confirmed
28	Thursday						Task work confirmed
29	Friday						Task work confirmed

Task completed
Task work confirmed
Task work probable

4. Master plan

For months: ...., ..., ..., 19....
Name of unit: ....

Activity / Time	Week 1	Week 2	Week 3	Week 4	Week 5	Week 6	Week 7	Week 8	Week 9	Week 10	Week 11	Week 12
Example: VI, I. Preparation of detailed course												

Bibliography

JOHNSTON, R.W. 1979. Seven Steps to Whole Organization Development. *Training and Development Journal*, January, p. 12–22.

REDDIN, W.J. 1971. *Effective Management by Objectives.* New York, N.Y., McGraw-Hill.

Chapter 19

Programme evaluation review technique (PERT)

Zenaida Domingo

Programme evaluation review technique, or PERT as it is commonly called, is one of the most widely accepted and used management tools in the implementation of complex, non-repetitive and one-time-through projects. PERT enables the project manager to plan and monitor the entire development–production–evaluation life-cycle of his or her work. He or she is able to synchronize and co-ordinate the multifaceted components of a project. Furthermore, PERT is a means of communication in that it reports and keeps the managers, as well as the project implementors, constantly informed on the favourable and unfavourable developments of the project. PERT has been found an effective tool for the implementation of project operations on schedule. With its built-in capability for providing vital information in project operation, PERT enables the manager to make decisions, to revise plans or to draw up new action points for the project.

Definition

PERT is a systematic method of scheduling and budgeting project resources, both human and physical, in order to accomplish a predetermined job on schedule (Levin and Kirkpatrick, 1966). It entails detailed planning and scheduling of project activities (PERT/time) and careful allocation of project resources (PERT/cost) in order to achieve the objectives of one-time-through or non-repetitive projects. With PERT, the complete work programme from inception to end is clearly identified and defined, specifically in terms of manpower/physical needs at any given point in time during the project, as well as of critical and slack work-loads by the various components of the project.

Assumptions

Planning the project implementation scheme is one major task of a project manager. Among other things, he or she should have the ability to plan the best possible use of human and physical project resources, to achieve the goals

387

of his/her project within time and cost limitations. The PERT as a planning/management tool stresses the need for built-in managerial planning skill, perceptivity, experience and judgement on the part of the project manager. Such qualities from the manager are required because of the great amount of detailed work needed in PERTing. Moreover, the manager should be thoroughly acquainted with the strengths and weaknesses of PERT as a planning, management and evaluation tool. Furthermore, PERT is primarily based on the presence of, or assurance of, the definite availability of resources, including human, physical and financial. Aside from the project resources identified, their volume/quantity must also be determined as well as when they will be available.

History

PERT's historical antecedents may be traced back to the early 1900s, when Frederick W. Taylor and his associates attempted to lay the foundations of scientific project management. Through planned observations and measurements, they firmly established the concept of direct-labour standards and control of direct-labour costs (Miller, 1963). Scheduling systems prior to the introduction of PERT included the Gantt chart and Gantt Milestone chart which refined the original Gantt chart. Both techniques were used within the context of military operations during the First and Second World Wars.

In the late 1950s, PERT was developed by the United States Navy Special Projects Office in co-operation with Booz, Allen & Hamilton, a management consulting firm. This was the time when the American Government was doing the Polaris project, a technical and engineering project on nuclear-powered submarines. It was stressed that what was equally as important as the technical/engineering facets of the studies was the need for careful planning, high co-ordination and control of all the resources required. The Polaris project staff worked with 250 prime contractors and 9,000 subcontractors. Such work pointed to the need for the Polaris project staff to co-ordinate the work of these contractors, to determine problem areas, to ensure that the deadlines were met and to orchestrate the tasks of several thousands of workers. PERT was evolved to meet with all these project needs.

For the past two decades, PERT has been used by management staff not only in the military but also in several other groups, in sectors such as education, social services, health, business and communication. It has been used in construction, product or project development, preparation of media strategies, feasibility studies and conducting research and evaluation work.

Main uses

PERT is best applied in development projects which have the following characteristics:

1. *Complexity*. These development projects entail hundreds or even thousands

of interdependent activities, to be accomplished by an equally large number of people. The technique is most usefully applied in work situations where there is a great deal of interconnection among the activities of individuals or groups of individuals.

2. *Non-repetitive or single-occurrence projects.* These development projects include tasks that are to be done only once, 'one-of-a-kind' in nature, as differentiated from repetitive production activities.

PERT has been acknowledged as having several uses. Perhaps its most important use is in providing the project manager with information that enables him/her arrive at highly informed decisions at the various levels of project planning, implementation and evaluation. One such type of information is the schedule of performance. The project manager is immediately able with this to assess whether the work is going on as scheduled or whether the project activities are behind. If they are behind, the manager is also able to obtain information on how far behind they are or will be if the work pace is the same. PERT provides a schedule-status profile of the project from start to finish.

Another type of project information made available by PERT is overall programme performance, together with considerable details to show possible problem areas, in terms both of manpower or physical resources. PERT also shows the cost status of the project. It tells whether or not the actual project cost is within the estimated amount at the inception of the project. Finally, data made available by PERT provide insights into overspending, that is, how much was overspent in the past, how much is being overspent in the present and how much will be overspent in the future until the project is completed.

PERT is a valuable communication planning tool (see 'Case example' below). It provides various types of useful information that will serve as guidelines in the decision-making activity of the project manager.

Limits and caution

PERT, like any other management technique, is not designed to do the problem-solving work for the project manager. The different types of information obtained from PERT charts and illustrations help the manager appreciate the nature and magnitude of the problems. Further, he/she can determine the needs of the project as well as the elements and considerations that bear on his/her decisions and any changes in action.

Since PERT is generally used in single-occurrence projects, one of its most noted limitations is the difficulty of making accurate work/cost estimates. It is a start-to-finish plan, and the manager should be flexible enough to make periodic overhauling and modifications in order to match the PERT plans with the actual realities of the project. The effective utilization of PERT requires constant review and action by responsible managers; for example, it should be examined on a fortnightly basis in a year-long project. The project manager must evolve various means to shorten critical time frames of the project by injecting new resources, whenever possible, from activities that can give away such resources because of their slack condition. The PERT system needs continuing re-analysis and updating. The project manager should accept the fact that a complex single-occurrence project is, by its very nature, constantly in a state of flux and uncertainty. He/she should, therefore, be ready to carry out reprogramming at any given moment for the duration of the project.

A frequently noted disadvantage of the PERT technique is the system's incapacity to yield quantity information. Therefore, there is a need to integrate the techniques of PERT with other established methods of production control, such as line-of-balance (LOB) or similar techniques to bring in the quantity factor (Miller, 1962).

Other techniques and product or result

Other major management planning and control techniques that are sometimes used in combination with PERT are the critical path method (CPM) and the line of balance (LOB) technique. The concerns of CPM, which are closely related to those of PERT, are to identify and shorten the critical path of the work schedule in order to improve the project operations. The use of PERT with LOB enhances the attributes of both techniques in that it provides better control of the critical transition phase between the development and actual production stages (Shroderbeck and Digman, 1967). Still other scheduling techniques closely associated with PERT are the Gantt chart and the Milestone chart, which are considered the predecessors of PERT, and the learning-curve technique, which also makes work-load projections primarily in terms of work-hour requirements.

The main output of a PERT activity is one or more charts that reflect the interrelationship between events and activities. An event represents a specified programme accomplishment at a particular instant in time. An activity represents the time and resources which are required to progress from one event to the next. For large-scale operations, computer runs may handle the large volumes of data involved.

Level of detail and level of confidence

As was earlier discussed, PERT helps the manager to view the project as an integrated whole instead of as isolated and unrelated tasks. A greater amount of detail is necessitated by PERT than by other techniques. The level of detail largely depends on the data deemed meaningful by the project manager and by the staff who will actually execute the work. It also depends on the extent of analysis needed in determining critical work areas or paths.

It is to be reiterated that one of the more critical concerns when using PERT is arriving at realistic estimates. Such estimates are achieved when manpower and physical resources are identified prior to PERTing. None the less, the project manager must constantly monitor project realities that will dictate possible revisions at any given point in time for the duration of the project.

Communicability and credibility of results, and time span

Communicability of results of the PERT technique is generally high. Assuming that project resources are known to the project planner and manager, the development of the PERT charts and schedules may be completed in a matter of hours after detailing of the project is finished.

The predictive quality of PERT is assured to be high if, as earlier stressed, the project resources are identified prior to PERTing. PERT charts based on knowledge of resources and validated by project realities are generally credible to project managers, implementors and planners of future projects.

PERT shows inception-to-end-of-project schedule/work estimates. It is therefore possible to plan the entire development, production and evaluation project life cycle. The span of estimates varies from project to project, depending on the life span of each. However, where resource availability is known for only part of the total long-term project, PERT will span only the period of known resource availability.

Resources needed

The key resource of PERT is the project manager and his/her planning staff who possess a high planning capability and who are knowledgeable of PERT as a management planning tool. But most important, they should have a good grasp of the nature of the project, its objectives and overall goals and its intended products or outputs. Likewise, they should be thoroughly familiar with inputs to the project, such as the availability of manpower and physical/financial resources obligated to the project, including the interdependency of resources and processes.

PERTing can be done with or without computerization. As in any large-scale data-processing work, a computer may handle PERT issues that involve a large volume of data. Manual handling of data is equally reliable and acceptable. Small-scale projects should not hesitate to adapt PERT merely because they do not possess high-volume data processing capability (Miller, 1962).

Procedures

In general, the procedure followed in PERTing is quite simple. Identification of all project resources, human and physical, and when they would be available is the initial step. The project planner and manager next identifies all the tasks involved in the planning, implementation and evaluation (quality control) of the project. Networking is one major step in PERT. After all the individual tasks are identified, they are put down in a network, which is composed of events and activities. An event represents a specific project accomplishment at a particular instant in time. An activity represents the time and resources which are necessary to progress from one event to the next. Networking requires clear and precise definition of events and activities in order to reduce the difficulty of monitoring actual accomplishments at the various points of project implementation, a clear enunciation of the interrelationship between events and the interdependency of activities. In networking, events and activities must be sequenced under a logical set of ground rules which allow the determination of important critical and subcritical paths (Miller, 1962). The general ground rule is that no successor event can be considered complete until all of its predecessor events have been completed. Furthermore, no 'looping' should be done, that is, no successor event can have an activity dependency which leads back to a predecessor event.

Finally, time estimates are drawn up for each of the networks on a three-way basis, namely, optimistic, most likely and pessimistic. An *optimistic* time estimate gives a minimum amount of time an activity will require. It is observed that optimistic time is possible to obtain only if everything 'goes right'. A *most likely* time estimate gives the normal time an activity will take. This estimate may be obtained if the activity could be repeated several times under similar circumstances. A *pessimistic* time estimate gives the maximum time an activity will take. This estimate foresees the possibility of initial project difficulties or failures. The three-time estimate recognizes the probabilistic characteristics of the project tasks of single-occurrence 'one-time through' and development-orientated programmes.

Case example

The following case illustrates how PERT has assisted the planning and implementation of an educational-communication project in the Philippines.

PLANNING THE PROJECT: THE PRE-INVESTMENT STUDY

In recognition of the potential of communication technology for educational reforms, the Philippine Government through the Educational Development Projects Implementing Task Force (EDPITAF), conducted a pre-investment study on the educational possibilities of mass media in the country. The major justification for the study was that, in order to provide the policy-makers with a sound basis for decision-making in the selection of a solid strategy for the introduction of an educational programme for the country, it was necessary to conduct a pre-investment study to assess the entry points and potential uses of communication technology for education.

The pre-investment study was conducted for one year, April 1976 to March 1977, and it underwent four phases: Phase I, Needs Assessment and Objectives Setting; Phase II, Options analysis; Phase III, Guidance/decision from government; and Phase IV, Preparation of a detailed project proposal.

In Phase I, a data base was established to determine the present 'lie of the land' in education and communication. The data base was the main source for the analysis and review of educational needs that would serve as entry points for educational communication. Phase II involved the detailing of various strategies to meet the educational needs identified in Phase I. These strategies were submitted to the Philippine Government for evaluation and review. In Phase III, the strategies were prioritized and decisions were reached on which areas were to be given focus. These were the use of communication technology to help support basic education and rural development. After the definite decision was reached, Phase IV entailed the preparation of a detailed project proposal to establish a pilot project as a first step in the implementation of an educational-communication programme for the country.

SEEKING THE PROJECT RESOURCES

The project proposal included a substantial amount of detail on the major tasks of the pilot project, its expected outputs and the resources needed. A second review was conducted in order to determine whether the Philippine Government could afford the project. The proposals were also negotiated with the World Bank for funding. By the early part of 1978, approval from both the Philippine Government and the World Bank was obtained. The availability of project resources was assured.

PLANNING FOR IMPLEMENTATION

Upon obtaining the assurance of the availability of project resources, the EDPITAF established the Educational Communication Office, to plan the implementation scheme and carry out the pilot project for three years, from 1978 to 1980. The operations plans for two major project thrusts, the Communication Technology for Basic Education Program (CT-BEP) and the Communication Technology for Rural Education Program (CT-REP), were prepared. The preparation phase entailed major PERTing activities.

IDENTIFYING THE PROJECT TASKS

Both the CT-BEP and CT-REP have several components. The CT-BEP has the Radio-Assisted Teaching in Elementary Schools (RATES) and the Continuing Education of Teachers (CET) which provide a multimedia-package instructional model in language teaching and teacher training. The CT-REP has non-formal-education distant-study courses for extension workers and local leaders/farm families. In addition, continuing research and evaluation work are needed to generate adequate data output that will serve as guidelines for expansion. This research and evaluation work includes formative evaluation to obtain feedback for improvement of the project materials,

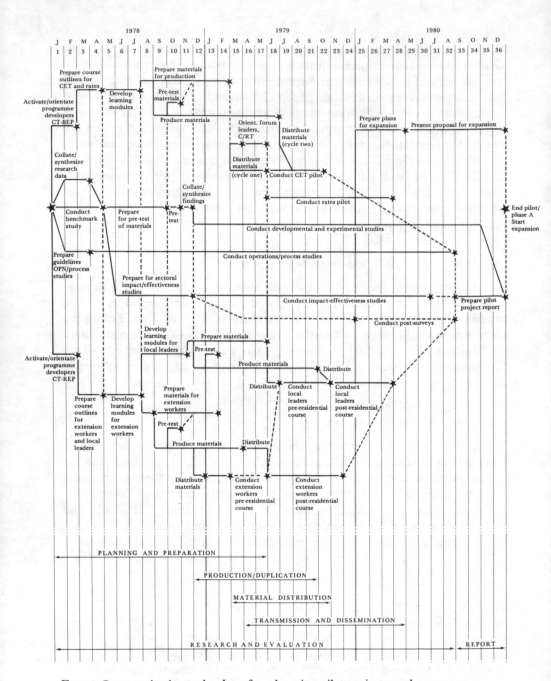

FIG. I. Communication technology for education pilot project: work programme

summative evaluation to gauge the learning gains of the target clientele, process/operations research and continuing technical/engineering studies, such as that for installing a small-diameter earth station for two-way administrative communication. All the tasks in each of these varied project components were identified, and their implementation envisaged.

NETWORKING

After the tasks were identified, they were translated into a network and time estimates were made. Although there are several unique tasks involved in each of the programmes, events and activities emerged that were common to the programmes. These are: identifying/prioritizing clientele needs; content planning and development; media planning/production; transmission/ distribution; research and evaluation; information campaign; clientele utilization of project outputs; and training of project staff. These events and activities were then drawn up into a work-programme chart, with time estimates made on a three-way basis.

PROJECT MONITORING

The initial PERT chart prepared prior to the actual implementation of the project was subjected to a weekly review and assessment during the first three months of project operations. Based on the work trends and patterns which emerged from these first three months (re-PERTing was done to match the project work plan with the actualities at hand—see Figure 1). Furthermore, on the basis of the project experiences during the initial stage, it became possible to make projections on the 'most likely' time estimate. The project staff therefore came up with a work-plan which primarily reflects this time estimate.

Annotated biliography

BRIDGES, F.J.; CHOPMAN, J.E. 1977. *Critical Incidents in Organizational Behavior and Administration*. Englewood Cliffs, N.J., Prentice-Hall. Primarily discusses several case studies that reflect critical incidents in organizational behaviour. The detailed descriptions are aimed to help managers broaden their managerial knowledge and better understand organizational activities that may be supported by structured and well-planned management techniques.

BURBRIDGE, J.L. 1978. *The Principles of Production Control*. London, Macdonald & Evans. Fairly detailed description of production planning and the day-to-day problem of production control, with the view that the principles which govern the flow of materials in production are universal, and that the engaged in distribution.

CHAMPION, J. 1975. *Management and the Behavioral Sciences*. Homewood, Ill., Irwin. (series.) Presents not only the established principles and concepts of professional management but also incidents that would help managers develop the frame of reference, the mental set, the perspective and the method of thinking needed to cope effectively with the value premises present in executive decisions.

FEDERAL ELECTRIC CORPORATION. 1963. *PERT*. New York, N.Y., John Wiley. A programmed text that provides an excellent practical introduction to PERT techniques.

LEVIN, R.; KIRKPATRICK, C. 1966. *Planning and Control with PERT/CPM*. New York, N.Y., McGraw-Hill. Describes the features of PERT as a method of planning and controlling non-repetitive projects and how it complements the CPM, which is a planning and control technique used in projects on which some past cost data are available.

MILLER, R. 1963. *Schedule, Cost and Profit Control with PERT*. New York, N.Y., McGraw-Hill. One of the early pieces of literature on the subject, this book gives a comprehensive description of PERT as mainly concerned with the problems, planning and control in the three dimensions of schedule, cost and profits, arguing that PERT's basic approach is founded upon the technique of networking. Also discussed are the strengths and weaknesses and the problems of implementation from the point of view of both top management and operating-level management.

——. 1962. How to Plan and Control with PERT. *Harvard Business Review*, March–April. Another early article on PERT, it describes the beginning of PERT and its relationship with CPM, its broad areas of application and when to use comluter services to enhance the capabilities of PERT.

SHRODERBEK, P.; DIGMAN, L. 1967. Third Generation PERT/LOB. *Harvard Business Review*, September–October. A concise, analytic discussion of the potentials of PERT/LOB in extending the functions of PERT in many activities related to research, development and quantity production. The authors describe the basic principles of LOB and PERT/LOB and show how the new technique would be used to help project managers plan and control work on a project.

Chapter 20

Flow charting

Jerry L. Brown

Flow charts are graphics that display the sequence of activities in a process. The preparation of flow charts is a useful planning aid that can help a planner to anticipate and avoid trouble spots in a project. They are useful management tools for tracking the progress of a project. They also can serve as aids when presenting information about a project, since they graphically present information that may be difficult to explain verbally.

Definition and history

Flow charts are graphic aids that illustrate the activities that comprise a process and the order in which the activities take place. Figure 1 presents a simple flow chart involving the preparation of a script for a television or radio programme. The flow chart is read from left to right. Rectangles represent activities. The arrows indicate the order of events within the process—the *flow*. Flow charts may be simple (as Figure 1) or complex, depending upon one's needs. They may use a variety of symbols the meaning of which varies from agency to agency, so that it is important for each agency to develop its own standards. Usually, however, rectangles are used to represent activities or procedures, while diamond-shaped boxes ($\Diamond$) are used to represent decisions that are made (as explained later).

The origin of flow charting is cloudy. It is associated with the invention of the computer. It has also been widely used in the construction industry for many years. With the growing popularity of systems approaches in the 1960s and 1970s, flow charting has been used in a wide variety of applications.

Main uses

Any project involves a series of activities. Some are *events*, such as the preparation of a radio or television script, others are *decisions*, such as whether or not to approve a script for production. Identifying and sequencing the major events and decisions in a planning project is an important, if not crucial, management task since it can influence the project's overall success in meeting

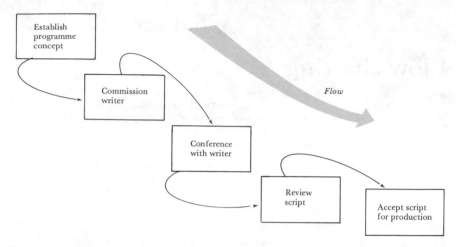

FIG. 1. Simple flow chart for preparation of a radio or television script

its goals. Flow charts can assist project planners and managers to find a sequence of events and decisions appropriate for their project. Analysing what activities are required in a project, and in what order the activities should be sequenced, is a difficult task. Flow charts can help planners quickly lay out alternative sequences for later analysis. In this sense they are facilitating devices for idea generation. Once ideas are down on paper, they can be compared. Since flow charts present ideas graphically, they help planners compare and contrast different alternatives. This, in turn, should help planners identify potential trouble spots and develop a sequence of activities appropriate for a given project. By experimenting on paper, planners can avoid many of the problems that arise when attempts are made to change procedures during an actual project.

Flow charts can serve as memory-joggers for planners and managers. Often in thinking through various alternative sequences for a project, ideas may be forgotten as one first explores one idea and then another. Flow charts summarize the essence of various ideas without requiring a great amount of time to prepare or using many words. They document what one was thinking so that there is a record which can be examined at a later time and which can help jog one's memory. There are two other uses for flow charts which should be in a planner's mind. They can be used as a reference point once a project has begun, in order to track the flow of events and decisions that are taking place. Comparing what was planned with what is actually happening can help a manager make corrections in the organization's operating procedures so that they better conform to what was planned—or, if inadequacies in the plan have been discovered, so that it can be changed. Flow charts can also serve as devices to help people outside a project understand how a project is organized. Often it is difficult to explain in words what type of work is being done and in what

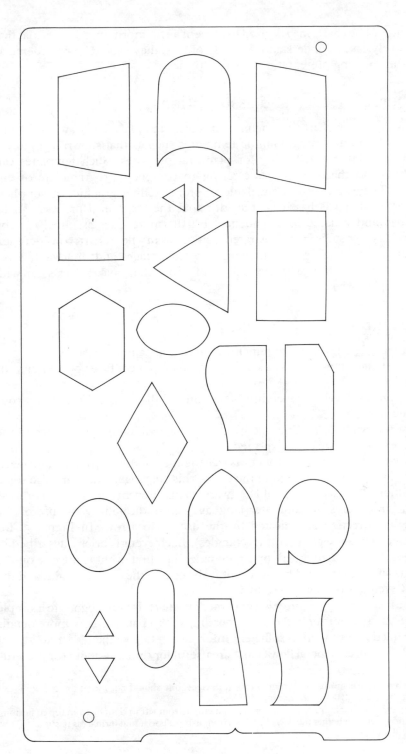

FIG. 2. Flow-chart symbols: computer programmer's template

sequence. Flow charts may be used to present such information in a format that is relatively easy to understand. Because of this, they should be considered as aids when making presentations about a project.[1]

Resources needed and assumptions

In making a flow chart, it is helpful to have a template for drawing various symbols. Computer-programming templates such as that shown in Figure 2 will be more than satisfactory for planning purposes. Such templates can usually be purchased in stores catering to computer programmers or engineers. They may also be available in stores selling graphic-art supplies.

Flow charting is based on the idea that the steps in a process can be identified and ordered in a sequence. Furthermore, it is assumed that by displaying these steps in an illustrated fashion, as in a flow chart, consideration of alternative sequences and their relative advantages and disadvantages is facilitated. Finally, it is assumed that use of a flow-chart makes discussion with other people easier.

Procedures

There are only a few rules to remember in making a flow chart:
Be consistent in how you use a symbol so you do not confuse yourself or your reader.
Decide on the level of generality or specificity that is appropriate for your needs.
Do not worry about finding 'the best' sequence: different approaches to the same problem are to be expected.
Although each individual or agency is free to invent its own symbol language, it is a good idea to be consistent in the use of this language. There are also some conventions of which one should be aware. Usually events or steps in a process (called 'procedures' in computer language) are indicated by the use of the rectangle. Direction is indicated by the use of an arrow. In Figure 3, for example, there are eight events (rectangles). Each event is briefly described in words and then 'surrounded' by a rectangle. The first event is the one on the extreme left of the page. The last event is the one on the extreme right, and the flow of events is from left to right.[2]

The flow chart in Figure 3 is a general flow chart. It is analogous to a simple outline that presents only the major headings for a paper. Many more details can be filled in, but there is sufficient information to give the reader an idea of overall structure. General flow charts are useful for thinking about (or present-

1. Since flow charts are useful communication devices, one should not forget the possibility of using them as instructional, training or job aids.
2. When using English, it is conventional to read either from left to right or from top to bottom, depending upon whether the flow chart is written using a horizontal format (as in Figure 3) or a vertical format.

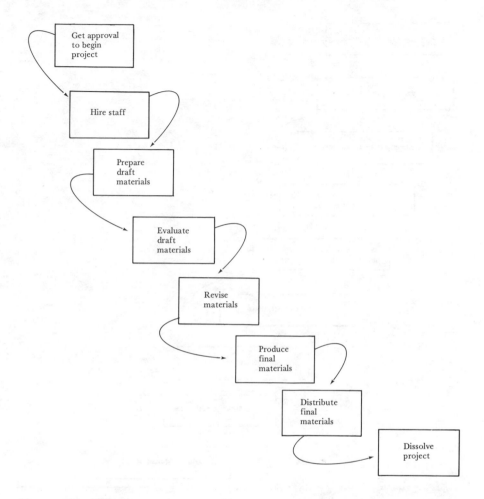

FIG. 3. General flow chart for a materials development project

ing information about) the gross structure of a project. If more detail is desired, then flow charts such as the one illustrated in Figure 4 can be prepared. Using the outline analogy, the flow chart in Figure 4 is equivalent to providing in-depth information about a subtopic with the broader category, 'Prepare draft materials'.

Sometimes it is necessary to choose between different pathways or sequences of activities in a project. When judgements or decisions are required, these conventionally are represented with the diamond symbol: ◇. For example, in Figure 5 a decision is made about whether or not there is sufficient time to permit a film to be field-tested in its 'rough cut' version.[1] The decision point is represented by the diamond symbol. The nature of the decision is written

1. A rough cut is a film that has been edited but is not in its final form.

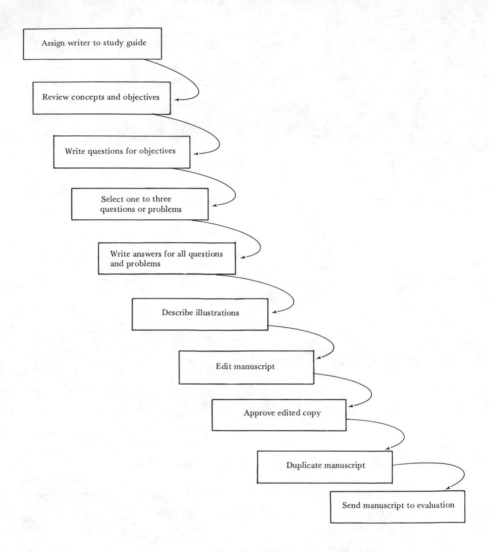

FIG. 4. Flow chart for preparation of a preliminary version of a study guide

inside the symbol and the choices ('yes' or 'no') are written outside the diamond symbol along the pathway which will be taken as a consequence of the particular judgement or decision. A 'no' decision leads to the pathway that results in staff subjectively deciding on what changes should be made in the rough cut. The 'yes' pathway leads to a series of events that, ultimately, provide staff with objective information about how well the rough cut performed in a field test.

It frequently happens in a project that a decision will require a series of previously completed activities to be redone or revisited. In flow chart lan-

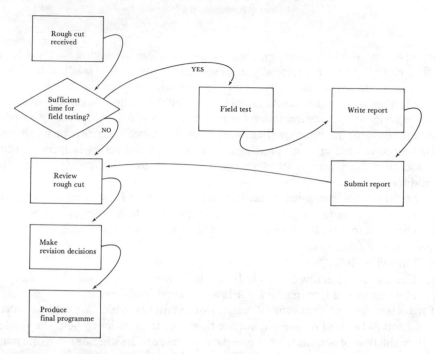

FIG. 5. Flow chart with decision symbol and alternative pathways

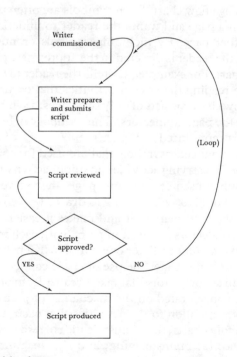

FIG. 6. Flow chart with a loop

guage this is called a *loop* and graphically is equivalent to moving backwards on a flow chart. Loops are pictorially represented by arrows that take one back to a previous point in the flow chart. Such a loop is illustrated in Figure 6 where the decision not to accept a script results in the writer having to continue working on the script and its resubmission for review and approval. Depending on how long it takes our imaginary writer to produce a successful script, one might use the loop one time or a hundred times: only when the script is approved for production does one proceed to the next step in the flow chart, 'Script produced'.

So far the following ideas relating to flow charting have been discussed:
1. The need to determine how general or specific a flow chart is needed.
2. The need to establish language conventions and to be systematic in the use of these conventions.
3. The symbols ☐ and ◇, and how they are used.
4. The use of the arrow (→) to indicate direction.
5. The concept of looping backwards after some decisions.

Two other conventional symbols exist. Both symbols, which are called *connectors*, tend to be used on more complex flow charts in order to help the reader follow the flow of activities from one part of a page to another or from one page to another page. These symbols, represented by the symbols ▽ and ○, are indexing devices and are used in pairs. The connector symbol, ▽, is usually used to 'transfer' the flow along the main branch of activity from one page to another in a multipage flow chart. Such symbols are often used when one has run out of space on a page and wants the reader to understand that the flow continues on another page. By including symbols or numbers within the connector symbol, the reader is directed to the appropriate place in succeeding pages of the flow chart. For example, ⟨3.5⟩ tells the reader to turn from page 3 to page 5 to continue reading the flow of activities that occurs along the major branch. When a flow chart consists of only two pages, a symbol such as ◿ will be included inside the page connectors. This symbol can be seen in use in the two-page flow chart reproduced as Figure 7.

Circles (○) are connector symbols that are used for connecting activities on the same page or for carrying activities on minor activity branches from one page to another. When used on the same page, they serve as substitutes for arrows and are often used to avoid having to draw a broken arrow. This keeps the appearance of the flow chart neat and makes it easier to read. Like page connectors, circle connectors are used in pairs, with each member of the pair containing an indexing number, letter or symbol so that pairs can be associated by the reader. Figure 7 illustrates the use of circle connectors both as single-page connectors and as connectors that take a reader from one page to another.

So far we have concentrated on the mechanics of preparing a flow chart. Now let us turn our attention to the activities that occur before we begin to make drawings. Before charts, there must be ideas. Two techniques are useful for generating ideas: (a) brainstorming; and (b) imagining. Brainstorming entails quickly listing as many ideas as one can without regard to their ultimate practicality. Individuals will find it helpful to list on index cards or slips of paper as many ideas as they can generate in a five-to-ten minute period. Groups will find it useful to follow a similar approach using one person as a recorder of all ideas and paying attention to the rule of 'no commenting on ideas' during the brainstorming. After ideas have been brainstormed, they can be evaluated and poor ideas discarded. (This is one of the advantages of working with index cards or slips of paper.) Applied to flow charting, brainstorming is a useful technique for identifying the events and decisions that comprise a project. It is also useful for generating many alternative ways to sequence activities in a project.

Imagining can be used in combination with brainstorming or by itself. It involves the use of mental pictures—as if there were a television programme playing in one's head. These pictures relate to the steps that compose a process and ways in which the steps may be ordered. For example, one can imagine seeing a product produced and, then, use mental vision to help generate a list or sequence of events or decisions. Imagining can also be useful in evaluating various alternative sequences; by trying to 'see' how the process would work, it is possible to identify potential trouble spots and to generate preferable alternatives. Figure 8 illustrates how brainstorming and imagining can be combined with flow charting to produce alternative sequences of activities in a process.

More complicated forms of flow charts

The flow charts in this chapter show the order of various events and decisions. It is possible to construct more complicated flow charts that add a time dimension—showing what happens in relation to the flow of time as well as activities. PERT and CPM are two such techniques.[1] PERT seeks to examine the flow of time from three perspectives: most optimistic, most likely and most pessimistic. CPM is primarily interested in identifying which activities are most important to the completion of a project as a result of their forming a pathway requiring more time than any other pathway. Since both topics are complicated, the interested reader is advised to consult the following books: Cabot and Harnett (1977) and Federal Electric Corporation (1963).

This paper has focused on the preparation of flow charts as part of the planning process. Preparing flow charts can be as simple or as complicated as one wants it to be. In most cases, users will find that simple flow charts serve their needs well. When preparing flow charts, one should seek to use symbols in a consistent manner in order to avoid confusing the reader. The planner who uses flow charts will find them useful tools for organizing and presenting information, both to him/herself and to others. Readers who wish to learn

---

1. PERT (see Chapter 19 above) stands for 'program evaluation review technique', which was developed by the United States Navy. CPM stands for 'critical path management' and is a tool used by the construction industry in a number of countries.

Activity screening and evaluation

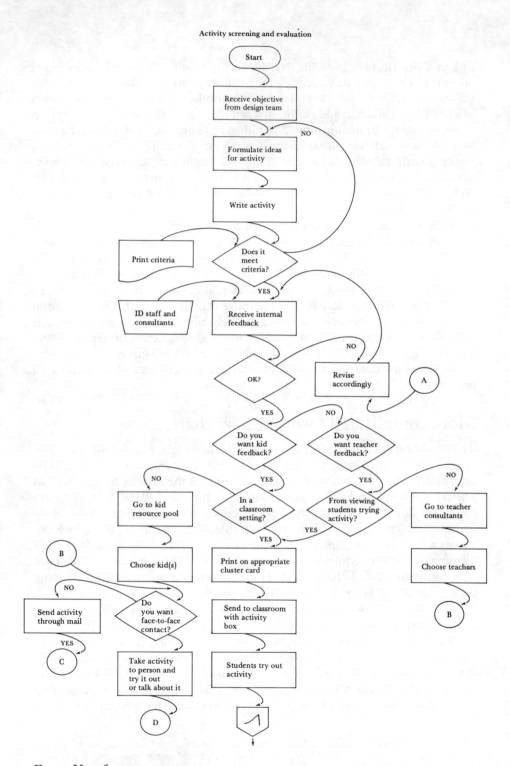

FIG. 7. Use of connectors: page 1

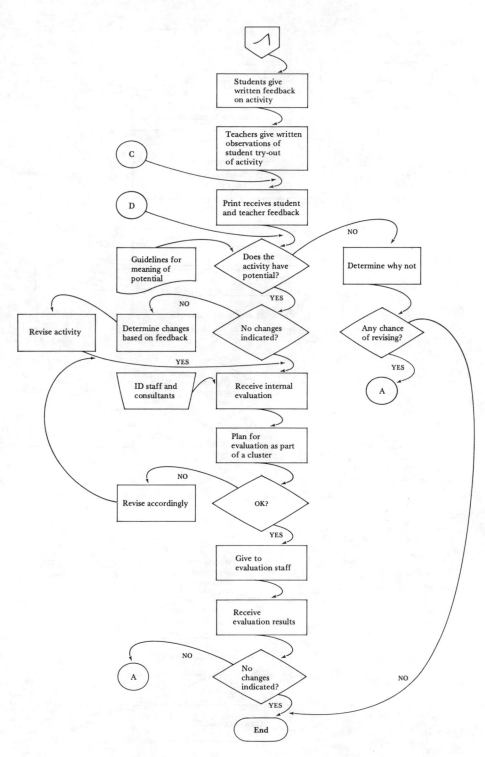

Students give
written feedback
on activity

Teachers give written
observations of
student try-out
of activity

C

D

Print receives student
and teacher feedback

Guidelines for
meaning of
potential

Does the
activity have
potential?

NO

Determine why not

YES

Revise activity

Determine changes
based on feedback

NO

No changes
indicated?

Any chance
of revising?

YES

A

YES

ID staff and
consultants

Receive internal
evaluation

Plan for
evaluation as part
of a cluster

NO

Revise accordingly

OK?

YES

Give to
evaluation staff

Receive
evaluation results

NO

A

No
changes
indicated?

NO

YES

End

Use of connectors: page 2

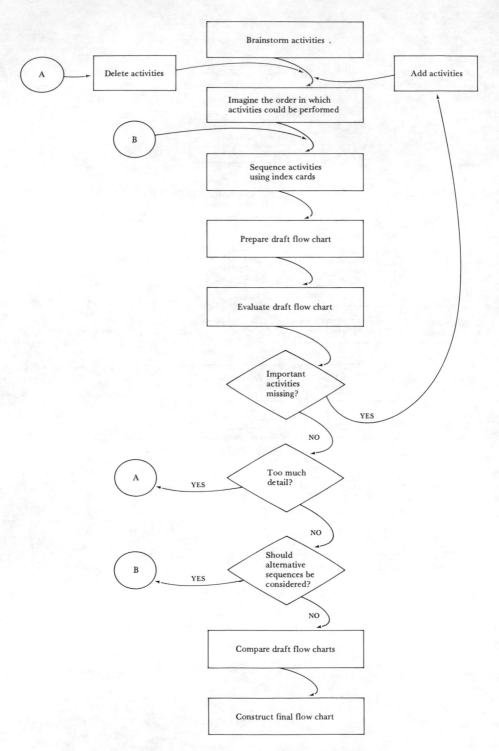

FIG. 8. Using brainstorming and imagining in the flow-charting process

more about the uses of flow charts and other graphic planning aids in training and instructional situations may want to consult the following sources: Brown (1978*a*), Brown (1978*b*), Carey and Briggs (1977) and Horabin and Lewis (1977).

Bibliography

BROWN, J.L. 1978*a*. Three Approaches to Describing the ID Work to be Done. *NSPI Journal* (Washington, National Society for Performance and Instruction), Vol. XVII, No. 2.

BROWN, J.L. (ed.). 1978*b*. Many Facets of Instruction Development. *NSPI Journal* (Washington, National Society for Performance and Instruction), Vol. XVII, No. 7.

CABOT, A.V.; HARNETT, D.L. 1977. *An Introduction to Management Science*. Reading, Mass., Addison-Wesley.

CAREY, J.; BRIGGS, L.J. 1977. Teams as Designers. In: L.J. BRIGGS (ed.), *Instructional Design*. Englewood Cliffs, N.J. Educational Technology.

FEDERAL ELECTRIC CORPORATION. 1963. *PERT*. New York, N.Y., John Wiley.

HORABIN, L.J.; LEWIS, B.N. 1977. Fifteen Years of Ordinary-Language Algorithms. *Human Performance Quarterly* (Washington, National Society for Performance and Instruction), Vol. 6, No. 2/3.

VI

Methods
for learning

Chapter 21

Communication development indicators

Majid Tehranian

The concept of 'communication development indicators', a derivative of the more general concepts of economic, social and cultural development indicators, owes much of its popularity to the normative theories of social change. Development indicators of whatever variety often suggest and quantify a desired model of social change. They tend therefore to reveal as much as to conceal the normative premises upon which much of their legitimacy rests. To select one set of development indicators as opposed to other possible alternatives suggests preferences, conscious or unconscious, for certain social goals as opposed to others. Indicators thus stand as intermediary variables which consist of a development theory, policy, planning, operations, research, evaluation and possible plan revisions. In other words, if appropriately used, indicators could provide signals to monitor the progress, efficiency and efficacy of certain development strategies and plans by supplying some answers to the following three questions: First, *what* are we doing in relation to some intended goals or unintended consequences? Second, *how* are we doing in relation to certain planning objectives and targets? And, third, *why* are we doing what we are doing, in relation to the implications of indicators of feedback for possible revisions in the prevailing development theories, policies, strategies and so on? However, indicators cannot alter the normative premises upon which they are based. They can bring those premises into question only if social problems (represented by such negative indicators as incidence of unemployment, violence or suicide) outweigh the apparent progress that is measured by the criteria of the positive indicators. Under such circumstances, then, a new set of theories, policies, plans and possible indicators is called for.

Definitions

As a subset of general development indicators, however, communications development indicators present some special problems of definition. Because of their interdisciplinary character, the boundaries of communications are not all that clear. A narrow definition of the term, implicitly used in the United Nations and Unesco statistical yearbooks, includes only the print and electronic media or media-related items such as newsprint consumption. A broader definition could include statistical data on all *technologically mediated*, *institutionally organized* and *spontaneously expressed* forms of social communication.[1] It is clearly easier to quantify the first set than the second and the third. General definitions given below for social indicators could be adjusted to fit the more specific case of communications development indicators:

Social indicators [are] statistics, statistical series and all other forms of evidence that enable us to assess where we stand and are going with respect to our values and goals, and to evaluate specific programmes and determine their impact. [Bauer, 1966, p. 11]

A social indicator, as the term is used here, may be defined to be a statistic of direct, normative interest which facilitates concise, comprehensive and balanced judgements about the condition of major aspects of society. It is in all cases a direct measure of welfare and is subject to the interpretation that it changes in the 'right' direction; while other things remain equal, things have gotten better, or people are better off. [United States Department of Health, Education and Welfare, 1969, p. 97]

However, the problem with the above definitions is that, while they recognize the normative content of social indicators, they also impart a concept of development that suggests a progressive, linear and unidirectional movement towards certain notions of social progress. The experience of history demonstrates, however, that social development is a dialectical process, replete with imbalances and forward as well as backward movements. If they are to be useful monitoring devices, therefore, indicators would have to measure also the contradictions and imbalances which are so characteristic of the developmental process. For this if no other reason, a more appropriate and comprehensive definition of communications development indicators may be suggested as follows:

Communications development indicators are those normative sets of quantitative or qualitative data that provide a link between communications development theory, and policy and planning, in order to assign numerical values or properties to social communication concepts. As such, communications development indicators could monitor the progress made or the bottlenecks reached on the path towards certain social objectives and targets in the field of *technologically mediated*, *institutionally organized* or *spontaneously expressed* forms of social communication.

Assumptions

The theoretical assumptions behind this particular definition are far-reaching. Development is here conceived as a dialectical process that involves three fundamentally different, concurrent and often contradictory processes. These

1. The term 'communications' is used in this chapter always in the plural whenever we are referring either to the study of communications or communications industries. By contrast, 'communication' will be used in the singular whenever we are referring to the communication process.

may be identified as the processes of accumulation, mobilization and integration.

The processes of *accumulation* involve a concentration of wealth, power and information. They often consist of capital accumulation, leading to higher levels of productivity of land, labour, capital, information and management, the accumulation of power in the hands of the modern bureaucratic corporation and state leading to the ever-increasing administrative reach and penetration of modern society, and the ever-accelerating accumulation of information and knowledge by the scientific-technological establishment.

Accumulation is thus essentially a top-to-bottom process. On the other hand, the processes of development also involve a concurrent and reverse bottom-to-top process of *mobilization*, which involves claims to wealth, power and participation on the part of those sectors of the population that feel disfranchised. In the economic sphere, the process of mobilization releases the enormous energies of the five factors of production (land, labour, capital, information and management) that have been often tied down to the traditional social and economic institutions. In the political sphere, the movement of vast numbers of people from the countryside into the cities, and their social and psychic mobility into new and modern professions and social status, bring pressures to bear on the modernizing political systems to make room for various forms of democratic participation. In the cultural sphere, the processes of mobilization have produced new forms of national and ethnic consciousness, with their own cultural claims and creativity.

In the meantime, the processes of integration are at work to establish communities of interest, authority and identity. Under historical conditions in which the rates of accumulation have been generally faster than the rates of mobilization (as often was the case in the western experience of industrialization), the social and political contradictions of development have been largely absorbed and integrated within the emerging economic, political and cultural institutions of modern industrial society. By contrast, however, whenever and wherever the rates of mobilization have outpaced the rates of accumulation and integration (of market demand and supply, of political pressures and opportunities for participation, of cultural claims and channels for recognition), the ensuing imbalances have produced revolutionary upheavals. The quickening of the processes of world-wide accumulation, achieved through the extraordinary reach of the transnational corporation and the modern bureaucratic state, has coincided with the even faster tempo of mobilization achieved through the communications revolution (mobility, literacy and media exposure). This combination has created serious imbalances everywhere, but especially in the Third World, between market demands and supplies, and between political and cultural claims and opportunities.

In the meantime, however, most theories and measures of development remain defined primarily in economic terms. They concentrate mostly on the indicators of accumulation (savings, investment, productivity, growth in output and in the communications field, mostly the management of consumer durables) and neglect to understand, let alone measure, the concurrent processes of mobilization and integration. As a result, the generally one-dimensional and unilinear indicators of development have tended to be more misleading than enlightening on the subject.

In the field of communications indicators, a necessary distinction must be made between the three different processes of communications development which correspond to the above three processes of general development. First, we may speak of the *development of communications* facilities and infrastructure, which corresponds to the processes of accumulation in general development. Most theories and measures of communications in development have concentrated their attention primarily on this aspect by measuring the expansion of transport facilities, newspaper circulation, broadcasting and telecommunications coverage and usage etc. Such expansion suggests primarily that power is being increasingly concentrated in the hands of the modern state and corporation. It does not necessarily mean general and balanced development. Communications in this context often perform the function of ideological legitimation of the prevailing forms of accumulation.

There is, however, a second aspect of the development of communications systems, which corresponds to the processes of socio-economic, political and cultural mobilization. It may be termed *development by communications*. This aspect coincides with the historical processes of the so-called revolution of rising expectations and pressures for democratic participation. Through their uses of communications, most governments and oppositions try to give shape and direction to these forces. Indicators of this kind of communications development would therefore have to focus more on software than hardware, more on the content and frequency of messages than on the media's coverage and circulation figures. Communications in this context provide the channels for mobilization and participation to increasingly differentiated audiences.

Third, and possibly most important of all, authentic social progress and development depends vitally on the processes of socio-economic, political and cultural integration; that is to say, on those processes which lead ultimately to a community of shared interests, ideals and identities. In this context, we may speak of *development for communications* which suggests a development policy aimed at social integration by giving adequate and effective recognition to the diversity of moral and material interests within society. Appropriate indicators in this category would focus on the extent to which the communication system gives satisfaction to the expression of the separate interests, identities, authority structures and ideological persuasions of the major sectors of population. The degree of integration achieved through communication is not only a milestone of how much social progress a society has made on the resolution of the inevitable contradictions and imbalances of the developmental process; it is also a measure of how much that process can be humanized. Communication in this context integrates the conflict of interests, authorities and identities that modern life imposes upon modern man and the difficult demands this makes on integrated social and personality systems.

Clearly not all these processes and their conceptualization can be measured quantitatively; the processes of historical development are ultimately qualitative in nature. Levels of social integration and disintegration in the process of development may not lend themselves to adequate measurement; but they can be felt, enjoyed or suffered. Development indicators may serve a useful purpose, as monitoring and planning devices, in focusing attention on those imbalances that are potentially disastrous. (For a critical review of the literature on development theory and communication policy, see: Taylor, 1979; Tehranian, 1979.)

History, theory and typology

The literature on communications development indicators *per se* is rather sparse, but there is an abundance of sources on economic, social and cultural indicators and they include reference to those indicators which could be considered specifically as communications indicators. In the same way that economic indicators can be traced back to the theories and measurement of economic growth and business cycles, the history of social, cultural and communications indicators is also traceable to the theories of social change that assigned a critical role to a certain set of variables. However, the organization of the United Nations system and the post-war world-wide preoccupation with problems of comparing the development and underdevelopment of nations also gave rise to a new generation of indicators that attempted to provide guides for development policy and planning. In reviewing their history and theory, we may therefore make a distinction here between three different types and uses of indicators: descriptive (statistically orientated), analytic (theory-orientated) and prescriptive (policy-orientated).

DESCRIPTIVE OR STATISTICALLY ORIENTATED INDICATORS

Descriptive indicators may be defined as those statistical time series that provide data on various aspects of economic, social and cultural life without suggesting necessarily any particular theoretical propositions or policy positions. Although one may argue that the very selectivity of such data reflects some conscious or unconscious theoretical biases (such as the choice of per-capita income as a measure of progress), the main urge behind this type of indicator is taxonomic. Most national and international statistical reference publications, based mostly on census data, are of this category. Unesco's *Statistical Yearbook*, as well as the five editions of *World Communications*, the latest of which was published in 1975, include much national and international data on communications indicators.

ANALYTIC OR THEORY-ORIENTATED INDICATORS

The relation between empirical data and theory construction is an interactive one. While statistical time series and indicators provide the raw material for the construction of certain theoretical propositions, certain theories also often lead to the generation of new data. Thus, the evolutionary views embedded in the grand theories of economic and social development of the nineteenth and early twentieth centuries may be considered as the godfather of indicators. However, the measurement of social change did not gain momentum until the twentieth century and the rise of empirical sociology (Land, 1971, 1975; Land and Spilerman, 1974). In sociology this led to the publication of the two-volume *Recent Social Trends*, under the direction of William F. Ogburn (1933), which included a comprehensive statistical report on social trends in the United States at that time. The search for quantitative measurements of social change is associated first with empirical studies of propaganda and public opinion (Lasswell, 1927; Pool, 1973). These in turn were influenced by Walter Lippman's classic study, *Public Opinion* (1922), that popularized the concept of stereotypes in the formation of public opinion. Lippman's book was part of an important literature in modern social science which may be called empirical criticism of democratic theory. Ostrogorski (1902), Michels (1939), Becker (1941), Burnham (1942), Schumpeter (1942) and Berelson, Lazarsfeld and McPhee (1954) have all documented 'the discrepancy between the norms of classical democratic ideology about how citizens should make up their minds, and the way in which they actually do' (Pool, 1973, p. 784). A general emphasis on the role of élites, charismatic leaders and opinion leadership is common to most of these theorists of public-opinion formation. Berelson, Lazarsfeld and McPhee (1954) carried these critiques further by a careful measurement of voter behaviour in United States presidential elections. The study of public opinion received its biggest boost, however, with the institution of polling. Public-opinion surveys received their first substantial start when George Gallup and Elmo Roper did rather well in predicting the 1936 election with small samples, using the principles of scientific sampling. Since that time, polling has assumed an increasingly more important role in modern societies and in a diversity of fields, including elections, advertising, propaganda and consumer research. Study of public opinion trends has thus become itself a most vital 'communications indicator' in most democratic societies.

Diffusion theory may be considered as a second strand of theoretical literature on communications indicators. The sociological studies of the diffusion of innovations have focused particularly on the measurement of the processes of social and attitudinal change in rural and urban areas with respect to the adoption of new seeds, practices, values, tastes etc. This research has been well summarized elsewhere (Katz, 1968; Lionberger, 1960; Rogers, 1969); we may refer to it here only briefly and to the extent that it may bear on communications indicators. Diffusion research has been used to measure and analyse the tempo and degree of adoption of innovations (Rogers, 1969; Fogers and Shoemaker, 1971); it has been also used to correlate innovation adoption with the degree of modernity or exposure to mass media; it has been further utilized to measure the psychological stages of the overall adoption decision by identifying five stages, conceived as awareness, interest, evaluation, trial and acceptance (Lionberger, 1960; Rogers and Shoemaker, 1971). The main contribution of diffusion research has been, however, to our understanding of the interaction between mass and interpersonal communication networks. The earlier models of one-step flow of communication, from the media to the audience (Coleman, Katz and Menzel, 1957; Katz and Lazarsfeld, 1955; Klapper, 1960; Lazarsfeld, Berelson and Gaudet, 1944); have been gradually supplanted by the two- and multiple-step flow models in which allowance is made for direct media effects as well as for indirect effects, for lateral communication among mass elements, for greater complementarity between mass media and interpersonal communications, for more reciprocity in the leader–follower relationship, for multiple steps rather than two and so on (Arndt, 1968; Ban, 1964; Frey, 1973; Katz, 1968; Lin, 1969; Rogers, 1971).

Communications development indicators also received a great boost in the post-war period by studies on modernization and development. In attempting to understand the causes of development and underdevelopment, some theorists focused particularly on social and psychological dimensions of social change with a direct or indirect bearing on communications. Some other theorists, however, were inventive enough also to suggest some concepts and methods for testing their hypotheses and measuring the causes and effects of social change. Daniel Lerner (1958) was perhaps the boldest of these theorists in proposing a general communications theory of social change. This in turn served as a basis for further research by a generation of American students of modernization. Lerner's main hypothesis is expressed in two key passages of *The Passing of Traditional Society*. The first states that 'everywhere . . . increasing *urbanization* has tended to increase *media exposure*; rising *literacy* has tended to increase media exposure; increasing media exposure has "gone with" wider economic participation (per capita income) and political participation (voting)' (Lerner, 1958, p. 46, emphasis added). Later in the book, the hypothesis is made a little more complicated by suggestions that media exposure feeds back to increase literacy in what Lerner (p. 60) maintains to be 'a supply-and-demand reciprocal in the communication market . . .'. Frey (1973) has illustrated the latter hypothesis in the following schematic form, where U stands for urbanization; L for literacy; P for participation; and M for media exposure.

Lerner's model had three main characteristics that made it quite attractive to the 'modernization' school of development theory. First, it provided a general theory that challenged the Marxist interpretations of social change by focusing on social and psychological processes rather than on economic structures and social class conflicts. Second, it bridged the gap between the macroanalytical (mainly economic and sociological) and microanalytical (mainly social psychological) models and theories of social change. The concept of 'empathy' or 'psychic mobility' served as Lerner's bridge between psychic and social modernization. Empathy, or the psychological ability to put oneself in the other fellow's shoes, according to Lerner, increased with the rise in urbanization, literacy, media exposure and various forms of participation. Third, Lerner's concepts and hypotheses were presumed to be capable of operationalization, quantification, measurement and testing. However, Lerner's basic hypotheses were somewhat qualified in his later discussions and revisions.

The last two decades of developments in many parts of the Third World had demonstrated the importance of impeding social and political structures, which were seriously neglected in the 'modernization' models, and which had focused too narrowly on the socio-cultural and psychological variables, on the one hand, or the economic factors, on the other. In the meantime, however, the indicators approach to modernization and development had received further refinement in the works of Adelman and Morris (1967), Alker (1966), Deutsch (1953), Frey (1973), Inkeles and Smith (1974) and McClelland (1961), among others. While the works of Frey, Inkeles and Alker were variations on Lerner's themes, Deutsch, McClelland and Adelman and Morris were following different conceptual schemes. Frey (1973, p. 403ff) provides a useful summary of the refinements on Lerner's hypotheses as well as some tentative conclusions based on the analysis of available national data on relations between communications and other development indicators.

Deutsch (1953) and McClelland (1961) are two other major theorists of the modernization school who have also assigned a special role to the media and communications indicators in the processes of social change. Indeed, Deutsch was a pioneer in the conceptualization, quantification and measurement of some highly complex phenomena such as nationalism, national integration and social mobilization. His view of the political system as an information and communication system led him to study how different national cultures produce, select and channel information in order to achieve national consciousness, social mobilization and cultural integration (Deutsch, 1953, Ch. 4). As a social psychologist, however, McClelland's central focus is on the motivational variables, their communication from one generation to the next and their impact on rates of economic growth. He identifies three major human needs that have played a central motivational function in history; these he labels as needs for affiliation, power and achievement. While the need for affiliation suggests an affective liaison between two hypothetical individuals, A and B, the need for power signifies a manipulative relationship, and the need for achievement implies a common functional task. McClelland's central hypothesis, buttressed by an abundance of historical and contemporary data, is that a rise in the need for achievement correlates significantly with a rise in the rates of economic growth. Periods of economic growth and cultural effervescence in history, McClelland holds, are often preceded by the rise of a generation that has been acculturated into a need for achievement, to do well, to surmount challenges, to be tested, to strive and to succeed in worldly endeavours. The significance of McClelland's hypothesis for communication indicators lies in that he also proposes some methods of measurement of the existing motivational patterns based on the content analysis of children's stories and thematic perception tests. In other words, he assumes that cultural values are transmitted by communication from generation to generation in ways that can be measured and correlated with historical developments.

By sharp contrast to the 'modernization' school, an alternative theoretical perspective has also emerged in recent decades that may be labelled the 'dependency' school (Amin, 1977; Baran, 1957; Frank, 1969; Taylor, 1979). Beginning with a critique of the modernization theories and methods as more ideological than scientific, this school has focused on the political, economic, technological and cultural dependence of the less-developed countries. Since the mid-70s, this theoretical perspective has also coincided with calls on the part of the less-developed nations for a new international and communication order (Brandt *et al.*, 1980; Erb and Kallab, 1975; MacBride *et al.*, 1980; Tinbergen, 1972). In the communications field, researchers with such a perspective have therefore focused primarily on the measurement and analysis of indices of dependence. Nordenstreng and Varis (1974), for example, examined the indicators of imbalance in the international traffic of television programmes, and the Unesco MacBride Report (1980) calls attention to the indicators of both economic and cultural dependency and suggests ways and means of redressing them.

There is also a vast and growing literature that employs the indicators approach in order to provide an inductive analysis of the comparative dynamics of development. Adelman and Morris (1967) and Chenery and Syrquin (1975) have been pioneering figures in this field, but O'Brien *et al.* (1979) provide a good review of such efforts, particularly with respect to the role of communications indicators. Constructing a 'Commindex' composed of five major communications indicators,[1] the latter also provide an interesting analysis of the correlations between the overall and separate communications indicators and GNP over a global range. The results suggest, not surprisingly, that all communications indicators are highly correlated with GNP per capita. Telephone and television receivers come first, while radio receivers show the lowest correlation. The results, based on 1970 global data, show further that

newspaper circulation increases steadily as GNP rises, the main exceptions to the trend being Hong Kong and Japan (both very high on newspapers) and Canada (very low). With telephones and GNP only New Zealand (high on telephones) shows a deviation from the trend line. Radio and GNP show a very interesting relationship; the range of radios does not appear to differ significantly (except in Canada and the USA) as GNP increases. This suggests a low income elasticity of demand for radios. TV shows a

1. These are newspaper (daily, general-interest) circulation per 1,000 population, newsprint consumption per capita, telephones per 100,000 population, radio receivers per 1,000 population and television receivers per 1,000.

TABLE 1. Commindex and core indicators (based on simple linear regression)

Indicator	Commindex		
	r	R^2	Level of significance
GNP per capita	0.9208	0.8479	0.00001
Literacy	0.6890	0.4748	0.00001
Primary and secondary school enrolment	0.7341	0.5389	0.00001
Motor vehicles	0.9100	0.8281	0.00001
Steel consumption	0.8517	0.7253	0.00001
Percentage GDP from manufacturing	0.6766	0.4578	0.00001
Percentage population in locations of 100,000 plus	0.6242	0.3897	0.00001
Expenditure on food	− 0.7514	0.5647	0.00001
Life expectancy	0.7154	0.5118	0.00001
Exports of raw materials as percentage of total exports	− 0.4312	0.1859	0.00003
Agricultural population as percentage of total population	− 0.7494	0.5617	0.00001

Source: O'Brien *et al.*, 1979.

steady growth with GNP (with the exception of Libya). Newsprint shows a steady growth with GNP, but there are more deviations from the trend line than with newspaper circulation. Notable exceptions are Argentina (very high on newsprint), France, East Germany, Czechoslovakia, and Libya (relatively low on newsprint). [O'Brien *et al.*, 1979, p. 28–9]

The authors subsequently provide a quantitative analysis of the relations between communications indicators and 'development patterns' (as defined by Chenery and Syrquin, 1975), communication and core development indicators, inter-temporal comparisons (1960–75), income distribution and economic dualism, and investment and production in mass communication. Tables 1 and 2 summarize some of the findings with respect to the correlations between communication and core indicators (1970), and Commindex and GNP per capita ranks. There are a few interesting variations, but no great surprises.

PRESCRIPTIVE OR POLICY-ORIENTATED INDICATORS

A third possible approach to the problem of indicators is to recognize their prescriptive assumptions and proceed then to construct indicators which are policy-orientated. This approach received a great boost with the quality-of-life movement of the 60s and 70s and at the policy level turned into what some observers have called 'the social indicators movement' (Land, 1975, p. 8). In the United States and Western Europe, this led to the construction of social as distinct from economic indicators and the publication of a variety of country social reports (Organization for Economic Co-operation and Development, 1973, 1977; United States, 1969, 1973). The United Nations system also followed suit by the establishment of the United Nations Research Institute for Social Development (UNRISD), in Geneva, that has pioneered many conceptual and methodological studies, while providing a data bank on social indicators (1974). The changing concepts of development in the 1970s have also prompted the United Nations system, as well as some governments and theorists, to recommend the abandonment of the earlier economic approaches in favour of a more unified, integrated or basic-needs strategy towards development planning (Adelman and Morris, 1967; United Nations, 1971). Finally, the United Nations University has also undertaken a project on 'Goals, Processes, and Indicators of Development' that promises interesting results (Galtung, 1978).

As the international agency primarily responsible for cultural and communications development, Unesco has also initiated some projects on development indicators that have generally followed the dominant trends in trying to establish links between economic, social and cultural factors (Unesco, 1975, 1976). However, Unesco's policy orientation with respect to communications development seems to have evolved during the past two decades from one of emphasis on quantitative indicators of media availability at the national level to the call for structural changes in the prevailing international information and communication system (MacBride *et al.*, 1980). While Unesco suggested in 1961 some minimal standards to be met by the Member States in mass media,[1] the MacBride Report called not only for the development of communications infrastructure but also for the endogenous production of messages and regional co-operation to establish collective self-reliance in the production of communications goods and services, training and research. One reason for this change of emphasis might be the fact, as reflected in the MacBride Report, that access to the media in the less-developed countries has either surpassed (in the case of radio) or approached some of the Unesco minimal standards. In the meantime, however, disparities within countries, between developed and developing countries and between developing countries themselves have dramatically increased (see Tables 3 and 4).

Three further trends in contemporary society, particularly in the advanced industrial countries, have also given rise to policy concerns with communications indicators. First, automation and the increase in leisure time in most

---

1. These urged that every country should provide at least the following media facilities per 1,000 population: 100 copies of daily newspapers, 50 radio receivers, 20 cinema seats and 20 television receivers.

TABLE 2. Comparison of Commindex[1] and GNP ranks (1970 data)

Country	Commindex	GNP per capita	Ranks by Commindex[2]	Ranks by GNP per capita[2]
Zaire	−1.02	90.00	1	3
Ethiopia	−1.01	80.00	2	1.5
Tanzania	−1.00	100.00	3	4.5
Saudi Arabia	−0.99	440.00	4	42
Pakistan	−0.98	100.00	5.5	4.5
Sierra Leone	−0.98	190.00	5.5	14
Ivory Coast	−0.97	310.00	9	31
Haiti	−0.97	110.00	9	6.5
India	−0.97	110.00	9	6.5
Uganda	−0.97	130.00	9	10.5
Nigeria	−0.97	120.00	9	8.5
Zambia	−0.95	400.00	12	39
Libya	−0.93	1 770.00	13	67
Kenya	−0.92	150.00	14	13
Senegal	−0.89	230.00	15	18.5
Algeria	−0.88	300.00	16	28.5
Honduras	−0.86	280.00	17.5	24.5
Zimbabwe[3]	−0.86	280.00	17.5	24.5
Sudan	−0.85	120.00	19.5	8.5
Ghana	−0.85	310.00	19.5	31
Morocco	−0.84	230.00	21	18.5
Tunisia	−0.83	270.00	22	23
Philippines	−0.82	210.00	23.5	16.5
Thailand	−0.82	200.00	23.5	15
Dominican Republic	−0.82	350.00	25	35
Indonesia	−0.79	80.00	27	1.5
Mauritania	−0.79	140.00	27	12
Paraguay	−0.79	260.00	27	22
Turkey	−0.78	310.00	29	31
Malaysia	−0.75	380.00	30	37.5
Nicaragua	−0.73	430.00	31	41
Guatemala	−0.72	360.00	32.5	36
Khmer Republic	−0.72	130.00	32.5	10.5
Egypt	−0.67	210.00	34	16.5
Mongolia	−0.65	460.00	35	44
Greece	−0.64	1 090.00	36	61
Jordan	−0.62	250.00	37.5	20.5
El Salvador	−0.62	300.00	37.5	28.5
Korea, Republic of	−0.61	250.00	39	20.5
Colombia	−0.59	340.00	40	34
Syria	−0.52	290.00	42	26.5
Brazil	−0.52	420.00	42	40
Peru	−0.52	450.00	42	43

1. 'Commindex' includes only newsprint consumption, televisions and radios per 1,000 population.
2. '1' is the lowest rank for both Commindex and GNP per capita.
3. Then Rhodesia.
Source: O'Brien *et al.*, 1979, p. 47.

Country	Commindex	GNP per capita	Ranks by Commindex[2]	Ranks by GNP per capita[2]
Iraq	−0.51	320.00	44.5	33
Iran	−0.51	380.00	44.5	37.5
Costa Rica	−0.41	560.00	46	46
Chile	−0.38	720.00	47	52
Portugal	−0.35	660.00	48	49
Romania	−0.32	930.00	49	57
Cuba	−0.31	530.00	50	45
Ecuador	−0.29	290.00	51	26.5
Yugoslavia	−0.17	650.00	52	48
Venezuela	−0.15	980.00	53	59
Panama	−0.13	730.00	54.5	53
Mexico	−0.13	670.00	54.5	50.5
Singapore	−0.04	920.00	56	56
Poland	−0.01	1 400.00	57	64
Hong Kong	0.03	970.00	58	58
Jamaica	0.04	670.00	59	50.5
Lebanon	0.06	590.00	60	47
Uruguay	0.10	820.00	61	55
Spain	0.13	1 020.00	62	60
Bulgaria	0.18	760.00	63	54
Israel	0.19	1 960.00	64	70
Italy	0.39	1 760.00	65.5	66
Hungary	0.39	1 600.00	65.5	65
USSR	0.49	1 790.00	67	68
Czechoslovakia	0.61	2 230.00	68	72
Ireland	0.66	1 360.00	69	63
Austria	0.84	2 010.00	70	71
France	1.02	3 100.00	71	82
German Democratic Republic	1.08	2 490.00	72	76
Belgium	1.23	2 720.00	73	78
Norway	1.24	2 860.00	74	80
Switzerland	1.35	3 320.00	75	84
Germany, Federal Republic of	1.45	2 930.00	76	81
Netherlands	1.55	2 430.00	77	75
Finland	1.60	2 390.00	78	74
Australia	1.62	2 820.00	79	79
Japan	1.63	1 920.00	80	69
New Zealand	1.65	2 700.00	81	77
Denmark	1.82	3 190.00	82	83
Argentina	1.86	1 160.00	83	62
United Kingdom	1.89	2 370.00	84	73
Canada	2.93	3 700.00	85	85
United States	4.97	4 760.00	86	86

TABLE 3. Media standards by level of GNP

Countries	Daily press	Radio receivers	Television receivers	Telephone[1]	Cinema attendance per inhabitant
	per 1 000 inhabitants				
A. With low GNP	19.2	56.0	5.4	1.3	2.7
B. With middle GNP	19.0	57.2	22.5	15.1	1.1
C. Developed	328.0	741.0	338.0	352.0	7.4

1. Data about telephones do not include China.
Source: MacBride *et al.*, 1980, p. 128.

TABLE 4. Television standards by level of GNP

Countries	Number of countries	Number of countries with television	Number of countries with colour television
A. With low GNP	45	28	3 (6% of countries)
B. With middle GNP	56	56	33 (59% of countries)
C. Developed	27	27	24 (89% of countries)

Source: MacBride *et al.*, 1980, p. 128.

industrial societies have led to a new genre of social research known as time-budget studies and indicators. In mass-communication research, time-budget studies have focused on the time spent on the comsumption of different media (radio, television, books etc.) and message types (drama, fiction, science etc.) by different sectors of the population (age, sex, class etc.). These studies have important policy implications in marketing, life-style, cultural trends etc.

Second, the rise in the sex and violence components of communication media in some countries has also sensitized some policy-makers and public-opinion leaders to the possibility of its link with deviant social behaviour. This has in turn encouraged considerable research, particularly in the United States, on the content analysis and effects analysis of the media (e.g. Comstock and Lindsey, 1975). Another more ambitious effort in this direction is represented by the cultural-indicators policy analysis proposed and conducted by Gerbner *et al.* (1973, p. 555–73). Cultural indicators as defined by Gerbner would try to deal with three areas of analysis:

How mass media relate to other institutions, make decisions, compose message systems, and perform their functions in society are questions for *institutional process analysis*; how large bodies of messages can be observed as *dynamic* systems with symbolic functions that have social consequences is the question of *message system analysis*; and what common assumptions, points of view, images, and associations do the message systems tend to cultivate in large and heterogeneous communities, and with what public policy implications, are problems of *cultivation analysis*. [Gerbner, 1973, p. 558; emphasis in original]

Content indicators can either include measures specific to particular issues, policies or symbolic functions (such as the television 'violence index') or they can deal with general features of the symbolic world—census figures, ranging over time, space, personality types and social roles. Indicators can also trace the reconstruction of historical memories, as well as the presentation of heroes and villains, victors and victims, fair means or foul, of the configuration of certain themes, actions and values over time and across cultures (Gerbner, 1973, p. 566).

Third, the rise of what some observers have called 'the post-industrial society' (Bell, 1973) or 'information society' (Porat, 1977), characterized in both instances by a predominance of production, consumption and employment in the communications industries and services, has led to a new kind of quantitative research and analysis that focuses on communications indicators. Indicators on knowledge and knowledge production (Malchlup, 1980), information production (Porat, 1977) and communication industries trends (Sterling and Haight, 1978) have provided the foci for different kinds of social analysis.

Methods and problems of application

Given the enormous diversity of communications indicators we have so far discussed, their methods and problems of application are also correspondingly diverse. A detailed discussion of such a multidisciplinary variety of methodologies, ranging from the simplest to the most complex, is impossible here. However, following the typology of the preceding section, the methodological problems of communications indicators could be generally discussed under the rubrics of the descriptive, analytic and prescriptive approaches. This may throw some light on the question of which methods are perhaps more appropriate to what purposes. It would be useful, also, to establish first some general criteria for constructing indicators.

THE CONSTRUCTION OF COMMUNICATIONS INDICATORS

There are at least five criteria which should be considered in the construction of any kind of indicator; these concern the problems of *content*, *validity*, *relevance*, *efficiency* and *efficacy*. Mukherjee (1976) has suggested and discussed the first four at some length; we may add here a fifth.

The *content* of an indicator refers to the set of phenomena of which that indicator is suggestive. The literacy rate, for instance, tells us about the parameters of written communication in a society. The number of telephones per thousand of population tells us about the parameters of oral communication mediated by telephone. The choice of these indicators as opposed to others inevitably suggests also a value preference for literacy and telephone communication which is not self-evident; the underlying concepts of development that have led to this choice should be therefore defensible on policy grounds.

The *validity* of an indicator depends on whether or not it is so constructed as correctly to represent its constituent variables. Does the literacy rate, for instance, adequately represent the access of the literate population to all written literature in a multilingual society? If one language dominates the others, literacy in a minority language does not necessarily ensure such access. We would have to supplement, therefore, the literacy rate in one language with other kinds of indicators to provide adequate and valid representation of the content of our indicator, which is presumably access to all written communication in its full diversity and complexity. As Mukherjee (p. 39) puts it:

An indicator may be valid in respect of the variables entering into its constitution (as an index, to begin with) and the conceptual relations drawn between these variables. But the association these constituent variables draw (or should draw) with the contingent variables in order to transform the index into an indicator: (a) may be wrongly assumed; (b) may be explicitly but wrongly stated; or (c) may be ignored.

In other words, the indicator could be valid but not relevant. Common religion is often taken, for instance, as an indicator of national solidarity. However, in certain situations (such as those of Pakistan and Bangladesh before separation), differences in language and ethnicity may be a more *relevant* indicator.

An indicator may be valid and relevant but not *efficient*. The efficiency of an indicator could be measured in analytic or economic terms. Analytically, the efficiency of an indicator would vary on two counts: (a) the treatment of its variables may be thorough enough in the existing state of our knowledge to depict the reality comprehensively; and (b) its value consideration, since it involves differential human relationships, may be ignored or by-passed (Mukherjee, p. 44). Economically, an indicator is most efficient when it produces the highest information/cost ratio. To make indicators more efficient, we may have to resort to paired or clustered indicators. A paired indicator would try to measure two, often contradictory, aspects of a single phenomenon such as industrialization which has both positive and negative consequences. Clustered indicators, such as that of Commindex discussed earlier, attempt to provide a global index on a highly complex phenomenon.

The *efficacy* of an indicator may be tested over time; an indicator could be valid, relevant and efficient for a time while losing its efficacy over time. Literacy rate may be an efficacious indicator of educational attainment in the earlier stages of development but certainly not for later stages.

THE DESCRIPTIVE APPROACH

The descriptive approach to indicators is based on methodologies that are atheoretical and taxonomic, attempting to discover regularities in certain phenomena without any necessary explication. Chief among such methods are population census, audience research, public-opinion surveys and statistical time series. Although with the introduction of computer facilities the potency and sophistication of such methodologies have enormously increased in recent years, frequent use being made of their data in social-science analysis, the methods in themselves are often aimed at a neutral description of the social reality. While audience research and public-opinion polls are explicitly tied to problems of communication and can therefore provide methodological tools for communication indicators, population censuses and statistical time series are broader in scope but can include some communications indicators. Items such as a census of consumer durables, including radio and television sets, audio and video tapes, telephones etc. could be easily built into census reports in order to provide a reliable set of communication data over time. Other items such as export–import data on communication goods and services (films, records, pre-recorded tapes, books, periodicals, news, hardware, consultancy etc.), and licence-fee payments on radio or television (if such be the case), could provide supplementary and sometimes corrective time-series data.

Audience surveys and public-opinion polls, however, provide other powerful tools for the construction of useful communications indicators. Both of these methods have been refined to a considerable extent in the advanced industrial societies such as the United States, where television ratings (such as Nielson's) and public-opinion polls are of such critical importance to the conduct of commercial and political life. In the socialist and less-developed countries where such tools appear to be of less importance, if they are used at all, a decision must be made as to what kinds of indicators can be employed usefully in the policy and planning process. Indicators of audience profile (age, sex, occupation, ethnic affiliation, ideological orientation etc.) as well as surveys of their daily habits and preferences can be very useful to programme planners. Content analysis of programmes can also provide indicators on the kinds of images (traditional versus modern, sexist versus non-sexist) and values (courage versus cowardice, patriotism versus treachery, collectivism versus individualism) that they impart. Similarly, public-opinion polls can provide useful feedback on the views and policy preferences of the different segments of the population.

A word of caution is, however, in order with respect to both of these methods when applied in contexts other than those of liberal democracies. The existence of 'public opinion' presupposes the presence of public forums in which a diversity of views and ideological tendencies confront each other. Such a development would have been inconceivable before the emergence of autonomous centres of power in mass political parties, voluntary associations, universities, the mass media and a value system that cherishes pluralism. Such conditions are not universally present in all countries. Consequently, methodologies that presume free expressions of opinions that are formed after an exposure to, if not an examination of, the alternative possible views on a single issue, are often doomed to findings other than of freely held opinions.

THE ANALYTIC APPROACH

Most of the methods in this category also use some of the time-honoured statistical and social-science methodologies. In contrast to the descriptive approach, however, the analytic approach is theory-orientated and attempts to test certain propositions, hypotheses or models against empirical reality. Chief among the methods we may take up briefly are interviews, random sampling, content analysis, Delphi, simulation modelling and experimentation.

Although the interview technique does not often lend itself to easy quantification, if combined with the content analysis method it can provide a useful tool for communications indicators. In open interviews, certain themes, images or words recur with considerable frequency and intensity. A sensitive interviewer can decode these messages in order to reconstruct the interviewee's conceptions of social reality. In closed interviews, however, the categories of analysis should be established before embarking on research. A combination of open and closed interviews, successively to explore first the categories of analysis and then on a larger scale and random sample to test certain hypotheses, would be perhaps most appropriate to the challenge of deciphering public-opinion trends under repressive conditions. Content analysis by itself is more appropriate to the coding and decoding of the content of media, but it requires considerable cultural sensitivity and understanding in its research design (Gerbner *et al.*, 1969).

Random sampling is one of the most frequently used methods of communication research, but subject to the cautions discussed in the preceding paragraph. Delphi, as discussed elsewhere in this volume, is a technique of forecasting. It seems most appropriate to technology trends, from which indicators on the future of communication technologies could be obtained by the use of successive interviews and questionnaires to elicit a consensus among the 'experts'. Where 'experts' are either wanting or in serious disagreement, Delphi cannot produce much. The growth of computing facilities has made simulation modelling a favourite method of some in planning. However, where data are inadequate or unreliable, the GIGO principle (garbage in, garbage out) applies. However, the growth of the communication infrastructure can be related to the different levels and stages of development and we may, therefore, use this method for limited (mostly infrastructural) aspects of communication planning.

Finally, the experimental method in communication research has a long history (see Comstock and Lindsey, 1975) and has been used primarily in media-effects studies. However, in view of the complexity of variables that determine social behaviour, it has largely proved ineffective in testing empirically the hypotheses proposed on media effects.

THE POLICY AND PLANNING APPROACH

In contrast to the descriptive and analytic approaches which contain policy preferences only implicitly, this approach begins with an explicit statement of policy preferences. As noted earlier, the quality of life movement in the 60s and the changing concepts of development in the 70s have particularly led to the construction of policy-orientated social indicators, of which cultural and communication indicators are often a subset. Given the diversity of methods proposed, it is difficult to provide here a comprehensive presentation. However, we may identify at least three distinctly different approaches, that may be dubbed *economic, systems* and *developmental.*

The *economic approaches* begin with economic models of the communication system, organizing cultural and communication indicators largely around the concepts of production, employment, ownership, consumption etc. Mowlana (1976), for instance, proposes an economic framework for comparative mass-media analysis that could be developed further to provide policy-orientated communication indicators. In its programme of cultural indicators, Unesco has also constructed an economic model of the flow of cultural goods and services which has direct relevance to the construction of communication indicators as well (Unesco, 1979). Porat (1977) and Malchulp (1980) have also approached the problems of information and knowledge indicators through basically economic models. The policy implications of most such models are also basically those of economic growth and stability models.

The *systems approach* often assumes an even broader framework for policy analysis, organized around input–process–output models of the communication system. Gerbner's cultural-indicators programme, discussed above, could be considered such an approach. While Gerbner's message system analysis looks at the inputs of the communication system, his 'institutional process analysis' focuses on the processes of decision-making, and 'cultivation analysis' concerns itself with the system output and impact.

The *developmental* approach to communication indicators covers a vast variety of methodologies that include both analytical (such as Lerner's) and policy and planning methods such as those proposed by the Organization for Economic Co-operation and Development (OECD), the United Nations University's Human and Social Development Programme and others. This approach often begins with some implicitly or explicitly stated normative concept of development. In the case of the OECD social-indicators programme, the concept revolves around measuring social well-being as reflected in 'the social concerns common to most OECD countries' (Organization for Economic Co-operation and Development, 1977). The indicators chosen are explicitly policy-orientated, but do not go into any detail with respect to communication indicators. However, 'time and leisure' (a category that might include communication indicators) is one of the nine goal areas set forth to measure social well-being. The United Nations University project on development indicators, directed by Johan Galtung, also begins with a normative concept of development that reflects the changing international 'concepts/theories' in recent decades. Galtung (1978), who proposes an 'integrated approach' to development in which the main focus should be on the satisfaction of 'human needs', places the methodological emphasis on 'dialogue' as the way of achieving a deeper understanding of the developmental problématique, with a correspond-ing methodological emphasis on a 'network' of research units involving insti-tutions and individuals well versed in the global developmental problématique as well as specific development activities in their own setting, and with good contacts with both people and planners/decision-makers. The five terms in quotation marks above (i.e. needs, concept/theory, dialogue, network and integrated approach) are the key concepts to define the United Nations pro-ject. However, the project has not as yet developed any specific set of indicators.

A DIALECTICAL APPROACH: SOME EXAMPLES

An alternative approach to development is to view the process as inherently contradictory and uneven in terms of, as proposed earlier, the dialectical processes of accumulation, mobilization and integration. Since in many less-developed countries the developmental process has often produced increas-ing levels of dependency, dualism, fragmentation and alienation as well, it would be necessary to construct those communication-development indi-cators which are appropriate to the measurement of all of these interrelated phenomena. From this perspective, the central developmental problem would be how to manage the imbalances and stresses of the process. The actual construction of communication-development indicators on this basis would require focusing on two different sets of analytic categories, in order to obtain indicators of structure and indicators of process, or stocks and flows, levels and rates. The first set provides us with a static view of where we are, the second set tells us something about the dynamics and direction of change. To cite an example, the rate of literacy as a communication indicator tells us what per-centage of the population can participate in written communication, but the annual rate of growth of literacy suggests what percentage of population is entering into a new form of consciousness and stream of social communication. As another example, GNP per capita tells us something about the level of average national income but the annual rate of growth in GNP per capita tells something about the comparative dynamics of income and population growth.

To view the levels and rates of change in time, a matrix can be constructed to show the change in the levels of accumulation, mobilization and integration etc. in a country between two or more points in time. To monitor and measure these processes, we need appropriate indicators for each. The following list of indicators under each category is, however, suggestive rather than exhaustive. It focuses particularly on communication-development indicators; it should therefore be supplemented with other types of development indicators to provide a fuller picture. Furthermore, in each different socio-cultural environ-ment, we should construct additional indicators appropriate to that environment.

Indicators of communications dependency

Ratio of domestic to foreign: authorship of books in print and per year; films shown; television programmes broadcast; radio programmes broadcast; news in newspapers, radio and television; textbooks in print and per year; authorship of scientific articles in periodicals; mail per year; produced paper consumption; produced media hardware; telegrams, telexes, telephone calls exchanged.

Indicators of communications accumulation

Growth rate of: printing presses by type and capacity; radio and television production and transmission centres by capacity and coverage; media hardware produced domestically by type; concentration of media ownership by categories (public/private, foreign/domestic); paper production by type.
Radio-television coverage by territory and population.
Books in print per 1,000.
Books published per 1,000.
Periodicals circulation per 1,000.
Letters exchanged per 1,000.
Telegrams exchanged per 1,000.
Newspaper circulation per 1,000.
Radio receivers per 1,000.
Television receivers per 1,000.
Telephone receivers per 1,000.
Telex machines per 1,000.
Computers per 1,000.
Cinema seats per 1,000.
Printing paper kg/per capita.
Libraries per 1,000.
Documentation centres per 100,000.
Records sold per 1,000.
Audio-cassettes sold per 1,000.
Video-cassettes sold per 1,000.
Video-discs sold per 1,000.

Indicators of communications dualism

Ratio of urban to rural ownership of the media (telephone, radio, television).
Ratio of urban to rural access to the media (libraries, cinemas, community radio and television).
Ratio of national to local/regional newspapers in numbers and circulation per 1,000.
Ratio of national radio-television networks to local/regional networks.
Ratio of urban to rural literacy rates.
Ratio of urban to rural educational participation rates at primary, secondary and tertiary levels.
Ratio of membership in traditional (e.g. religious) to modern (e.g. political party) organizations.

Indicators of communications mobilization

Rate of literacy by age, sex, language groups, urban rural categories.
Rate of urbanization by size of cities.
Rate of educational participation by categories of primary, secondary and tertiary level.
Rate of labour participation by categories of age, sex, profession.
Rate of internal migration by categories of age, sex, profession, location.
Rate of external migration by categories of age, sex, education, profession, location.
Rate of social mobility by horizontal and vertical categories (professional and income mobility).
Rate of media exposure by categories of information-intensive versus information-extensive media (e.g. scientific media versus entertainment media, or books versus television).
Rate of participation in traditional associations, e.g. mosques, churches, folk dances, sports houses, tea houses, other voluntary associations.

Rate of participation in modern associations, e.g. labour unions, political parties, professional associations etc.

Rate of psychic mobility by categories of population, compositely measured by such indices as capacity to project oneself into a diversity of social roles other than one's own.

Rate of psychic ambivalence by categories of population, compositely measured by such indices as feelings of conflict between tradition and modern values and life-styles.

Indicators of communication fragmentation

Ratio of actual political groupings (exile, underground) to officially recognized ones.
Ratio of literacy in the national language to literacy only in sub-national languages.
Ratio of broadcast stations in national to sub-national languages.
Ratio of newspapers in the national to sub-national languages.
Ratio of schools in the national to sub-national languages.
Ratio of religious to secular schools.
Ratio of autonomous military groupings to the unified military command.
Ratio of foreign to domestic radio-television audiences.

Indicators of communications integration

Rates of speaking knowledge of national language(s) by linguistic categories of population.
Rates of literacy in the national and sub-national languages by national and sub-national categories of population.
Rate of national newspaper(s) readership by categories of major ethnic/linguistic groups.
Rate of national radio(s) listenership by categories of major ethnic/linguistic groups.
Rate of national television network(s) listenership by categories of major ethnic/linguistic groups.
Rate of electoral participation in national, regional, local and municipal elections.
Rate of membership in national political parties.
Rate of personal identification with national citizenship.
Rate of acceptance of the prevailing system of justice.

Indicators of communications alienation

Rate of personal access to state officials.
Rate of suicide, anomic violence, police violence, criminal violence, political violence.
Rate of critical letters to the editors.
Rate of critical commentaries on radio-television public-affairs shows.
Rate of knowledge of the names of the most important state officials and current political issues.
Rate of feelings of efficacy at national, regional and local levels.
Rate of non-participation in state elections.
Rate of reported psychic disorders.

It is clear that the above indicators are not easily obtainable in all circumstances. However, some of the more conventional ones (literacy and educational participation rates, for example) are part of the national statistical time series in most countries. Others, such as ownership of radio or television sets, might have to be obtained in some countries through other channels. Still others, of a more subjective nature, such as the rate of personal identification with national citizenship as defined by the state (Iranian as opposed to Azari Turkish, Iraqi as opposed to Kurdish, British as opposed to Welsh), would have to be obtained through specially designed random samples of the population. Beyond this, to test specially constructed hypotheses on positive or negative correlations between any of the above indicators in isolation or in aggregates, a further refining of our concepts and indicators might be necessary. Generally, however, we need a plurality of indicators to provide us with maximum flexibility in responding to a diversity of policy or theoretical needs. As Karl Deutsch (quoted in Taylor, 1980, p. 17) aptly puts it:

When we have two indicators, we look for six, eight, ten or twelve indicators. Later when we find twenty or thirty indicators, we may then have to look for methods of *complexity reduction*. We may go back to factor analysis and other methods trying desperately to reduce the amount of evidence. In these fields, what is intended to be a science may very easily become an art once more. But this is a problem that we share with many of the natural sciences as well.

Information resources: varieties and requirements

Given the enormous human and material resource requirements of establishing a national system of reliable statistical time series, the less-developed countries face the perennial problem of how to allocate their limited resources to achieve the highest possible social returns in the indicators field. The dilemma often lies in the choice between comprehensiveness and descending degrees of selectivity, based on the competing merits of different sets of indicators. Each country would have to make a compromise between the universal and the particular, the sets of indicators proposed by the United Nations system and those peculiar to its own conditions and development objectives. Communication-development indicators are, however, scattered among numerous administrative bodies and can be gathered through different methods and procedures. In so far as a comprehensive approach can serve a variety of purposes, descriptive as well as analytic and policy aims, the following major sources of information collection may be identified.

STATISTICS OBTAINED FROM ADMINISTRATIVE DOCUMENTS

There is an abundance of information, some of it of a statistical nature, buried in most administrative documents. The problem in using this type of information is essentially how to sift through the terminological disparities, overlaps, duplications and contradictions of a mine of information in order to arrive at a coherent and meaningful picture of the situation. To do this as best as the circumstances allow, particularly in the less-developed countries where such information is gathered on a piecemeal and haphazard basis, one needs a clear definition of the problem at hand. We need, for instance, a picture of the traditional communications systems, e.g. coffee shops, religious centres, sports houses, social and professional associations etc., before data about their numbers and activities can be extracted from administrative documents. Knowledge about the types and varieties of communication goods and services traded can lead to a monitoring of the export/import data of customs departments.

STATISTICS OBTAINED BY USE OF QUESTIONNAIRES

Questionnaires are used either to provide new information or to supplement information supplied by administrative documents. For useful results to be obtained, questionnaires must be drafted very carefully, and must be sensitive to the rules of economy, clarity and relevance. In the less-developed countries, where illiteracy presents barriers, carefully selected teams of questionnaire re-porters should be trained to undertake the task. Questions which are too sensitive or taboo should be avoided; reporters should be assigned to households and areas in which they would not face prejudice and could be reasonably received. A questionnaire should elicit precise replies which clarify the situation and provide the decision-makers with additional information. The collection of information of too general a character or that was not suitable for immediate use should be avoided as far as possible.

DATA OBTAINED FROM SURVEYS AND PUBLIC-OPINION POLLS

Population surveys such as the census provide a rich source of information for communication indicators. Items such as ownership of radio and television sets, readership of newspapers and books, telephone ownership and usage etc. could be included in such surveys. However, as noted earlier, the conduct of public-opinion polls in the fashion of western democratic societies presupposes the existence of a relatively free media system as well as autonomous centres of power (labour unions, political parties, voluntary associations) that can provide effective support for dissent or opposition to the government or dominant views. In the absence of such conditions, informed opinions cannot be easily formed and opinions held privately cannot be easily made public. Public-opinion polls conducted under conditions of repression often result in such enormous distortions that little value can be attached to their scientific credibility. Open and unstructured interviews would therefore be a better, more effective technique for obtaining credible results.

CONTENT ANALYSIS OF THE MEDIA

The technique of content analysis provides an incomparable method for establishing and monitoring communication indicators. However, as most practitioners of the art know, the construction of appropriate symbolic codes to decode the media messages requires considerable linguistic and cultural knowledge and sensibility. It also requires considerable patience and practice, as well as team-work. Content analysis is particularly useful when and if a particular policy problem has to be addressed, such as the image of women in the media. It would provide an especially effective feedback to producers and policy-makers alike on what conscious or unconscious values and preferences are going into the media messages and how possibly to correct them.

EFFECTS ANALYSIS OF THE MEDIA

By contrast with content analysis, effects analysis is far more difficult to design and far less certain of results. Nielson's ratings are perhaps the best known and least complicated example of effects analysis. Modern communications technologies have further simplified the task of random sampling of a population on their media behaviour. The telephone provides ready access to vast numbers, but in places where its possession is limited to small élites, it would be of limited value. Radio and television sets can now be installed with electronic feedback mechanisms that report the choice of stations and channels at any given moment back to a central switchboard. Letters to the editors, combinations of telephone and radio or television programming, as well as two-way audio and video technologies have provided other examples of immediate feedback on media effects. The computer technologies have also vastly simplified the tasks of collection, storage, processing, retrieval and analysis of large stocks of data. The experimental efforts on media effects have also made great strides in the design of ingenious methods and techniques of effects analysis. One such technique is called 'fidgetometry', in which the subject viewing a film or a television programme sits on a chair that is tied to electronic nodes recording the degree of his or her fidgeting!

Despite all these technological advances, however, the answers to the sociological problématique of media effects are sparse and intermittent. The literature on the subject has grown by leaps and bounds, with the increasing recognition that the media constitute only one among many other social institutions and forces that shape the individual's behaviour (Comstock and Lindsey, 1975). It is extraordinarily difficult if not impossible to say to what extent and in what form the media programmes are responsible for certain types of social behaviour. This is particularly so because most of the media-effects experiments are conducted under laboratory conditions on isolated individuals. Their findings cannot therefore be extended easily to society and social behaviour. Originating mostly from behaviourist psychology, such experiments often ignore the influence of social structures on human behaviour and the fact that the same individuals can behave differently under different social conditions. Nevertheless, experiments can be designed to test the immediate impact (rather than the long-run effects) of certain programmes on representative groups of the population, i.e. children, workers, women, youth etc. This technique is often used to measure the immediate impact of media software, and is known by two general names: *formative evaluation* of software and *pre-testing*. The intent is to use empirical observation of media at work on a small scale in order to modify software until desired effects are achieved. Information collected in these processes, however, can be used both to estimate probable effects of full-scale implementation and to construct more precise indicators for subsequent measurement of effects.

SURVEYS OF PRODUCTION AND CONSUMPTION

If we assume information and communication to consist of a variety of goods and services in the market that are produced, distributed and consumed, surveys could be conducted to find the patterns of supply and demand. However, because information and communication are not often subject to the same laws of scarcity that other commodities are, a solely economic perspective on the problem would be too confining. Nevertheless, the economic dimension applies with respect to certain types of information/communication goods and services, particularly the hardware. Regional and social distributions of information goods and services, for example, correlate highly with income distribution patterns. Surveys of this kind would have to be designed to cover a vast variety of good and services, and at least those in the following categories (Bohner, 1979):

Cultural heritage. This category covers statistics relating to archives and documentation centres, museums and historical sites, archaeological excavations; also statistics on all specialized employment in the field of history, palaeontology and archaeology, as well as all expenditures for particular forms of the cultural heritage, such as festivals and popular folk events. Statistics on the use made of the components of the cultural heritage by categories of the population should form an important part of the information classified.

Printed matter and literature. Production, circulation and content of printed material (books, periodicals, newspapers etc.). This category covers the paper, printing and publishing industries from the level of the semi-finished product to the final consumption of products and services. Also included in this category are libraries, the creative activities of authors, monetary flows and transfers linked with intellectual property of books and other printed materials (i.e. copyright, royalties etc.), as well as information on the cultural content of printed material and of the use made of the 'printed material' and 'literature' by categories of the population.

Music. Production and dissemination of music, participation of the population in musical activities and use of music halls. This category includes the production and commercialization of all relevant forms of hardware: musical instruments, gramophones, records, sound recorders and reproducers, cassettes etc. It also covers the creative activities of musicians and other professionals as well as amateur performance of musical works.

Performing arts. Production and dissemination of performing-art activities, participation of the population in those activities and use of performing-art amenities. This category covers all scenic arts (e.g. theatre, dance, circus). It also includes the construction and upkeep of facilities, the creative activities of artists, amateur performing and participation, as well as the intermediate consumption and activities which are necessary to organize the performances.

Pictorial and plastic arts. Production and dissemination of the arts of painting, sculpture, art handicrafts and adornments, as well as use made of these by the population.

Cinema and photography. Production and distribution of cinematographic and photographic material. This category covers all relevant forms of hardware (cameras, photographic apparatus, projectors etc.), supports for still images, moving images and motion pictures, and the buildings or facilities used for the projection of films. It also covers the activities of professionals and amateurs and intellectual property, as well as information on the use made of these amenities by categories of the population and by region.

Broadcasting. Production, dissemination and content of radio and television communication. This category includes the production, setting-up and commercialization of various forms of hardware for broadcasting and television (e.g. transmitters, networks, receivers etc.). Also included are: the activities of professionals employed in radio and television institutions, together with creative activities, and statistics on the content of radio and television programmes, their accessibility and information on the use made of these amenities by categories of the population and by region.

Socio-cultural and religious activities. Informal channels of communication are often a neglected aspect of the communication system. Under social conditions where the formal channels are completely controlled by the government, however, the informal channels assume a critical importance. In this category are: provision, accessibility and use of cultural facilities; and activities of organizational and social services, including community services (coffee shops, sports houses, cultural centres, youth clubs etc.) and professional associations. The category covers ceremonies and social practices, and activities connected with religious beliefs. It also covers services of private non-profit institutions and household as well as general expenditure for the public administration of culture and communication.

Advertising. Production, dissemination and content of state and commercial advertising, including the number and variety of advertising firms, employment, financial outlays, media outlets, subject-matter, audiences reached, effects on consumer behaviour etc., all fall within this category. Information of this kind is not readily available in most countries and would have to be gathered through a variety of channels and methods.

Data processing. The introduction of computers has revolutionized the communication system of many countries, and yet indicators on data-processing facilities are often neglected. This category includes information about computer facilities by type, ownership and use, 'bits' of information stored and processed (potential as well as actual), costs of hardware and software, varieties of applications and users etc.

News services. Varieties of foreign and domestic news and feature services, employment, income, users etc.

Office communication facilities. A variety of modern communication facilities have transformed life in modern offices, including mimeographing machines, copying machines, adding machines, intercoms, word processors, typewriters, micro-computers etc. However, this kind of information is often neglected in official statistics and would have to be collected perhaps by specially conducted surveys.

Miniaturized media. There is an increasing variety of miniaturized communication technologies which slip by the statisticians but which have had a profound impact on contemporary social and cultural life. This category could include such items as transistor radios and cassette tapes, citizen-band radios, pocket calculators, mini-computers etc. Once again, official statistics are of little help and specially conducted surveys would be needed.

Export/import data. This is a category that cuts across all the others, but is needed in order to establish the situation of a country with respect to its communication and cultural trade. In countries where smuggling constitutes a significant portion of this trade, customs data should be supplemented by surveys of under-the-counter trade.

Communications infrastructure. Last but not least, the communication system is dependent upon an infrastructure that includes transport, power, education, and the ethnic and linguistic composition of the population. Data in all of these categories relevant to the operation of the communication system is indispensable to the compilation of comunication indicators. Such items as literacy rate, roads/railways/airports, electrical-power facilities, languages spoken and written etc. are the most obvious examples among them.

SURVEYS OF ACCESS AND PARTICIPATION

Although production and consumption surveys include some indications of the level of access and participation, communication is a uniquely two-way process and cannot be assumed to be taking place entirely because of the presence of a developed print and broadcasting system. Mass-communication technologies are notoriously one-way and do not elicit feedback or participation on their own. For this reason, surveys of access and participation are necessary. Such surveys should perhaps begin by an assessment of the legal and political environment for communication access and participation, including the provision of guarantees of free speech, existence of autonomous political parties, trade unions, voluntary associations etc. But the surveys should also go on to establish such indicators of access and participation as the level of attendance at cultural, social and political meetings, the ideological, ethnic, linguistic and regional (including rural) diversity of the press, electoral freedom and participation, membership of voluntary associations, membership of and access to cultural and educational facilities etc.

Conclusion

Communication-development indicators are a vast and as yet unexplored territory; they touch on virtually every aspect of life in modern society. However, as tools for communications policy and planning, the concept can be narrowed or broadened to serve specific policy and planning objectives. Apart from the basic distinction made in this chapter between descriptive, analytic and prescriptive indicators, certain policy concerns call for the monitoring of specific well-defined indicators. A concern with the position of women in society, for instance, calls for the monitoring of indicators of the media images of women. A concern with problems of national integration likewise calls for the construction of those communication indicators (such as literacy in the national languages), use of major languages of the country in the national media, employment of ethnic and racial minorities in the media, degree of consensus on national identity, political legitimacy etc.) that are relevant to integration. A policy preoccupation with the social effects of sex and violence in programming would require a monitoring of those communication indicators that concern the content and effects analysis of media programmes, and the like.

Discounting those communication indicators that are generally incorporated into the United Nations statistical yearbooks, there is therefore no consensus on what communication indicators are the most critical and relevant to the processes of development. Every country and every communications planning body would have to make its own choices on the basis of its policy objectives, financial and administrative resources and the immediate problems at hand. Intimate knowledge of the problem at hand, clarity of objectives, flexibility in the choice of methodology and imagination in the construction of relevant communication indicators are, therefore, of the essence.

Annotated bibliography

ADELMAN, I.; MORRIS, C.T. 1967. *Society, Politics and Economic Development: A Quantitative Approach.* Baltimore, Md, Johns Hopkins University Press. An early quantitative approach to the problems of development indicators, interesting both conceptually and methodologically.

ALKER, H.R., Jr. 1966. Causal Inference and Political Analysis. In: J. Bernd (ed.), *Mathematical Application in Political Science.* Dallas, Tex., Southern Methodist University Press.

AMIN, S. 1977. *Unequal Development.* Brighton, Harvester Press.

ARNDT, J. 1968. A Test of the Two-Step Flow in Diffusion of a New Product. *Journalism Quarterly*, 1968, Vol. 45, p. 457–65.

BAN, A.W. Van der. 1964. A Revision of the Flow of Communications Hypothesis. *Gazette*, Vol. 10, NO. 3, p. 237–49.

BARAN, P. 1957. *The Political Economy of Growth.* New York, N.Y., Monthly Review Press.

BASTER, N. (ed.). 1972. *Measuring Development: The Role and Adequacy of Development Indicators.* London, Frank Cass. One of the earliest introductory collections of articles on the subject.

BAUER, R.A. 1966. Detection and Anticipation of Impact: The Nature of the Task. In: R. Bauer (ed.), *Social Indicators.* Cambridge, Mass., Massachusetts Institute of Technology Press.

BECKER, C.L. 1941. *Modern Democracy.* New Haven, Conn., Yale University Press.

BELL, D. 1973. *The Coming of Post-Industrial Society: A Venture in Social Forecasting*. New York, N.Y., Basic Books.

BERELSON, B.; LAZARSFELD, P.F.; McPHEE, W. 1954. *Voting*. Chicago, Ill., University of Chicago Press.

BOHNER, L. 1979. *Indicators of Cultural Development within the European Context*. Paper presented at a meeting of experts on statistics and indicators of culture, Vienna, December 1979.

BRANDT, W., *et al.* 1980. *North–South: A Programme for Survival*. London, Pan.

BURNHAM, J. 1942. *The Machiavellians: Defenders of Freedom*. New York, N.Y., John Day.

CHENERY, H.; SYRQUIN, M. 1975. *Patterns of Development, 1950–70*.

COLEMAN, J.S.; KATZ, E.; MENZEL, H. 1957. The Diffusion of an Innovation among Physicians. *Sociometry*, 20 December, p. 253–70.

COMSTOCK, G.; LINDSEY, G. 1975. *Television and Human Behavior*. Santa Monica, Calif., Rand Corporation.

DEUTSCH, K. 1953. *Nationalism and Social Communication*. Cambridge, Mass., Massachusetts Institute of Technology Press.

ERB, G.F.; KALLAB, V. 1975. *Beyond Dependency: The Developing World Speaks Out*. New York, N.Y., Praeger.

FRANK, A.G. 1969. *Capitalism and Underdevelopment in Latin America*. New York, N.Y., Monthly Review Press.

FREY, F.W. 1973. Communication and Development. In: I. de S. Pool (ed.), *Handbook of Communication*. Chicago, Ill., Rand McNally. Review of the theories of communication and modernization, largely from American perspectives, also including, in the appendix, some useful maps, charts and tables on available cross-national communications-development indicators.

GALTUNG, J. 1978. *Goals, Processes and Indicators of Development*. Tokyo, United Nations University. Outlines of a United Nations University research project on development and development indicators, reflecting the author's original ideas.

GERBNER, G., *et al.* 1969. *The Analysis of Communication Content: Developments in Scientific Theories and Computer Techniques*. New York, N.Y., Wiley & Sons.

——. 1973. Cultural Indicators: The Third Voice. In: L. Gross and W. Melody (eds.), *Communications Technology and Social Policy*. New York, N.Y., Wiley & Sons.

INKELES, A.; SMITH, D.H. 1974. *Becoming Modern: Individual Change in Six Developing Countries*. Cambridge, Mass., Harvard University Press.

KATZ, E. 1968 Diffusion. III. Interpersonal Influence. In: D.L. Sills (ed.), *International Encyclopedia of the Social Sciences*. Vol. 4. New York, N.Y., Macmillan.

KLAPPER, J.T. 1960. *The Effects of Mass Communication*. Glencoe, Ill., Free Press.

LAND, K.C. 1971. On the Definition of Social Indicators. *American Sociologist*. November, Vol. 6, p. 322–5.

——. 1975. Theories, Models and Indicators of Social Change. *International Social Science Journal*, Vol. XXXVII, No. 1.

LAND, K.C.; SPILERMAN, S. 1974. *Social Indicator Models*. New York, N.Y., Russell Sage Foundation.

LASSWELL, H.D. 1927. *Propaganda Technique in the World War*. New York, N.Y., Knopf.

LERNER, D.; PERSNER, L.W. 1958. *The Passing of Traditional Society*. Chicago, Ill., Free Press of Glencoe.

LIN, N. 1969. Information Flow, Influence Flow and the Decision-Making Process—testing a New Conceptualization of the Communication Flow. Unpublished revision of a paper presented at the meeting of the American Association for Education in Journalism, Berkeley, 1969.

LIONBERGER, H.F. 1960. *Adoption of New Ideas and Practices*. Ames, Ia., Iowa State University Press.

LIPPMAN, W. 1922. *Public Opinion*. New York, N.Y., Harcourt Brace.

MACBRIDE, S., *et al.* 1980. *Many Voices, One World: Communication and Society Today and Tomorrow*. Paris, Unesco Press. The controversial Unesco report calling for a New World Information and Communication Order that includes many tables on cross-national communications-development indicators in the context of its arguments for a new balance in the international flow of news, views and images.

McCLELLAND, D. 1961. *The Achieving Society*. Princeton, N.J., Van Nostrand, 1961.

MALCHUP, F. 1980. *Knowledge and Knowledge Production*. Princeton, N.J., Princeton University Press.

MICHELS, R. 1939. *Political Parties* (transl. Eden and Cedar Paul). New York, N.Y., Free Press.

MOWLANA, H. 1976. A Paradigm for Comparative Mass Media Analysis. In: H. Fischer and J. Merril (eds.), *International and Intercultural Communication*. [Place and publishes to be added.]

NORDENSTRENG, K.; VARIS, T. 1974. *Television Traffic—A One-Way Street? A Survey and Analysis of the International Flow of Television Programme Material*. Paris, Unesco.

O'BRIEN, R.C., et al. 1979. *Communication Indications and Indicators of Socio-Economic Development*. Paris, Unesco. A statistical analysis based on the UNRISD Data Bank (1960–70) to test hypotheses on correlations between communication and other types of development indicators. Conclusions are not all that surprising but suggest that communication indicators should be chosen and made a part of a system of national accounts in relation to a country's development strategy and communication policies.

OGBURN, W.F. 1933. *Recent Social Trends*.

ORGANIZATION FOR ECONOMIC CO-OPERATION AND DEVELOPMENT. 1973. *List of Social Concerns Common to Most OECD Countries*. Paris, OECD.

——. 1977. *The OECD Social Indicator Development Programme*. Paris, OECD.

OSTROGORSKI, M. 1902. *Democracy and the Organization of Political Parties*. New York, N.Y., Macmillan.

POOL, I. de S., et al. 1973. *Handbook of Communication*. Chicago, Ill., Rand McNally.

PORAT, M. 1977. *The Information Economy*. Washington, D.C., United States Department of Commerce, Office of Telecommunications.

RAO, M.V.S.; PORWIT, K.; BASTER, N. 1978. *Indicators of Human and Social Development: Report on the State of the Art*. Tokyo, United Nations University. A series of articles from a diversity of perspectives on development indicators with some relevance to communication indicators.

ROGERS, E.M. 1969. *Modernization among Peasants: The Impact of Communication*. New York, N.Y., Holt, Rinehart & Winston.

ROGERS, E.M.; SHOEMAKER, F. 1971. *Communication of Innovations*. New York, N.Y., Free Press of Glencoe.

SCHUMPETER, J.A. 1942. *Capitalism, Socialism, Democracy*. New York, N.Y., Harper & Row.

STERLING, C.H.; HAIGHT, T.R. 1978. *The Mass Media: Aspen Institute Guide to Communication Industry Trends*. New York, N.Y., Praeger Publishers. A comprehensive first attempt at a compilation of communication indicators for the world's most advanced country in communication industries.

TAYLOR, C.L. (ed.). 1980. *Indicator Systems for Political, Economic, and Social Analysis*. Cambridge, Mass., Oelgesschlager, Gunn & Hain. A review of the state of the art from a diversity of American and European perspectives.

TAYLOR, J.G. 1979. *From Modernization to Modes of Production: A Critique of the Sociologies of Development and Underdevelopment*. London, Macmillan.

TEHRANIAN, M. 1979. Development Theory and Communication Policy: The Changing Paradigms. In: M.J. Voigt and G.J. Hanneman (eds.), *Progress in Communication Sciences*, Vol. 1. Norwood, N.J., Ablex Publishing. A critical review of the most important theories of development in the liberal, Marxist and Third World traditions and their relevance to the problems of communication policy and planning.

——. 1980. *Socio-Economic and Communication Indicators in Development Planning: A Case Study of Iran*. Paris, Unesco. A systems approach to communication-development indicators and its application to the case of Iran in the revolutionary 70s, demonstrating the predicative value of communication indicators.

TINBERGEN, J. 1972. *Towards a New World Economy*. Rotterdam, Rotterdam University Press.

UNESCO. 1975. The Social Indicators Programme at Unesco. *International Social Science Journal* Vol. XXVII, No. 1, p. 195–7.

——. 1975. *World Communications: A 200 Country Survey of Press, Radio, Television and Film*. Paris, Unesco. The latest edition in Unesco's periodic publication of world-wide statistical time series on the state of communications-development indicators.

——. 1976. *The Use of Socio-Economic Indicators in Development Planning*. Paris, Unesco Press. A series of articles on the theories, methodologies and applications of development indicators to problems of planning.

——. 1979. *Indicators of Social and Economic Change and Their Applications*. Paris, Unesco.

——. DIVISION OF STATISTICS. 1979. *Preliminary Study of the Scope and Coverage of a Framework for Cultural Statistics*. Paris, Unesco. (CES/AC, 44:8.)

443

UNITED NATIONS. STATISTICAL OFFICE. 1971. *A System of Demographic, Manpower and Social Statistics Series, Classification and Social Indicators*. New York.

UNITED NATIONS RESEARCH INSTITUTE FOR SOCIAL DEVELOPMENT. 1974. The Measurement of Real Progress at the Local Level. *Research Notes* (Geneva), Vol. 4.

UNITED STATES. DEPARTMENT OF HEALTH, EDUCATION AND WLFARE. 1969. *Toward a Social Report*. Washington, D.C., United States Government Printing Office.

——. OFFICE OF MANAGEMENT AND BUDGET, OFFICE OF STATISTICAL POLICY. 1973. *Forward Indications*. Washington, D.C.

Chapter 22

Surveys

H. Dean Nielsen

Surveys are highly structured data-collection procedures which allow researchers to make generalizations about a human population based on information from a sample of respondents. The method involves the use of interviews or questionnaires in collecting answers to carefully constructed questions from a sample of respondents usually drawn at random from a predefined population. Surveys are most often used in describing populations, providing causal explanations of social phenomena, predicting future social conditions, evaluating social programmes and measuring social indicators. Large amounts of data are generally collected which are analysed (often with the assistance of computers) using inferential statistics, which allow one to generalize to a population within known limits of error.

Definition

Although to many the term *survey* means the 'general overview' of a subject or a set of techniques for establishing land boundaries, in contemporary social planning and inquiry the term is most often used to refer to a particular method of gathering information about groups of people. More precisely,

a survey is a method of collecting information about a human population in which direct contact is made with the units of the study (individuals, organizations, communities, etc.) through such systematic means as questionnaires and interview schedules. [Warwick and Lininger, 1975, p. 1–2]

A survey, then, is basically a method of data collection. As a method it serves many different kinds of research needs and disciplines. It is used in market research, in public-opinion polling and in scientific inquiry. In scientific inquiry surveys are often incorporated into the research designs of studies in such fields as sociology, political science, economics, social psychology, social anthropology, demography, public health, agriculture and communications.

Survey research is a particularly attractive approach to data collection for those who would like to be able to make generalizations about an entire human population but who do not have the time or resources to question each of the

445

population's members. This is made posible through the use of carefully drawn samples and through analysis using inferential statistics which allow one to estimate population attributes or characteristics within known limits of error. A 'population' can be defined as broadly or as narrowly as the scope and purpose of the study demand, for example: all voters in a national election; all owners of video tape in a certain metropolitan area; all schools adopting a certain curriculum in a state or district etc. The units in a population are typically individuals, though they may be organizations, such as businesses, schools or households, or communities, such as villages or neighbourhoods.

Collection of data through systematic means implies that surveys are pre-planned and highly structured. The questions posed have been distilled through a process of conceptual clarification, variable specification and oper-ationalization, consultation and pre-testing. In scientific inquiry, survey structure is often derived from social-science theory, data collection being used to confirm or refute hypotheses concerning relationships among socially relev-ant variables. As the above definition points out, survey information is gener-ally collected through questionnaires or interview schedules (scripts). Although a great deal of survey research involves face-to-face contact between an interviewer and a respondent (representing himself/herself or an organiz-ation), surveys may be conducted by mail, by telephone or be administered to groups at places like schools or offices.

A survey as defined above is distinguished from a census by virtue of the fact that it uses only a fraction of a population in making inferences about the population as a whole, whereas a census requires the direct participation of all (or virtually all) of the members of a particular population. For this reason this method of data collection is often referred to as the 'sample survey'. Polls and market research are particular varieties of sample surveys. Polls generally deal with issues of public opinion, and are thus transient and descriptive in nature. Market research is used to investigate phenomena such as the nature and scope of markets and the acceptability of products. Such information may be of vital interest to a certain company or class of companies, but it is rarely of general or public interest. The use of surveys in the various public, commercial and scientific modes mentioned above is often referred to as survey research. In practice the terms *sample survey, survey research* and *surveys* are often used synonymously, and will be so used in the discussion which follows.

History

Survey research as we know it today is rooted in eighteenth- and nineteenth-century England and France, where social reformers used it as a means of revealing the deplorable working and living conditions of urban dwellers. During this period efforts to use survey research in the process of social and economic planning were already apparent, as in the work of the French economist, Frédéric LePlay (Young, 1944). Such efforts culminated in the work of the English statistician, Charles Booth, who between the years 1886 and 1897 documented the results of surveys of urban poverty in his seventeen-volume work, *Life and Labour of the People of London*.

The 1930s and 1940s saw new breakthroughs in survey research methodology, which led to the scientific foundation that it has today. The most important breakthrough was the coupling of probability sampling (first used in agriculture) with controlled-interview techniques. Academics like Rensis Likert (who eventually established the Survey Research Center of the University of Michigan) applied this powerful combination in the study of attitudes and behaviours of large human populations. Others, like Paul Lazersfeld of Columbia University (founder of the Bureau of Applied Social Research) began to apply the above methodologies in hypothesis testing and pioneering explanatory research (Warwick and Lininger, 1975, p. 2–4).

Further developments came during the Second World War, when scientists from a variety of disciplines were mobilized to co-operate in solving various logistics problems. One particular development was the use of single-sample surveys for a variety of purposes, e.g. for simultaneous economic forecasting, opinion polling, needs assessment etc. Finally, the development of computer technology and software appropriate to social science problems in the 1950s and 1960s led to breakthroughs in the size, speed and analytical depth of survey research, allowing researchers to process enormous amounts of data quickly using the most sophisticated of statistical techniques.

Main uses

According to Warwick and Lininger (1975), survey research is most frequently used in: (a) the description of populations; (b) causal explanation; (c) the prediction of future conditions; (d) the evaluation of social programmes; and (e) the measurement of social indicators. Each of these uses will be elaborated upon below and, when appropriate, related to the framework of communication planning described in this book. This section will then conclude with a brief description of the common abuses of survey research.

Description of populations. The most common use of survey research is to provide descriptions of populations. This use is most appropriate during the analysis stage of communications planning (see the ASDAL model in 'A conceptual framework for communication planning'—Chapter 2 above). During this stage surveys can be effectively used to describe the social characteristics of potential programme participants (i.e. in developing baseline data). In addition, surveys can reveal much about the socio-economic environment of a proposed communications project, and much about the needs and resources of the target population in a communications intervention. Such uses of survey research are most appropriate within the comprehensive-planning approach, since they assume a relatively stable environment and communications system and a population which is capable of identifying and articulating its needs, resources, attitudes and values. In less stable situations where incremental-planning approaches are more appropriate, highly structured surveys are clearly not possible and other forms of data collection should be employed.[1]

Causal explanation. The researcher can use surveys in developing explanations for social conditions and phenomena. Generally, this involves the relatively formal process of hypothesis testing, but it may also involve various kinds of causal modelling using survey data in sophisticated statistical procedures such as path analysis. Such use of survey research is possible in both the strategy and the learning stages of communications planning, although it is more often used for less applied purposes, e.g. theory-building and the creation of knowledge.

Prediction of future conditions. It is often the explicit purpose of public-opinion polling, market research or economic forecasting to predict conditions that will exist in the future. The pollster, market researcher or forecaster is interested in how the public might react if, say, a certain candidate were nominated for public office or a certain product were introduced into the market. Since it often requires that respondents respond to hypothetical conditions ('How would you feel if . . .'), the results are not always highly accurate predictors, especially since dissemination of the survey results is in itself likely to influence future behaviour (self-fulfilling or 'self-defeating' prophecies). Nevertheless, such predictions are often used in the development of communications strategies, as for example, by predicting how many television receivers there will be in a certain area within a given time period.

Evaluation of social programmes. During the past decade, as programme administrators have been more and more often held accountable for the resources they use in a project, survey research has become increasingly important in evaluating social programmes. Evaluation is the process of 'delineating, obtaining, and providing useful information for judging decision alternatives' (D.L. Stufflebeam, in: Worthen and Sanders, 1973, p. 129). Surveys are effectively used in obtaining information, especially that relating to the knowledge, attitudes and practices of individuals. Survey results can help decision-makers assess the effectiveness of an intervention and the extent to which processes operate according to project plans. They can be used by decision-makers in formulating revisions and improvements during the course of project implementation (formative evaluation) or in making judgements about overall programme worth and sustainability (summative evaluation). Within the communications planning framework of this volume, evaluation is most

---

1. One such form is called the 'rapid reconnaissance survey', which combines network analysis with semi-structured interviewing to form a quick portrait of a project context. For a description of this methodology, see Honadle (1979) and Mickelwait (1979).

appropriate at the learning phase. Typical areas of evaluation in communications planning can be seen within the KAP[1] framework:

KNOWLEDGE: Reception of a message; recall of the content; understanding of the content.
ATTITUDES: Acceptance of a message or point of view; change of attitude.
PRACTICE: Change in social behaviour; change in media use; adoption or innovation.

Measurement of social indicators. Survey research as a tool for measuring social indicators emerged in the 1960s as the result of pressure to monitor the social and political equivalents of familiar economic indicators (such as the wholesale price index). A social indicator is, essentially, one of a number of indices which reveal social trends and conditions, and which must be measured at regular intervals. Examples could be job satisfaction, health status, leisure-time activities, satisfaction with government services etc. Such indicators are often collected by governments (census bureau) to assist them in the planning of government policies. Communications planners would be interested in only those social indicators having a direct relationship to media use. For example, the social indicator on leisure-time activity might indicate a change over time in movie-going or television-viewing among certain segments of the population. This information could then aid communications planners with decisions relating to media extension.

ABUSES OF SURVEY RESEARCH

Survey research is used inappropriately almost as often as it is used appropriately. Since it is a popular and relatively straightforward research method, it is often used when other means of social inquiry would be more appropriate. It is also possible for researchers to violate the norms of survey research through carelessness in safeguarding the confidentiality of data, or by neglecting to feed survey results back to respondents. Some problems for which survey research is an inappropriate research method are:
Problems which require the judgement of experts. As an example of this, it would be inappropriate to ask classroom teachers to assess the extent to which a particular text book is consistent with the official curriculum if they were to have only a vague notion of curriculum requirements. Such assessment should rather be elicited from those in the educational system, curriculum-development specialists or others, who are thoroughly familiar with curriculum requirements.
Problems relating to the implementation of a particular procedure. A respondent

1. The KAP survey was pioneered by demographers and population researchers to assess the success of family-planning campaigns. Its has subsequently been applied in other areas of social research and planning.

449

will generally try to show himself/herself in the best possible light. There may well be, therefore, a tendency to exaggerate the extent to which desired behaviours have taken place. The best way to assess the implementation of a procedure is through direct observation.

Problems involving historical events. The best way to find out what happened in the past is to refer to appropriate historical documents, not to survey individuals concerning what they remember of particular past events. For example, to find out whether all levels of government were involved in a planning process it is more reasonable to check the minutes of planning meetings than it is to ask participants to try to recall who was present and who did what at a meeting.

Problems involving complex behaviours under controlled conditions. Sometimes survey researchers attempt to collect information which can only be accurately obtained in a laboratory setting, e.g. information about certain kinds of learning disabilities. The respondent may him/herself be unaware of certain problems (such as vision impairment, colour blindness etc.) or, if aware, may be unwilling to acknowledge or reveal them to an interviewer whose background and intentions are not well understood.

Problems of a highly personal or sensitive nature. There is considerable cross-cultural variation in the extent to which certain topics are open for discussion with outsiders. The researcher must be sensitive to cultural norms and values in order to avoid asking questions in areas that are taboo.

Advantages and disadvantages

The main advantages and disadvantages of survey research are listed below. It should be noted that some features which appear to be advantages from one point of view can be seen as disadvantages from another. For example, the highly structured nature of survey research is an advantage from the point of view of administrative control and data coding, but from the point of view of flexibility—the ability to respond to unexpected conditions in the field—the highly structured nature of survey research is a constraint.

ADVANTAGES

1. Surveys yield *'grass roots' information* from and about a population which is inaccessible through other means. This information can often correct mistaken assumptions based upon conventional wisdom or wishful thinking.
2. Surveys are *highly structured*, thereby providing the researcher with considerable control over the data-collecting situation and allowing him/her to determine in advance a reasonable range of response categories. Such structure also allows for relative ease in replication and in conducting longitudinal studies.
3. Results of survey research can be *generalized to the target population* through the use of proper sampling techniques and inferential statistics. It is also

possible, using statistical means, to determine population parameters so that the levels of confidence in the findings can be known.

4. Since surveys involve only a fraction of a population, they are *relatively inexpensive* and require much less time for data collection and analysis than a full census of the population.

5. Survey research can be used for *hypothesis testing and other forms of causal analysis*. For example, surveys can produce data on both the social characteristics of respondents and on their attitude and/or behaviour changes. The relationships between these two kinds of variables can then be examined further if desired.

DISADVANTAGES

1. Survey research lacks certain kinds of flexibility—this is the dark side of being highly structured. Survey research is not amenable to the constant adjustments in approach and point of view that characterize grounded or ethnographic research. It may also, by its very structuring of responses, push people towards a mind set much closer to that of the investigator and away from the respondent's own.

2. Survey research lacks the qualitative depth of other kinds of studies. The emphasis on quantifiable variables and extensive coverage of a population means that there is little opportunity for survey researchers to pursue topics in depth by probing beneath the surface of responses to survey questions.

3. Survey research carries a relatively high administrative burden. This is a disadvantage not shared by case studies (which are often conducted by one individual), laboratory research and historical or library research. The administrative burden includes the long process of instrument development, the training and supervision of field-workers (interviewers) and the management of a large volume of collected data.

4. Survey research is subject to various kinds of systematic bias which threaten the validity and reliability of the data. Besides the biases introduced by the structure of the survey itself, biases from the interviewer and biases from the respondent may also occur. Unless the interviewer is experienced or well-trained, he/she may have a tendency to add a personal touch to questions, to coach or tip the respondent towards particular answers, record answers according to his/her own preferences, encourage certain responses by giving an undue amount of approval etc. These biases can be overcome by careful training, but since the supervisor cannot be present at each interview, he/she can never be sure how much interviewer bias is entering. There are a number of respondent biases: the courtesy bias, the ingratiation bias, the social-desirability bias, the 'sucker' bias.[1] In general these biases result in responses which represent something other than the respondent's

---

1. An in-depth discussion of each of these biases is beyond the scope of this section. For such, see Warwick and Lininger, 1975, p. 201–20.

true feelings, stemming from the desire to be polite, to please, to seem reasonable or to trick or make a fool of the interviewer. Such biases can generally be avoided by careful instrument construction, although one must be aware that the tendencies or pressures towards such biases are stronger in some cultures than in others (see, for example, Jones, 1963).

5. Surveys are often met with certain forms of resistance. In the western industrialized countries surveys have become so commonplace that they are often seen as a nuisance. For that reason, and because people are sometimes suspicious of interviewers' motives, there tends to be a high refusal rate among participants. In other countries surveys might be so much of a novelty that advance publicity leads either to response bias or to forms of social/political resistance.

Resource requirements

The most important resource for carrying out survey research (and the one most often neglected) is a solid set of well-defined concepts and purposes. Next in importance are the human resources: experts in research design, sample selection, questionnaire construction, data collection, management and analysis; interviewers and field supervisors; office personnel; coders and tabulators; and, if necessary, computer programmers.

The decision whether or not to use a computer for data processing needs to be made in the survey planning stage. If a computer will be used, access to one of appropriate size and configuration, as well as access to appropriate software (computer programs), must be assured. In addition an important, and sometimes neglected, resource is access to respondents. This is best assured by acquiring all necessary authorization or at least endorsement from the proper authorities. In some societies, for example, letters of introduction or authorization are mandatory before survey research can be initiated. Finally, there must be sufficient finances to cover staff salaries, costs of printing and distributing questionnaires (if not by interviewer), office expenses, transportation-to-field costs and costs associated with report production and distribution.

Level of confidence

If the best survey research techniques are rigorously followed, relatively high levels of confidence can be placed on survey results. One of the advantages of survey research over less-structured research forms (case studies, historical analysis etc.) is that, with surveys, various estimates of error or bias can be calculated at important steps of the research (e.g. sample selection, data collection and data analysis). For example, if random-sampling procedures are carefully followed, one can compute a measure (called the standard error of estimate) that will indicate the extent to which a smaple attribute is representative of that of the population. In addition, developers of scales for the assessment of attitudes and values can determine coefficients of reliability (internal consistency and stability over time) and validity.

Finally, analytical results which compare groups of respondents or which test hypotheses can be tested for statistical significance. The results of such tests (e.g. *chi*-square, *t*-test, *T*-test) indicate the probability that a certain finding could have occurred by chance. Those findings which have a greater than 5 per cent probability of occurring by chance are usually rejected as not statistically significant.

Procedures

There are no strict conventions in the conduct of survey research. Many of the details depend upon the purposes of the survey and the resources of the organization which is administering it. There are, however, some general steps which time and experience have shown to be basic, namely:

1. Conceptualization and design.
2. Sample selection.
3. Instrument development.
4. Data collection.
5. Data management and analysis.
6. Reporting and feedback.

These steps need not be strictly sequential. For example, it is sometimes advisable to suspend final decisions on sample composition until instruments have been drafted and tried out. In some surveys certain data-management tasks (e.g. coding) can proceed at the same time as data collection is under way. Or, as it is often helpful to have a vision of the final product from the beginning, some survey researchers may even find it useful to construct 'dummy tables' of the kind of data they intend to report, and then to work backwards in planning the developmental steps. Each of the above steps will now be described in more detail.

CONCEPTUALIZATION AND DESIGN

Clarifying purposes and goals. Before anything else, survey researchers must clarify the purposes and goals of their survey; in other words, they must specify the reason for which the survey is being conducted and what the expected outcomes of the survey are. This is especially crucial if the survey is being conducted for another party—a school district, government agency, business concern etc. This clarifying process is made easier for the researcher when the decision-makers (those requesting the survey) articulate or write down the questions which they intend the survey to answer.

Establishing definitions. In most cases the decision-makers' questions will be stated rather generally and imprecisely. The researcher, in consultation with the decision-makers, must establish precise definitions of terms and concepts in order to clear up any conceptual ambiguities that might otherwise arise. The researcher must then create operational definitions, further elaboration of terms and concepts for the express purpose of suggesting possible survey questions. Let us consider a hypothetical management question. Managers often ask questions like, 'How effective was the radio campaign on family planning?' The researcher must first of all determine what the decision maker means by 'effective'. Would the decision-maker consider the campaign effective if a high proportion of the target population simply received the campaign message, or is the decision-maker interested in attitude change or even behaviour change? Let us assume in this example that for the decision-maker 'effectiveness' includes all three of the above. The problem the researcher now faces is that of determining the decision-maker's concept of 'effectiveness' in each of those three areas. For example, with respect to reception of the above campaign message, the researcher must determine whether merely hearing the radio broadcast constitutes 'effective' reception as far as the decision-maker is concerned, or whether 'effective' reception must include understanding that message. Is hearing one broadcast enough, or is it necessary for a series to be heard (and/or understood)? Perhaps by the time all such probing has been completed, the original question will have been broken down into many sub-questions written in operational terms which make clear what data needs to be collected. Returning to the example, one step in assessing the effectiveness of the family-planning radio campaign might consist in answering the question, 'What proportion of the target population correctly identified the main themes of the three radio broadcasts on family planning during the past month?'

Developing a research design. Once all important terms and concepts are carefully defined and operationalized, it is essential that the researcher develop an appropriate research design. Again it should be pointed out that the survey may be only one part of the overall research project. If such is the case, then the basic research design may already be specified. In other cases, the survey will stand by itself and the researcher will need to develop his/her own design.

There is a wide variety of survey-design possibilities, ranging from a simple, one-time-only cross-sectional design, to a highly complex longitudinal design involving one or more control groups. Once again, the choice depends on the purpose of the survey and the resources of the sponsor. In general, surveys which are intended to be descriptive or predictive (polls, market research etc.) require relatively simple designs—sometimes a single data collection is enough. Surveys which purport to explain or evaluate often require a series of data collections over time so that change can be measured. Some surveys of this latter type are conducted to determine whether or not an intervention or treatment produced certain desired outcomes. In such situations, researchers should survey not only those receiving the treatment, but also a comparable group of people (a control group which did not receive the treatment) in order to establish whether or not change was associated with the treatment or was likely to have happened anyway.

Much has been written on the various research designs, their strengths and weaknesses (see especially Campbell and Stanley, 1963), and a detailed discussion of them is clearly beyond the scope of this section. The following is simply a list of possible design types, ordered roughly in terms of complexity and rigour:

1. *Single cross-section.* The collection of data at a single point in time from a sample chosen to represent a population.
2. *Successive samples.* The collection of data from a series (two or more) of samples drawn from the same population. (Sometimes used in trend analysis).
3. *Panel studies.* The collection of similar sets of data from the same sample on two or more successive occasions.
4. *Experimental designs.* Collection of data before and after a 'treatment' from both a treatment and a control group. 'True' experimental designs are achieved only when respondents are randomly assigned to either the treatment or the control groups.

Planning the survey. Surveys are highly structured data-collection events involving a series of rather complex steps which must be carefully co-ordinated. This means that surveys must be well planned. Planning a survey involves deciding what tasks need to be done, estimating the length of time needed to do each, assigning the various tasks to appropriate staff members and estimating costs. Once a plan has been drafted it should be possible to see whether the available resources—time, human and financial—are sufficient to carry out the tasks envisioned. If not, efforts to increase resources or, if that is not possible, to cut back on the scope of work may be necessary.

The general survey task categories are, again: conceptualization and design; sample selection; instrument development; data collection; data management and analysis; and reporting and feedback. In a well-planned survey, each of these will be broken down further into specific activities.

SAMPLE SELECTION

One of the most critical tasks in survey research is that of selecting an appropriate sample, a sample which is sufficiently representative of a population to permit the research to generalize about the population as a whole. In general, the subtasks involved in sample selection are:

Defining the target population. A target population is the group of individuals, organizations or communities about which conclusions will be drawn. Among factors contributing to the definition of a target population are location, age and time parameters, and the unit of analysis (individual or group). Target populations could include, for example: the mothers of all students enrolled in the third grade in Washington County schools during school year 1981–82; all manufacturing organizations in the state of São Paulo employing more than

100 employees in 1980; all Indonesian subscribers to *Newsweek* magazine during the period 1975–80.

Compiling a list of elements of the population. The researcher needs a list of all individuals of groups about which conclusions will be drawn. Often such lists can be obtained from organizations such as census bureaux, chambers of commerce, schools or school boards, or business organizations. Where there are no ready-made lists, however, the task of compiling one rests with the researcher.

Determining the number/proportion of the population which is to be included. This determination is a matter of judgement and should be based upon such considerations as: (a) the homogeneity of the population (the more homogeneous the population, the smaller the sample size need be for valid generalizations); (b) the level of precision demanded (the higher the precision demanded the larger the sample size required); (c) the complexity of the analysis design (some statistical procedures require a minimum number of cases); and (e) the human, financial and temporal resources available. For beginners in survey research, a general rule of thumb is that samples should represent not less than 10 per cent of a population.

Drawing the sample. It is usually preferable to draw a sample from the population in such a way that any one element has the same chance of being selected as any other element. This procedure is known as probability (or random) sampling; not because it is haphazard or unsystematic, but because the elements are chosen by chance—by flipping coins, drawing numbers out of a hat or using a table of random numbers. Variations on simple random sampling are *stratified sampling* (in which subgroups or strata are sampled separately), *area sampling* (in which sampling is done in contingent stages, areas first and then units within the selected areas) and *cluster sampling* (in which elements for a sample are chosen from the population in groups or clusters—like classrooms—rather than singly).

INSTRUMENT DEVELOPMENT

The survey instrument is the means by which the researcher structures the data-collecting situation. Instrument development is basically a process of drafting questions and of then refining them through review, pre-testing (piloting), revision and further pre-testing. A general idea of questions to be asked will already have been indicated by the operational definitions arrived at during the conceptualization of the survey. However, before any questions are drafted, a few preliminary steps should be taken.

Preliminary steps. First, the researcher must decide whether to collect data through face-to-face interviewing or by some other method, such as telephone interviewing, mailed questionnaires or self-administered questionnaires in group settings (e.g. schools, offices, workshops, shopping centres etc.). The decision will have an influence on the format and language of the instrument (for example, interview schedules are generally more conversational than questionnaires, whereas questionnaires can use more visual aids). Second, the researcher should comb the research literature related to the subject of the survey to see if there are already questions or scales available which adequately cover certain aspects of the survey (attitude scales, for instance). Third, the researcher should determine whether a variable is to be measured using a single item or a series or set of items, sometimes called scales, remembering that scales are much more stable or reliable in measuring a construct than single items. Finally, a researcher must decide whether to design questions as open-ended or closed (having fixed alternatives).

Writing questions. The real art in question writing—and good questionnaires clearly are works of art—comes in designing closed or fixed-alternative questions. In most cases, however, the questionnaire developer will not need to invent completely new question types or formats. A wide variety of formats are already available, including:

1. The simple yes/no, agree/disagree format, which generally allows for a 'don't know' response.
2. Check-lists of various kinds, for example, 'which of the following kinds of reading have you done during the past week? (check as many as apply)'.
3. Forced choice, which generally have the following kind of format, 'which of the following most closely represents your opinion about ...'.
4. Intensity scales, such as the popular Likert scale, which presents a statement and then asks the respondent to choose among 'strongly agree, agree, uncertain, disagree or strongly disagree'.
5. Frequency scales, which present a behaviour (or series of behaviours) and then ask the respondent to tell 'how often' they do such things, using such categories as 'often, sometimes, rarely, never'.
6. Semantic differential scales, requiring the respondent to rate items (persons, institutions, events, commodities etc.) on a seven-point scale with each end-point anchored by an adjective or phrase, usually contrasting pairs like good–bad, pleasant–unpleasant, restrained–spontaneous, active–passive.
7. Ranking questions, in which the respondent is asked to arrange a series of options in order according to personal preference or judgement.

In writing questions it is important that vocabulary be at the appropriate level (to ensure comprehension), that meaning is clear and unambiguous, that appropriate grammar is used and that questions are not leading or 'loaded', thereby nudging the respondent in the direction of a particular response. First drafts of questions should be sumbitted to colleagues for review or given preliminary try-outs. After obvious vocabulary and grammar errors, ambiguities and biases are eliminated, a pre-test instrument, in which sequencing and layout have also been considered, should be constructed.

Pre-testing. The only way to judge for certain whether or not a set of questions will 'work' is to pre-test them with a small but representative group of respondents. In addition to demonstrating the adequacy of questionnaire items and instructions, pre-tests also yield important information about the quality of interviewers, the length of time required for data collection and the approximate rate and reasons for refusal. In assessing the adequacy of items questionnaire developers should be on the look-out for questions that are embarrassing, confusing, ambiguous or too difficult. In addition, local use of language is sometimes a problem, especially in localities composed of different ethnic groups. A well-designed questionnaire/interview should quickly put respondents at ease. It should cover the range of possible responses for each issue or topic. Response categories which prove to be unused in the pre-test should, in most cases, be eliminated or revised. Problem questions, once revised, should be pre-tested again, if possible.

DATA COLLECTION

There are two basic approaches to survey-data collection: by interviewing, either face-to-face or by telephone; or by the use of questionnaires, which are either mailed or personally administered to groups or individuals.

Like question-writing, good interviewing is as much an art as a science. It is therefore important that much care be taken in the selection and training of interviewers. A crucial consideration in the selection of interviewers is an appropriate match between the prospective interviewer and the prospective respondents, especially with respect to age, sex, education, race or ethnicity and personal appearance. In addition, some consideration should be given to intangibles such as personability, thoroughness, trustworthiness and ability to follow instructions. During training each question should be reviewed so that interviewers thoroughly understand both question content and purpose. Interviewers should be taught not to deviate from the written text of the questions unless the answer is unclear or incomplete, at which point they should be urged to 'probe' with a neutral follow-up question like, 'Could you tell me more?' Role-playing and practice runs are helpful in building the skill and confidence of interviewers. Once data collection is under way, thorough field supervision, involving daily debriefings, quality reviews and spot-checking, is advisable. If there are omissions or discrepancies in the data, a return visit is much easier during this period than at a later date.

The use of mailed or self-administered questionnaires generally involves fewer logistical problems than interviewing, but of course, these procedures present challenges of their own. The main challenge with mailed questionnaires is attaining a sufficiently high response rate. This can often be facilitated by the use of a well-written cover letter and follow-up reminders by mail or telephone. With questionnaires administered to groups the researcher must make sure respondents answer independently, without comparing or sharing answers. With questionnaires that are either mailed or administered to groups there is a danger that respondents will fail to understand or adequately answer a question. If this occurs during an interview, the interviewer can probe for a more adequate answer. With self-administered questionnaires, one of the only ways to overcome such a problem is for the researcher to present the questions one by one by reading them aloud to the group and then watching members of the group as they attempt to answer them. If confusion is detected, brief clarifications may be given.

DATA MANAGEMENT AND ANALYSIS

Data management. Prior to analysis, survey data must be checked, labelled, classified and stored. This is the problem of data management. As soon after collection as possible the researcher must check the results to see if answers are clear and complete. In addition, questionnaires or interview schedules should be assigned an identification number so that they can be easily accessed and so that the confidentiality of responses can be safeguarded. In cases where computer analysis is required, numerical values should be assigned to each response category of each question (the process of coding). Sometimes survey researchers like to place the numerical code for a particular response on the questionnaire itself. This is called 'pre-coding' and makes the process of data management easier. Computerized data processing also requires that data be punched on to computer cards or entered on to tapes or discs by key punching. Once the data has been punched, a listing of that data should be made. Listings can then be examined and 'cleaned', by eliminating punches which are out of place or beyond the range of possible values for each particular item. Cleaned data which will be processed by computer can be stored on cards, tape or disc.

Analysis. The type of data analysis employed depends in large part on the purposes of the survey. Surveys which are largely for descriptive purposes (polls, market research, social indicators) will often require nothing more complex than measures of central tendency (means, median, mode, standard deviation) or frequency distributions (proportions of respondents choosing a certain response category). Slightly more complex, but still descriptive, are cross-tabulations of various kinds, in which frequencies on one question are tabulated separately for each category of another question (e.g. attitude-question responsed broken down by the age, sex or socio-economic status of the respondents).

Surveys used for explanatory purposes or for evaluation will often employ more complex procedures, including cross-tabulation using three or more variables, analysis of variance or covariance, simple and multiple correlation, simple and multiple regression analysis, canonical correlation and path analysis. The purpose of most such complex statistical procedures is to allow the researcher to assess the strength of association among two or more variables while holding constant or controlling for the influence of other variables.

Although theoretically any of the above procedures could be done by hand,

hand calculation is enormously time-consuming for any but the simplest of descriptive statistics. Mini-computers can adequately handle the analysis demands of relatively small surveys (e.g. fewer than thousand respondents). But for speed and overall ease in handling data with larger samples, or for surveys with a large number of questions (e.g. more than one hundred), a large mainframe computer is preferable. Computer programs for appropriate analysis are often provided by the manufacturers (in the case of minicomputers) or are available in one of the widely used statistical packages, usch as the Statistical Package for the Social Scientist (S P S S).

REPORTING AND FEEDBACK

There is no standard report format for survey research. However, most reports provide explanation of purposes and design of the survey, describe procedures used for sample selection and data collection and summarize survey outcomes. Generally findings are summarized in the form of tables and graphs. Surveys for explanatory, predictive or evaluative purposes also require narrative summaries which discuss interpretation, conclusions and implications (policy and theoretical). In some cases (e.g. polls, market research, evaluation research) the timing of reporting is crucial, since survey results might influence the results of an election or policy decisions about the future of a certain programme.

Case example

The Indonesian Government, in its efforts to achieve universal primary education, is currently developing an innovative primary education delivery system called the Pamong Primary School System. Pamong uses programmed materials and procedures, small-group interaction and peer- and cross-age tutoring. Such innovations allow the school to operate with fewer professional teachers than are traditionally required, thus freeing some teachers to visit village learning centres to bring educational opportunities to village youth (school drop-outs) during times when they are free from work.

Evaluation of Pamong during its pre-dissemination phase involving schools throughout an entire regency in Bali requires the assessment of student achievement and attitudes. Attitudes were assessed through the use of an attitude survey.

Conceptualization. In conceptualizing the survey, care was taken to determine just what attitudes were considered by Indonesian educators to be important outcomes of primary schooling. A review of documents revealed that the acquisition of the attitudes contained within the state ideology called Pancasila was considered highly desirable. A study of the Pancasila revealed five principal themes. A research design was created in which participants in Pamong-system schools were compared with students in conventional schools with respect to the change in their endorsement of attitudes consistent with

Pancasila over the course of an academic year. The basic hypothesis to be tested was that there would be at least the same amount of attitude change in a positive direction in the Pamong schools as in conventional schools (even though Pamong schools had fewer professional teachers).

Sample selection. The population within the Pamong system for the year in question consisted of fifth- and sixth-graders from twenty-one schools, three in each of the seven subregencies of the target regency. Researchers decided to draw a cluster sample involving all of the fifth- and sixth-graders from one school of the three in each subregency. Comparable clusters would be drawn from conventional schools in the same area, matched as closely as possible with Pamong schools in terms of facilities, teacher experience and community socio-economic status. In sum, the sample included the pupils (thirty-five/forty per class) from twenty-eight classrooms representing the the fifth and sixth grades from seven Pamong and seven non-Pamong schools, or approximately 500 students from each.

Instrument development. Fortunately, an instrument with items covering each Pancasila theme had already been drafted by an education ministry team for use among teenagers in Java. The main instrument-development task was to adapt this instrument for use among elementary-school children in Bali. A set of items was first given to a Balinese anthropologist who analysed it for cultural biases and non-Balinese use of national language. Once the gross cultural problems were eliminated, the items were tested with small groups of school-age children through in-depth interviews, in which the children could suggest better ways to ask the questions. After revision the full set of questions was tried out during a pre-test in two representative classrooms. The try-out served two purposes: to find items which were still difficult for the children to understand; and to see how well and how quickly local teachers could administer the questionnaire to children in their classrooms.

Data collection. Data were collected with self-report questionnaires administered simultaneously to all members of a classroom by a classroom teacher. The teacher read the questions one by one while the students followed along. The teacher then observed as each student checked one of the answers provided. Questionnaires were administered at both the beginning and the end of the school year.

Data management and analysis. After data collection each questionnaire was inspected for obvious discrepancies and assigned an identification number. Back at the main office the questionnaires were coded and values were entered on to a 'floppy' disc. Frequency distributions were computed for all items for both the Pamong and conventional school samples using a minicomputer. Data from the year-end collection will be similarly analysed. The comparison of change between the Pamong and conventional group will be done by analysis of covariance, in which post-test data will be compared holding pre-test data constant. A report on the affirmation or refutation of the basic hypothesis (that attitude change in Pamong would be at least as positive as that in conventional schools) would be included as part of the summative evaluation of the Pamong system during its pre-dissemination phase.

Bibliography

CAMPBELL, D.T.; J.C. STANLEY. 1963. *Experimental and Quasi-Experimental Designs for Research.* Chicago, Ill., Rand McNally.

HONADLE, G. 1979. *Rapid Reconnaissance Approaches to Organizational Analysis for Development Administration.* Washington, D.C.

JONES, E.L. 1963. The Courtesy Bias in South-East Asian Surveys. *International Social Science Journal,* Vol. XV, No. 1, p. 70–6.

MICKELWAIT, D.R. 1979. Information Strategies for Implementing Rural Development. In: Honadle and Klauss (eds.), *International Development Administration: Implementation Analysis for Development Projects.* New York, N.Y., Praeger.

SINGARIMBUN, M.; EFFENDI, S. 1981. *Metode Penelitian Survai* [Survey Research Methods], 2nd ed. Yogyakarta, Indonesia, Center for Population Studies, Gadjah Mada University. (In Indonesian.)

WARWICK, D.P.; LININGER, C.A. 1975. *The Sample Survey: Theory and Practice.* New York, N.Y., McGraw-Hill.

WORTHEN, B.R.; SANDERS, J.R. (eds.) 1973. *Education Evaluation: Theory and Practice.* Belmont, Calif., Worthington.

YOUNG, P. 1944. *Scientific Social Surveys and Research.* Englewood Cliffs, N.J., Prentice-Hall.

Chapter 20

Case study

John Middleton

Case study is a form of a naturalistic inquiry useful in studying complex social processes from a holistic prospective. The method involves the study of processes as they occur in the social environment, without intervention of the researcher either to control variables or to impose predetermined units of measurement of outputs. The purpose of the method is to increase understanding, not to verify prior hypotheses and propositions. As such, the method is well suited for a variety of purposes where planners and decision-makers are concerned with learning about process and context. The method is weak in studying communication effects, or where generalization beyond the instance studied is required.

Definition and purpose

A case study is a detailed analysis and description of some real-life process or phenomenon in the context of its environment (Anderson and Ball, 1975, p. 60). Its purpose is to organize ' . . . the details of life in search of patterns and insights' (Schramm, 1971). It may focus on an institution or organization, on a social process or on a project or activity. It often centres on a decision or set of decisions, seeking to explain why those decisions were taken and with what effect (Schramm, 1971). Cases may be done after the fact, after a communication project has been completed for example, or they may be done while a process is under way.

Case-study methodology is often defined in contrast with other forms of research and evaluation, notably experiments and surveys. The principal difference lies in the purposes for which the different methods are used. Experiments and surveys are typically used to test hypotheses, propositions and models advanced by the researcher. Case studies, on the other hand, are used to expand understanding of complex phenomena, not with testing previously developed propositions.[1] These differing purposes reflect the different philo-

---

1. Both purposes, and both kinds of research, are valid and important. The discussion here is not meant to favour one approach over the other, but rather to increase understanding of the case-

sophical or epistemological bases of the two approaches.[2] Experimental and survey research has a positivistic basis, in which the investigator seeks to identify the 'facts' about a social process, and their causal relationships, as external and scientifically verifiable elements of reality. Thus social researchers apply scientific method to the study of society in the same way that physicists apply it to natural phenomena. Case study, on the other hand, is a typical methodology of a research approach known as *naturalistic inquiry*, which has a phenomenological basis. It is concerned with understanding social reality from the point(s) of view of people engaged in the process under study. It is concerned with subjective reality.

In sum, conventional inquiry is concerned with verifying propositions and theories with a view to establishing objective 'truths' or laws about social processes independent of the subjective perceptions of people engaged in the process. Case study, as a form of naturalistic inquiry, is concerned with increasing understanding of reality as people perceive it. Naturalistic inquiry through case study is concerned with helping key actors in a process tell their story, and verifying and integrating these stories to come up with a coherent and verified story of the whole. These very fundamental differences in purpose are reflected in the types of research and evaluation problems for which the two approaches are used, the way research is designed, the way in which data are collected and analysed and the way in which results are used.

Conventional research approaches are employed when the researcher seeks to establish laws or patterns which can be generalized from the research to other instances of the processes or problems. Thus, there is great concern for such things as sampling, experimental design, control or measurement of variables in the process being studied, and quantification of measures to permit the establishment of associative or causal relationships through the combined force of design and statistical analysis. Case study, on the other hand, is primarily concerned with achieving understanding of a particular process or phenomenon. Case-study researchers seek to generalize about the case, portraying—with data and analysis—patterns of relationships and causation which explain how a particular process functions. Occasionally, generalizations will be made from a case to similar cases, as when a case study of an educational-media project is used as a guide to planning or decision-making for a similar project in a different place and at a different time. When such generalizations are made, the relevance of the case for the new situation is judged by the decision-maker by comparing the elements of the case with the elements of his/her own situation. This is a main reason why cases must be rich in description and detail. In conventional research, the generalizability of findings is determined by the adequacy of the methodology employed: there is

---

study method in contrast with some more widely practised approaches to research and evaluation. Moreover, researchers, especially evaluators, are increasingly combining elements of both approaches.

2. For a more complete discussion of these ideas, see Guba (1978).

tacit agreement between the researcher and the users of research on the degree to which a particular research design and statistical analysis can be trusted to yield objective truth. With case study, generalization from the case to other situations rests not on the methodology, but rather on the appeal of the case data to the reader's own knowledge and understanding.

In conventional research, such as experiments and surveys, the researcher typically manipulates—changes, controls or creates—the conditions of the process being studied or imposes limits on the range and kinds of responses that are measured as outputs of the process, or does both. This is most clearly seen in experimental research, where the researcher limits the number of variables to be measured, creates a 'treatment' which embodies the propositions to be tested, controls and limits the environment in which the treatment is allowed to function and measures the effects with predetermined categories and types of measurement. In evaluation, this is exemplified by a field experiment testing a particular project (say an instructional radio model). The evaluator decides in advance which aspects of the project and the project audience are to be studied; establishes experimental and control groups to make controlled comparisons possible; requires the treatment (the radio project) to remain unchanged during the experimental period; and measures results with tests and questionnaires prepared before the experiment is run.

Case study deals with the situation very differently. As a form of naturalistic inquiry, the emphasis is on understanding processes as they occur in a natural environment. Rather than seeking to limit and control variables, the researcher/evaluator seeks to gain as much understanding as possible of all the factors operating in the situation: the emphasis is on expanding, rather than reducing, the scope of the inquiry. The concept of treatment is not utilized. Instead, the process is studied as it naturally occurs and as it changes during the period of study. There is, in fact, emphasis on seeking explanations for such changes as part of generating understanding. The case-study method emphasizes continual observation and analysis of processes, drawing the categories of such analysis from the research process, rather than relying on pre-developed measurement instruments which may limit the investigator to hypothesized effects at the expense of other outcomes.

Data collection in conventional research tends to be carried out at prespecified times—before and after tests, cross-sectional surveys etc. Data collection for a case study is continuous, limited only by time, resources and the continuing utility of newly generated information. Analysis of data in conventional research follows predetermined rules and procedures, with tests of statistical signficance typically being used to establish the existence of associative or causal relationships. Analysis is usually a one-time, after-the-data-is-collected phase in research. In case-study research, data analysis is a continuous process through which patterns and propositions are continually surfaced, tested and reformulated. In conventional research, analysis ends when the appropriate statistical tests have been applied and the results interpreted. In naturalistic case-study research, analysis ends when the patterns and propositions identified are seen as 'true' by a significant majority of the actors in the process. There is no clear and predetermined stopping-point.

Finally, the two approaches differ in the way in which results are used. Results from more conventional forms of research are, if the research is well done, generalized to the class of instances of which a sampled number have been studied. Thus experimental research findings on the processes of learning are generalized to learners typical of the population that has been sampled. In an evaluation research effort, effects of a programme as measured for a sample of the programme clientele are generalized to the client population. Case-study findings, however, are normally limited to the case itself. A case study of a mediated education project leads to the identification of patterns of relationships and activities within the project; these patterns are generalizations about the case, and can help decision-makers with the task of modifying or improving that particular programme. The patterns may be generalized to other situations, as noted above. But in such cases the responsibility for such generalization rests not on the researcher, but on the research user. It is the latter who must make the critical judgements about the relevance of the case studied to the new situation addressed.

Main uses

The case-study method may be used to generate insight and understanding which assists planners and decision-makers at several points in the planning process:

Analysis of the environment in which a planned activity will function. For example, case studies of villages where audiences for a particular communication campaign live can be very useful in strategy development, supplementing survey data.

Analysis of needs. While surveys can give a broad but essentially shallow view of client needs, case studies can explore these in great depth, helping the planner see the complex causes on which needs rest, and thus be able to develop richer action strategies.

Analysis of planning and management process. Case-studies of planning, of decision-making, inter-organizational relations, implementation systems and programme operations can generate insights useful to improving action. Case analysis of complete systems can not only serve for system improvement, but also provide a useful introduction to the system for outsiders and new employees.

Enrichment of evaluation of effects. Cases can be used to provide the detail necessary for full understanding of evaluation findings developed with survey or experimental research.

History

The case study has long been part of the research tradition of many fields. Ethnographic cases have been extremely important in anthropology. Cases have been a main approach in psychiatry and medicine. And case analysis is an important tool in management and organization research. Case study as a method has received new attention in the last fifteen years as part of increased interest in forms of naturalistic inquiry, from the appearance of the field of ecological psychology to the evolution of educational evaluation models which rest on the naturalistic-inquiry approach or combine several research approaches (Guba, 1978, p. 31–41). An important impetus came with the publication of key work on 'grounded theory' in sociology (Glaser and Strauss, 1967). This new attention has emphasized the value of the case study and other naturalistic research not only to generate hypotheses and propositions for testing through more conventional methods, but also as a significant research tradition—albeit one with radically different assumptions—in its own right. This latter position is not without criticism, however, from researchers and evaluators who have serious reservations about the reliability—and hence utility—of case study findings (Anderson and Ball, 1875, p. 60–2).

Advantages and disadvantages

The case study has both advantages and disadvantages. Taken together, these would seem to indicate that the case-study approach is most useful for studying complex whole processes, such as the environment of programme clients, the full operation of a project or significant project components. The approach seems less useful for measuring *effects* of planned action, although case studies may illuminate causes for effects—or lack of effects—discovered through other research methods. Needless to say, the advantages listed below assume that the case is well and rigorously done! Poor cases are no better than poor research of any kind.

ADVANTAGES

Case studies are 'natural'. That is, they can portray a process in its natural setting without manipulation and intervention by the researcher. By eliminating such manipulation, they can strengthen the relevance of findings to the real world of action, avoiding the problem often encountered in generalizing from highly controlled and manipulated pilot projects to large-scale field implementation.

Case studies embrace complexity. In seeking constantly to expand the scope and coverage of a study, the case-study researcher avoids the strait-jacket of preconceived propositions and variables. This enables complex processes to be considered in their entirety, including factors not anticipated before the study is began.

Case studies are strong in 'reality'. The emphasis of case studies on detailed description and expansive approaches to data collection leads to studies which give the user insight into complex reality. This in turn helps the user relate the findings of the study not only to the case at hand, but also to similar cases and problems. The point has also been made that the form of

467

the case study makes it easier for non-technical research users to comprehend, thus strengthening its utility in decision-making (Stake, 1976). The data in case studies are thought to be more readily accessible to public audiences as well.

The case method encourages participatory research. When properly done, case-study activity involves the key actors in the process under investigation in determining the nature and findings of research. Persons who would be 'subjects' in a piece of survey research become rather more like 'partners' in the conduct of a case study.

DISADVANTAGES

Case studies are difficult to do well. As will be shown in the discussion of procedures below, the conduct of a case study is—and should be—every bit as rigorous and systematic as other forms of research. This alone prevents case studies from being the 'quick and dirty' method they are often thought to be. The difficulty is increased by the case-study emphasis on complex, holistic reality. This leads to the collection of a great deal of data of different kinds, requiring careful attention to data organization and analysis. Finally, case studies require a great deal of care in the presentation of description and analysis: it is often more difficult to describe a complex process with words (or pictures) than it is to display a table of statistical analysis.

Case study requires special skills. The methods of case study are eclectic. A wide range of data collection tools can be used, ranging from observation of behaviour through document analysis and interviewing to secondary analysis of existing statistical data. The writing of a case to show clearly the dynamics of a complex process is often considered an art. The case-study researcher is thus called upon to possess a wide range of skills, and the training of good case-study workers is far from easy.

Generalization from cases is limited. Part of the debate about the usefulness of case studies centres on the degree to which we may generalize from a specific case to other specific situations. Detractors of the case method, usually researchers of the positivistic school, believe that generalization from a case is, by and large, not possible. Others hold that it is possible, provided the case-study researcher has (a) demonstrated sufficient rigour in data collection and analysis and (b) explained the relationships between the process studied and its environment well enough to enable the research user to form judgements about the relevance of the lessons of the case for his/her own decisions or problems. Both types of researchers would probably agree, however, that the case study is not the strongest method for testing or confirming hypotheses or propositions about the population of processes of which the case is one instance. In other words, it is dangerous to draw firm, 'scientific' conclusions about all communication campaigns from one case study, or even from a series of cases. Generalization about a specific case, as we have noted, is a different matter. This is much more possible, and although there are problems in establishing the internal reliability of case-study data, there are procedures for doing so which can greatly increase the confidence of research users that the case truly portrays the process it studies.

Case studies place special obligations on the researcher. Conventional research methods have been developed to guarantee, in so far as is possible, the objectivity of the research process. These methods help the researcher to avoid personal bias in the collection and interpretation of data, and enable other researchers to confirm findings by replicating studies. Case-study research, whether carried out by an individual or team, has fewer methodological protections against possible bias. As a result, case studies should explicitly recognize potential biases or preconceptions held by researchers. Finally, the very nature of case-study research or evaluation places the researcher in a position of extreme responsibility with respect to the problem of anonymity of sources of data. It is almost impossible to mask the identity of key people in processes studied. The requirement of full display of data can collide sharply with the difficulty of protecting individuals who may be associated with 'bad' elements of a process. This can often limit the extent to which cases can be published or otherwise widely circulated, which may be one reason why they are not too popular with university researchers.

Resources required, product and communication of results

The principal resource required for case-study research is well-trained case-study investigators. There must be access to documents and to all levels of the process being investigated. As with any research, adequate funds are required for site visits, interviews and observations. A critical resource is time for several rounds of interviews and observations in the conduct of the case, and for preparation of the final report.

The typical product of a case study is a report document, although case studies have been reported via film and other media. As noted earlier, one of the strengths of a case study is its ability to describe and analyse complex social phenomena in terms readily understood by the decision-maker or public audience. The ability of a well-prepared case to appeal to the tacit knowledge of the reader, enabling him/her to draw conclusions and generalizations, is a strong point of the method. This effect, however, does not come automatically by calling a piece of research a 'case study'. The case writer must be able to demonstrate how conclusions have been reached, displaying the various kinds of data used as well as the reasoning followed. Thus a good case weaves together many kinds of information—interviews, document analysis, critical incidents, statistics—to tell the story of a social process as perceived by key actors in the process and as verified by the case-study investigator. Like any good story, a case study must be well written and interestingly presented to be most effective.

Level of confidence

The level of confidence one can have in a case study depends on the uses to which it is put. If a case study is used to increase understanding of a particular process among relevant decision-makers (generalization about the case), the level of confidence is determined by the research user by assessing the quality of the analysis. Of particular importance in this assessment is the internal reliability of the case data. Internal reliability rests on the quality of the relationship between the data presented and the conclusions drawn.

If the purpose is generalization from one case to another similar process or problem (generalization from the case), the level of confidence depends on the degree of correspondence between the case study and the new situation. Again, this assessment is the primary responsibility of the research user, who must decide if the features on the case studied are relevant to the new decision situation.

Procedures

Like all research, case-study investigation can be broken down into phases. Five phases are discussed below: conceptualization; choice of data sources; choice of data collection methods; conduct of the case study; and preparation and negotiation of the report. The procedural suggestions noted in the discussion of each phase are drawn from the literature of case study and naturalistic inquiry, and from the author's personal experience as a case-study researcher.

CONCEPTUALIZATION: THE STRATEGY OF INQUIRY

The central problem of conceptualization in a case study is defining the boundaries of the process to be studied, and hence of the study itself. In instances where the case-study methodology is used for research, the problem can be difficult indeed. Unlike the experimental or survey researcher, the case-study investigator cannot limit the investigation to a predetermined set of propositions to be tested. Instead, he/she is confronted with the possibility of dealing with an ever-increasing set of processes and variables as more is learned about the phenomenon under study and its relationships with its environment. In evaluation uses of case-study methodology, however, there is a ready approach to the problem of boundary definition. Simply put, the boundaries of study are determined from the nature of the problem or issue out of which the evaluation arises. If the case-study evaluation is to deal with a particular communication process, activity or organization, the boundary of the study can be determined from the boundaries of the process, activity or organization. To continue our earlier example of a radio education project, the initial boundaries of the study would be determined by (a) identifying the concerns or issues which have led decision-makers to request the evaluation and (b) the elements of the project as determined by its originators, as well as the relationships among the elements and between them and the environment in which the project operates.

A related issue is the degree to which the case-study researcher prepares an *a priori* conceptual map (or a study 'outline') before undertaking data collection. Some proponents of naturalistic inquiry hold that the researcher should begin with as few preconceptions as possible, letting direct experience with the phenomenon being studied determine the first tentative outline of important categories of information. While this approach is appealing from the perspective of theory generation, it seems unnecessarily 'pure' for evaluation purposes. Among other things, evaluatory case studies will almost always be undertaken to respond to particular issues or concerns. There will be considerable accumulated 'common knowledge' of the process to be studied. Thus it seems reasonable for the evaluatory case-study researcher to develop an initial general outline of categories of information to be sought. Most likely, these categories will correspond to readily identifiable elements of the systems to be studied. In a radio project, for example, these would include the learners, the materials, the learning environment, the delivery system, the management structure and so on, as well as the issue giving rise to the evaluation—such as the question, 'Are people learning?'

As an alternative to either the 'no outline' or the 'element plus issue' approaches the researcher may choose to apply a general systems framework as the initial inquiry paradigm, looking for inputs, processes, outputs and environmental relationships. Thus the conceptualization phase should result in (a) a statement of the boundaries of the study and (b) an initial outline or conceptual map to guide the study during initial stages.

SOURCES OF DATA

One of the strengths of case studies is their ability to use any and all types of data. In studying a planned process, the range of data that can be used is indeed broad. Primary sources of data are the key actors in the process being studied. Direct observation of key elements of the process is important, as is secondary analysis of documents and existing statistical data. At certain stages of the inquiry, surveys may generate additional data.

Adequate logistical planning, if nothing else, requires the researcher to identify the various sources of data to be drawn on in the course of the study. It is useful to identify data sources for each element of the conceptual map prior to beginning a study to identify areas where little data may currently exist, and where data-generation efforts may have to be emphasized. Thus this second phase of the study should result in a list of sources of data of different types for different elements of the study.

METHODS OF DATA COLLECTION

Case studies can employ a variety of data-collection methods. Interviewing key actors in the process is a central method. These interviews may be unstructured or semi-structured. A usual procedure is to begin with relatively unstructured interviews, perhaps focused on one or two basic questions designed to elicit the respondent's overall view of the process being studied and to define his/her own role in that process. Ideally, several rounds of interviews are possible, enabling the researcher to probe with increasingly specific questions based on data generated earlier in the study, both from the individual respondent and from other sources.

Participant observation methods are also useful, and check-lists and other observation forms may be appropriate. Document analysis is also important, both as a source of information on intentions regarding the programmes (i.e. from plans and budgets) and for information regarding the nature and content of the programme or process (i.e. from communication materials, administrative guidelines, monitoring and other 'evaluatory' information). Popular accounts of the phenomenon, such as newspaper and magazine articles, should not be overlooked.

While unanticipated opportunities for data collection will arise during the source of most studies, the careful researcher will prepare for the major anticipated kinds of data collection prior to initiating field study. Thus this phase of the research should result in a specification of data-collection methods, and the preparation, in rough form at least, of any instruments needed. In many cases, this may only be a list of key persons for the first series of interviews, together with a short list of initial questions for each.

CONDUCT OF THE STUDY

Constant comparison, inductive analysis and triangulation

While a researcher may begin a case study with a conceptual map, a list of data sources and a set of data-collection methods, he/she must be willing to interact constantly with the data as it is gathered, formulating and reformulating categories and relationships. Good case-study research rests on constant examination of the data for emerging categories and patterns of explanation. These in turn are formulated and tested against new data. The researcher always seeks alternative explanations for observed relationships, and continues to gather data until an established pattern 'holds up', and is not significantly altered by new information. Central to establishing the internal reliability of the case study is triangulation of data sources. To the extent that a pattern is supported by data from several sources it may be considered relatively reliable. If three key actors independently provide complementary and mutually supportive information about some aspect of the process under study we begin to have confidence that we can portray that element reliably. If their testimony

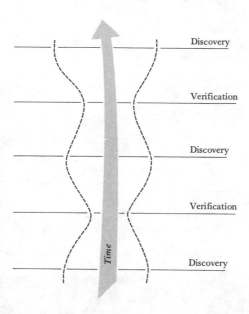

FIG. 1. Modes of analysis

diverges, the researcher must examine the data for other, underlying explanations.

The researcher constantly checks the ideas, insights and conclusions being generated with key actors in the process. The goal is to get agreement among a wide range of participants regarding the factual elements of the study. This is done as tentative conclusions emerge from the data. These are put in the form of a *research memo*, which in essence says to key actors: 'This is what appears to happen and why. What do you think?' Research memos are the basis for *en route* verification of tentative findings and the source of new directions for data collection.

Thus, patterns and insights grow inductively during the course of the study through a research process that alternates between discovery modes, which emphasize data collection and exploration, and verification modes, in which the researcher draws partial conclusions and seeks to verify these with key actors. The process is shown in Figure 1 (Guba, 1978, p. 7).

Finding a starting-point

The study must begin somewhere, both in time and space. The researcher must choose both an initial set of actors for interview and a point in the life of the project around which to initiate discussion. There are several options. It is usual to begin interviews with leaders of the process under study. It has also been suggested that, especially in evaluations, early interviews include critics of the activity. Most researchers seek to interview at all levels, often working

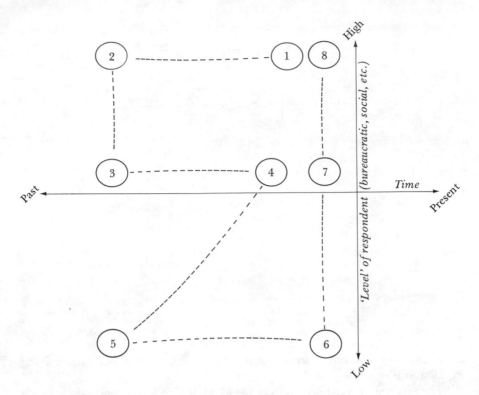

FIG. 2. Dimensions of inquiry

down and then back up the bureaucratic or social ladder in order to trace out relationships between individuals or classes of individuals involved in the process. The starting-point in time can be the time of the investigation, in which case the initial questions are usually about the current situation of the process. A useful alternative is to start with some significant past event, such as the initiation of the process, a key decision to change, a notable success or failure. Regardless of the starting-point chosen, the investigator will seek to move back and forth in time. What happened before? What happened after? Moving the inquiry through time helps establish causal relationships within the project as it has evolved.

Thus, the inquiry proceeds along two key dimensions. One is the dimension of key actors in the process; the other is the dimension of time. This process is illustrated in Figure 2, showing a possible conceptual plan for interviewing. The pattern in Figure 2 shows eight rounds of interviewing, beginning with interviews with relatively 'high'-level persons focused on the present situation. These are followed by interviews at the same level about past events and their relationship to the present. The interviewer continues learning about the past with interviews administered to 'lower'-level persons, beginning with the present situation, and then down to past and future at the 'lower' levels of the process. He/she ends by working back up through the levels.

Interviewing

The researcher must be highly organized in conducting interviews. While questionnaires may be used, they tend to be intrusive and to offer both the researcher and the respondent an easy way out of the interview. I have found note cards with a few key questions to be more useful. Tape recording is a good procedure if the researcher has time to transcribe and the respondent doesn't object. The researcher should constantly ask respondents to provide evidence to support their view of processes or events. This evidence can come in the form of explanation; it can also be in the form of artefacts (reports, memos, test instruments, media materials) which support the respondent's analysis.

Respondents should be asked to assist with the process of triangulation. They can be asked to name other persons with knowledge of the process being studied. The researcher should find out why the respondent is recommending that a certain person be interviewed: this will shed some light on the nature of the relationship between the two persons. It is useful in this context to ask respondents to assess the roles that other actors play in the process. Cross-checking of role perceptions often uncovers important underlying dynamics in the situation.

Building a data base

A case study generates a great deal of data, which must be organized, coded and constantly combined and recombined in the process of generating inductive insights. The data can readily be stored on index cards, which facilitates the process of formulation and reformulation of partial conclusions. It is extremely important to know, for example, whether certain information came from a first or later interview from a respondent.

PREPARATION AND NEGOTIATION OF THE REPORT

The process of cross-checking conclusions with key actors in the process extends to the preparation of the final report. Ideally, this is prepared in sequential partial drafts from research memos that are developed relatively late in the process, and which are relatively unchanged by additional data. These drafts should be circulated to key actors in the process for comment and review. If possible, face-to-face discussion should be arranged. While it is unlikely that the researcher will get complete agreement on the report, he/she should strive to achieve agreement at least on the observable facts of the process.

In preparing the final report, the researcher should be careful to support conclusions with both data and agreement. Key quotes from interviews and small critical incidents can be worked into the text. Extensive data citations and examples should be referred to and put into an appendix. Care should be taken to write the report in a straightforward and interesting way, without technical jargon. It is often useful to separate clearly desceiption and analysis from evaluation or 'judgemental' aspects of the report. The researcher may be able to get agreement on the former but not the latter, but the report will still serve a valuable purpose in stimulating thought and action at the decision level.

Case example

A North American instructional television (I T V) planning agency had evolved a set of organizational processes for (a) the design and development of I T V materials and (b) co-operative funding and planning with consortia of users of the agency's services and materials. These processes were working rather well, involving up to twenty different organizations at once in co-operative efforts. However, because they had developed informally over several years, no coherent descriptions of the processes existed outside the collective minds of the top agency personnel. And even among them differences of perception might exist.

PURPOSES OF THE STUDY

The agency commissioned the investigator to conduct a study of its co-operative planning and development processes. The study had general purposes: (a) to increase understanding of these complex processes among key actors in the central agency and in the seventy or more co-operating agencies; (b) by surfacing and analysing these processes, to point towards ways in which they might be strengthened; (c) to portray the processes of co-operative funding and development sufficiently well that other educational agencies might gain insights for their own operations; and (d) to serve as an introduction to agency work processes for new staff during an anticipated era of expansion. Thus, the situation called for naturalistic case study. Decision-makers wanted to increase their understanding of holistic, complex processes, for several purposes. They wanted to generalize *about* the case to improve the system and to increase understanding among participating agencies and new employees. They were willing for other agencies to generalize *from* the case.

PROCEDURES AND CONCEPTUALIZATION

The boundaries of the study were relatively easy to define. Given the goals of the study, the boundaries would include the core agency and its co-operators in those aspects of operation in which they interacted with the core agency: in short, in their I T V operations. These boundaries thus excluded much of the broader work of co-operating agencies.

An initial concept map was developed after two weeks of initial interviews with key actors in the core agency and analysis of major agency planning documents. This map was based on an initial systems viewpoint, and was presented as a partial outline of the work processes of the agency. Some categories in the outline were more developed than others; some categories had no information to support them, but were included because other data pointed to their existence. This outline was discussed for a half day with key actors, and radically revised. The revised outline held up in its major categories for the balance of the study, although sub-categories changed constantly. The outline served to guide document analysis and interviewing.

SOURCES OF DATA

The study drew on interviews with key actors in both the core and co-operating agencies. Additional interviews were conducted with experts outside the agency network. A literature review was conducted to set the historical context in which the agency developed. More than one hundred agency planning, design and research/evaluation documents were analysed, as were several years of internal correspondence. Instructional materials produced by the agency were also used as a data source. Key elements of agency processes were observed in action.

METHODS OF DATA COLLECTION

Methods used included: (a) unstructured and semi-structured interviews; (b) document analysis; (c) participant observations; (d) literature review; and (e) analysis of media materials. No formal instruments were used. Some interviews were tape-recorded. The majority of interviews were conducted with three or four key questions prepared in advance on note cards. Care was taken to write up interview notes immediately after interviews were completed.

CONDUCT OF THE STUDY

The study took two years, primarily because the researcher worked only part time and lived some 4,000 miles (6,400 km) from the agency studied. Three rounds of interviews were conducted in agency headquarters, each round lasting five days and involving multiple interviews with each respondent. Key questions were mailed to respondents prior to interview rounds. These interview rounds also enabled the investigator to participate in daily work processes, meetings etc. Research memos expanding and modifying subcategories of the outline were prepared after each round and mailed to key actors for review and clarification, and to raise new questions. Cost prohibited personal interviews with key actors in co-operating agencies across North America. Telephone interviews were conducted with some twenty such persons, who were prepared by receiving a letter from the agency requesting co-operation and a letter from the investigator listing general areas to be discussed. The investigator also did in-depth interviewing with a co-operating agency in his home city.

The investigator served as a consultant during the course of the study on an agency I T V project, enabling him to participate directly in the processes under study. The sequence of interviewing was similar to that shown in Figure 2. Initial interviews were conducted with the agency leadership following several days of document review. These interviews began with the current situation of the agency, then turned to agency origins and development over time. Subsequent interviews were conducted with middle-level agency staff. Interviews with co-operating agencies followed. Throughout the process, however, the investigator moved back and forth between levels, cross-checking ideas and insights, and seeking triangulation of data.

After three rounds of interviewing and document analysis (discovery mode) and two interviewing verification modes with research memos and expansion/ modification of the general outline, new data began to have little impact on the understanding that had emerged. Thus, a first draft of the study was completed and sent to key actors for review. This draft was discussed in detail at several meetings at the agency, and was also subject to written review by key actors. Throughout the study, data and emerging patterns/categorizations were re-corded on standard index cards, with annotation of sources and dates. This facilitated the combination and recombination of data in different ways as understanding of the process grew.

PREPARATION AND NEGOTIATION OF THE REPORT

The final draft of the report was prepared following feedback on the first draft. The framework of the report was a systems flow chart of agency work pro-cesses, with a chapter on each major subprocess. A wide range of evidence was used to support conclusions about patterns of action. A typical pattern would be supported by descriptive data from interviews, excerpts from key docu-ments, work-flow analyses developed from documents and observations, and small sub-cases or 'critical incidents' illustrating how particular processes operated.

One of the several large I T V projects completed by the agency was analysed in great detail as a separate sub-case. Placed in the appendices, this sub-case was referred to often as a major source of detail in supporting conclusions. The report included a separate role analysis of key actors, and a final section analysing the descriptive data in the report and offering a set of generalizations about the case. The study was eventually published by the agency (Middleton, 1978) and was distributed widely throughout the agency network.

COMMENT ON THE CASE

The case could have been completed in six months of full-time effort by an investigator closely located to the agency being studied. During the course of the investigation a number of insights into agency processes were obtained which were of immediate use to key actors in strengthening procedures. Insights such as these enabled the agency to achieve, at least partially, one of the purposes of the study.

Annotated bibliography

ANDERSON, S.B.; BALL, S. 1978. *The Profession and Practice of Program Evaluation.* San Francisco, Calif., Jossey-Bass.
GLASER, B.G.; STRAUSS, A.L. 1967. *The Discovery of Grounded Theory.* Chicago, Ill., Aldine. This book provides a full rationale and method for a relatively pure naturalistic-inquiry approach in sociology. Contains an excellent discussion of the process of constant comparison for the inductive development of theories and propositions from emerging data.
GUBA, E.G. 1978. *Toward a Methodology of Naturalistic Inquiry in Educational Evaluation.* Los Angeles, Calif., University of California Center for the Study of Evaluation. (CSE Monographs in Evaluation Series No. 8.) A thorough philosophical and mid-range methodological review of the uses of naturalistic inquiry in educational evaluation.
MIDDLETON, J. 1978. *Cooperative School Television and Educational Change.* Bloomington, Ind., Agency for Instructional Television.
SCHRAMM, W. 1971. *Case Studies of Educational Media Projects.* Stanford, Calif., Stanford University Institute for Communication Research. (Mimeo.)
STAKE, R.E. 1976. *The Case Study Method in Social Inquiry.* Champaign, Urbana, Ill., University of Illinois Center for Instructional Research. (Mimeo.)

Notes on contributors

George M. Beal obtained a Ph.D. in sociology from Iowa State University in 1953, where he taught from 1947 to 1977. He was Chairman of the Department of Sociology and Anthropology, 1968–75, and Charles F. Curtiss Distinguished Professor. He joined the East–West Communication Institute as a Research Associate in 1977. Dr Beal, who has specialized in adoption-diffusion and communication, complex organizations and inter-organizational relations, social change and social action, and communication planning, is the co-author of four books, two of which are *Dynamic Leadership and Group Action* and *Social Action and Interaction in Program Planning*. He has contributed chapters to five books, and is the co-author of over eighty monographs, twenty journal articles and one hundred popular articles. Among his recent publications (as co-author) related to the chapters in this book are: *Organizational Communication and Coordination in Family Planning Programs* (1975); *Knowledge Production and Utilization* (1977); *Communication Planning at the Institutional Level: A Selected Annotated Bibliography* (1979); and *The Development Communication Planning Simulation Game* (1979).

Dr Beal has worked in India, Burma, China and Guatemala, and has held consultancy and training assignments with over five hundred private companies, co-operatives, voluntary associations, agencies and organizations. He has been President of the Rural Sociological Society, a council member of the International Sociological Association and one of the organizers of the World Congress of Rural Sociology.

Jerry L. Brown is a Project Officer and Director of Instructional Design for the Agency for Instructional Television (AIT). Dr Brown specializes in managing instructional television projects and the design of instructional materials in general. Prior to joining AIT in 1974, Dr Brown was a member of the faculty of Indiana University, where he taught courses in curriculum development, instructional design and programmed instruction. He was also director of the Population Education Project. Dr Brown's interests are wide-ranging and he has worked in a variety of curriculum areas. Topics of particular interest to him include management of large-scale instructional-development projects and the development of instructional materials for strengthening learners' reasoning and problem-solving skills.

Lertlack Burusphat is a planner/programmer of health and population programmes, United Nations Development Training/Communication Planning Office (DTCPO), Bangkok, Thailand. She obtained her Ph.D. degree in instructional technology and educational psychology from the University of Indiana. Her past experience includes research, teacher-training, curriculum development and college administration in Thailand. Her present duties include programme/project development in health and population, field-worker training and conducting workshops for planners and trainers.

Chee-wah Cheah obtained his degree of Bachelor of Economics with first-class honours from the University of Malaya, Kuala Lumpur. He has worked as an economic analyst in a management and planning consulting firm in Kuala Lumpur, specializing in project evaluation and financial analysis. In 1979, he completed his Master's degree in urban and regional planning at the University of Hawaii, Manoa, under the sponsorship of an East–West Center grant. Mr Cheah was a research intern at the East–West Communication Institute in 1981. He is currently a graduate assistant and Ph.D. candidate in economics at the University of Hawaii, Manoa.

Wimal Dissanayake is currently Research Associate and Assistant Director for Participants at the East–West Communication Institute in Honolulu, Hawaii. He was formerly Chair of the Department of Mass Communication, University of Sri Lanka, and Visiting Fulbright Research Scholar, University of Pennsylvania (1975–76). Dr Dissanayake, an author of three books, has an M.A. from the University of Pennsylvania and a Ph.D. from Cambridge University in England. He has served as an adviser to the Ministries of Broadcasting, Cultural Affairs and Education, Sri Lanka.

Zenaida T. Domingo is the Project Director of the Educational Communication Office of the Educational Development Projects Implementing Task Force in the Philippines. She is responsible for the overall planning and implementation of a World Bank-assisted project on educational technology. Ms Domingo has served as a project planning and evaluation consultant on information/education/communication work in other government agencies such as the National Media Production Center and the Bureau of Agricultural Extension. She has also managed several national research projects funded by the Philippine Government and international agencies. She is also a lecturer in communication research and media planning at the Ateneo University Department of Communication.

Ms Domingo comes from the Philippines and is an M.A. graduate from Ateneo University. She has been a recipient of various international fellowship grants from Unesco, the Friedrich-Ebert Stiftung and the Philippine Government. She has also undertaken several planning projects under the sponsorship of the East–West Center, Hawaii.

Jim Herm is a training specialist at the United Nations Development Training/Communication Planning Office (DTCPO). He has worked as a rural radio/television producer and population, agricultural extension and programme planner in Thailand, Turkey and India. Currently, he is developing training components of projects, advising on the design and operation of training programmes and conducting training workshops. His educational background includes a B.Sc. in agricultural communication, University of Illinois, and an M.Ed. in educational communication and technology from the University of Hawaii.

Manuel Gomez-Ortigoza is Assistant to the Vice-President for Expansion, Televisa, in Mexico City. He holds a Master's degree from the Annenberg School of Communication,

University of Southern California, Los Angeles. His duties entail the preparation of expansion projects for new ventures in the telecommunications field and planning the introduction of new communication technology, such as satellite-television transmission and the study of a teleconference system for Mexico.

Alan Hancock, who was educated at Oxford, spent eleven years as a radio and television producer, specializing in educational broadcasting; his last assignment in the United Kingdom was as a senior producer with the Open University, where he was responsible for programming in the social sciences. In the 1960s, he worked for several years in South–East Asia, where he collaborated on the planning and development of educational media services in Singapore, Malaysia and Hong Kong, and helped to establish the Asia–Pacific Institute for Broadcasting Development in Kuala Lumpur. He joined Unesco in 1969 as Regional Broadcasting Planning Adviser for Asia, and moved to Paris in 1972, where he has worked principally in the communication-planning field, and was responsible for two major media-planning surveys, in Thailand and Afghanistan. In 1980 he transferred to the International Institute for Educational Planning, also in Paris.

Alan Hancock holds a doctorate in educational technology from the Open University. He is the author of numerous publications, including, most recently, *Producing for Educational Mass Media* (1976); *Planning for Educational Mass Media* (1978) and *Communication Planning for Development* (1981). He is currently working in Thailand, where he is Chief Technical Adviser to an educational-radio development project.

Barclay M. Hudson is a planning and management consultant with specializations in compact, accelerated methods of planning, project development and programme evaluation. He has undertaken state-of-the-art research on planning methodology for numerous agencies including Harvard University, the Japan Economic Research Institute (Tokyo), the East–West Center (Hawaii), the International Institute for Educational Planning (Paris), the World Future Studies Federation (Rome), the United States Office of Education, the Ford Foundation and the National Science Foundation. Author of numerous publications on planning theory and policy research, he taught planning theory, systems analysis and evaluation methodology at the University of California at Los Angeles (UCLA) for eight years before establishing his own consulting firm, specializing in fast-track methods of planning, forecasting and programme evaluation.

Dr Hudson received his B.A. in economics from Harvard University, studied history at the École Libre des Sciences Politiques, Paris, and finished his graduate work at the Harvard University Center for Studies in Education and Development, receiving his doctorate in 1971.

Meheroo Jussawalla is a Research Associate at the East–West Communication Institute in Honolulu, Hawaii. She holds a Ph.D. in economics from Osmania University, Hyderabad, India, and was Professor of Economics and Dean of the Faculty of Social Sciences at Osmania University before migrating to the United States in 1975. She served on the Research Programmes Committee of the Planning Commission, Government of India, from 1968 to 1970. From 1971 to 1975 she was a member of the board of directors of the State Bank of India. In 1957–58 she was awarded a grant under the Wheat Loan Program for studies at the University of Pennsylvania. In 1969–70 the

American Council on Education awarded her a Visiting Professorship at Hood College, Frederick, Maryland. During that period she gave guest lectures at Vassar, Elmira and Cedar Crest Colleges. From 1975 to 1977 she served as Professor of Economics at St Mary's College in Maryland and joined the Communication Institute in January 1978. Meheroo Jussawalla has published books and articles in professional journals on development economics, money and banking. Her recent publications are on communication economics. Her special interest is in the field of communication policy and planning.

Bruce McKenzie is a Senior Lecturer in Psychology at the Warrnambool Institute of Advanced Education in Australia. During the first half of 1980 he was a Research Fellow at the East–West Communication Institute in Honolulu, Hawaii. While at the East–West Center he was co-author (1981) of a student text on communication planning. Other academic papers written during this period were in the areas of international news flow, the economic dimensions of development communication and the teaching of development communication in undergraduate programmes. In recent years, Mr McKenzie's publications have concentrated on the application of planning principles to various fields in the social sciences, particularly social welfare and environmental psychology. Mr McKenzie completed his undergraduate studies at Melbourne University and graduate programmes at London University and the University of New England. He worked in community development projects in Papua New Guinea and Northern Australia before taking up an academic position at Warrnambool.

John Middleton has been a Research Associate of the East–West Communication Institute since 1972, and was Assistant Director from 1975 to 1980. On leave from the Institute in 1980–82, Middleton served as Planning Adviser to the Indonesian National Center for Communication Technology in Education and Culture. Prior to joining the Communication Institute, he served with the Peace Corps in Korea, Micronesia and Washington, D.C. In 1977, he spent six months as a Research Fellow at the Asia and Pacific Development Administration Center in Kuala Lumpur, Malaysia. John Middleton holds a doctoral degree in educational planning from Harvard University. His publications have covered a range of problems in training, non-formal education and communication planning. Among his recent publications are: *Planning Family Planning Communication* (with Y.S. Lin, 1975); *Cooperative School Television and Educational Change* (1978); *Perspectives on Communication Policy and Planning* (with S.A. Rahim, 1978); *Approaches to Communication Planning* (1980); and *The Development Communication Planning Simulation-Game* (with Gus Root, George Beal, Meheroo Jussawalla and Meow Khim Lim, 1979). He has been consulted by numerous Asian, American and international agencies on communication planning.

Gerald E. Moriarty is a telecommunication engineer and currently holds the position of Supervising Engineer, Planning and Development, in Radio New Zealand, a service of the Broadcasting Corporation of New Zealand. He has been responsible for the implementation and operation of a new decentralized engineering organization for Radio New Zealand and also for the introduction of the first automated radio presentation and network distribution systems within the organization. In 1980 he spent eight months as a participant in the East–West Communication Institute's Project on Communication Policy and Planning and on his return to New Zealand was seconded to the Communications Policy Research Unit formed by the New Zealand Commission for the Future to recommend a government policy on national communication develop-ment. Prior to graduating as an engineer, Mr Moriarty was a telecommunications technician on a number of radio and television stations in New Zealand.

H. Dean Nielsen is Senior Research Scientist with the Institute for International Research Inc. and Chief of Party for the USAID-supported Self-Instructional Learning System Project (Proyek Pamong) in Indonesia. Previous positions have included that of Professional Associate at the Educational Testing Service, Princeton, New Jersey; Research Adviser and Team Leader in the Unesco Education Development Programme at the Research and Development Office of the Indonesian Ministry of Education; Research Associate at the Social Ecology Laboratory of Stanford University, California, and Visiting Assistant Professor in Education at the Federal University of Brasilia, Brazil. He is the author of numerous articles, primarily on educational environments and evaluation/research methods, and the book *Tolerating Political Dissent: The Impact of High School Social Climates in the United States and West Germany* Dr Nielsen received his doctorate in International Development Education from Stanford University in 1976. His dissertation research was conducted during the previous year in Stockholm, where he was a Pre-doctoral Fellow with the International Association for the Evaluation of Educational Achievement (IAEEA).

Marc U. Porat, who holds a Ph.D. in communication and economics from Stanford University, is Director of Film Projects and Fellow at the Aspen Institute, where he was the executive producer, writer and on-camera host of the film, *The Information Society*. From 1975 to 1977 he worked as an economist for the United States Department of Commerce and served as principal investigator on the Information Economy project.

Gus Root, who holds Bachelor degrees from Middlebury College (1942) and the Massachusetts Institute of Technology (1943), has spent sixteen years with the General Electric Company as a development engineer and a consultant in engineering edu-cation. To further his understanding of human learning and behaviour, he attended Syracuse University to complete a Ph.D. in psychology (1967). He remained at Syracuse as a Professor of Instructional Technology until 1978 and is now an in-dependent consultant in communication and health planning, and engineering edu-cation. Working with the United States Bureau of Education for the Handicapped, he prepared a simulation-game to represent the ways in which the many agencies, schools, research centres and publishers interacted to affect the flow of educational materials and methods from research and development centres to classrooms and teachers. Other simulations which he has designed and operated include a model of the School of Graduate Education at Syracuse University, the Educational Television network serv-ing the middle schools throughout Iran and the Communication Planning Simulation-Game which is the central experience for the five-week workshop on communication planning that was developed for Unesco and the East–West Communication Institute. He is currently working to develop the data base for a simulation of the community-health system within the region in which he lives in northern Vermont in the United States.

J.K. Satia has a Bachelor's degree in engineering from Bombay University, India, and a Master's degree and Ph.D. in industrial engineering from Stanford University.

California, United States. He is now a Professor in Production and Quantitative Methods and a member of the Public Systems Group at the Indian Institute of Management, Ahmedabad. He was a consultant in the Population, Health and Nutrition Department at the World Bank during the year 1979/80, and was Chairman, Public Systems Group, in the Indian Institute of Management for the period 1978–79. During the period 1973–77, he was Co-ordinator of the Population Project Unit, an interdisciplinary group working on the Problems of Population programme at the institute. He has published several papers and has been a consultant to many organizations, including several government departments. His current interest includes the application of quantitative techniques to the problems of managing public systems.

John Spence is a member of the Board of W.D. Scott & Co., an Australian-owned international management consulting organization. He is also a member of the Australian National Commission for Unesco and lives in Sydney. He has degrees in electrical engineering and in science from the University of Sydney and has responsibility for his company's development of approaches to strategic planning for governments, international agencies and private corporations. With W.D. Scott, John Spence has been working for the last twenty-four years in the field of resource allocation, utilizing computer models and communications, work which initially concentrated on energy models and transportation (including the evaluation of alternatives for South–East Asia in the major regional transport survey undertaken by the Asian Development Bank). For the last ten years, he has been responsible for communications planning. This work has included the optimization of international cable and satellite options for OTC (Australia), the assessment of future communications development and strategies for both Telecom Australia and for Australia Post, the definition of the appropriate data-handling system for the Asian Development Bank and the development of the organization, structure and management for Intelsat in Washington, D.C.

Benjamin E. Suta is a Senior Operations Analyst with SRI International (formerly Stanford Research Institute), Menlo Park, California. His major field of interest is the application of statistical and operations research techniques to environmental problems. This has included forecasting, risk assessment, statistical analysis and the management of environmental assessments. He has worked on a number of research projects requiring the development and application of forecasting techniques. These include: an assessment of future national and international problem areas; a handbook of forecasting techniques; a mathematical evaluation of the KSIM procedure; and a number of applications of forecasting techniques to specific problem areas. He is currently doing research on risk assessments of environmental substances for the United States Environmental Protection Agency.

Majid Tehranian holds a B.A. in government from Dartmouth, an M.A. in Middle East studies and a Ph.D. in political economy and government from Harvard. He has taught and researched for the past seventeen years at universities in the United States, Iran, United Kingdom and France, including Harvard, Massachusetts Institute of Technology, Oxford, Stanford and Tehran. He has also held positions with national and international public agencies, including that of Director of the Prospective Planning Project of National Iranian Radio/Television, director of Iran Communications and Development Institute and Programme Specialist at the Unesco Division of Development of Communication Systems in Paris. He has served as consultant, planner and director for several telecommunications development projects, including the Free University (a multi-media open-learning system), the Iran Telecommunication Satellite Project and the Information and Communication Commission of the Sixth Plan of Iran. Dr Tehranian's publications include some ten books and over forty articles in scholarly journals, including the volume *Communication Policy for National Development: A Comparative Perspective* (1977). As well as in English, some of his publications have also appeared in Persian, French, Spanish and Indonesian. He is a Fellow of the East–West Communication Institute and a Visiting Professor at the Department of Communication, University of Hawaii.

Victor T. Valbuena is a Research Associate and Operations Manager of the Cooperative Research Program at the Population Center Foundation in the Philippines. He is also a Professorial Lecturer at the Institute of Mass Communication, University of the Philippines. Dr Valbuena received his B.A. (journalism) and M.A. (communication) from the University of the Philippines and a Ph.D. (Philippines studies) from the Centro Escolar University in Manila. He was written articles for Manila newspapers and magazines and has done research in the areas of media distribution and utilization, public-health communications and theatre as development communication. He is co-author or *Effective Ways to Communicate Family Planning* (1978) and *Clinic Education* (1977). Dr Valbuena has served as Consultant for Communication Planning and Training upon projects of the Philippine Ministry of Health, Ministry of Labor and Employment, and at the Institute of Maternal and Child Health.

Dan J. Wedemeyer is an Assistant Professor, Department of Communication, University of Hawaii, and a Fellow in the Policy and Planning Project, East–West Communication Institute, Honolulu, Hawaii. His Ph.D. in communication theory and research from the Annenberg School of Communication, University of Southern California, emphasized such areas as forecasting methods, communication policy and planning, communication technology and international communication. Dr Wedemeyer teaches classes in human communication futures, perspectives in telecommunication and forecasting methods. His recent publications concern such topic areas as: emerging communication technologies and services; communication needs, supplies and rights; and long-range communication policy and planning. He has served as editor of the Pacific Telecommunication Conference proceedings (1979–82) and is co-editor (with John Middleton) of the present volume. More recently, he has served as a telecommunication consultant to the State of Hawaii, for which he drafted the State Telecommunication plan.